KWAME DAWES' *PROPHETS*

A READER'S GUIDE

JEREMY POYNTING

KWAME DAWES' *PROPHETS*

A READER'S GUIDE

PEEPAL TREE

First published in Great Britain in 2018
Peepal Tree Press Ltd
17 King's Avenue
Leeds LS6 1QS
England

ISBN13: 97818452323413

Supported using public funding by
ARTS COUNCIL
ENGLAND

CONTENTS

PREFACE

Prophets can be read with understanding and pleasure, without the aid of annotations and critical commentary. However, based on my own experience of looking deeper into the poem's contexts, sources and allusive resonances, this book is written with the belief that a reading informed by such knowledge can be even more rewarding. I was the editor and publisher of *Prophets* in 1995, but I know now that my understanding of the poem at that time was in some respects superficial and faulty. Even so, I thought it one of the most important works of poetry to have come out of the Caribbean and worthy of international recognition as a narrative in verse of exceptional quality. Now, even amongst Kwame Dawes' very substantial body of work, I believe that it has a special place, not least because it is the book that shows the first coming together of the various elements of Dawes' creative mission, the strands that later work has pursued in deepening cycles of maturity.

When *Prophets* first came out it was warmly albeit scantily reviewed,[1] but since then it has generated a disappointing level of critical response, and even within the Caribbean has not achieved a place in the literary canon equal to its quality and importance. It is not, for instance, being much taught. One can only speculate why this should be. Is it the distinctly unromantic, unheroic setting – the context of a self-invented Charismatic church[2] and a *dramatis personae* of the aspiring petit bourgeois of suburban Kingston with a prophetess who has visions as she sits on the toilet? Is it because its range of local Jamaican reference, so pertinent to the poem's meaning, lies outside the repertoire of the international reader? Is it because some readers (and critics) may have sensed that there are depths and resonances in *Prophets* that only a fairly thorough knowledge of the Bible would enable them to grasp?

There has undoubtedly been a fragmenting of the knowledge of biblical narratives (perhaps to an even greater extent than of classical mythology) that poets and novelists could once take for granted amongst their readers. As the son of an Anglican clergyman, my childhood (already, I confess, a non-believing one) included Sunday school and exposure to Bible stories. That was more than sixty years ago. Now, no one who has taught otherwise well-educated young people in the UK is likely to be surprised about how little they actually know of what you might think are the most commonly known Bible narratives. Could this be true even amongst some Caribbean readers? Even with what I suspect are better than average antennae for biblical allusion, there was much in my earlier readings of *Prophets* that passed me by. Rereading and tracing the biblical and other literary allusions in *Prophets*, my admiration for the poem and its beauties has increased because I understand so much more of what is going on than I did twenty years ago. It is, of course, possible that some of those who did read *Prophets*, who had the depth of biblical knowledge it builds on, may have been offended by the poem's treatment of those narratives. About that kind of response one can do nothing, except to assert that poetry is the place for freedom of thought.

Whilst I have had many hours of pleasurable conversation with Kwame Dawes about *Prophets*, and he very graciously corrected some of my misapprehensions about the place and the time – he was there, I wasn't – this is in no sense an authorised reading, and I've no doubt there are particular interpretations with which Kwame Dawes wouldn't agree – or at least wouldn't remember that he was thinking in this way or was conscious of making some particular allusion. I know that at times, when he read earlier drafts of this manuscript, he has been surprised as he looked once more at his poem and seen it as something imperfectly remembered.

I hope the notes and summaries in the latter part of the book offer both navigation through the poem and helpful information on the poem's range of reference to the Jamaica of the mid to late 1980s and to the biblical and other literary sources it draws on. I make no claim that all the allusions noted were in Kwame Dawes' mind and I hope this book offers as much a creative reading as a practical guide. Not least I wanted to show how much *Prophets* was engaged with other literature – and how a rewarding reading of this poem is about the connections made with often half-remembered fragments in the reader's mind, in this case mine.

In practical terms, the notes assume, a) that not all readers are Jamaicans or have an intimate knowledge of Jamaica; b) that not all Jamaican readers under the age of thirty will necessarily know much about the milieu and times of *Prophets*; c) not all readers (from wherever they come) will possess the poem's range of biblical and literary reference. Of course, if some notes seem obvious, pat yourself on the back.

The critical commentary which occupies the first part of the book has more conventional literary-critical objectives. It looks at *Prophets* in its relationships to both the world and the books it is in dialogue with, and in terms of its formal construction as a literary work.

CRITICAL COMMENTARY

ONE: INTRODUCTION

Prophets, Kwame Dawes' third book, published when he was thirty-three, is a remarkably assured work, an ambitious poem in structure, in its play with multiple points of view and its frequently striking imagery. It maintains a sustained energy throughout its 3132 lines, displaying great variety of tone and prosodic virtuosity within its tercet form. It achieves a dynamic flow between its levels of dramatic focus: an autobiographical strand that traces the involvement of an "I" figure, a student at the time, with a new Charismatic church and his eventual departure both from that church and from Jamaica; the narrative unfolding of events within that church and the rivalry of two prophets, Clarice and Thalbot, who represent different – Old and New Testament – models of prophecy; a trenchant portrayal of the state of the Jamaican nation in the late 1980s and early 1990s; ingeniously inserted reflections on the fate of some of Jamaica's brightest and best literary and musical talents; post-hoc reflections from a place of greater maturity and geographic distance on the nature and meaning of the experience of the younger "I"; and a metatextual discourse on the literary choices made in writing the poem. It is a work that captures with great exactness the political, cultural and ideological manifestations – across race, class and gender – of a society in a state of flux. As such, it is a work essential for the understanding of its time, but because it displays a profound sense of Jamaican history, *Prophets* has since lost nothing of its pertinence in tracing how that country's racial, social and cultural fissures continue to manifest both publicly and in the privacy of the heart.

It is also a poem that engages in a risk-taking way with issues of gender, both as a reflection on Jamaican society and, self-reflexively in the construction of the poetic narrative. *Prophets* emerged at a time when a powerful women's literary presence had been a salient element in African American writing since the 1970s – Alice Walker and Toni Morrison (themselves drawing on Zora Neale Hurston) are writers Dawes particularly attends to. It was also a presence emerging in the Caribbean in the 1970s and 80s in the work of Lorna Goodison, Merle Hodge, Olive Senior, Erna Brodber, Dionne Brand and others. As a male author to write a narrative poem that has a female character as its protagonist was to invite a particular kind of inspection, especially when that character is the object of erotic speculation on the part of the poem's quasi-autobiographical "I". How *Prophets* deals with the reality of the male gaze, both observed and inherent to the poem, is discussed in the third chapter.

This critical commentary attempts several things. Throughout, it sets out why *Prophets,* as a Caribbean verse narrative, in addition to its intrinsic merits, is a path-finding poem in creating an aesthetic that is natively Jamaican, making a poetic epic out of specifically local materials. Since one of these materials is the Bible, the question of how the Bible can be regarded as local material is a legitimate one, but one for which I think there are convincing answers. The poem is also considered in the context of earlier Caribbean writing and, briefly, its place in the development of Dawes' own body of work.

Secondly, I offer what I hope are coherent frameworks for the specific information presented in the notes in the second part of the book concerning the poem's non-literary contexts, and discuss how the poem treats this material. These include those elements of biography pertinent to the poem; aspects of its historical setting in mid-1980s Jamaica; the significance of the poem's social geography; and, perhaps most necessarily, an elucidation of the poem's religious context, in particular how it relates to both biblical and Jamaican notions of prophecy and to the upsurge of Charismatic and independent Pentecostal churches in this period.

Thirdly, because like all really significant literary works, *Prophets* is as much in dialogue with other literature as it is with the external world of people in social structures, cultural institutions and time, the introduction looks selectively at *Prophets'* relationship to some of the books that were important in its gestation and to which there are references of various kinds. Here, discussion with Kwame Dawes confirms what books these were; but what *Prophets* took from them, how it transformed and in some cases implicitly critiqued those sources, are matters of my own critical judgement.

Fourthly, because above all else *Prophets* is a poem, the introduction explores formal aspects of its composition. It looks at the poem's structure, its play between narrative and lyric modes and its departures from linear sequence. It explores shifts in genre and point of view, between realism and the magic of constructed myth; and between a quasi-autobiographical "I" who is a character in the poem, an "I" who speaks as Clarice, an "I" who is an unnamed, goddess-like avatar who makes a self-propelled flight over Africa, and the implied author who at a later point in time reflects on the experiences of his younger self. It traces some of the tropes and patterns of imagery that provide both cohesion and meaning to the poem, such as madness, flight, birds and the cinematic. Both the critical commentary and the notes draw attention to the presence of the poem's wit and humour, in the frequency of irony, punning and other kinds of verbal play that signal

Prophets' rich ambivalences of tone and meaning. It notes how, within *Prophets'* tercet form, variety in the patterns of sound and rhythm reinforce meaning and offer pleasure. It notes the thread of metatextuality that runs through the narrative, the poet's reflections on the choices made in its writing, not least on the poem's relationship to its society and responsibilities to the church community from which it draws some of its raw material.

Fifthly, because *Prophets* is such a richly allusive poem, the critical commentary explores the different ways allusions to classic and contemporary literature, the Bible and reggae are used. And because the poem's use of allusion varies between the explicit and the sometimes opaquely implicit, the commentary looks at allusiveness as a matter of both communicative risk and reward – particularly in the context of a potential readership that is both national and international. Again, since allusion is a device that foregrounds the presence or absence of a shared communicative context of writing and reading, my discussion deals both with those prompts that one can confidently locate as intended elements in the text, and those textual elements that bring into play other texts located in the reader's memory, in this instance mine, which are not necessarily part of the writer's conscious intention.

This critical commentary also looks at *Prophets'* use of allusion's bolder cousins, adaptation, parody and pastiche – or in Jamaican terminology, versioning[1] – where the poem takes on and transforms several biblical narratives for its own purposes – for instance, the stories of Jesus, Legion and the Gadarene swine; Lot's angel-assisted flight from Sodom; Jonah's encounter with the belly of a whale; and the conflict between Jezebel and Elijah.

Finally, this commentary discusses how, as an imaginative poem about religious faith and practice, about politics and literature, about a filial relationship to the Bible and Jamaican culture, *Prophets* asks how both it and the Bible – its predominant intertext – are to be read. The young man whose experience is at the centre of the poem questions what has been fraudulent, what true in his experience of the church. Beyond that, the poem asks what is more truthful: the supposed, remembered experience or the conscious creation of myth? What is the connection between the spiritual truths that we may assume the poet Kwame Dawes searched for in his heart, and the ironic, speculative, even satirical treatment of some of those biblical narratives which are regarded by at least some Christian believers as divine truth?

These have been interesting questions for me as a reader who long since parted company from Christian faith, who has rarely thought about what kind of a text the Bible was, who has not been shaken from his conviction that the materialist dialectics of Marx, at his least deterministic, and of his most imaginative followers,[2] still offers the best approximation about how to make sense of the human, social world, but who not only finds the poetry of *Prophets* emotionally and intellectually engaging, but came away with a new awareness of what a mysterious, poetic and tumultuously gigantic body of writing the Bible is, and how central its narratives and visions have been, and are, to both Caribbean and Western ways of understanding ourselves and the world. *Prophets* invites us to reread the Bible as a master literary text, but also as a text that has been constructed to convince, a text that puzzles, that offers images of the divine that are deeply perplexing, a text that connects the Caribbean to world discourse in the widest possible way. As one of the characters in Sylvia Wynter's novel, *The Hills of Hebron* (1962) ponders: "Where had she heard that? It must have come from the Bible. Everything came from the Bible" (p. 255).

Whilst I repeat my advice to read the poem first – and much of what follows is written in the hopeful assumption that the reader has a working knowledge of the poem – I know from my own reading habits that readers don't always follow good advice. What immediately follows is a brief synopsis of the recoverable narrative and the plot structure of *Prophets*. Readers will also find more detailed synopses and discussions of the content of each chapter in the section of notes that makes up the second part of this book.

TWO: STRUCTURE AND NARRATIVE

Prophets is divided in four parts with twenty-eight chapters of varying lengths. It has a narrative that can be reconstructed, but is not told in a linear fashion. Briefly, *Prophets* tells the story of a young man's involvement with a small independent Charismatic/ Pentecostal church that holds its services on the university campus. The church is led by a preacher and prophetess, Clarice, who possesses the gift of being able to see into the hearts and the secret and often shameful thoughts and motivations of her congregation; of being able to induce shame, repentance and psychic reconstruction; of being able to arouse the worshippers to the point of ecstatic transcendence signalled by speaking in tongues; of being able to heal physical and psychological ills. It is a new church, without premises of its own, though it has recently bought the decaying home of Castleberry, an old white man of the upper class, who stays on after his death as an amiable ghost, clearly visible to Clarice.

Into this church also comes a character called Last Night, in flight from what he regards as the insatiable and improper sexual demands of the woman he has been living with. Last Night is saved in the spirit by Clarice, who takes him into her home to support him. When it becomes apparent to the senior church brothers that there is a sexual tension between Clarice and Last Night, the church insists on his baptism (by immersion) and their separation. As a priestess in the church, Clarice is forced to deny her sexuality, to live in a state of virginal purity.

There are two episodes that focus on the presence of the narrating young man in the church. In the first, he confesses his relief that Clarice offers spiritual support and material help to rescue him from his distress, rather than exposing his sexual indiscretions. In the second episode, the young man confesses to a poet's distraction from whole-hearted spiritual involvement in the act of worship, though surrounded by people possessed by the holy spirit, and speaking in tongues.

Running parallel to this narrative is the figure of Thalbot, first seen as a madman living on the streets, or squatting in whatever empty residence he can find, including Castleberry's old house, from which Clarice ejects him. We learn later that Thalbot has once been a political informer, working with the CIA, though when they offer him the chance of exit from Jamaica to the USA, he declines. Thalbot also enters Clarice's church, where she casts out his demons and for a brief period his sanity is restored. However, as Jesus warns, as reported in Matthew's gospel (12: 43), when an evil spirit comes out of a person, unless the space is filled by the holy spirit, it leaves a vacuum open for occupation by other invading spirits. This is what happens to Thalbot who is inhabited, one after the other, by the wandering spirits of four artistic figures (three deceased), all of whom have either broken down in psychic distress or fled Jamaica – through a lack of appreciation or outright rejection of their art, the stress of dealing with Jamaica's fissures of class and race, and their own mental fragility or hubris in their attitudes to the inequalities of race and gender.

The narrative is resumed several months later when the church temporarily leaves Kingston to engage in an evangelical mission to save souls at the resort of Annotto Bay on Jamaica's north coast. In the meantime, it is evident that Last Night has risen in the church to become a preacher, no doubt through convincing displays of spiritual fervour, apt biblical quotation and speaking in tongues. At this point, as a man, Last Night, now "the Preacher", is senior in the church hierarchy to Clarice, though it is through her prophetic preaching that the mission is triumphant. Her converts to the true God include a Rastafarian, an obeah woman and members of African-oriented Revival churches, all regarded as heathens and idolators. However, at the height of Clarice's success in winning these souls, her sexual attraction to Last Night surfaces and they "sin" on the beach. Last Night is mortified to have succumbed to the temptations of the flesh, but Clarice is unrepentant, believing that on the evidence of her power to win these heathen souls, she must still have God's favour. She concludes that there is no reason why she should not also delight in sexual desire and pleasure, and she employs words from the Song of Solomon to equate these two kinds of transcendence: spiritual and erotic. Unfortunately for Clarice, the episode on the beach has been observed by Thalbot, who reacts with all the misogynistic fury of an Old Testament prophet.

Then, the narrative moves its focus to Thalbot who, in a re-enactment of the story of the Prophet Jonah, is instructed to go to Nineveh (Kingston) to preach of God's wrath to come. Like Jonah, Thalbot resists this command and decides instead to go to Joppa (Montego Bay) because he fears the violence that awaits madmen/prophets in Kingston. But just as Jonah is thrown overboard from the ship to Joppa – because the seamen conclude that the storm God sends is connected to his presence – Thalbot leaves the bus to Montego Bay (which has broken down) but is then virtually kidnapped by a coach driver (the coach playing the part of the fish that swallows Jonah) and taken to Kingston. There Thalbot discovers that though the inhabitants of the Babylonian city persist in their wickedness, God has failed utterly in his part of the bargain and spared them. Like Jonah, Thalbot quarrels with God and takes himself off in a dudgeon to languish on the seashore.

Meanwhile, it is evident (though this takes place "off-screen") that Clarice's indiscretion with Last Night has become known to the senior brothers in the church, but she is saved from the disgrace of disfellowshipping and expulsion because she is privy to their embarrassing secrets. Instead, influence is used to get her a visa to go to Canada. This is not how Thalbot imagines what has happened to her. He, now playing the part of another disappointed prophet, Elijah, imagines her first as a raven who brings him food in the desert, but then as a bird that falls to its death when he stones it. He conflates the bird's fall with that of the iconic figure of Jezebel, Elijah's persecutor, whose name signifies the misogynist male's worst nightmare of the treacherous woman, who in the Bible narrative is cast from the walls of the city to be eaten by dogs.

In the last, fourth part of *Prophets*, the poem moves from narrative to lyric, with three first-person monologues that complicate the notion of "I" in the poem. First, it is Clarice, speaking as a figure of poetic myth, renouncing the narrow path of self-denial to heaven, and proclaiming her joy and exhilaration in falling from heaven's door to rise into her full womanhood. Clarice speaks as "I", but in a register that is manifestly the poet's. Then, in the very last chapter (XXVIII, *Flight*), the "I" is an unnamed prophetess (not Clarice, because she has gone to Toronto) making a mythic (and self-propelled) flight over Africa to bring the gospel to South Carolina. She reflects on the contradiction between her commitment to the fundamentals of Christian faith and her attraction (in distinction to Clarice with her blue-eyed Jesus) to the cultural imagery and world-vision of Rastafarian and other Afrocentric systems of belief. After this flight to the USA, the prophetess confronts the challenge of being a black woman in the racially segregated institutions of the Southern church, where she hopes to find a space where her New World African cultural desires and her Christian beliefs can find harmony. This is, of course, the journey that Kwame Dawes made in reality to South Carolina in 1992. We can read this "I" as a kind of avatar for the poet, reflecting the blurring of identity between poet and character, creating the prophetess he would most have wished Clarice to be, and pointing to his attempt to embrace the female in his epic. In having a woman make this mythic flight, Dawes also pays homage to Toni Morrison's *Song of Solomon* in its challenge to the idea that the flights of the enslaved back to Africa were a male preserve.

Finally, the "I" can be heard as the poet reflecting on what he can take from his experience of the church, and on the impulses that have moved him as writer to transform the image of Clarice from the realistically drawn figure who has enjoyed a somewhat ambivalent power in the church, into becoming the ascendant figure of myth who can embrace both the spiritual and the erotic.

It should be clear from this that the narrative of *Prophets* moves variously among the realistic, the surreal or magical, the mythic, the parodic and the metatextual. Further, the implied narrative is not always presented sequentially. For instance, Part Two, Chapter XIV, *The Making of a Prophet*, takes place long before any of the events of Part One. It becomes clear, particularly in Part Four, which contains several short lyric poems, that the structure of *Prophets* is as much driven by a lyric impulse as a narrative one. There is, too, an element of play in the sequencing, where, for instance, the poem titled "The Last Poem" is not in fact the final one.

Prophets, then, has a four-part structure that is more thematic than linear. Part One, from the Prologue to Chapter XIII, establishes the narrative in the context of the political, social and cultural changes in Kingston in the 1980s. The chapters that focus on Castleberry serve to show how an older Kingston has disappeared. This first part begins with the arrival of the worshippers for the service and ends with an episode that signals that the young student's devotion to the church is on the wane as the rival distractions of sex and poetry take hold of him. In this part there is a focus on Clarice's conflicted attitudes to her blackness and a flashback to the sexual abuse and desperate poverty she suffers as a child, and her abandonment of the Rastafarian faith of her abusive father, once a famed musician, now derelict. The narrative peaks of this part come with the arrivals and spiritual experiences of the three male figures who come to Clarice's church – the student, Last Night and Thalbot. Their fates are different. Last Night rises in the church, Thalbot is only temporarily cured of his madness, and the student is won for the dubious battles of poetry.

Part Two focuses mainly on Thalbot's back story – told in a parodic versioning of the biblical narrative of Lot's escape from Sodom – his arrival in Clarice's church, and then his possession by the four artistic apparitions, four chapters quite outside the main narrative. The second part ends with the dramas of Clarice's mission to Annotto Bay, the "sinning" on the beach with Last Night, Thalbot's witnessing of the act and his descent into madness again.

Part Three focuses on Thalbot's passage, in the guises of righteous Jonah and misogynist Elijah, from the coast back to Kingston, no doubt to expose Clarice and Last Night. He is too late. Clarice has already arranged her comfortable exit from the church and Kingston. Part Three ends with the two rival prophets vanquished – Clarice in exile, Thalbot in defeated silence.

Part Four moves from narrative to speak in three lyric, first-person voices. Clarice speaks "for the first time"; the unnamed prophetess makes her flight over Africa; and the presumed author looks back at his younger self and wonders what the whole experience, including the writing of the poem, has meant.

THREE: CONTEXTS

1. The "Autobiographical"

The reader who has some knowledge of Kwame Dawes' life, or who has followed the flow of his work, will be drawn to supposing that the poem contains elements of autobiography. That, of course, does not guarantee that what is written is true. *Prophets*, as a narrative poem, is as fictive in character and incident as any novel. If there are "characters" in the poem who point to or draw on actual figures recognisable from recent Jamaican history, they are no less fictive for that. This is equally true of the woebegone young man who emerges from behind the authorial voice to speak as an "I", whom Clarice first rescues, then later flirts with and into whose troubled soul she sees. This "I" is revealed in the prologue as "…secure as / a victim, broke and hungry as never / before, my stomach growling; / maybe it was the cake of tears // in my eye-corner that she saw, or the sway of my broken body/ which made her prophesy my need" (ll. 9-15). Readers of Kwame Dawes' fiction know just such a young man from his story, "The Clearing", in *A Place to Hide* (2003), an episode repeated in his quasi-autobiographical novel, *Bivouac* (2010). Yet whilst there are connections with the student Kwame Dawes, who was once an active member of just such a Charismatic/ Pentecostal church, who records of this time that "all my work was deeply religious and sometimes quite evangelical in its polemics. … I was then a very devout university Christian",[1] what is pertinent in the poem is the dramatic play amongst a number of narrating voices, including that of the experiencing "I". That experiencing "I" is not simply a figure of need. When he reappears in Chapter XIII, *Sunday Morning*, he is both an involved participant and a somewhat ironic observer. The congregation notes his "wandering eye" as signalling his loss of faith: "they think I have died inside / unfeeling to the prophecy coming like the wind" (XIII, ll. 49-50).

And this is only one of a number of different narrating voices and tones, invested with varying degrees of spirituality and secular irony, marshalled by the organising authorial presence. There is the unnamed prophetess who makes her flight over Africa, who is given some aspects of Dawes' actual biographical experience, and also the "I" who speaks as the poet of his desire for some certainty about the significance and meaning of his experience.

As the editor of *Prophets*, I also know that at a fairly late stage in its original publication, the name of the prophetess was changed (to Clarice) because the original name would have pointed too obviously to the woman on whom the portrayal was based. Clarice's church is, incidentally, the same one (portrayed at an earlier period) that Kei Miller has written about in *Writing Down the Vision* (2013), and a conversation between Kei and Kwame I was party to in Barbados in 2012 identified some of the same leading members of this church. Even so, it is important to recognise that Clarice is a fictive creation whose trajectory in the poem is shaped by the poem's dramatic needs and the biblical resonances these bring into play. In his *A Far Cry from Plymouth Rock* (2007), subtitled a "personal narrative", Dawes confirms that he remains a committed Christian.[2] What will strike readers of *Prophets* is the poem's creative slipperiness between a commitment to take the "convinced" saints of the church entirely seriously, on their own terms, and a degree of irony that throws matters of faith and belief up in the air.

This questioning strand no doubt arises from the reservations that Dawes arrived at in his evaluation of this particular independent "Charismatic" church, but equally, and perhaps more fundamentally, it seems to me to grow out of his recognition that he was writing about something that lies at the heart of Jamaican/Caribbean religious culture, a nexus that is both inseparable and a point of conflict. This is the unstable coming together of the Protestant ethic of sanctification through moral purity (with its origins in Europe and European North America) and the West African vision of the trickster god. This is the figure through whom, by ritual, by arcane knowledge or by the practice of magic, the polarities of "rational" discourse (life/death, sickness/health, the spiritual and the sensual, male/female, humans and gods) may enter into liminal states of convergence. Anansi is, of course, the trickster god who made his way to the Caribbean and the figure of the Anansified trickster (generally male) is regularly attached to those who claim the power to heal, who have the charismatic capacity to influence others and turn situations to their own advantage. Diane Austin-Broos, whose thesis in *Jamaica Genesis: Religion and the Politics of Moral Orders* (1997) this discussion is indebted to, argues that this provisional merger is at the heart of the success of Jamaican Pentecostalism – aspects of which are discussed further (pp. 32-37) below. Austin-Broos records seeing both the "trick" (the performance of the apparently logically inexplicable) and the tricksterish in the personas of a number of the (male) Pentecostalist pastors she observed. She notes elements of irony in the responses she heard from some of the more established women leaders of such churches to the performance of male pastors – particularly in the ambivalent performance of a sensual masculinity when surrounded by the admiration of often younger women, and the public assertion of sexual continence.

Kwame Dawes went on to explore his fascination with trickster figures in *Jacko Jacobus* (1996) and in the reggae prophets of *Shook Foil* (1997), and one can see in *Prophets* an embryonic exploration of the ambiguities of this figure and the ideas it contains – the manipulator who uses her/his gifts to control others and the divinely inspired figure who is able to manage apparent contraries. Clarice is a trickster in both senses, a woman who uses her capacity to heal, her prophetic skills, her uncanny sense of what secrets people hide, or what they are planning to do, to achieve power and influence within the church, but who, ultimately, in myth at least, lives with both her spiritual gifts *and* her sexuality as a woman. Within the Charismatic Protestant church these are seen as polar opposites; within a West African spiritual framework they can converge.

This point of connection, dissonance and flow between African and European, Protestant and West African spirituality is central to Dawes' writing from *Resisting the Anomie* (1995, but actually his first book) through to *Impossible Flying* (2007) and more recently in *Wheels* (2011). At its heart is personal experience. Dawes grew up in Ghana, experienced prejudice as an African youth in a still Afrophobic Jamaican society, and spent his adolescence attending Jamaica College, a deeply colonial (male, homophobic) educational institution,[3] though one that was beginning to experience some shock-waves from the decolonising upsurge of 1970s Jamaica. His father was a politically committed atheist Marxist, but the rest of his family members were devout, convinced Christians. At university he was, as noted above, an actively evangelising Christian, and the Charismatic church he became involved with propagated a puritan attitude towards sexuality as the most dangerous of temptations for the would-be saint. His poems in *Progeny of Air* confess to a young man's very normal (if sometimes conflicted) recognition that sexuality was an essential part of his being. As a young man he had also discovered – celebrated in *Shook Foil* (1997) and the subject of analysis in his *Natural Mysticism: Towards a New Reggae Aesthetic* (1999) – in the most Rastafarian strands of reggae a synthesis that provided him with an aesthetic that validated Africa, was actively decolonising in its language, musical forms and cultural reference, that sang in a prophetic voice about the deep ills of Jamaican society and which had no problem with harmonising the spiritual and the erotic. The problem was that for a convinced Christian, the fundamental belief of Rastafarianism in the divinity of Haile Selassie was profoundly blasphemous and idolatrous.[4]

I think, too, that as the son of a Marxist father, who made no secret of his view that Jamaica needed to go through revolutionary change to overthrow its grossly unequal economic arrangements and its Eurocentric social and cultural hegemony, Kwame Dawes must have thought about the contradictions between the emphasis on the very individual, inward and personal kinds of salvation sought by the church as portrayed in the poem and the social redemption that political radicals could now only dream about in the

"New World order" in which 1980s' Jamaica found itself. These are issues discussed further in the section on prophecy, below.

Prophets dramatises these personal conflicts between spirituality and sexuality, sin and sensuousness, between individual salvation and social redemption, between Christian doctrines and Rastafarian culture, between the trick and the trickster. As in the best kind of (poetic) fiction, there is no neat resolution of those conflicts, and it is out of their dramatisation that the poem's continuing energies flow.

I read *Prophets* as the coming together of a number of important strands in Dawes' work that form the frameworks within which his later work has developed. But since this is a book about *Prophets*, these are outlined only briefly here, and dealt with in the course of the more specific notes. I see these to include: a focus on the personal and the familial (brought forward from *Resisting the Anomie* and *Progeny of Air* and developed in *Impossible Flying* and *A Far Cry From Plymouth Rock* and *Bivouac*); the historical (in *Requiem* and *Wisteria*); the social dimensions of race and gender (in *Wheels* and *City of Bones*); the body in sickness and health (in *Back of Mount Peace* and *Hope's Hospice*); the geographic (*Jacko Jacobus*); the artistic (*Shook Foil*, *Wheels*, *City of Bones*, *A Place to Hide*); the religious and the roots of faith (*Jacko* et al.). And whilst these may be the dominant concerns of particular books, there is scarcely one that does not take forward some aspect of all these areas of focus.

2. Gender, misogyny and the male gaze

As is discussed in the introduction, *Prophets* was written at a time when African American and Caribbean women writers had been and were revising the premises of how the lives of women of colour in the New World could be portrayed. As a male writer, Jamaican/Caribbean in nurture, but then living in the USA, there is ample evidence of Dawes' keen awareness of that development. The discussion of *Prophets*' intertextual relationship with the work of Zora Neale Hurston, Alice Walker and Toni Morrison in the next chapter (pp. 65-73) and the notes on allusions to their work in the second section of this guide point to his close reading of their novels as an encouragement to the writing of a strong female character and to the demolition of patriarchal thought.

As a doctoral student at New Brunswick University (he was awarded a PhD in 1992), it is evident that Dawes was also familiar with the new currents of women's critical writing about Caribbean and African American literature. Much of the Caribbean critical work published at that time, as is documented in Evelyn O'Callaghan's pioneering *Woman Version* (1993), deals with the emergence of Caribbean women's writing and the rediscovery of forgotten women writers. Dawes was also no doubt aware of the emerging critique of the gender biases of male Caribbean writing that drew on such critical concepts as Laura Mulvey's "male gaze", first developed in her essay, "Visual Pleasure and Narrative Cinema" (1975). Belinda Edmondson's *Making Men: Gender, Literary Authority and Women's Writing in Caribbean Narrative* (1999), though published after *Prophets*, was part of a wider feminist scrutiny of earlier Caribbean male writing and its assumptions. As George Lamming had belatedly admitted in *Natives of My Person* (1972), women were "the future" that men "must learn" (p. 351). Dawes' awareness of these critical trends is indicated in his essay "Violence and Patriarchy: Male Domination in Roger Mais's *Brother Man*" (1994, see also the note on p. 203), so it should come as no surprise that *Prophets* not only has a strong female character at its centre, but portrays patriarchy, male chauvinism and misogyny in sharply critical ways. But then, whilst we rightly expect male writers to show an awareness of the gendered nature of male behaviour, writing insightfully and self-reflexively about women is a challenge of a different order. How well does Dawes meet this challenge?

Prophets is forcefully explicit in its portrayal of the misogynist mentalities and behaviour of Thalbot and Last Night, prophet and preacher respectively, and of the four artistic apparitions who invade Thalbot. The poem questions the patriarchy of the Charismatic-Pentecostalist churches in giving an unquestionable priority to male leadership. It points to how misogynist narratives in the Bible are still used against women (see pp. 73, 97, 100, 218), and to elements of misogyny in Jamaican popular culture (see pp. 103, 188). In presenting all these aspects of toxic maleness, the poem is entirely clear about the damage done to both women and men.

Both Thalbot and Last Night are deeply conflicted about sexuality and women. Our first view of Thalbot is as the naked madman "exposing the branch of his circumcised penis/ to the women too curious to look away, too shy to stare/ on its ungodly size – 'What a waste, what a waste!'" (V, i, ll. 10-12). Later, after witnessing Clarice and Last Night on the beach, Thalbot's language in representing what he has seen confirms his distaste both for sex and for women's sexuality in particular. He identifies with Last Night's agonised and guilty point of view, sees Clarice as "milking him, milking him" and imagines in disgust the "thin membrane" of her "drying sex" being picked over by a soldier crab. When Thalbot moves from playing the role of Jonah to the role of Elijah in mortal conflict with Jezebel (see XXIII, xii, ll. 3-18 and xv, ll. 1-17, and the notes on pp. 250 and 254-255) we see just how misogynist a prophet he is. In the references to Jezebel, *Prophets* also notes the place this iconic target of misogynist hatred and contempt occupies in Jamaican popular culture.

It is also worth noting how, after the episode on the beach with Clarice, Last Night uses the story of David and Bathsheba (XXI, iv; see notes on pp.

192-193 and 223) to comfort himself, reflecting on a narrative that suggests that God is ready to forgive his male favourites for their morally appalling behaviour.

This use of allusion to narratives outside the poem is one of the ways *Prophets* gives resonance to how we read the misogyny of its male characters. For instance, as I argue (see p. 186), all the four artistic apparitions who invade Thalbot fail at some point in their lives in demonstrably male ways. The first of these, the musician who murders the woman he loves but wants to control, is read through allusions to Othello's murder of Desdemona. This allusion plays on the intersection of race and gender in the murder, and also responds to two earlier Caribbean poetic allusions to *Othello*, by Derek Walcott and Kamau Brathwaite. Here, Dawes rejects both the racial alarm and the misogyny masquerading as a self-justifying racial assertion explored, respectively, in those earlier poems (see p. 189).

By contrast, we may note how *Prophets* alludes to the one unequivocal expression of women's sexuality in the Bible, when Clarice uses the Song of Solomon to justify her sexual being.

However, in writing about a woman who seeks both spiritual and sexual realisation, the poem enters more hazardous territory, particularly since the figure of Clarice is the object of male desire and gaze, including, at one point, that of the young man who is the "I" of the poem. The prologue to *Prophets* begins with his confession of mingled fear, respect and desire for the prophetess. He recalls how, fearful that she will expose his sexual indiscretions during the church service, her pointing finger "stirred bumps on my flesh". She has been for him the "priestess of the pure" and yet in the writing of the poem he admits, "I reach for her tarnished flesh" and that he has dared "to imagine her coupling/ in the blackness of the beach" (Prologue, ll. 6, 19, 46, 49-50). In the metatextual operation of the prologue, the poet is both the autobiographer who can safely make admissions about his gendered imperfections (his own conflicted feelings about the relationship between sexuality and religion, his guilty weeping and wailing (XII, i, ll. 28-29)), but also the writer who must take responsibility for how he portrays Clarice.

There are sharp observations of the male gaze in operation in the poem, but also, I think, sometimes expressions of it in the narrative voice. The first image of Clarice portrays her as asexually demure: "In her blue chiffon dress and white head-tie,/ she carries her virgin body like a saint" (I, I, ll. 10-11), yet the church brothers who have come to collect her for the service have to "recite their verses to ward off/ the lust, seeing Clarice like that, her curve of breast/ and wet, dipped lips" (I, i, ll. 43-45). The poem, though, has to risk going further than this kind of safe observation of shamefaced male desire, because it needs to portray the reality of Clarice's sexual desires as the basis for her challenge to the church's imposition of virginal abstinence, to establish her as a sexual being. The poem could have had Clarice expressing her desires verbally, or representing her thoughts as inner speech, but it does not – not until she becomes a figure of myth in the last part of the poem. Clarice, as social actor, is observed, rather than given the words to speak on her own behalf, and this almost inevitably forces the poem to construct her sexuality through male eyes. One can argue that since Clarice knows what is at stake with the church, it is psychologically truthful that she is not open about her feelings, that she is forced into indirection, even apparent hypocrisy in her halting seduction of Last Night. Even when Clarice has a voice, when she justifies the seduction, she is more comfortable with the idea that what has occurred is "that abandonment of self […] the succumbing of my limbs to the nerves'/ attack" (XXII, viii, 2-4) than with admitting to any conscious desire on her own part. Given her past history as a victim of incestuous abuse and her enmeshment in the values of the church, this seems realistic.

One can see a dramatic movement from observed action, without internal commentary, to the point where, in Part Four, the prophetess "speaks" for the first time. I put *speaks* in inverted commas because Clarice both speaks and doesn't speak – in the sense that the register of the words she uses is manifestly not her own. It is a point where the poem reminds us that it is a poem and not a realist novel (see the summary on p. 258), but also where it confesses that it has not felt able to give the Clarice of social reality an inner voice, and has portrayed her sexual desires through describing her body – even at the risk of eroticising it in a way that might sometimes look suspiciously like male wish-fulfilment. This comes in the scenes when Clarice is alone in Castleberry's old house, where under the appreciative eye of this benign old ghost, "she feels the looseness in her thigh" (II, l. 24), and where her viewing of the TV soap *Hawaii Five O* is eroticised in sexually suggestive language, describing her imagined perceptions as she watches the canoeing boys "rippling their humping bodies over the frothing sea,/ their paddles parting, dipping, withdrawing, horning…" (ll. 26-27). The image of her profile in the mirror, "the breast and nipples, the stomach's curve", is ambivalently caught in her own, the ghost's and the poet's eyes.

If the eroticisation of Clarice's body remained simply the object of an external viewing eye, then it would be hard to deny several Susannah and the Elders (Daniel 13) moments in the poem. But Clarice does not remain the passive object of external view. In the scenes with Last Night (Chapter VII, *The Old Man* and Chapter IX, *Confessional*) she emerges as the most powerful actor in the process of a seduction that will end with the realisation of her desires to bring together the spiritual and the erotic. When we enter Last Night's fevered imagination while he is present in her apartment receiving counsel ("He has heard the shower, but dares not think/ of the water beating her exposed skin,/ her private stepping out of her damp panties" (VII, I, ll. 3-6), the focus is primarily on the ambivalence of his sexuality, stirred to erection by his imagining of Clarice's vulnerability, though as we know from his escape from Thelma, "a black woman with a bold bright eye", he is a man who cannot deal with the sexuality of a woman with her own sexual agenda and direct style (IX, i). The other element in these episode is their undoubted humour – a humour that both complicates Clarice and puts us on her side. This works to defuse the element of voyeurism in the scene-setting in Chapter VII where "Clarice entertains Last Night with Bible verses/ and prayers, casual in her yellow nightdress" (VII, I, ll. 2-3. We realise that Clarice is anything but casual in her strategies, even if she does not admit them.

In addition to the satire on the pious brothers praying to ward off their feelings of lust, there is also a strong element of reflexive self-satire in the poem. It arises from the metatextual play with the roles of an "I" who is both a character in the narrative and the poet who is the creator of the narrative and all its characters. In Chapter XII, where the "I" who is a character confesses his fear that Clarice will see prophetically into his guilt over his own sexual indiscretions, he records how he tried "to force a purer image into my mind,/ as if Clarice's prophecy *required my writing*// a digression of bright images into my brain" (XII, I, ll. 10-13, my italics). It is clear, though, that the young man's image of Clarice is far from pure – "my/ fantasy, flaming with its startling detail" (ll. 23-24). This is confirmed in Chapter XXVI, *The Perks of Prophecy*, where Clarice speaks in her own voice, recalling the incident from her perspective: "…he thought I could see into his heart./ He was right. I was naked there…" (ll. 2-3). There is a male gaze, but the poem both admits it and Clarice, as principal woman character, stares back.

Whatever one's views on how successfully the poem escapes the male-ness of its gaze, there can be no question that *Prophets* is a poem with a strong woman at its centre, and that it unambiguously rejects male chauvinism. This was undoubtedly still a new note in male Caribbean writing and one that chimes with the changing gender politics of the historical moment in which the poem was written. But then again, this is the reading of a male critic.

3. History and Politics

Prophets is set in the 1980s, the Caribbean's low dishonest decade when the 1970s' hopes of radical decolonisation collapsed with the return of right-wing Washington- and CIA-supported governments in Jamaica (in 1980) and Grenada (following the 1983 collapse of the PRG government in fratricidal killings and the US invasion); the collapse from inner corruption of the state socialist experiment in Guyana and the presence of unashamedly neo-colonial governments in, for instance, Barbados and Dominica, both loyal subjects of the Reagan administration.[5] The 1970s began with the promise to address the huge economic inequalities of Jamaican society, but ended when rising debt resulted in the imposition of IMF-enforced austerity on the poor, which was estimated to have cut living standards by around 40%. It was a decade when the decolonising energies released by Michael Manley's People's National Party's (PNP) election victory in 1972 ended in the out-of-control violence of the 1980 election when over 750 people died in inter-communal political warfare in the nine months between the election's announcement and the polling date. In this period, Manley's PNP, no less than the conservative opposition Jamaica Labour Party (JLP), lost control of the dons, the community enforcers to whom both sides forwarded guns. This was done, allegedly, to protect the housing areas dominated by their own party supporters, but in reality to enforce the clientelism that both parties relied on for electoral support. Popular disillusionment with "democratic socialism" and the massive decline in living standards, along with the widely believed and probable complicity between a senior PNP minister and elements in the army to set up and murder JLP supporters in the Green Bay incident,[6] the divisions between left and right in the PNP and its subsequent demoralisation, saw the return to power of the free-market JLP in a landslide election victory and the return of at least some of the light-skinned elite whom Manley's "communism" had scared into taking flight to North America, along with upwards of $300M US taken out of the country illegally.[7]

The 1970s was a decade when the first Michael Manley government played a role in the upsurge of pride in blackness (and sometimes Africa) that spread in both the USA and the Caribbean from the outsider voices of militant minorities into the political mainstream. There was a belated recognition that Jamaica was, in fact, a country whose majority ethnic heritage was African and that the slogan of "one out of many" was a myth that did not disguise the reality that Jamaica's "official" culture was still that of the European elite, and that the culture of the African majority was regarded as primitive and uncivilised by that elite. It was an irony of the times that Michael Manley was himself a part of that elite. It was a period when, from being a community of the despised and outcast, Rastafarians found an articulate international voice in roots reggae through Bob Marley, Burning Spear and many others, and for a time had a cultural influence massively disproportionate to the actual numbers of people who, in census terms at least, identified themselves as Rastafarians. It was also a time when both political parties shamelessly exploited the popular credibility of reggae in their own more narrow interests. In the 1980 election campaign, the PNP was mortified to hear Bunny Wailer's truth-telling single "Crucial"

(Solomonic, 1980) being used by the JLP against them.[8] It was a time when an unsuccessful attempt was made to murder Bob Marley (1976) – followed a decade later by the actual murder of Peter Tosh (1987).

In truth, the socialist slogans of the 1972 PNP government sounded more militant than they were in practice, bringing in what was actually a modestly social democratic programme, though the leading conservative newspaper, *The Gleaner*, and columnists such as the novelist John Hearne (who features as one of the four apparitions) told the Jamaican people that if they didn't vote the PNP out of power in 1980, they would never have the chance to vote again and that under the communism the PNP would install, Jamaicans would suffer more than under the slave-master of plantation days.[9] Whilst the PNP was accused of anti-white and anti-brown racism by *The Gleaner*, the expressions of black pride didn't translate into any structural change in the coincidence of race and class privilege. What brought the democratic socialist experiment to an end was the economic collapse that came as a result of the quadrupling of world oil prices, the consequent inflationary pressures and its devastating impact on the value of the Jamaican dollar (devaluing eight-fold between 1973 and 1990) and the consequent debt burden that Jamaica, like most Third World countries, was unable to avoid. In 1980, 30% of the labour force was out of work. Whilst this 1970s period of decolonising hope (flawed as it was) is not the period in which *Prophets* is set, it lies behind the poem's present and stands as a contrast to it.

Prophets refers to this decade in some ironic lines ("…Long gone is the socialist puritanism, gone/ the old revolutionaries who have/ discarded their bush jackets, (hand-me-downs to/ gardeners) who now concede without fanfare to// the pragmatic wisdom of the IMF" (XIV, ii, l. 31)) and a few throw-away details (the white Jamaican sellers of the mansion that Clarice's church buys after Castleberry's death are noted to be on their way back to Toronto). Now, Clarice sleeps "to the symphony of gunshots in the tenement", and this is a time "with its pragmatics of finding the right price every time./ Infidels skank to the visionless platform/ of sweet-mouthed politricksters looking a contract// for their twilight years on the stump…" (III, i, l. 21). The consequences of the collapse of 1970s' hopes reverberate through the poem, not so much in any overt political statement (beyond those just quoted), but in the accumulating details of cultural change in musical expression, dance styles, styles of dress and which recreational drugs became most popular – all caught in the poem's sharp eye for the telling image. Not least of the changes, as a response to the collapse of hopes in the political kingdom, the poem portrays a corresponding investment in the comforts of religion – whilst also suggesting ways in which the ethos of religious practice was itself changing in tune with these free-market times.

In the 1980 election, the evangelical churches had been vociferous in their opposition to the PNP's allegedly godless communism, "the politics of the devil",[10] and as Chapter III of *Prophets* suggests, the right-wing politics of US televangelism, with its acquisitive prosperity gospel, had found fertile ground in these churches. This is dealt with further below, but suffice to say that *Prophets* observes a church at a point of ambivalence, as very much part of the every-manjack-for-himself politics of the time. This is the conflict between the conviction that "saintliness" in this life is about preparing for the imminent hereafter (and the irrelevance of worldly things), and the hope that "saintliness" might bring God's favour, signalled by access to worldly rewards. Right at the beginning of the poem, the image of the church's senior brothers with their "off-the-wharf" – and hence expensive – cars signals a coincidence between religious fervour and acquisitiveness.

The particular phenomena of cultural change and their significance are identified and discussed in the notes, but if there are themes that link them it is the coming together of hedonism (with an edge of desperation) and a cult of violence. Whilst Jamaican music has always been as much about pleasure, sensual abandonment and (mostly) male sexual aggrandisement, as about social justice, spiritual consciousness and racial pride, the mid- to late-1980s' soundtrack of *Prophets* signals the dominance of the former over the latter. As a venue, the dancehall was where Jamaicans sought bodily pleasures long before the naming of the musical styles that emerged in the 1980s as "dancehall" and later ragga. Even so, there are distinct changes in the style and content of Jamaican music from the conscious reggae of the 1970s to the styles of the later 1980s. This was reflected in the speed of the music, the use of computerised elements ("the rapid digital basslines"), and the focus on an ever-changing range of dance styles – which chiefly turn on the display of the female body. This was the period of the "dancehall queen" in her batty-riders and sequinned bralet. As the tone and imagery of Chapter III in particular shows, these were not political or cultural changes with which Dawes, the admirer of Marley and roots reggae, felt much in sympathy.[11]

Even so, as my discussion of the religious milieu of the poem argues, in the stoned dancehall queens and the ecstatic dancing in the church, the poem suggests a shared desire for transcendence from the harsh realities of Jamaican life. *Prophets* portrays the church hall and the dancehall as driven by the same cultural sensibilities: by the irrepressible germ of Africa and the Creole Jamaican urge to transform whatever enters its national space. The same dub sensibility that creates versions galore in reggae, is also the one that drives churches like Clarice's to the spiritual eclecticism described below.[12]

4. The Social Geography of Prophets

As a colonial city dating back to 1692, Kingston's topography is deeply marked by divisions of class and race, wealth and poverty and successive waves of settlement.[13] The city grew massively in the 1940s and 1950s when its population virtually doubled with inward migration from the countryside. As a seaport, its expansion could only move in one direction, and even this has been limited by the city's mountainous surrounds. Only the wealthy have been able to invest in the expense of the elaborate engineering needed to turn these hilly areas into zones of elite housing, such as the "balconied mansions of Beverly Hills". From the 1940s, what had once been the prosperous commercial sector by the waterfront rapidly became a deteriorating downtown, and West Kingston became a byword for the squalor of overcrowded slums and squatter settlements. But as sectors of the non-agricultural economy grew in the postwar years, Kingston grew a middle and lower-middle class of office workers, supervisory management, teachers, nurses and middle-range public servants. To meet their needs, large-scale new housing settlements developed to the north of Kingston, above Half-way Tree – the very precise point that divides downtown from uptown.

The specifics of place and how the events of the poem are mapped onto them are more fully detailed in the notes to the poem, but I mention here several ways in which place enters into the poem's meaning. Firstly, it is a marker of the historical shift from the decay and destruction of the old colonial Kingston and the emergence of the free-market materialist consumerism of the present. This is seen in Thalbot's tribulations in Chapter V, where he is rudely expelled from squatting first in the "jaded pink mansion", the old colonial house on Old Hope Road (after the conservationists fail to save it) and then in the replica American shopping mall of Sovereign City with its "bubble-gum scented air", and "Marley in a can [watered down] to muzak" that replaces it.

Place also enters the poem in tracking Clarice's movement through Kingston's social geography. At the beginning of the poem we learn that she has been installed as the caretaker in an old St Andrew's house (the gradually decaying area of old white and brown privilege). As is made clear in Chapter X, which flashes back to her youth in the Rastafarian squatter encampment on the hills of Wareika, this represents a huge uplift in her fortunes. The fact that the church's services take place in the Guild Hall of the University of the West Indies at Mona signals a number of things: that this is a very new church that doesn't yet have its own premises and that geographically and socially the campus is a crossroads setting, not far from decaying Old Hope Road, but also a route to middle-class status. Other more passing locations that signal social setting include the charitable sybil mother's reference to her good works on Oxford Street (III, ii, l. 24) which all Jamaicans would know is where Kingston Public Hospital, destination of last resort for the poor, is located, or Knutsford Boulevard signalled as a place of both foreign embassies and prostitution in Chapter XIV, ii.

The actual physical geography of Kingston is also a signifier. For instance, when Thalbot gets the call to go to Kingston to prophesy God's wrath to come, even when he eventually finds himself in the capital, and when he finally does preach to the Kingstonians, he does it from the "marl of the Edgewater coast" – in Portmore, one of Kingston's overspill settlements, which is in fact safely separated by the sea from the wicked city, across the bay from Palisadoes.

Geography also enters the poem in more imaginative ways, though it has ample precedent in the rhetoric of Rastafarianism and reggae. This is the mapping of biblical locations onto Jamaica. This happens in the parallel geographies of the dub version of the Jonah narrative where Thalbot is in Joppah (Annotto Bay) when God tells him to go to Nineveh, but instead flees to Tarshish (Montego Bay). This is more than just a witty play with allusion in the narrative; it records a truth about the millenarian imagination in Jamaica. It is not just the naming of Jamaica as Babylon, or that the descriptions of the city of Nineveh at war in the prophetic book of Nahum had a chilling applicability to Kingston at this time (see the notes on pp. 126-127), but *Prophets* connects to the kind of geographical mapping of biblical image onto Jamaican soil found in popular culture. Prince Far I has come from Bozrah in his song, "Wisdom" (Clinch records, c. 1975): "Prince Far I/ Come from Bozrah to show you the way/ Listen what he really has to say/ Behold, Behold/ Prince Far I." So too Prince Alla takes the Rastaman to Bozrah in his song of that name: "Now the Rastaman came from Bozrah/ With his garment dipped in blood…" (Stars, 12", 1976). But it is perhaps Max Romeo's "Valley of Jehoshaphat" (on *Open the Iron Gate*, 1978) that makes the mapping most explicit. He sings: "When Jah come from Bozrah/ With his garment dipped in blood/ It a go red hot, red hot, red hot/ Down in Jehoshaphat […] It a go jamdung, jamdung, jamdung/ Down in Jehoshaphat, yeah". Jamdung is, of course, one of the patwa names for Jamaica and 1978 was a year of political violence (387 murders), including the infamous Green Bay massacre of JLP supporters and the Bob Marley peace concert that didn't bring peace. In *Prophets*, one element of Thalbot's delusion is his fantasy (XXIII, xii, l. 6ff) of himself as a persecuted Elijah sojourning in the desert wilderness of Damascus – he is on the Edgewater coast – and that he has chopped down Clarice along with the idolators of Baal in the Kishon valley, when he is in fact chopping down flowers in one of the city's municipal parks.

I think, too, that in the poem's emphasis on place, one can read *Prophets* as a kind of wounded love letter to Kingston in all its horrors and charms by a poet who had, like many young, educated people, been forced to leave the country to look for work, and, as his alter ego, the unnamed prophetess in Chapter XXVIII (*Flight*) indicates, is looking to make a connection with another landscape, the piedmont of South Carolina. In Chapter XIII (*Sunday Morning*), a pivotal chapter in exploring the competing pulls of religious faith and poetry, there is a rich abundance in the description of the sights, sounds and smells of the university campus that suggests a poetic abundance of lost love.

5. The Charismatic Churches and Revival Zion: Prophets' Religious Setting

The narrative core of *Prophets* concerns the struggle for salvation and meaning in one of the many independent "Charismatic" churches which, by the 1980s, together with the more mainstream Pentecostal Church of God, had become the repository of the faith of the majority – and growing – of Christian Jamaicans, and in particular of those from the lower-middle and working classes and of predominantly African heritage.

Romantic outsiders might imagine that Jamaica as a country dominated by Rastafarian cultural energies (and it is a striking acknowledgement of the reach of those energies when we recognise how disproportionate it is to the number of Jamaicans who actually identified themselves as Rastafarian (14,249 in 1982) in comparison to the numbers who identified as either Church of God (400,379) or the many hundreds of independent Charismatic/Pentecostalist churches (113,570). By 1982, these two denominations vastly outnumbered any other Christian denomination (though it's worth noting that the second biggest category in the census was of Jamaicans who acknowledged no faith), including the churches of the elites (Anglicans, Roman Catholics and Methodists), the Baptists (the denomination historically associated with bringing Christianity to African Jamaicans and formerly the church favoured by the black working and peasant classes) and the African-Jamaican churches that have been grouped under the label of Revivalist Zion.[14]

However, to attach any definitive label to the church that Clarice leads – such as Charismatic or Pentecostalist – is convenient, but not exact. It is not part of any wider institutional structure such as the Baptists, Seventh Day Adventists, or even the Church of God, the largest and most centrally organised of the Pentecostal churches, which has a formal hierarchy and headquarters in the USA. The heirs of Castleberry, from whom the church buys his old home, snottily describe it as a "New Age" church – and whilst this is wholly misleading if it suggests some hippyish, Age of Aquarius eclecticism across a variety of world religions and spiritual practices, Clarice's church *is* eclectic within a much narrower Protestant Christian range of Bible-based practice. It would no doubt regard New Age teachings as quite literally emerging from the pit of hell.[15] But the actual inventiveness in inspiration and practice of Clarice's church is initially both its attraction to the young man who falls into its orbit, and ultimately seen as its fatal flaw. It is Pentecostalist in the sense that it sees itself in a direct line from the first Christians, the disciples who received God's apostolic gift and mission in the tongues of fire that appeared above their heads, enabling them to speak the languages of the diverse nations of gentiles (Acts 2: 2-3); and speaking in tongues (glossolalia) is frequently the climax of this church's act of worship.[16] It is a Charismatic church in the sense that its only hierarchy is that of manifest spiritual gifts – principally in the signs that the worshipper displays of possession by the holy spirit – speaking in tongues, the gift of healing powers and of prophecy (in senses that will be discussed below). Individuals with such gifts can rise rapidly in the church, as Last Night evidently does in his transformation from outcast waif to preacher. It is an evangelical church in the sense that it sees its prime function as being the missionary task of going out to preach the gospel to win souls to God and save them from eternal damnation. It is a fundamentalist church in that it believes the words of the Bible are literally and historically true, though how the Bible's often puzzling words are to be interpreted is a matter of individual interpretation, divinely inspired, rather than that of the authority of any accumulated body of institutionalised teaching. In this respect, the church manifests the radical democracy of the most anti-clerical traditions of Protestantism. Even so, on the basis of the ability to readily and pertinently quote the Bible, chapter and verse, individuals acquire authority in this church. As a literalist church, its members see themselves as the direct inheritors of the first apostles (with a similarly embattled sense of fighting for truth in a hostile world where satanic powers are very real). It displays the same apprehension of the early church that the end of the world and the second coming might well be near, that as true believers they might well be "rapt" away from Earth to be with Jesus and separated from the damned.

On the other hand, as Dawes acutely observes, as the church grows and attracts a more lower-middle class following (the brothers with their "off-the-wharf cars"), it is no less immune to the shifts in ideology between the "socialist" 1970s and the free-market capitalist 1980s. As Chapter III, I, l. 24-25 has it, "every Christ is fixing/ a tidy nest up in the sky for the greying times." Even the most pious, for instance, the testifying "sybil mother" we meet in that chapter appears to confuse the heaven of a green card to the USA with the heaven of the saved soul's afterlife.

Like the Baptists of old, the church practises adult baptism by total immersion; it envisages sin as the very real physical occupation of the body by evil spirits, but believes in the possibility of the body and soul being cleansed and the individual being born again – which is a necessity for salvation. The church also believes – and this distinguishes it from the spectrum of conventional Christianity from Catholicism to Calvinism – that it is possible for the born-again, spiritually-infilled person to achieve the living status of a saint. As such, the saints exist on a narrow tightrope of perfection with neither the regular sacrament of confession and absolution of the Catholic church to manage human "sinfulness", or the bleaker pessimism of Calvinist Protestantism that hope rests only in God's grace after death. In Clarice's church, backsliding in the faith is taken as a sign that God does not intend this sinner to be saved. This is Clarice's explanation to the congregation of Thalbot's failings.

Yet if Clarice's church is not part of any institutional order, it has a virulently sectarian sense of it own rightness and the heretical, idolatrous wrongness of all other churches. As a new church, it has very probably split off from another similar church over some matter of intensely felt doctrinal schism. Its fate is very probably to split again and again.

As Diane J. Austin-Broos shows in *Jamaica Genesis*, the phenomenal growth of the Pentecostalist churches (with origins in the 1920s and rapid expansion in the 1960s) raises fundamental questions about the nature of Jamaican culture and society, questions that are at the heart of *Prophets*. As noted above, she argues that the success of Pentecostalism both points to and, after a manner, heals the deep fissure between West Africa and Europe in the island's culture and religious practices (in both cosmological and institutional terms). This is a fissure that goes back to slave society and the "civilising" mission of 19th- and 20th-century colonial rule, and the way those divisions mapped onto Jamaica's race/class hierarchy and social and cultural inequalities. What she means by the fissure is that on the one side there have been the churches whose gospel teachings appealed to African Jamaicans, but whose cultural and institutional practices either denied their cultural selfhood, or excluded them from any positions of power and influence. On the other side were the churches and belief systems that arose out of creolised treaties between radically reinterpreted forms of Christianity and cosmologies, beliefs and cultural practices that derived from survivals of West African spirituality.[17] In the period in which *Prophets* is set, this includes the Revival churches such as African Zion, the more purely, though creolised, African spiritual practices of Kumina and the more autonomous inventions of Rastafarianism – some sectors of which related to the Ethiopian Christian church and almost all to consciously "African" Jamaican interpretations of the Bible, particularly the prophetic Old Testament – as well as to the more political vision of Marcus Garvey. However, except for brief periods (such as the Myalist spiritual upsurge in the immediate post-slavery period, 1840-1850s) these have never been institutions that attracted more than a minority of Jamaicans, and these mainly amongst the poorest and most marginal communities. Colonialism was remarkably effective in inoculating at least some black Jamaicans with a contempt for things African and for those who followed such faiths. This is not to say that Christian African Jamaicans were wholly obedient to the pressures of Eurocentric respectability. To the constant despair of the churches, they steadfastly refused the command to marry – either not until it suited them, or not at all.

On the surface, the Pentecostal churches entered the Jamaican cultural fissure on the Eurocentric side. They were white-led, American missionary churches and *Prophets* notes the new forms of cultural imperialism in the way that Clarice constantly denies her Africanness, with her blue-eyed, white Jesus and her conviction that those groups whose belief systems have any connection to Africa are irredeemably damned. But what *Prophets* dramatises (and Austin-Broos documents) is the way that worshippers in the independent churches Jamaicanised Pentecostalism in ways that kept hold of its authority as a Bible-based Christianity with white American origins, whilst embedding some of the practices of West African spirituality in forms of worship in their churches. Possession by spirits – divine or malevolent – and the bodily performance of "labouring" to reach a state of divine possession (see the summary and notes for Chapter XXII, p. 225), psychic healing, ecstatic bodily worship involving dance, communal "call-and-response" styles of interaction between priest and congregation were all forms of worship drawn from the very Revival churches the Pentecostalists regarded as pagan, or in Old Testament terminology, idolatrous because they revered ancestors and natural forces and sometimes involved animal sacrifice. As Barry Chevannes noted in his essay, "Revivalism: A Disappearing Religion" (1978), from the 1960s onwards, the Pentecostal churches were absorbing the congregations of the Revival churches at a existentially threatening rate. But they were also evidently absorbing those churches' practices, which is why they were proselytising their congregations so successfully.[18]

Austin-Broos writes about these issues within Pentecostalism as a struggle to find a meeting point between the pulls of a "rational" ethical morality as defined by the European churches, and a Jamaican eudemonism[19] with roots in West Africa. She describes this as bringing together an extreme Protestant emphasis on sinfulness (particularly of a sexual kind) and sanctification through faith (and the demonstration of that sanctity through, for instance, sexual abstinence outside marriage) and the Jamaican creolisation of a West African spirituality which displays a ready belief in the corporeal reality of spirits (good and bad), and of attaining present spiritual joy through those African derived forms described above. Austin-Broos points to a contrast between a world-view where there is a rationally ranked hierarchy of behaviours, good and bad, and primarily legal or morally-agreed ways of dealing with harmful behaviours when they arise, and, on the other, a world-view where the goal of happiness (or avoidance of misfortune) is to be achieved by whatever means is most likely to succeed, whether rites for the ancestors, acts of sacrifice, pleas to God or the gods, or the casting of spells. In truth, it is ultimately within this second world-view that Clarice operates, though the language she uses suggests the first. For instance, whereas Last Night, as a good Protestant, is mortified by his failure to resist the temptation to "sin" on the beach, because he sees it as a clear breach of the church's moral rules (as well as his hang-ups about sex), Clarice persuades herself that God can't think that badly of her if he has permitted her to win so many converts during the Annotto Bay mission. This play between cultural orders is central to the drama of *Prophets*, and the ironic eye it sometimes casts on the process. In Chapter XXII, *The Saints Return Triumphant*, when Clarice's church wins many sinful souls to the true church, it is clear that Merle, the obeah woman, though now "captive sister of the crusading Clarice", feels no sense of defeat but instead "is giddy with this new reckoning. For power like that / which she has seen at the hands of the prophetess / is power to bring supplication" (XXII, ii, ll. 27-30). In other words, Merle is only too pleased to ally herself with someone she thinks has superior magical powers, and it is clear that the crowds observing these "impossible occurrences" interpret them in the same, creolised West African way.

Whilst this is a church located at the radically democratic end of Protestantism, readers of Keith Thompson's classic *Religion and the Decline of Magic* (1971) will see echoes of the ways that the radical Protestant sectarian churches that emerged in the period (1640-1660) of the English civil war and the Protectorate tended to rediscover elements of popular Catholicism, forms of magical thinking that encompassed faith healing, miracles, divination, prophecy and millenialism. As Thomas notes at one point of a slightly earlier period, "The reign of Elizabeth produced a small army of pseudo-messiahs" (p. 157). Dawes echoes this in his lines: "the market is glutted with sybils and clarices/ cornering the ready congregation with miracles" (V, iv, ll. 20-21). The poem maintains a creative ambivalence between the suspicion of tricks and self-deceptions and an appreciation of the radical energies of tambourines celebrating "the joy of faith rewarded" (XXVIII, v, l. 11), and, like the work of Thomas, Christopher Hill and E.P. Thompson, pays respect to the often poetic logic of popular culture.[20] This is a topic addressed further in the next chapter in the discussion of the connections between Prophets and Sylvia Wynter's *The Hills of Hebron* (1962).

Implicit in *Prophets'* recognition of the success of this kind of church in making converts is the counter-view of the poem's several reiterations of the fragility of Jamaican sovereignty in the post-independence era, even as British colonialism gave way to the new hegemony of US capitalism and its religious and cultural exports, of which the missions of American Pentecostalist churches were significant parts. The poem has a creative ambivalence in suggesting that whilst in some respects Jamaicans infallibly Jamaicanised the meanings and forms of these ideological/spiritual imports, they were unable to dismantle the political hegemony of their source.

The rise of these independent churches is also connected in the poem to the class and gender inequalities of Jamaican society. At one level, these are churches in which the poorest and most African of Jamaicans can find personal status as well as God, yet in their practices these churches also enshrine the scriptural obedience of women to men, for as *Prophets* notes, "... the power is in the channelling,/ the clear path without static and pride from/ God to man to woman" (XXI, ii, ll. 17-19). Yet as both the poem and Austin-Broos observe, many of the independent churches have at their centre strong women with charismatic personalities and spiritual gifts. Conversely, as noted above (pp. 23-24) the poem has a sharp eye for the misogyny and mental fragility of its two male priestly or prophetic figures, Last Night and Thalbot.

Ironic as it is at times about the posturing, occasional hypocrisies and deceits of the faithful, the poem as a whole supports the respectful account given by Austin-Broos about the way membership of such churches could bring order, self-respect and dignity to lives otherwise lived on the margins of disorder – the way church members live by strict codes of sexual behaviour and insist on marriage.[21] Yet it is the demand for Clarice's total sexual abstinence which, of course, brings her into conflict with the church and provokes one of the central themes of the poem: the case it makes for the compatibility of spiritual and erotic transcendence. Yet if this suggests a miserably repressive church, this is very far from the truth, and this, perhaps, is the church's Jamaican genius. There is a not dissimilar church in George Eliot's *Silas Marner* (1861), the small independent Protestant sect of Lantern Yard, of poor but aspiring working people, where "the poorest layman has the chance of distinguishing himself by the gifts of speech". Silas Marner, like Last Night and Thalbot, "had fallen, at a prayer-meeting, into a mysterious rigidity and suspension of consciousness".[22] This is accepted by all, except the false friend, William, as evidence of "an accession of light and fervour". What is utterly dissimilar about the two churches is that one is all gloomy earnestness, in a perpetual state of fearful anxiety about their unworthiness for salvation, whereas Clarice's church, for all its restrictions on sexuality, frequently manifests joy, as when the church triumphs over the unbelievers at Annotto Bay: "...Oh, they have seen/ the work of the Lord, and there is rejoicing in the pews./ There is leaping in the hall of light this morning,/ spirited dancing among the saints..." (XXII, i, ll. 10-11).

In this perception of the African Jamaican propensity for the expression of bodily joys, *Prophets*, as hinted above, makes connections between the practices of the church and the culture of pleasure-seeking in secular

Jamaican society. At the beginning of the poem, analogies are drawn between the enjoyments of the student body on the campus, who have had the pleasures of a night of dancing, Guinness, curried goat and ganja in the very same building in which the Clarice's church has come to worship – with an equal spirit of abandon. In the episode at Annotto Bay, the poem links the worlds of dancehall and the church compound. On the surface they are rivals, but what the poem suggests are their similarities:

> ...The thump of
> the man-high speaker boxes below mainstreet
> rattle the dry bamboo of the church's fence.
>
> The sisters wait for the prophetess to electrify
> like a pole in the balm yard catching the current
> from the sea and then, rooted like that
>
> in the soil of ages, to speak. (XXI, ii, ll. 7-11)

This is an image that locates Clarice in the space between the dancehall (the huge sound-system speakers pumping out ragga music, courtesy of the JPS electricity supply), and the Africa of the centre pole (the *mitan*) where the electricity that connects the earth and heavens is divine. It signals another connection between this church and the African-centric Revivalist churches that the mission has come to vanquish and to the dancehall world it no doubt regards as irrevocably damned. Here Dawes points to what is irrepressible in the African roots of Jamaican popular cultural and religious expression. It is the dub sensibility at work, where both church hall and dancehall are rooted in a transformative eclecticism, where Africa is the referent of the "soil of ages".[22]

6. Versions of Prophecy:
The Old and New Testaments and the Jamaican Tradition

The Africans who were forcibly taken as enslaved people to the Caribbean came from societies with developed spiritual roles and practices that in some respects equate to those of Clarice's church. Scholars have identified a number of related but distinctive priestly roles in traditional societies: spirit mediums, diviners and prophets.

Spirit mediums were the receivers of messages from the gods, often women, and these messages were quite frequently relayed in vocalisations and not in the language of the people. These had then to be interpreted by the male priest. In Chapter XXI, these are the roles played respectively by Clarice and Last Night, now preacherman, as the congregation waits for Clarice to catch "the current".

Diviners read signs from nature, or from chance, such as the casting of cowrie shells in Yoruba divination. Divination reached the Caribbean in the practice of obeah, in the Yoruba-focused religions of Cuban Santeria and Trinidadian Orisha and in the private consultations that were parts of Kumina practice. Whilst the Pentecostalists would have rejected such practices as pagan and idolatrous, private consultations for the church brothers over spiritual matters were evidently part of Clarice's role, and it appears that amongst the independent churches, the Bible, as a sacred text, was sometimes used as a form of divination. There is no suggestion that Clarice's church engages in such ritual uses of the Bible as the "Book and Key" practice, a form of divination to discover a guilty party[24] – as the Lantern Yard congregation in *Silas Marner* cast lots to determine Silas's guilt – but amongst the independent churches there are accounts of believers lighting on random verses from the Bible, sometimes in dreams (as in the account of Claudius Henry below) where those verses are interpreted as divine instruction for future behaviour. What *Prophets* does allude to is the ritualistic use of the Bible in the "reading out", when Thalbot is expelled from the church.

There are clear linkages between African forms of prophecy and the creolisation of that role in African Caribbean Christian practice. It began from the moment that Baptist missionaries brought the Bible to the enslaved in the late 18th century, the role of prophets in the Old Testament being as readily absorbed into the African Jamaican world-view, as in the narrative of Moses leading the Jews out of slavery in Egypt. From Paul Bogle (1820-1865),[25] "Shakespeare" (H.E.S. Woods)[26] prophesying circa 1876, Alexander Bedward (1848-1930)[27] to Marcus Garvey (1887-1940)[28] and Leonard Howell (1898-1981)[29] and then to Claudius Henry (1903-1986),[30] and through to Bob Marley (1945-1981),[31] there is a clear line of prophecy in its Old Testament oppositional sense. In Jamaica, this involved the merging of a message of spiritual salvation with the call to black people to throw off their white and brown oppressors. Beyond these publicly recognised figures with significant followings, there was the regular appearance on the streets of the warnerman or warnerwoman (Chevannes, 1994) who predicts disaster to come and instructs the wicked population to repent and mend their ways, sometimes ringing a bell, and usually dressed in the robes and headwrap of the Revivalists (Revival Zion and Pukkumina).[32] Whilst Kwame Dawes told me that he was not aware of the existence of the prophet Shakespeare, there is an uncanny resemblance between this forgotten figure and Thalbot. As Thalbot does when he channels the desert prophets in Chapter XXIII, Shakespeare, according to A.A. Brooks (Bedward's first biographer), "was very peculiar, and lived in a stone hole or cave in the wilderness; whence he habitually came on missions of love, preaching the word of God and prophesying: for prophet indeed he was." On one occasion he prophesied a flood, which entirely destroyed the local Wesleyan chapel of Dallas Castle, St Andrew; on another occasion he came to August Town, as Thalbot comes to Kingston, to tell the people, "Thus saith the Lord behold the sins of August town have come up before me, and I will destroy the place as I did Dallas Castle, except the people repent." This time they do, and August town is saved.[33]

In reggae, the figure of the Old Testament prophet is sung about as if he is very much part of the present, as Peter Tosh sings in "Moses (the Prophet)" (*Bush Doctor*, 1978): "Remember Elijah./ Do you remember Elijah?/ Him no dead, him no dead,/ Him no dead.// The man deh on earth still./ The man a trod earth still, younger than ever." Max Romeo's "Blood of the Prophet" (*Revelation Time*, 1975) is more despairing: "Rachel mourns for her children!// They have killed the prophet,/ And burned down the altar./Whooah, what a slaughter!/ The blood of the prophet,/ Is on the shore of Babylon./ Whoah, what a woeful situation!" In Burning Spear's borrowing of "Estimated Prophet" from The Grateful Dead (*Jah Kingdom*, 1991), the singer is the prophet whose "time coming", making allusions to Ezekiel in the wheel of fire: "We are standing on the beach, the sea will part before me/ Fire wheel burning in the air/ You will follow me, and we will ride to glory".[34] Israel Vibration's "Prophet Has Arise" (*The Same Song*, 1978), gives the reassurance that in bad times the prophet will come, "So the people shall never run short/ Of a King or a prophet."

But this is only one side of the Jamaican prophetic tradition, since in the case of Garvey, Howell and Claudius Henry, the biblical word was also channelled into social action. Indeed, in the case of Claudius Henry, the word became revolutionary action intended to overthrow the Jamaican state. Since, I think, there are parody resonances of Claudius Henry in the figure of Thalbot, and since to the non-Jamaican (or young Jamaican) reader, the figure of Thalbot may seem a manifestly less real character than Clarice, it seems worth saying a little more about that tradition, to locate the character of Thalbot in Jamaican historical reality.

Thalbot is in the tradition of Paul Bogle, who preached "Cleave to the Black" to his followers in the church at Stoney Gut in 1865;[35] of Alexander Bedward who preached, "There is a white wall and a black wall. And the white wall has been closing around the black wall: but now the black wall has become bigger than the white";[36] and of Claudius Henry who along with the gospel preached, "This is black man's time".[37] All this is filtered through the forthright language of a Peter Tosh (1944-1987), when Thalbot preaches against the "canker of colonialist edifices" – the Sovereign City shopping mall:

As long as they break down that slavemaster castle
where a wild mad black man, naked as any Kojo,
been shitting and pissing and coming each morning

to desecrate the legacy of the whip and the chains,
as long as them wipe away the remembrance
of this artefact of the past instead of defecating on

its rass right there, so that our children won't forget,
then is this kind of shithouse imperialist
bloodsucking monstrosity going to rise from the ashes. (V, iii, ll. 25-33)

Thalbot's vision is historical, collectivist, Africanist in the reference to Kojo, and as such it is worth looking briefly at Henry's story, as documented by Barry Chevannes in his essay, "The Repairer of the Breach: Reverend Claudius Henry and Jamaican Society" (1976). Now, whilst the Henry uprising took place in 1960, a good many years before Kwame Dawes' arrival in Jamaica from Ghana, Henry was very much part of the political reportage of the 1970s and Dawes has confirmed his awareness of Henry's activities. Henry was also undoubtedly in Kwame's father, Neville Dawes' mind when he wrote his second novel, *Interim* (1978) about a failed revolutionary insurrection in Jamaica in the late 1940s, which is defeated by naivety, betrayal and an American invasion. In its narrative of guerrillas in the hills, *Interim* echoes the actuality of the military and insurgent side of the activities of Claudius Henry's son, Ronald, with his African American supporters, though *Interim* excludes any religious framework for the uprising, which is perhaps not surprising for a Marxist. Indeed, it is interesting that the two significant accounts of Claudius Henry's life, that of Barry Chevannes and Brian Meeks' chapter in *Narratives of Resistance* (2000), address almost completely alternative sides of the story. Meeks is most interested in the serious reality of the physical rebellion focused on the son, Ronald, (and on how the story has disappeared from the Jamaican historical narrative), whilst Chevannes is primarily interested in the father, Claudius, and the way his prophetic pronouncements reveal both the powerful spiritual/political/racial tradition in Jamaican prophecy, and its impact on mainstream politics.

Briefly, Claudius Henry's story is this. He was born in 1903, was given to receiving visions and, like Bedward earlier, he was arrested for lunacy around 1930. His most important vision came when he heard God speak to him, after a fast of three days and nights (whilst he was in prison being investigated for lunacy), instructing him that he should read Isaiah 58 when he was released. This verse told him: "Thou shalt raise up the foundation of many generations; and thou shalt be called the repairer of the breach". Thereafter, this is the title Henry took. At some time in the 1940s he migrated to the USA, not returning to Jamaica until 1957, on the instruction of another vision. This informed him that he was the Cyrus destined to lead Israel back to the promised land.[38] When he was back in Jamaica and a woman addressed him as Cyrus his mission was confirmed. Back in

Jamaica, Henry, who had once been an Anglican, now identified himself as believer in the divinity of Haile Selassie and saw himself as "Another Moses leading Israel's scattered slaves Back Home to Motherland Africa" (he also at times declared himself divine, a black Jesus). He made connections to some elements of the Rastafarian movement (with which he had a vexed relationship since he was anti-locks and anti-ganja) and built a church with a significant congregation and a much wider following through pamphleteering and itinerant preaching. When he announced his prophecy that a ship would come to Jamaica on October 5th 1959 and take Africans back to Ethiopia (he issued blue card passports), over 500 people turned up at his Kingston headquarters ready to leave. (It is an episode that Orlando Patterson uses in his novel *The Children of Sisyphus* (1964) when Brother Solomon makes just such a prophecy.) After the failure of this prophecy, Henry abandoned the back-to-Africa mission on the grounds that his visions told him that Jamaica, as a black country, "was a part of Africa".

Meantime, his son Ronald Henry was in the USA, recruiting followers (largely African Americans) and acquiring weapons, still focused on the mission of a return to Africa. When Ronald arrived in Jamaica with his group of militant followers, Brian Meeks' account indicates that this was a very serious if naive attempt to build a revolutionary movement to take over the Jamaican state (it depended to a large part on Rastafarians joining his rebel army). In April 1960, the police raided Claudius Henry's church and found a considerable quantity of arms and explosives. Letters seen by Meeks make it clear that Henry senior was fully party to his son's mission. In June that year, the police, in pursuit of armed guerillas in the hills around Sligoville, who had shot dead two British soldiers, were informed by a shopkeeper in Orange Grove that four heavily armed men were sleeping in his shop. It soon emerged that Ronald Henry and one of his close allies had murdered five of the African Americans with whom serious splits over ideology and tactics had arisen. Ronald Henry and Albert Gabbidon were tried for murder and hung. Claudius Henry and other leading members of his church were put on trial for treason, for complicity in the armed plot and the intention (there was the evidence of a letter) that they would invite the recently victorious Fidel Castro to take over Jamaica. Claudius Henry was sentenced to ten years' hard labour and other lieutenants, including his common-law wife, to shorter periods in jail.

As Chevannes observes, the Henry movement ought to have collapsed at this point and dwindled away. But it did not. His supporters concluded that Henry's "persecution" was predicted in the Bible, with a precedent in the ill-fortunes of the prophet Ezekiel, and that he would emerge to lead the movement again. This indeed happened when Henry was released after seven years of his sentence in 1968. His followers had been leading a precarious quasi-communal existence in Clarendon, and Henry, with evident vision and organisational skills (and now a declared commitment to peaceful, democratic action), developed successful brickmaking and bakery businesses, built houses for his followers and a stone church that could hold 300 congregants and a schoolhouse in Sandy Bay, Clarendon.[39]

This, though, was not the end of the story, since, according to Chevannes, Claudius Henry's prophecies, and the credence in which they were held, played a significant role in the popular support for the PNP in winning the 1972 election. In 1969, Henry issued a pamphlet declaring that Michael Manley was God's chosen to lead Jamaica out of "high society injustices and victimisation". In a rather idiosyncratic interpretation of biblical sequence, the son Michael (Joshua) was compared to the father, Norman W. Manley (biblical David, who was unworthy to fulfil God's work because of his bloodstained hands – Norman Manley had been chief minister when Henry was sent to prison). Michael Manley had for some time been known as Joshua to his followers following the flamboyant part he had played (lying down in the road and prophesying that the walls of Jericho would tumble down) during a bitter 97-day strike at the Jamaica Broadcasting Corporation in 1964. There was also the crucial iconography of the rod, and one of Henry's pamphlets featured photographs of himself, Haile Selassie and Michael Manley, each holding a rod. Manley's had, according to Henry, been given to him by Selassie. This connection was picked up in reggae songs such as Clancy Eccles' "Rod of Correction" (Trojan, 1969) who instructs: "Lick im wid di rod of correction, Faada", and in Eddie Ford's "You Wrong Fe Trouble Joshua" (Pressure Beat, 1972), with the lines, "Joshua is the lion/ lion will devour you" and "You wrong to trouble God's son/ God's son is rod man, Rod man will lick you down." Claudius Henry's pamphlet claimed: "Now the time for a change has come. This change will be brought about by Moses, Joshua, and the King of Kings and Lord of Lords, 'Trinity of the God-head.'" Whilst this was regarded as blasphemous by orthodox Christians, the message evidently lent, in Chevannes' words, "ecclesiastical authority" to the PNP campaign, and though they weren't expected to win, they did so.

Now whilst Thalbot is not to be regarded as a portrayal of Claudius Henry, Henry's story indicates the prophetic/ political world in which Thalbot operates. But then, as indicated in the account of *Prophets*' setting in the post-1980s' context (see above, pp. 26-29), this is no longer a time for political prophets like Thalbot. Now "the market is glutted with sybils and clarices/cornering the ready congregation with miracles". Theirs is not the gospel of black resistance but of individual salvation. For the Thalbots of now, "… the city is deaf to the curve of their words;/ just the spectacle of verbal acrobatics and scandal" (V, iv, ll. 21-22). So if the characterisation of Thalbot has a relationship to Claudius Henry, it is a parodic one. When Thalbot goes out to fight, he is likened to a fighting Maroon, but his cutlass is not stained with blood: "…Then Thalbot had// awakened, ready for battle, black skin glowing,/ like a maroon on a raid into a redcoat camp/ with his machete slick and sticky// with the crystallising syrup of cane juice, and the mad/ buzz of bees like a garland or talisman around his head" (V, ii, ll. 24ff). However, like the Ronald Henry fugitives, Thalbot is defeated in his sleep. Searched for by around 1000 police and army, Ronald Henry and three of his men are found in deep sleep in the shop of Septimus Higgins, "having cleaned themselves of ticks and parasites", as Brian Meeks quotes from state papers.[40] Thalbot, having defended his pitch for three days, is taken at three in the morning as he is sleeping off "a gift of potent weed".

No doubt theologians would offer a more nuanced view of the difference between Old and New Testament than I am trying to make with respect to the models of prophecy exemplified by Clarice and Thalbot. In the context of the Bible, rather than in their social and political manifestations in Jamaican life, it appears that evangelical Christians make the distinction between the Old Testament prophet as being the true prophet, whereas the post-New Testament prophet is an altogether less reliable proposition. This is because the OT prophet must, *de facto* speak truth because his books have been included in the Bible, which is God's unquestionable word, and because much OT prophecy is about the future coming of the messiah, which is a prophecy come true. The post-New Testament prophet can have no such role, because God's word has already been brought to all people through Jesus's incarnation and the offer of salvation to all through the holy spirit. The New Testament prophet, therefore, does not have any privileged access to God's word, but is at best an interpreter and capable of error. As Matthew warns (24: 24), "For false messiahs and false prophets will appear and perform great signs and wonders to deceive, if possible, even the elect."[41]

In comparison to this theological distinction, *Prophets* displays an equally questioning attitude towards the figure of the prophet, whether Old or New. The OT biblical figures who provide models for Thalbot, or as whom he appears as a contemporary incarnation, are those who have a quarrelling relationship with a notably capricious God. Nahum is a vengeful character, hoping for God's support against his enemies; Jonah is a passive-aggressive sulker, bitterly disappointed with God when he fails to lay waste to the Ninevites; Elijah is a miserably misogynistic loner; and Isaiah walks around naked for three years in order to make his point. As their inheritor, it is perhaps no accident that Thalbot moves in and out of madness and nakedness, and no accident that he is a misogynist who is deeply phobic about sexuality in general. And yet, Thalbot speaks a social, communitarian gospel that Clarice does not.

She is a New Testament prophetess in the sense that her concern is with the inner person, with individual salvation. She has been "born with [a] seer's eye", "eyes that penetrate/ the sinew and bone", a quality revealed in the episodes where she displays her acute understanding of the distresses that Last Night (and also the narrating young man) brings into the church service, when Clarice, "on a roll,/ points her tender finger at his forehead/ and speaks his mind" (IV, ii, ll. 6-8). That this is a divinely inspired insight is suggested in the poem's allusion to Hebrews 4: 12 ("For the word of God is living and active. Sharper than any double-edged sword, it penetrates even to dividing soul and spirit, joints and marrow...") in the image describing Clarice when she is preaching on First Sunday, of "the power of the word/ now cutting through bone, marrow,/ the word resurrecting Lazarus,/the stone moving" (XVI, ll. 29-32). And yet, not much later, Clarice uses the same metaphor to justify herself in refusing to feel guilty after the night on the beach with Last Night. She tells herself that God cannot be displeased with her because it is so evidently God who is the source of her visions. As she asks herself, rhetorically: "whose are these precise visions/ of the indiscretions of the believers – these truths/ on my tongue, cutting the bone and marrow/ of closeted secrets?" (XXII, vii, ll. 4-7). The ambivalence of the verse is that, whilst the poem is sympathetic to Clarice's erotic self, the last phrase about "closeted secrets" points to what we discover later, that Clarice, as "confessor of the wayward", is quite prepared to use those secrets to save her skin when the church threatens to make her affair with Last Night public.

Yet though they are powerful manifestations of Jamaican life, neither the prophetic spirit of Clarice nor that of Thalbot appears to offer much hope for the future. Only in the mythical passage of the unnamed prophetess in *Flight* (Chapter XXVIII) does the poem offer a vision of the fusing of the erotic and the spiritual, of Christian faith and the centrality of African culture.

By the end of *Prophets* (XXIII, xv), Clarice and Thalbot have cancelled each other out. She has lied to make Thalbot an outcast, and he (in his imagination) has stoned down the bird he pictures Clarice to be. She has succumbed to the temptation of using her prophetic gifts for selfish ends; he has become trapped in life-denying misogyny. Ultimately, though, he has to acknowledge that no one is listening to his message.

> ...Thalbot weeps

> for the prophecy he cannot speak, this curse
> upon him, the path of disobedient prophets
> now stuck with powerless clairvoyance.

> The seer tongue, once fire,
> now damp coals,
> has lost the will to speak.

FOUR: LITERARY DIALOGUES

As the notes to the poem indicate, the wide range of allusions to be found in *Prophets* show that Kwame Dawes is a poet who not only displays the evidence of extensive and retentive reading, but has never concealed the fact that he draws the inspiration for his poetry as much from literature, music and art as he has done from directly encountered life. There is no attempt here to engage in full-blown genetic criticism, to reconstruct all of the reading that went into the writing of *Prophets*, or the processes of textual invention that transformed those sources. However, there are three areas of engagement with other writers' texts that focus rather neatly, respectively, on the three main characters in the poem. Firstly, in constructing the role of the narrative "I", as well as in deriving a real but contested formal inspiration, there is Derek Walcott's epic poem, *Omeros* (1990). Secondly, in constructing the character of Thalbot, there is not only the history of actual prophetic figures in Jamaican society, but a body of Caribbean imaginative writing that has created fictional analogues for such figures, the most important of which, in relationship to *Prophets*, is Sylvia Wynter's novel, *The Hills of Hebron* (1962). Again, whilst the figure of Clarice, as indicated above (p. 20), has real life sources, the other inspiration for this fictive character owes a good deal, as Dawes has confirmed, to his reading of several African American women's novels, including Zora Neale Hurston's *Jonah's Gourd Vine* (1934) and *Their Eyes Were Watching God* (1937), Alice Walker's *The Color Purple* (1983), Toni Morrison's *Sula* (1973) and *Song of Solomon* (1977), and Ntozake Shange's "Choreopoem", *for colored girls who have considered suicide/ when the rainbow is enuf* (1975), finding in these books images of strong and sexually engaged black women, such as had not really begun to emerge in Caribbean writing. In the poem's focus on the inner workings of a small, independent black church, Dawes also acknowledges the impact of James Baldwin's play *The Amen Corner* (1968).

1. The Epic Form and the Self-Reflexive "I": *Omeros* and *Prophets*

As a narrative in verse, *Prophets* joined a small number of prior Caribbean works in this genre: Saint-John Perse's *Anabase* (1924), Aimé Césaire's *Cahier d'un Retour au Pays Natal* ('Notebook of a Return to my Native Land', 1939), Édouard Glissant's *Les Indes: poèmes de l'une et l'autre terre* ('The Indies: poems of one and another world', 1955) and Frank Martinus Arion's *Stemmen uit Afrika* ('Songs from Africa', 1957), and to Derek Walcott's *Another Life* (1973) and *Omeros* (1990).[1] But it is to Derek Walcott's *Omeros*, published just five years earlier, that *Prophets* has the most obvious and acknowledged connection.

Kwame Dawes has not written about *Omeros*, but he has evidently read it closely. In a much later interview[2] he records how, "I was likely influenced… not so much for its metric patterns and rhyme, but for the way that the three-line stanza seemed to lend itself to stretches of narrative verse that were as much interested in capturing the landscape as in creating the cadence of an epic tone and manner". The critical silence suggests that Dawes' relationship to *Omeros* was more intimate, a dialogue that could only be expressed fully in the writing of *Prophets*.

Here is Dawes, with two collections of poetry to his name, who is twenty-eight at the time of *Omeros*'s publication and thirty-three when *Prophets* came out, taking on the acknowledged technical master of Caribbean poetry, who was then aged sixty with thirteen collections of poetry, multiple prizes and the Nobel (awarded as *Prophets* was in germination) to his credit. In his implicit statement of acknowledgement and ambition embedded in *Prophets* – the kind of response one expects of all significant writers to what has gone before – Dawes makes absolutely no attempt to disguise what he has taken from *Omeros*, not least because the poetic sensibility and cultural aesthetics behind *Prophets* are so different that he can afford to make a series of affectionate "homages" to *Omeros* – beyond the borrowing of the tercet – without in any way suggesting that he lacks a signal and distinctive voice and vision of his own. On the contrary, because *Prophets* so openly plants its flag in the territory mapped out by *Omeros*, its differences, and the sense in which it pushes back against Walcott's aesthetics become all the clearer.

So what does *Prophets* take from *Omeros*? First, the permission to combine the narrative and the lyric and a structural framework where the thematic or metaphoric connection is frequently a much more important determinant than the linearity of narrative. Very obviously, *Prophets* follows *Omeros* in going to Dante's *Divine Comedy* for the tercet as a poetic form. Unlike Dante and Walcott, Dawes does not attempt rhyme and he goes further than Walcott in carrying the narrative thrust across the stanza, whilst preserving a sense of regularity through the visual appearance of stanzaic repetition and the use (generally) of a four-beat line.

What Dawes also takes from Walcott is an unabashed pleasure in displaying the fertility of his poetic imagination. As he said in the same interview of 2007, Walcott "gave me the permission to indulge in the richness of language and the grandness of poetic ambition". This is seen not only in the range of allusive literary reference *Prophets* draws on, but also in employing a voice that regularly calls attention to itself in the surface texture of the poem. Dawes happily follows Walcott in his delight in verbal play; like Plunkett, Walcott's writerly alter-ego, he "puns relentlessly" (*Omeros*, p. 30).[3]

Prophets also takes from *Omeros* the permission to combine a sometimes confessional personal narrative with the dramatisation of the stories of a core group of characters. These are both characters in their own right, with their own stories and motivations, but they are also dramatic representatives of an inner authorial debate. Here, though, I think that Dawes is more evidently respectful of the autonomy of his characters. The character "Walcott" is unquestionably the real hero (and anti-hero) of *Omeros*; his Homeric fishermen, Achille and Hector, and his white alter-ego, Major Plunkett, are at times cipher figures in a way that Dawes' Clarice and Thalbot are not.

Like Walcott, Dawes is both sometimes the speaking "I" and sometimes, in Walcott's phrase, the "phantom narrator", the authorial presence behind the poem as a whole. Like Walcott, Dawes uses this division of voices to pursue a self-reflexive metapoetics, reminding the reader that there is a shaping vision behind it all, who weaves strands of the narrative and invents aspects of character at will. Like Walcott, Dawes employs a self-questioning voice – though quite differently. Walcott's self-questioning ("Didn't I want the poor/ to stay in the same light so that I could transfix/ them in amber…" (XXXVIII, ii, l. 227)) frequently seems concerned with defending his poetics against encircling, hostile critics. Dawes' self-questioning is about how to interpret the experience recorded in the narrative (how, ultimately was the "I" to make sense of the "miracles" of faith and the counter-evidence of "the tricks, the sin, the betrayals" (XXVIII, v, ll. 1-2)?).

These difference between the two poems in the relationship between their authors and their *dramatis personae* are aesthetic, social, cultural and political in motivation. Compare, for instance, the portrayals of the central female character in each poem. Helen in *Omeros* is a woman who is sought, pursued by others, the object of male desires, who, though presented as a strong figure in her rejection of male patronage, is only ever seen from outside, and ultimately as the womb carrying Hector's child. Indeed, the poem admits rather ambivalently that both Plunkett and the "phantom narrator" have loaded Helen with a symbolic weight that is not hers. (There is also a distinctly masculinist strand in *Omeros* where the "I" figure, in bewailing the breakdown of his marriage, whilst admitting shared responsibility for the failure, describes the woman's role in uncomfortably misogynist terms – in, for instance, the analogy with dung beetles where the male leaves "its exhausted mate hysterical" (p. 240).) By contrast, Clarice is a seeker with her own very specific goals, whose inner thoughts we in time become privy to, and where the authorial admission is of his anxiety as to whether he has done justice to Clarice's autonomous strength of character.

This is part of a larger difference between the two poems with respect to their respective social and cultural positions. It is impossible not to recognise, for instance, how much more at home and inward Walcott is with his portrayal (it is a genuinely moving one) of the Plunketts than he is with his peasant characters – Achille, Hector, Philoctete – who are so much more one-dimensional – signified by a wound, a rivalry, the urge for modernity – in their characterisation, so that despite Walcott's assertions to the contrary, they depend on the Homeric resonances loaded onto their characters to have a metaphoric weight in the poem. This is scarcely surprising. As Walcott notes, "There was Plunkett in my father, much as there was/ my mother in Maud" (*Omeros*, p. 263). This is the world he grew up in, whereas the world of Achille and Hector is not his. As he admits of similar figures in *Another Life*, "if these heroes have been given a stature/ disproportionate to their cramped lives, / remember I beheld them at knee-height…" (p. 41). In *Omeros*, the view the "Walcott" figure has of this village world is most frequently from a hotel balcony, or as a passenger in a taxi from the airport.

Prophets has none of that distance. The "I" of the poem is no less a supplicant, a seeker of a safe harbour, than the bedraggled character of Last Night in Chapter IV. One cannot imagine Dawes writing, as Walcott did in his Nobel speech, of "the island's life, [as] illiterate in the way leaves are illiterate; they do not read, they are there to be read, and if they are properly read, they create their own literature" (n.p.).[4] Dawes' characters in *Prophets* read voraciously, and interpret and quote their reading with great eloquence and vigour – even though sometimes in self-deceiving ways. Of course, what they read is the Bible, not the canon of great Western literature, and as indicated at various points (pp. 106-107 262-264), in its portrayal of its four artistic apparitions, *Prophets* is not inclined to make any grandiose claims about the writer's role as the elevated interpreter of an otherwise "illiterate" Caribbean reality. Again, as the notes on allusions and references in the poem make clear, whilst the literary (which includes Walcott as well as Shakespeare and others from the Western canon as well as the Bible) is part of the dialogue, what is perhaps most distinctive about the allusiveness of *Prophets* is the equality it grants to the lyrics of reggae –

and beyond that to the way Jamaican speakers have made the language and narratives of the Bible part of their daily exchange and way of seeing the world. When Walcott makes an allusion to a Bob Marley lyric ("Buffalo Soldier"), one senses he is catching up with the new poetic voices announced by, for instance, *Savacou 3/4* in 1970 – poetry he had mostly dismissed as Afro-centric and without craft.[5]

Another hint Dawes may have found in *Omeros* is the trope of the cinematic or the filmic (discussed below, see pp. 81-83). As Jean Antoine-Dunn's *Derek Walcott's Love Affair with Film* (2017) convincingly shows, the cinematic trope has been central in Walcott's poetry, including *Omeros*. The filmic, both as a narrative and metatextual device, is an even more extensive element in Dawes' poem. Whether Dawes drew consciously on Walcott's example is immaterial, but if he did, then he displayed both critical acumen and a writerly imagination in seizing on what was then an unremarked motif in *Omeros* and extending it into an effective poetic device in his own poem. The most explicit filmic trope in *Omeros* comes in Chapter XLV, iii, p. 230, a sequence where Walcott uses Eisensteinian montage as a summarising, contrastive and harmonising device, yoking elements from the recent and epic past in the poem: "Cut to a leopard galloping on a dry plain/ … Cut to the spraying fans/ drummed by a riderless stallion…" At the time of writing *Prophets*, Walcott's attempt to write a film treatment for *Omeros* lay well in the future.[6]

Of course, the most obvious difference between the two poems is in the literary models they draw on, though *Omeros* can be seen as sanctioning the consumption and creolising of the literary past. Yet whilst Walcott constantly subverts the model of the Homeric epic with his (faux?) admission that he has never read *The Odyssey* all through, and with his self-questioning of the need for the "Homeric shadow" or "All that Greek manure under the green bananas" (*Omeros*, p. 271), he must have been aware that the Homeric echoes would draw admiring readers to the poem, and that he was making a statement about the location of Caribbean writing within one version, at least, of the Western literary tradition.

By using the Bible as the source of several of his sub-narratives, Dawes establishes *Prophets'* independence from *Omeros*, not least in connecting to a text that can, in a real sense, be described as belonging to the Caribbean's own popular cultural traditions. In engaging with the Bible, Dawes riffs off a text that (even before its translation into Jamaican patwa) has long been part of the common culture of Jamaica – in its speech rhythms, aphorisms, allusions, characters (from brave Daniels to deceitful Jezebels) and popular song. Further, because Dawes treats the Bible in this popular cultural way, as a repository of diverse narratives with a potential range of uses (rather than as the unitary text of the religiously orthodox who see the individual books of the Bible as parts of an indivisible whole)[7] he frees himself to employ a whole variety of approaches to those different books – dub versions, allusions, re-readings and parodies – as well as bringing contemporary Jamaica and biblical narrative into a mutually dynamic relationship.

Omeros is Walcott's record of a homecoming, his attempt to effect a closure of the Caribbean's social, historical and cultural divisions (where his work has been seen as located on one side of that divide in a predominantly Euro-Creole space)[8]. Dawes' *Prophets* is a record of having always been there. *Omeros* undoubtedly records the genuine distance Walcott travelled from the mocking images of African otherness in early poems such as "Tales of the Islands" (*In a Green Night*, 1964), or his rage against the Afrocentric spirit of the 1970s in Chapter 19 of *Another Life* ("those who explain to the peasant why he is African")[9] towards the sympathetic treatment of Achille's inner journey back to Africa, or of Ma Kilman's African-derived healing skills. It was a somewhat belated arrival. The theme of entry into the African-Caribbean spiritual world is one that goes back to Claude McKay's *Banana Bottom* (1928), and to George Lamming's *Season of Adventure* (1960), written thirty years before *Omeros*. Like the journey of Lamming's Fola (who comes to the world of the tonelles from a position of light-brown, mulatto, upper-class ignorance), Walcott's proxy engagement with Africa, via Achille, also reads as an *adventure* of discovery of an Africa whose description, in Walcott's case, seems to me to owe more to Conrad than experienced reality or to the living presence of Africa in the Caribbean that Fola experiences.[10] By contrast, the three journeys made to Africa in *Prophets* are to an actual place and involve a relationship, even in myth, that is realistically defined in time. In *Prophets* there is no space for a sentimental linkage to an Africa of the pre-slavery past. When in Chapter VI, *Denial*, the writing "I" imagines how he would like to transport Clarice back to the Africa her religion has taught her to deny, it is to a contemporary Africa, not the lost past. With regard to that, he cannot get past the image of Elmina (the slave fort) where "the bones grope blindly for missing joints". There is, too, the reference to the Africa visited by Jamaican missionaries in the early 20th century. This is an episode based on the actual missionary work of Dawes' grandparents (see the notes to Chapter X, pp. 160-161), who are the source of the sculpture with which Last Night is, in his imagination, unfaithful. Even from the recent past, what they have brought back is "transported exotica" from an Africa no less altered by colonialism than Jamaica, "artefacts" now gathering dust in a museum.[11] Finally, the journey that the unnamed prophetess makes across Africa to the USA in Chapter XXVIII, *Flight*, whilst it is a journey as imaginary as Achille's – as a literally self-propelled flight – and whilst it resonates with the folk narratives of the flights of enslaved people back to Africa, it is across an Africa that is contemporary and real. There is an abandoning of "the museum of broken dreams" to hear, instead, the "antiphonal howls of the

Mahotella Queens" – the South African township mbaqanga group whose albums were popular amongst world music listeners in the 1980s.

Again, if in *Omeros* Walcott makes a new space for an African dimension in Caribbean life, it is part of an argument for a Caribbean in which the Eurocentric cultural presence is dominant. In *Prophets*, a creolised Africa is a constant presence in the speech, body movement, dance, spirituality and music of the Kingstonians who people the poem. It is not an unchallenged presence, nor even sometimes a recognised presence; the forces of white American cultural imperialism are a constant threat to self-image.

The movement towards reconciliation in *Omeros* – the poem's autumnal glow – is no doubt one of the elements that give Walcott's poem its appeal to many readers – including me. It embraces the magical fulfilment of desire, the kind of healing of wrongs done that is to be found in Shakespeare's late romances, such as the bringing back to life of a statue in *The Winter's Tale*. Ma Kilman's folk remedy (the only image of the Caribbean African presence other than Philoctete and Achille's cross-dressing as Christmas masqueraders), the herbal bath that cures Philoctete's unhealing shin, seems to cure not only that wound, but the grief of 300 years of slavery, the centuries of contempt for Africanness – and even to assuage the "I" figure's grief over his lost love and broken marriage. There is no such comforting closure in *Prophets*. Whilst Dawes ends the poem with a psalmist's note of joy ("their feet skip on the mountains"), the very fact that the line references a psalm points to likelihood of struggles and lamentations beyond the poem's end.

These differences can be seen as having their source in biography, ideology and aesthetic commitments. Walcott is a man of sixty returning home after a lifetime of wandering. Dawes writes about the experience of his late teens and early twenties from the point when, like many Jamaicans, he has been forced to leave the island of his youth to seek employment in the USA. Walcott also returns to an island which, whilst it shares with Jamaica a history of external conquest, slavery and colonialism, is in many respects a distinctively different place. In *Omeros*, change is introduced as one of new features of St Lucian life recognised by the returning "I", particularly the impact of tourism on the island (though as Garth St Omer's novel *Nor Any Country* (first published in 1968) makes clear, this kind of change was already happening in the 1950s[12]). It is not just a matter of size (a population of 2.5 million to 165,000) but a significant difference of political and cultural character. By the time Dawes wrote *Prophets*, Jamaica had been independent for thirty years and had been engaged in combative, and latterly violent, mass politics for almost fifty years. St Lucia had only been independent for eleven years at the time of *Omeros*' publication; it was evidently still possible for Walcott to see St Lucia at an emergent point in its history, to see it as a world still to be born. His St Lucia remains primarily rural (the urban character of Castries where over a third of St Lucians live does not feature in *Omeros*). Dawes' territory in *Prophets* is almost wholly urban; it is a fallen world where political innocence has long departed and it is inconceivable that Dawes could have praised any of his characters for their heroic simplicity. There are no fishermen in sight. Dawes' characters are complex, conflicted, noble and ignoble, all at once.

Though Walcott constantly urges his narrative self to avoid sentimentalising or romanticising his characters, this seems to me somewhat disingenuous because it is of a piece with the desire expressed in the poem for the reconciliation of Caribbean peoples with their history, and with the divisions of race, class and culture that have grown from that history. (Walcott has little to say about the inequalities of gender.) In *Prophets*, any such movement towards reconciliation would have to be seen as an act of wish-fulfilment profoundly out of character with the Jamaican world that the poem so acutely anatomises. In *Omeros*, Dennis Plunkett's movement from left-over relic of Empire to becoming the settler who is wholly integrated into St Lucian society is movingly and, in its own terms, convincingly portrayed. Such a narrative would be inconceivable in *Prophets*, where the equivalents of the Plunketts had been abandoning Jamaica for North America, and the character closest to Plunkett in role (Castleberry) is a ghost, a relique of a Jamaica that is fast disappearing. In *Prophets*, there is no denial of the power of the somatic norm of whiteness and Euro-American cultural values in the mentalities of some of the characters, but it is an ideological force which is seen as profoundly harmful to their psychic wholeness. Colonial Englishness may be dead, but this is a society where the mixed messages of American evangelism and consumerism, beamed into the satellite dishes of the island, exert a powerful influence. This is a society where everything about Clarice is African and black, except her thoughts, her image of a blue-eyed Jesus. For Dawes, the cultural war for sovereignty is still being fought, and *Prophets* expresses the sharp angst of battles lost and a world still to be won. His is a world divided between a hunger for transcendence and the temptations of a cynical self-serving politics, public displays of righteousness as the hoped-for route to wealth, and the escapes of hedonism, consumerism and the promise of the green card to the heaven of the USA.

Besides the contrasts of these larger themes, there are elements in *Prophets* where the relationship to *Omeros* is allusive rather than permissive or critical, that are part of the wider literary dialogue that *Prophets* engages in. For instance, there are parallels in the relationships between Plunkett and Helen, and Castleberry and Clarice, where personal qualities (both men have a gentle generosity of spirit) and differences of age and race mesh ironically with the history of the abuse and exploitation of black women by European men).

Both poems make use of the epic resonances of apparitions (echoing, for instance, Odysseus' descent into the underworld in Book 11 of Homer's *Odyssey*, and his conversations with Elpenor and Tiresias, or Aeneas's descent into the underworld in Book 6 of Virgil's *Aeneid*). *Omeros* features the presence of Warwick Walcott, and *Prophets* has Castleberry and the four artistic "visitations" or "hauntings". (One may note here Dawes' self-discipline in not bringing his own father into *Prophets* – except through the most oblique of allusions – since Neville Dawes was, in reality, a much more powerful literary mentor to Dawes than Walcott's father could ever be.

Walcott's sometimes parodic relationship to the "epic paraphernalia" becomes a double parody in *Prophets*. For instance, Walcott gives over part of Chapter XV to a rather stilted account of the Battle of the Saints, the naval battle between France and Britain that settled St Lucia's future as British – since no good epic should be without a battle. *Prophets* perhaps alludes to Walcott's battle in Chapter XXII, *The Saints Return Triumphant*, where the military metaphors relate to religious conquest.

There are, too, obvious connections between Walcott's Ma Kilman who is described as "gardeuse, Sybil, obeah-woman" (p. 56) and later as "the caverned prophetess" (p. 243) and Dawes' Clarice who is "this Sybil" (VI, I, l. 19). *Prophets* is peopled by sybil figures from the testifying "sybil mother" (III, ii, l. 17), and is indeed "glutted with sybils and clarices" (V, iv, l. 20).

There are other allusions to *Omeros* (if indeed they are) that operate at an even further remove. In *Prophets*, behind the description of the canoeists Clarice is watching on television (Chapter II), there perhaps lies an oblique allusion to the canoes that take to the sea at the beginning of *Omeros*. In Walcott, the echoes are Odyssean or point to ancient Caribbean ancestry – the voyaging of the Aruacs. In *Prophets* the reference is to a trashy American soap opera, *Hawaii Five-O* – a sign of the poem's conscious postmodernity.

We may imagine, too, that Dawes, like Walcott, reflected on his literary heritage in constructing a modern, anti-heroic epic. Here, he echoes Walcott in his homage to "Mr Joyce" in Chapter XXXIX of *Omeros*. Like Joyce, Dawes locates his characters in the daily flesh and blood specifics of the body. Like Leopold Bloom in *Ulysses* (1921), Clarice communes on the toilet.

2. The Writer and the Logic of Popular Culture: *Prophets* and *The Hills of Hebron*

The character of Thalbot has a clear literary ancestry that includes Sam Selvon's embedded narrative of Brackley and the Cross in *The Lonely Londoners* (1956), V.S. Naipaul's Man-Man in *Miguel Street* (1959) and Preacher in *The Suffrage of Elvira* (1958), Andrew Salkey's Dada and Mother Johnson in *A Quality of Violence* (1959), Sylvia Wynter's Moses

Barton in *The Hills of Hebron* (1962), Orlando Patterson's Shepherd John in *The Children of Sisyphus* (1964) and Manko in Ismith Khan's *The Crucifixion* (1987, but written much earlier). These are all prophetic figures, leaders of small, nativist churches. All are seen from an external and often satirical point of view. They are phenomena of curiosity, at best the subject of a kind of anthropological interest, at worst the subject of ridicule. Most are shown as motivated by monetary gain and the desire for power; several are misogynist sexual predators; all are destined to betray their followers. Whether seen from a perspective of ethnic prejudice (V.S. Naipaul[13]), class anxiety (Andrew Salkey[14]) or a secular and radical political critique (Wynter and Patterson[15]), the African-centred prophet is variously portrayed as pathological, atavistic, delusional, anomalous – at best a vehicle of false consciousness who leads his followers to folly and ruin. These are deeply entrenched colonial perspectives, inherited by the Eurocentric Caribbean middle classes, and even, it seems, by some literary radicals. *Prophets* has elements of irony; it explores the interface between the figure of the spiritual outsider and the nature of madness, perceived and real (a connection discussed at greater length below (pp. 84-91)); it displays no reluctance in depicting the misguided and the hypocritical, as well as the sincere, the ecstatic and the transformative, but it takes its prophetic figures entirely seriously, and portrays them empathetically from within (if also sometimes ironically from without). What makes the difference in treatment is not only Kwame Dawes' own immersion in the kind of Charismatic church portrayed in *Prophets*, but, as he has acknowledged in his study, *Natural Mysticism: Towards a New Reggae Aesthetic* (1999)[16], the example and inspiration of the prophetic voice in reggae. For whilst *Prophets* makes no explicit reference to the aesthetics of reggae, as do later books such as *Jacko Jacobus* (1996) and *Shook Foil* (1997), reggae's world vision resonates through the poem, and, in particular, in its network of biblical allusion.

There is no act of self-crucifixion in *Prophets*, though there are several allusions to the New Testament narratives of Christ's crucifixion, but one image of Thalbot, at a moment when he feels persecuted, standing with "his arms spread, his eyes giving their last passion of tears" (XXIII, xiii, ll. 44-45), points clearly to his connection to the self-dramatising figures in the several literary narratives mentioned above.

Of all the novels that explore this figure, the one that Dawes engaged with most deeply is Sylvia Wynter's *The Hills of Hebron* (1962). This novel is treated somewhat dismissively in *Natural Mysticism*, but I think that *Prophets* reveals a more intimate dialogue, a reading that fed into the poem.

The Hills of Hebron is a deeply flawed novel. This is Wynter's own view, made in a 1980 interview with Daryl Dance,[17] but I think that Dawes found rich material for reflection in the novel's confusions about how to tell the story of its prophet, Moses Barton. At the time of writing *Prophets*, Dawes was undoubtedly thinking about the relationship of the artist/writer to the African Creole world that lay outside and in opposition to the hegemony of Europe in the Creole mix and he would have found in Wynter's novel an engagement with the phenomena of religious prophecy, madness and the black revolt against Euro-Creole supremacy and its somatic and cultural norms. Not least of its attractions, Wynter's novel has a level of seriousness that goes far beyond the comedy, say, of Naipaul's Man-Man or Selvon's Brackley.

Set rather vaguely in the years between c. 1914 to the 1938 labour rebellion in Jamaica, in the outward lineaments of Moses Barton, Wynter draws on the life of Alexander Bedward (c. 1848-1930, and see above, p. 39 and below, p. 195). Moses' first manifestation is as an itinerant prophet who leads some of the poor black people of Cockpit Centre to worship in his church, promising them an intimate relationship with God, because he is his returned Son. This first phase ends when Moses declares he will fly up to heaven from where he will send back golden chariots for his followers. From the top of a tall tree, Moses crashes to the ground and breaks his legs. He is arrested, tried by a mocking and biased court and sent to an asylum for five years as a lunatic. On his return, mocked by ribald folk songs about his ignominious fall and his fame as the sexual exploiter of the women of his flock, he explains that his fall was a merited punishment from God for his hubris in seeking to assume his place at God's right hand. Moses also privately concludes that the god whose favour he had assumed is still a white god. The publicly chastened Moses, now literate and better aware of how the white world works (he has been the recipient of the drunken confidences and support of the patronising but anti-colonial Irish doctor at the asylum), leads his flock to squat on a vacant and unproductive piece of crown land in the hills to establish the quasi-utopian community of Hebron. Rather than ascension in golden chariots, what Moses envisages is "a new kingdom, a kingdom here on earth" (p. 136) and a God who is black. On the one hand, this is a conscious act of rejection of the colonial world, but it also becomes clear that this is a community that echoes the colonial world in the authoritarianism of its leadership and structure.

Here the narrative fictively parallels the settlement of Pinnacle that Leonard Howell (1898-1981), founding father of Rastafarianism, set up in Sligoville in 1940. Howell, too, was incarcerated by the colonial Jamaican state, first on sedition charges and then for his alleged lunacy.[18]

All goes quite well in Hebron, until Moses, on a visit to Cockpit Centre, encounters Bellows, a quasi-communist agitator straight out of early John Steinbeck, who is whipping up the crowd with a purely secular and class-oriented message about how to fight against injustice. Moses protests that there is no mention of a black God in this speech (he is even more concerned that there is no room for him in Bellows' anti-clerical vision).

He is recognised by the crowd as the mad prophet, is verbally and physically abused, and challenged by a woman "…why don't you crucify yourself, black Jesus?" This tips Moses over into renewed madness when he decides that he will redeem himself and his community by doing just this. Unlike the crucifixion of Naipaul's Man-Man, which ends in calypsonian farce, Moses dies on the cross, seemingly prepared for sacrificial death, until, in his last moments, he begs his ambitious and insincere follower, Aloysius Matthews, to cut him down, a plea that for his own purposes Matthews ignores.

It is not the particular narrative of Moses Barton that feeds into *Prophets*, but the novel's treatment of prophecy as an oppositional force, of prophetic delusions of grandeur, of madness and the likelihood that the prophet is as likely to encounter hostility as respect, undoubtedly does. There are some narrative and thematic parallels, but most often *Prophets* makes an implicit critique of Wynter's novel. In *Natural Mysticism*, Dawes links Wynter with Andrew Salkey and Orlando Patterson as producing novels in which:

> the prophet is rarely seen as a figure whose voice is not only necessary to the society, but emerging from the soul of the community. On the contrary, these figures are almost always imposing their egos on their followers, their manic delusions of grandeur inflicting harm on the community. In its turn, the community is seduced and then comes to its senses (p. 249).

Dawes' argument is not that Caribbean societies are immune to immense damage by charismatic fake saviours of the people,[19] but that Salkey, Patterson and Wynter:

> all stand distant from the spirituality that they observe in their characters and, from that position of distance, take cynical pot-shots at the belief systems of the working-class community. It is a chasm that was only bridged when reggae began to offer a language which could speak simultaneously of spiritual and political notions without embarrassment (p. 253).

Dawes' critique can undoubtedly be backed up by closer reference to *The Hills of Hebron*, though I'd argue that there is an argument, albeit ambivalently expressed, for the necessity of the prophetic, even as a mad voice, in Wynter's novel. I think, too, that there are things that Dawes may have drawn from Wynter's novel that are not suggested in his critique in *Natural Mysticism*. One is the encouragement to be found in the poetic richness of biblical language that Wynter's characters use, and the way they locate their experiences in biblical narrative, as Aunt Kate does when she dreams that she has wrestled with Moses, like Jacob with the angel (p. 153). As she concludes at one point, "Where had she heard that? It must have come from the Bible. Everything came from the Bible" (p. 255). Nevertheless, the broad sweep of Dawes' criticism is one that Wynter herself backs up in the 1980 interview when she says, "I think that some of my book, where it fails, also fails because of an insufficient awareness *of the logic of the popular culture* we were trying to write about" (p. 302, my italics). But I also think that in the novel's contradictions and confusions ("there were lots of unsolved problems", Wynter adds (p. 301)), and in particular the elements of revealing self-reflection she embeds in the latter part of the novel, Dawes found material that could have informed his writing of *Prophets*, particularly in writing the figure of Thalbot.

Wynter's uncertainty is firstly about whether to treat Moses Barton as the object of satire or tragedy – whether she wants to stress his deviousness as self-invented community leader or his sincerity in being open to the voices that incite his revelations and delusions. She seems uncertain about how his madness is to be regarded, to the point where the words mad and madness are used in so many different ways that they cease to have heuristic meaning.

But even as she was writing *The Hills of Hebron*, it is evident that Wynter was aware of the difficulties with which she was engaged. Late in the novel (by which time the tone has shifted from satire to tragedy), she makes use of the character Isaac Barton to explore the question of how the story is to be written. Isaac is Moses' son, who has been sent away from Hebron by his mother, Gatha, to acquire the education and knowledge of the world that she thinks will enable him to lead the community towards modernity and self-respect – in a way that Moses could not do. Wynter creates Isaac as a would-be writer (it is a rather suddenly introduced narrative strand), and through him expresses the problems of perspective the novel is struggling with. Away at a teacher training college, Isaac contemplates writing about Hebron. With the distance of absence, "his father's story returned to him free from mockery, from the petty interpretation of the unbelievers of Cockpit Centre; freed, too, from the ignorant and indiscriminating glorification of the Believers in Hebron" (p. 243). But when Isaac makes an actual return to Hebron from the college, "nothing in Hebron was as he imagined it". Hebron is "too loud, too violent, too farcical to trap on paper, except perhaps with the bold outlines of satire" (p. 244). This is a judgement that connects to how the earlier part of the novel is written, where Moses appears as a plausible, womanising rascal who then tilts into hubristic madness. The problem, now, is that Isaac's colonial education has taken him too far from Hebron. This is despite the radical, anti-colonial sentiments that get him into trouble at the college. Isaac is also undermined by wondering for whom he is writing and why. He asks himself why he is writing, "For a people who could not read… And for the few who could, so suborned by the false coin of shallow dreams that they would deny Moses and his visions. And to strangers outside he could only speak across great distances" (p. 243). Although Wynter locates Isaac in the late 1930s, his anxieties no doubt express her own for Jamaica on the cusp of independence (an implicit point of reference in the novel). She no doubt saw power falling into the hands of a political class that was still firmly located within a neo-colonial mould. Much as she would have wished it otherwise, she appears to see no new beginnings, and this is expressed in Isaac's lament: "He should have come at the end of a tradition and not at the beginning... his was more a lyric talent than an epic one" (p. 244). This implied comparison of lyric and epic is one that connects neatly to the movements between these modes in *Prophets*: the epic narrative of realistic event, and the lyric metaphors of myth.

Wynter is convinced of the nation's need to have writers with the creative vision to stimulate its people on their journey from colonialism to genuine sovereignty, but she is also unconvinced that the nation's writers, including herself, have the skills and vision to provide that guiding light. She evidently thinks, too, that a decolonising vision is meaningless unless it overturns the nation's inequalities of class, race and gender, and its Eurocentric biases, and can communicate this vision to the African Jamaican mass of the people. This is the view expressed in *Natural Mysticism*, and is implicit in the portrayals of the four artistic apparitions who inhabit Thalbot in *Prophets*. Each – as is explored more fully in the notes and commentary (see pp. 186-196, pp. 197-206, pp. 207-212, and pp. 213-217) – is deeply flawed by their position on matters of gender, race and class, and by their self-deluding or self-destructive tendencies. None of the writer apparitions (the one exception is the apparition modelled on the jazz/ska trombonist Don Drummond) has been able to breach the divide between the educated elite and the mass of the people, and the Drummond figure is flawed by his misogyny.

In *The Hills of Hebron*, how the writer might build that bridge is both exemplified and pessimistically denied by Isaac's example. He begins to write a story based on the unassuming, artless narrative ("simple, graphic") that Obadiah tells his wife Rose about his boyhood in Cockpit Centre. Isaac writes this story in the first person, "and his identification with the young boy was complete". For the first time, "words came to him new-minted, in their pristine innocence, with all the dross of centuries, the tawdriness and disillusionments, discarded" (p. 245). But before Isaac reads the story to Obadiah and Rose, he has crippling second thoughts: the story will reveal too much of himself to them and he will be "implicated with them in a conspiracy of understanding that, binding him to them, would bind him to Hebron for ever, and to the image that Hebron had made of him" (p. 245). He tears up the story and behaves furtively when next he meets them. The allegorical significance of the incident is clear and needs no explanation. This act of denial clears the way for Isaac's betrayal of Hebron when he steals Gatha's concealed money and rapes Rose.

As I have already suggested, the issue of connection and self-revelation is very much at the centre of *Prophets* in the importance of the role of the

"I", the young man who is also the implied author, who very frankly reveals his woeful misery and desire for spiritual healing.

There is a further revealing indication of Wynter's anxieties about what is problematic in her novel. This comes in the account of Obadiah's discovery of his creativity in his inspired carving of an African head. However, it isn't clear whether the point is that Obadiah has made something that reveals to the people of Hebron their true African selves ("in carving the doll, Obadiah had stumbled upon God" (p. 259)), or whether he has stumbled on a lucrative business in selling mementoes to raise money for Hebron. One guesses, though, that Wynter's shift from literature to the plastic arts was a response to the emergence in the 1950s and 1960s of artists such as Mallica "Kapo" Reynolds (1911-1989), Ralph Campbell (1921-1985) and Osmond Watson (1934-2007), whose inspiration was visionary and arose directly out of the African-Jamaican spiritual tradition without any sense of cultural separation from the Jamaican working class and peasantry. Here was an art that was in touch with the logic of popular culture (with its non-Western spiritual cosmology) and expressed in forms that bypassed the colonial traditions that separated it from the black majority.[20] This is Obadiah's conclusion when he recognises that to communicate his new vision of the social and the spiritual for Hebron, "he would need the words and rhythms, not of a sermon, but a song" (p. 279). Writing in c. 1960, when the explosion of popular (and sometimes spiritually inspired) Jamaican music from ska and rocksteady through to the conscious reggae of the 1970s was still to come (the epochal release on disc of the Folkes Brothers' "Oh Carolina" with Count Ossie came out in 1961), this was a truly prophetic recognition, and one that Dawes could have seized on.

As with the relationship with *Omeros*, the connection between *The Hills of Hebron* and *Prophets* is both one of signposts and very fundamental revisions.

Prophets shares with *The Hills of Hebron* an emphasis on the malign legacies of slavery. The early part of the novel records that for the people of Cockpit Centre, "The instinct for survival was as strong in them as in their slave ancestors" (p. 52) but it is an instinct that comes at a horrific cost. They "carried the ghosts of dark millions who had perished, coffined in the holds of ships, so some could live to breed more slaves". They are "a waiting people, striving for nothing, accepting all" (p. 44). Folk memory and learnt instincts imprison them in a sense of total loss and the impossibility of escape from history's malign fatefulness. The authorial voice reproaches them as people who accepted their slavery and were complicit in it, as people who, in history, "haunted the pages, imprisoned in mute anonymity, the done-tos who had made possible the deed" (p. 55). The novel's references to the African Jamaican past are pointedly unheroic, as in the story Aunt Gatha's grandmother tells of Cato Randall, Gatha's great-grandfather, a slave who gains his freedom and is rewarded when he betrays both his fellow slaves in a revolt that he himself has fomented, and the master who has trusted him as a favourite (pp. 81-82).

What survives of the African cultural inheritance is seen in equally negative ways. Obadiah, for instance, still carries with him the terror of his mother's involvement with Kumina, described in colonial and racist ways as "pocomania, the little madness which used to seize his mother when the drums beat their frenzies into her limbs" and he recalls her "terrible fits" when she is possessed (p. 24). These "pocomania" followers – loosely described later as "voodoo followers"[21] – are led by an "obeahman" – another slack confusion of spiritual identities – believe in "the malevolent, cruel spirits opposed to man". As the authorial voice explains: "Theirs was a lost god of Africa" with whom they can only commune when possessed by "the 'spirit'". At first, the Kumina/Pocomania followers flock to Moses and dismiss Ambrose the obeahman as "an incarnation of the dark spirits", though after Moses' failed flight, Ambrose's flock returns to him. The furthest Wynter's narrative will go in recognising the African presence, and its possibilities, is in its persistence, expressed in Gatha's feeling that "the white man's church and all the words in his Bible could not destroy that seed" (p. 82).

Prophets begins with the image of the "stale renk" of the Guild Building, where the new church's service will be held, described as like the air in "the drifting carcass of an old slaver/ after the liberation of the encumbered souls" (I, ii). Then, the camera perspective moves up and outwards, to the shores of Kingston/ Nineveh lapped by "the Atlantic turned foul/ with the restless spirits of abandoned slaves" (III, i). However, what follows in the poem puts the emphasis on "liberation" and "restless", rather than the passivity of Wynter's poor black people. *Prophets* also echoes *The Hills of Hebron* in the connections it draws between the slave past, the present of disillusionment with the independent nation and the psychoses that afflict Thalbot and other figures in the poem (a discussion taken further below, see pp. 84-91). However, whilst Wynter's Moses comes "with a message from God to stir His people out of their apathy... He had come to break the neck of cowardice and slavery... out of bondage and into the Promised Land", his church offers only a new form of bondage to his will, and for his congregation, madness (for which they "had a respect") is not the urge to change the seemingly impossible, but "a private nirvana a man could reach when he was pushed beyond the limits of human endurance, when his spirit was so troubled that his body became a temple of dreams" (p. 60).

This is very far from Thalbot's liberatory mission when he seeks to rouse the people from their evasive amnesia about the past, in his witness as "a wild mad black man" who seeks to "desecrate the legacy of the whip and the chains" [...] "so that our children won't forget" (V, iii). Thalbot is unquestionably "mad" when we first meet him (in Chapter V), and the poem shows him as disabled by his madness, under the pressures of a society that has denied his hopes. This is in contrast to the somewhat romantic gesture Wynter makes (in seeing madness itself as a liberatory force) when she has Isaac "begin, dimly, to understand the necessity of his father's madness" (p. 261). Whilst there are further parallels between Thalbot and Moses in that both "hear" the voice of God telling them to undertake their respective missions, there are also significant differences in how that trope is handled. At the beginning of the novel, Wynter presents Moses's announcement of his divine call as part of his self-invention when he tells Liza (whose land he wants for his church): "He speak to me stern, but He called me… Son! He told me to shake the dust of Kingston off my feet…" (p. 108). It is only much later in the novel that Wynter signifies that Moses might genuinely be the hearer of voices. This comes after the confrontation with Bellows' supporters: "The Prophet stood up and pressed his fingers against his temples. Voices were calling to him, beating against his brain like wings, clamorous as birds in startled flight. But soon, very soon, he knew the turmoil would die down, and a voice, like the first sound of morning, would speak to him sweetly" (p. 214).

What I think Dawes really learnt from Wynter's awkward clashing of modes was to remove his narrative from a connection with conventional realism, which, of course, he does by writing a poem rather than a novel. This can be seen in the portrayal of Thalbot's instruction by God to go to Nineveh (Kingston) and warn the city of its coming judgement. By making this a parodic version (a poetic one) of the Jonah narrative, the poem is able to move fleet-footedly between humour and seriousness. Within this overtly meta-literary, non-realist narrative, Dawes is able to move seamlessly between the humour of Thalbot's quarrel with God (because he knows what kind of ill-treatment he will receive on the streets of the capital); the satirical treatment of Thalbot's misogynistic imaginings of Clarice's downfall; the sharp common sense of the sermon that he never actually delivers to anyone ("If a liar and deceiver comes and says,/ 'I will prophesy for you plenty wine and beer'/ he would be just the prophet for this people" (XXIII, ix)); and the pathos of his final silence ("The seer tongue, once fire/ now damp coals,/ has lost the will to speak").

It is a strategy that Wynter herself identified when she reflected on the problems with her novel: "…I failed with it because I wasn't bold enough to have broken away from the format of the realist novel" (Dance, p. 300).

There are other connections and differences, but a couple of further comparisons will suffice. I have noted the battle Moses fights with Ambrose, the "obeahman" leader of the "pocomanians" and the negativity of the novel's descriptions of African-centred spirituality. There is an echo of this battle in Chapters XXI and XXII of *Prophets* in the spiritual war Clarice's church wins against various representatives of African-oriented groups. But, as already suggested, this is a Christian victory only on the surface (see above pp. 36-37). This is an insight that draws on Dawes' participation in the church, a closing of the distance between writer and people, but about which Dawes makes no smug, self-congratulatory claims, as is clear in Chapter XIII, *Sunday Morning*, which explores the distractions of the poet-to-be during the church service.

My final observation concerns the difference between the two books in their approach to the "logic of popular cultures" (which Wynter identifies as a failure of vision in her novel). Even though she writes at what ought to have been a moment of possibility (on the eve of independence) and about a period (c. 1938) when the "starvelings" of the Jamaican working class had arisen,[22] whereas Dawes writes at a time when deep pessimism about the failure of decolonising politics (discussed above, pp. 26-29) was an entirely logical response to the times, the two books have radically different approaches to the way African-Jamaicans express their spirituality. When Wynter describes Moses' church as one that buries "carnival and careless laughing, eating, drinking and making merry", which endures "terrible days of expiation, of mourning" (p. 36), her description may encompass one truth, which *Prophets* also encompasses in its images of guilt and expiation ("how deep my weeping, / my lamenting before the altar" (XII, i)). But what *The Hills of Hebron* wholly omits is the energy and joy that can sweep up Clarice's church: its "intoxications" of the spirit, her "transported" reveries and "her rocking waistline/ […] balancing her sway to the bassline" (VI, i, ll. 22-24), the "rejoicing in the pews... bright arcs of tambourines" (XXII, i, ll. 1-2), "the dancing brothers,/ sweat pouring, clothes sticking to their torsos,// as they leap naked in the eyes of the maidens of God" (XXII, iv, ll. 2-4).

Prophets is deeply invested in the logic of popular cultures in a way that *The Hills of Hebron* self-admittedly fails to be. Nevertheless, I am sure that, like *Omeros*, Wynter's novel was one of the gateways Dawes walked through.

3. Clarice, the Church, the Bible and Sexuality:
Prophets and the novels of Zora Neale Hurston, James Baldwin, Alice Walker and Toni Morrison

The relationship between Dawes' reading of Zora Neale Hurston, James Baldwin, Alice Walker, Toni Morrison, and to a lesser extent Ntozake Shange, and the writing of the figure of Clarice may not be as clearly apparent as the dialogue *Prophets* has with Walcott's *Omeros* or Wynter's *The Hills of Hebron*, but it is a crucially important one for several reasons.

It speaks of Dawes' desire to create a strong black woman who is nevertheless complex, even at times conflicted. It shows him drawing from Hurston and Morrison, in particular, the permission and encouragement to engage in a dialogue with the Bible that is utterly open and without constraints of propriety, anxieties over blasphemy or the need for obviousness. He takes from Shange's *for colored girls who have considered suicide when the rainbow is enuf* (1975) the example of the choreopoem, the series of lyric poems that combine to create a whole. He finds in Baldwin, in particular, the impetus to regard the doings of a small black church as worthy of literary investment.

There are several elements in Baldwin's published play, *The Amen Corner* (1968), that would have connected with what Dawes was attempting. Baldwin's small black church, in its independent, self-fashioning Pentecostalism, situated above the flat of its pastor and leader, has many similarities to Clarice's church. Dawes would have seen the sensitive negotiation between insider and outsider views. The play takes the "saints" of the church entirely seriously at their own self-evaluation, recognising their sincerity and the dignity they derive from their efforts to live by their faith. But Baldwin also shows the suspicions, jealousies, malice and power struggles inside the community and the way that other messy human realities – like the return of Pastor Margaret Alexander's dissolute husband – intrude and complicate the integrity of the community. In the way that Baldwin allows Sister Boxer to say entirely sincerely, but self-servingly, "I ain't got no brothers or sisters on the road to hell… every soul I come in contact with is saved…"(p. 73), Dawes could have found the literary restraint that allows him skewer, by indirection, the hypocritical self-righteousness of the testifying "sybil mother" in Chapter III, ii. He could have recognised the same motivations towards control that trap Pastor Alexander in the uneasy space of holding on to her authority by her sharp-tongued put-downs of her flock's misdemeanours, such as Brother Boxer's unwillingness to give up his driving job for a company that sells alcoholic drinks. In *Prophets*, there is an acknowledgement that Clarice's authority in the church comes as much from her knowledge of the congregation's inner secrets as from her spiritual visions. Dawes would have seen in *The Amen Corner*, as well as from direct experience, that this is the kind of church in which the elect can rise and fall with great rapidity. We deduce Margaret Alexander has at some point overthrown the church's previous pastor. Now, because her own family life is falling apart she is under threat. As Brother Boxer says, "She rose overnight. She can fall overnight" (p. 72). This, too, is Clarice's trajectory. Dawes could have seen in Baldwin's alter-ego character, the young David Alexander, who is increasingly restless with the church's narrowness, a parallel with his own alter-ego characterisation in *Prophets*, particularly in the scene in Chapter XIII when the student is distracted into poetic reverie from the serious business of prophecy. Dawes could have noted the strain of misogyny in Brother Boxer that he portrays in both Thalbot and Last Night, when Boxer attacks Margaret on the grounds that she was "a woman who run off from her husband and then started ruling other people's lives because she didn't have any man to control her" (p. 84). Dawes could have found in Baldwin's play the same embedding of biblical reference in the speech of the saints. Indeed Sister Boxer's "The truth is a two-edged sword" is an allusion that both works share. Above all, in *The Amen Corner*, Dawes could have found the theme that is at the heart of *Prophets*: the confusion in the church about the relationship between love and sexuality and its narrow vision of the sexual purity necessary for achieving a relationship with the divine. Though spoken in hypocrisy, Sister Boxer's rhetorical question can serve as an epigraph for both Baldwin's play and Dawes' poem: "If you don't love your brother who you can see, how you going to love God who you ain't seen" (p. 47).

But it is in the work of African American women writers that Dawes found his greatest literary inspiration for his writing of Clarice. It is not that there was not yet a Caribbean women's writing to be acknowledged and admired; traces of Lorna Goodison's poetry are to be found at several points in *Prophets*. However, there isn't really a figure like Clarice in the emerging women's fiction from the region. There are striking quasi-autobiographical figures in the novels of writers such as Erna Brodber, Michelle Cliff, Dionne Brand, Merle Hodge, Elizabeth Nunez, Jamaica Kincaid and Merle Collins, amongst others, emerging in the decade or so before *Prophets* was written, but these tend to involve characters emerging through education into a conflicted relationship with their society's social divisions. There is Mother Gatha in Wynter's *The Hills of Hebron*, but she is, in truth, whilst strong, a single-dimensional character chiefly obsessed with supporting her son's rise to power. In some respects, the fictional character who bears at least some faint resemblance to Clarice, in her social emergence from rural poverty into a position of urban achievement (though without Clarice's prophetic gifts and ambitions), is the figure of Jane in H.G. De Lisser's novel of 1913, *Jane's Career*, written before De Lisser became the racist reactionary revealed in his later fiction. This is a novel that Dawes studied as part of his doctoral thesis.

Nevertheless, it was in the work of African American women writers that Dawes found a mature, achieved and ambitious writing that dealt with some of the issues that challenged his ambitions as a young male writer: to write a strong, complex black woman, to deal with the interface between spirituality and sexuality, and to engage with the role of religion and the ambivalent power of the Bible in black people's lives.

Whether he came to Zora Neale Hurston via Toni Morrison's championing of her work, or found it independently is both immaterial and lost in memory, but it is clear that Dawes found in two of Hurston's novels, *Jonah's Gourd Vine* ([1934] 1990) and *Their Eyes Were Watching God* ([1937] 1986) a number of inspirations for *Prophets*. Ironically, the connection between the title of *Jonah's Gourd Vine* and the parodic narrative of Jonah in *Prophets*, including the scene when Thalbot (in Chapter XXIII, xiv), shelters under this "mesh of vine" (the gourd), is the least significant of the echoes between these two works. In Hurston's novel the allusion to Jonah's story is used by one of John Pearson's enemies to justify bringing about the preacher's downfall. The man swears, "I'd cut down dat Jonah's gourd vine in a minute" (p. 147) – an example of a man hubristically playing God. (In the Jonah narrative, God first provides the gourd vine as shelter, then destroys it to teach Jonah a lesson.) More pertinent is the language of Hurston's novel, its focus on prophetic inspiration, the role of misogyny and sexual adventuring in the trajectory of the preacher's fall, and the relationship between Christianity and survivals of West African spirituality in South Florida. As a reader, Dawes must have been bowled over by both the poetry and the parodic energy of Hurston's use of biblically inflected language. There is the astonishing sermon, with its mix of poetry, Blakean vision and self-serving justifications, that John Pearson preaches when his philandering has finally exhausted the patience of his flock (a sermon that Hurston acknowledged she had mostly transcribed from a black preacher in a little rural church).[23] This sermon is set out like free-verse, marked with the kind of rhythmic stresses that suggest the actual rhythms of the preacher in interaction with the congregation – what Cheryl Wharry calls "textual boundary markers, rhythm markers, and spiritual maintenance markers"[24] – the rhythmic breaks signified by the printed lineation, and interjections of "ha" that Pearson uses for emphasis and building to an emotional crescendo:

> "When God said, ha!
> Let us make man
> And the elders upon the altar cried, ha!
> If you make man, ha!
> He will sin
> God my master, ha!
> Father!! Ha-aa!
> I am the teeth of time
> That comprehended de dust of de earth
> And weighed de hills in scales..." (p. 175)

It is just that kind of rhythmic effect that Dawes achieves in the tour-de-force of his lines in section v of Chapter XXII, *The Saints Return Triumphant*, lines discussed below as an example of the range of prosodic invention in *Prophets* (see pp. 80-81).

As in all the African American texts Dawes acknowledges as influences on *Prophets*,[25] one of *Jonah's Gourd Vine*'s themes is the vexed relationship between spirituality and sexual desire. As Pearson says, with a measure of truth, but a failure to acknowledge the misogyny embedded in his ill-treatment of his wife, Lucy: "You see dey's ready fuh uh preacher tuh be a man uhmongst men, but dey ain't ready yet fuh 'im tuh be uh man uhmongst women" (p. 182).

Again, it is clear that Hurston preceded Dawes in being deeply interested in the connection between the "trick" and the "divine trickster". John Pearson is convinced that "De words dat sets de church on fire comes tuh me jus' so. Ah reckon de angels must tell 'em tuh me" (p. 112) – which is very much Clarice's logic when she sets out to justify her "sinning" on the beach. But there are also doubts cast on the sources of Pearson's inspiration, when the reader remembers the earlier scene when he parodies a sermon he has heard, when "he aped the gestures of the preacher so accurately that the crowd hung half-way between laughter and awe" (p. 107).

With her roots in South Florida, Hurston was familiar with a territory with cultural resemblances to Jamaica (which she did, of course, visit and write about its black folkways in *Tell My Horse* (1938)). In *Jonah's Gourd Vine*, she writes about the meeting of Pentecostalist black Christianity and Hoodoo, where one of her characters declares that biblical Moses was "de greatest hoodoo man dat God ever made" and that "De Bible is de best conjure book in the world" (p. 147). It is just this fluidity between world-views that Dawes addresses in Chapter XXII in *Prophets*.

But it is undoubtedly Hurston's *Their Eyes Were Watching God* (with its flow a generation later into Morrison's *Song of Solomon* and Walker's *The Color Purple*), from which Dawes drew most as he took on the challenge of creating a female character who will not settle for any circumscription of her life. In Hurston's novel he found a bold examination of the nexus between black female sexuality and religion, and a model – which is a matter of tone – for taking on the Bible in a way that acknowledges its centrality and importance to black lives, but also finds ways of humanising it – through irreverent parody, through confronting its misogyny, through asserting a gendered female space within it. In biblical tone there is Teacake's joking reference to himself as an apostle of sexual love ("Ah'm de Apostle Paul tuh de Gentiles. Ah tells 'em [women] and then agin Ah shows 'em" (p. 158)), but there are also the images that channel the poetry of the Bible when, after the storm, death with "His pale white horse had galloped over waters and thundered over land" (p. 249). There are in *Prophets* occasional allusions to *Their Eyes Were Watching God* that are dealt with in the notes below, but what Dawes' poem takes on above all is the logic of Janie's injunction to her friend Pheoby: "Two things everybody's got tuh do fuh theyselves. They got to go tuh God, and they got tuh find out about livin' fuh theyselves" (p. 285). Janie's God is a god of love and "Love is lak de sea. It's uh movin' thing, but still and all, it takes its shape from de shore it meets, and it's different with every shore" (p. 284). Not least, in reading Hurston, Dawes could have seen her influence on Alice Walker and Toni Morrison as a model of the creative use of appropriation and development.

From Alice Walker's *The Color Purple* (1983), there at least three strands that feed into *Prophets*. Firstly, like Walker's Celie, Dawes creates for Clarice the most unpromising beginnings, scarred by her father, Ras Pedro's incestuous abuse (though the man who abuses Celie and takes her children from her turns out to be her step-father). Whilst we see none of Clarice's life between the point where she hands herself over to "the Government Office to declare/herself delinquent and whore" (X, ii, ll. 42-43) and her emergence as the new prophetess of the church, we must suppose that this past enters into "Her caged mind/ cracking on the quiet" when she is confronted by Last Night's emotional and sexual vulnerability. There is in Celie's narrative a trajectory towards the point where she can embrace her New World Africanness, her sexuality and her ease with the idea of the divine – material that offers inspiration to Dawes. Again, whilst there are no direct allusions in *Prophets* to the conversations that Celie has with Shug Avery, where Shug tells her about the pleasures of sex and the erotic uses of her "button" and breasts (*The Color Purple*, 1983, pp. 68-70), there are parallels in the way Clarice's sexual frustration is imaged in the physicality of her "sweating thighs" and "damp panties", until "The priestess waits for his [Last Night's] arrival at her temple / with her satchel of penance and her chastisement" (XI, ii) – though we may note that sexuality in *Prophets* is wholly heterosexual, unlike the relationship between Celie and Shug. Again, there are echoes of this couple's discussions of religion, when Shug points out that Celie's problem with God is that she thinks He's white, and Celie admits later that until she "chase that old white man out of my head… I never truly notice nothing God make" (p. 168). She includes sexual pleasure in the list of things she refused to notice whereas, as Shug says, "That's some of the best stuff God did" (p. 167). Now, whilst *Prophets* does not follow the detail of *The Color Purple*'s arguments with respect to race, gender and religion, it does engage directly with the question of godliness and sexuality, and with the existence of concepts of God that are deeply racialised; we see this in the conflict between Clarice's denied but deeply rooted Africanness and the vision of the blue-eyed Jesus that cramps her spirit.

The other encouragement that Dawes found in Walker's novel is the long epistolary narrative of Nettie's missionary sojourn in West Africa. This strand quite possibly encouraged Dawes to bring his own family history of African missionary work into the poem (in Chapter XI, *Infidelity*, and see the notes below, pp. 160-162). Here, the careful realism of Nettie's account chimes with Dawes' treatment of Jamaica's connection to Africa in *Prophets*. In *The Color Purple*, Nettie informs Celie that in both America and Africa patriarchy keeps women in subjection and that though the African villagers live without racial oppression – until the white road-builders arrive – there is really no meeting of minds with the African Americans. The Olinka villagers are not interested in their Christian, Westernised message, because they still have a coherent world vision of their own. As the leader Samuel complains, "The Africans don't even see us. They don't even recognise us as the brothers and sisters they sold" (p. 201). *Prophets* shows a similar refusal to sentimentalise pre-slavery connections with Africa, as is discussed above (pp. 52-53).

There is a climactic scene in *The Color Purple* when Celie finally frees herself from psychic bondage to Mr——, when she curses him, telling him that "Until you do right by me, everything you touch will crumble" (p. 176). There are two echoes of this in *Prophets*, which can perhaps be seen as implicitly criticising this act of cursing. Thus, whilst Clarice has every reason to curse her father, Ras Pedro, for his incestuous abuse, and though she can see no hope of salvation for him as an unregenerate Rastafarian, she, in her imagination, "carries a balm for his head and ministers it" (X, ii, l. 52). The other moment comes when Clarice and Last Night curse Thalbot's "inconsistency and disobedience", as part of the formal act of disfellowshipping him from the church, but in reality to silence him. Here, the act of cursing is far from admirable.

But it is with the work of Toni Morrison that *Prophets* displays the deepest engagement. There are permissions, allusive engagements – and evident differences, though perhaps of all *Prophets'* intertexts, Morrison's are closest in aesthetics and cultural location, certainly in comparison to Walcott and *Omeros*.

There is a direct allusion to Morrison's *Sula* ([1973] 2002) in Chapter XVI, ll. 44-45, where Clarice witnesses a "rain of crows from the sky", an echo of the plague of robins that accompanies Sula's return to Medallion,[26] a phenomenon that the townspeople associate with the curse of her presence. What Dawes found in *Sula* – in the portrayal of a woman who refuses all accepted parameters of black life in Medallion – was a way of envisaging his own heroine as a morally complex character, who is prepared to destroy Thalbot and blackmail the church brothers.

It is with *Song of Solomon* ([1977] 1995) that the most profound links can be found. Most directly the connection comes in the trope of flight. In *Song of Solomon*, the half-remembered stories and garbled songs about flight are one of the mysteries that Milkman must tease out. When he goes down South to uncover his family roots, he discovers the story of his grandfather Jake as "one of those flying African children" (p. 346), though his teller, Susan Byrd, also adds, "that's just some old folks' lie they tell around here…" But as she continues her account, it is clear she half-believes that "Some of those Africans they brought over here could fly", and when he challenges: "When you say 'flew off' you mean he ran away, don't you? Escaped?" she makes it clear, "No I mean flew" (p. 346). But then Morrison complicates this myth of an enslaved man's triumph in escaping from slavery, because in the process, Solomon/Shalimar both abandons his wife Ryna, who loses her mind, and leaves behind his twenty-one children, including Jake, who he has carried with him but is forced to drop. The dropped child and the abandonment suggest a breach that cannot be repaired, that what Milkman can connect to is not a vanished Africa, but to the family left behind who are making an African New World life for themselves in the South. Later, when Milkman tells his aunt Pilate about his discoveries, he realises that what is also wrong is the idea that flight was something only men could accomplish. This he realises was the significance of Jake's words: "You just can't fly off and leave a body" (p. 358). This caution was something that Dawes evidently responded to, since in *Prophets* it is the unnamed prophetess who makes the mythical flight not so much back to as over and embracing Africa. Here, *Prophets* shares with *Song of Solomon* the perspective that it is with the living Africa *in* the New World that connection must be made, or with the contemporary Africa that shares the same post-colonial challenges, not with "this museum of broken dreams" (XXVIII, l. 49), the imagined and mythically whole Africa before the breach of slavery.

Dawes draws, perhaps, his greatest inspiration from Morrison's treatment of the Bible. He begins by sharing with Morrison a powerful awareness that he lives in a society where people lead lives that are enmeshed in the Bible as the most ubiquitous and profound guidance for living, as a source of narratives that speak in living ways to current circumstances, and as provider of iconic symbols of human types as well as proverbs and phrases that are parts of daily speech. If Morrison sees the Bible in worksongs, spirituals and blues, Dawes finds it in reggae. But like Morrison, he is aware that its narratives are sometimes puzzling and contradictory, and open to racialised and gendered interpretations that can entrap their readers as much as offer any kind of salvation. From Morrison, Dawes found the encouragement (which he no doubt also found in Jamaican oral culture) to parody, to play with, to freely version, to challenge the teachings and narratives to be found in the Bible. A couple of examples illustrate this common playfulness. There is, of course, Morrison's play with naming in *Song of Solomon* – the Dead family's habit of naming their children by random searches of the Bible, so children are given such names as First Corinthians, and Pilate, the latter named thus, despite the nurse trying to persuade her father that the name of the Roman emperor who washes his hands of Jesus was not an appropriate name for a baby girl. But Pilate is also the pilot who conducts Milkman to his salvation. This kind of serious playfulness finds its way into *Prophets*. There is, for instance, the scene of the mission at Annotto Bay which plays on the words of Christ: "I will make you fishers of men", to describe the converts as "freshly heaved from black water of St Thomas", like landed fish, "mouths still gasping for air" (XXII, i, l. 15-16).

Dawes also draws from Morrison the willingness to take communicative risks with the reader in making allusions that are not available on the surface. It is there in the naming of Morrison's novel, where the Solomon turns out to be quite other than the biblical figure, and the connection to the the Song of Songs is not made by textual allusion, but through the novel's moral discourse on the nature and necessity of love. Here, whilst Dawes would have been well aware of the way the institutional church, throughout history, had overlaid a layer of allegory on the Song of Songs, in order to de-eroticise it,[27] he follows Morrison in discarding those allegorical layers and responding to the book as the expression of sexual love.

Sometimes Morrison's allusive use of the Bible can be even more devious. As Agnes Suranyi notes in her essay "Bible as Intertext",[28] one of the sleights of allusion that Morrison pulls is the scene when Pilate comes to the police station to secure the release of Milkman and Guitar after their arrest for breaking into her house and stealing what they think is gold, but is in fact human bones. There is the clue of Pilate (who is tall and strong) pretending to behave like a little old black mammy of racist stereotype, who uses a biblical quotation, giving chapter and verse, as support for her plea for the return of the bones and two men's release on the grounds that they have taken nothing of monetary value. But, as Suranyi shows, the quote Pilate uses (the injunction that what God has joined let no man put asunder – the implication being that the bones are her late husband's) is not from the chapter and verse she cites. The cited verse has a quite different, but in the context funny, slightly blasphemous and apposite meaning. It actually refers to Jesus's command to the disciples to go to a village to find an ass and colt, and "loose them and bring them unto me" (Matthew 21: 2) – the events that precede Jesus riding into Jerusalem on an ass, as celebrated on Palm Sunday. It is very clear, here, who the asses are that Pilate wants released.

Dawes does this kind of thing on a number of occasions. One occurs when he brings on stage a series of prophets who attempt to give his first apparition good advice on the basis of their own misfortunes with women. But as the notes to Chapter XVII show (see below pp. 192-195), the versions of the stories given are deliberately inaccurate versions of the actual Bible narratives, so that, not surprisingly, the first apparition ignores the advice and the episode becomes a display of biblical misogyny. Above all, as is discussed below in the notes to Chapter XV (*Legion*), there is Dawes' parodic deconstruction of the narrative of Jesus, Legion and the Gadarene swine, where Jesus plays the role of trickster in a Hollywood-style movie shooting-script. Toni Morrison was another of the gateways through whom Kwame Dawes passed to arrive at this kind of imaginative freedom.

FIVE: *PROPHETS* AS POEM

Another book could be written about *Prophets* as a poem, but this chapter confines its focus to four aspects of the poem's form – in addition to the account of its structure and plotting given above (pp. 15-18). These include the way the poem locates its aesthetics through the variety of language registers it employs; the way it is a poem in the purest sense of being expressed through a repertoire of prosodic and sound patternings; and the way the coherence and meaning of the poem is achieved through the patterning of imagery and a number of key tropes.

1. Language Register and the Writing of a Caribbean Epic

In his tart account of Milton's *Paradise Lost*, Samuel Johnson writes that the task of the epic poet is to achieve variety and appropriateness of linguistic register, to the "level" of the subject matter – for Johnson, of course, within the Enlightenment concept of refinement. He writes how "In every work, one part must be for the sake of others; a palace must have passages; a poem must have transitions. It is no more to be required that wit should always be blazing, than that the sun should always stand at noon."[1] This is a precept Dawes instinctively follows. Whilst the 18th century concept of refinement may only faintly linger, the goal of variety and appropriateness is no less true for the Caribbean poet, with the particular challenge of locating the epic in relationship to the socio-linguistic registers that mark those fissures and confluences of class, race and gender in Jamaican society, which are amongst *Prophets'* themes. This is a goal with a particular framing in a poem that stakes its claim to being an expression of a Caribbean aesthetic vision that brings poetry *closer* to the popular traditions of orality (for Dawes, located in the radical aesthetics of reggae) than tutelage to the Euro-Western poetic tradition. *Closer* to Jamaican orality, but not in any exclusive sense, because in *Prophets* Dawes draws from all points between these poles to achieve the richest range of poetic language.

What he is up to is signalled early in the poem in lines such as:

> ...In the air the stale <u>renk</u>
> of spilt <u>Red Stripe</u>, curdling vomit, ganja and

sweat is thick as in the drifting carcass of an old slaver
after the <u>liberation</u> of the <u>encumbered</u> souls... (I, ii, ll. 5-8, my emphasis)

where the word choice moves from the patwa of "renk" to the latinisms of "*liberation* of the *encumbered* souls". This kind of register shift is a standard element in the poem, made as appropriate to the context or presumed speaker. For instance, in the passage introducing Thalbot, when he is squatting in the decaying colonial mansion due for demolition, the language moves from the bureaucratic tones of "This was before the city decided against preserving this legacy/ of the past" (V, ii, ll. 8-9), to the exasperated tones of the police charged with removing him: "before all else had failed short of the police doing// what they said they would do and shoot the focking mad man/ in the head" (V, ii, ll. 18-19). Again, in a poem which, like all proper epics, at times introduces the voice of the writer in asides, apostrophes and rhetorical questionings, Dawes achieves a further variety in the narrating voice that is appropriate to circumstance. There is the tenderness of address to Clarice:

For though our heaven may be all nostalgia and created myth
it is my gift to you, sybil, while you sleep
to the symphony of gunshots in the tenement. (VI, ii, ll. 21-24)

There is also the created voice of the nameless prophetess travelling to South Carolina, putting on the tones of a less educated woman, and alluding to the slave auction, because that, she supposes, is how her white interlocutors see her as a black woman bringing the gospel to the old slave state of South Carolina:

Finger me now, I don't

give a damn who sees. I won't <u>cause no</u>
<u>trouble</u>. Tell the ushers to stay cool. I will smile
<u>'cause</u> I come to find a path – and this won't be

a path you make, it will be a path you may offer... (XXVIII, iv, ll. 3-7, my emphasis)

Having established this range of socio-linguistic register, Dawes is then able to play with ideas of impersonation in the poem. For instance, in Part Four, the poem introduces Clarice, "speaking for the first time". But what we hear is very far from Clarice's voice (whose "Africa clogs thick in her tongue" (VI, i, l. 9)), and the register used reinforces the play between Clarice as physical being and Clarice as an authorial invention of poetic myth:

"To speak my words would be to fracture
the wings of a myth and send it careering
to the sun-baked earth." So said the prophetess. (XXIV, ll. ll. 1-3)

Elsewhere, when the poem introduces a direct speaker, such as the

street-preaching sybil mother, the language is exact both to person and
the performative function of sermonising:

> An is not one somebody me pray up dem stairs
>
> t'rough the raw smell and stink a dem ole neaga a try
> defy the way of the Lawd fe de visa – People,
> when time neaga a fret is a foul smell dem give off. (III, ii, ll. 25-29)

It is not merely that the woman speaks a patwa that is socio-linguisti-
cally exact, but that it is a patwa that catches both the intimacy of ad-
dress (from one black person to another) but also the ambivalent
self-perception of "neaga". And adding to the complexity, the lines also
allude to Edward Baugh's poem "Nigger Sweat" (see the note, p. 129).
Beyond appropriateness to persons, *Prophets* is exact in attuning its language
to situation, in particular through its use of allusion. When the poem
visits Clarice's father, Ras Pedro, in the squalor of his Wareika cave,
the language echoes the very battered dignity of the Rastafarian speaker,
mocked by those who bring him gifts of pork:

> The dread accepts
> the <u>degenerate</u> flesh – only, he says, to protect
> another from <u>partaking</u> of its poison: "I shall
>
> burn it on this holy mountain, as a <u>fragrant</u>
> offering to Satan!" He does not touch the bloodied
> newspaper. "Res' it over yonder in my shrine
>
> to the <u>shitty of Nineveh</u>." He points to his latrine...
> where the groan of sluggish blue flies emanates. (X, i, ll. 19-26, my emphasis)

Here the language register both recognises Ras Pedro's belief system
and its archly enobled language (degenerate, partaking, fragrant) and
part shares, part ironises the old rastaman's wordplay (the shitty of
Nineveh). Similar shifts in contextual register can be found in the episode
that narrates the would-be rescue of Thalbot by the CIA from Kingston
(playing with the narrative of the rescue of Lot by angels from Sodom
– see the notes to this episode on pp. 172-174) where the hard-boiled,
clipped language of the telling is in an opposite register from the Jacobean
cadences of the original: "But word carry fast in this city/ and a bunch
of serious fellows/ gather like military front of Thalbot house" (XIV,
iii, ll. 57-60). There is a shift, too, in the versioning of the Gadarene
swine episode (XV) where the language plays with technical cinematic
terminology and the cynical voice of an American movie producer. In
contrast to these two episodes, the closure of the breakneck journey
Thalbot (as Jonah) makes into Kingston (Nineveh) in the belly of a
coach (whale), ends in appropriately biblical pastiche:

> And the Lord commanded the bus
> and it vomited Thalbot onto dry land;
> and the city grunted, then turned over (XXIII, vii, ll. 1-3)

Many more instances of Dawes' varied and effective use of language register could be cited, but it is worth pointing briefly to three that reflect the way register conveys the varied emotional and sensory impact of different parts of the poem. For instance (and there are many other examples of punning and wordplay), in the episode of the mission to Annotto Bay (Chapters XXI-XXII) the poem enacts the hedonistic raucousness of the seaside resort through the ganja/maritime punning playfulness of the "weed-infested buoys" and the invention embedded in Jamaican naming of dance movements:

> In the rumshop, the revellers bob like weed-
> infested buoys, tams and head-ties just keeping
> afloat over the wave of rapid-fire dancehall;
>
> and their bodies contort and fall back into the bogle
> while their legs flap in flamboyant butterfly (XX, i, ll. 7-11)

Elsewhere the poem employs the register of epic lamentation:

> In Kingston's orange glow, the worm swallows
> its last morsel and the gutter closes like a grave
> on another corpse, daily slaughtered souls (XXIII, xiv, ll. 45-48)

Whereas at moments of emotional intensity, the poem moves to a prosaic starkness of expression, as when the flash of attraction passes between Last Night and Clarice when he stumbles into her church and is smitten by the spirit and she by his need:

> Through the raised hands
> Last Night searches for her eye.
> Her womb leaps. (IV, ii, ll. 43-45)

2. Prosody and Poetic Effect

As noted above, *Prophets* follows Dante and Derek Walcott in using the tercet form throughout, a form that lends itself to the onward flow of narrative by its capacity to allow for extensive use of enjambment across stanzas as well as across lines. In Dawes' case the tercet is unrhymed and, whilst syllabically irregular, generally follows a four-stress line. Within this structure, through variations of stress and patterns of sound – assonance, consonant and vowel clusters, alliteration and a variety of rhetorical devices anchored in repetition and the convergence of sense and sound – *Prophets* achieves a musicality that carries the reader through the poem. Anyone who has been lucky enough to hear Kwame Dawes perform sequences from the poem will attest to its word sound and power.

Again, whilst the number of verses where one could draw attention to beauties of poetic craft is large and the number selected for commentary small, I want to point to the musicality of a composition that brings together the narrative and the lyric. Of course, one of the goals of a narrative poem is to achieve a base layer of unmarked plainness that carries the poem forward and stands as a foil to moments of heightened intensity. An instance of this can be seen in an early expository stanza such as:

> And <u>yet</u>, from a <u>ladd</u>er <u>in</u> the <u>clouds</u>,
> her <u>m</u>emory descends <u>m</u>ysterious
> and <u>m</u>iraculous in its detail. (*Prologue*, ll. 55-58, my emphasis)

Here only the cluster of initial "m"s and the four-stress scansion (on <u>yet</u>, <u>ladd</u>(er), <u>in</u>, <u>clouds</u>) distinguishes this stanza from the patterns of unheightened speech. By contrast, the pair of stanzas describing the arrival of the congregation at the church at the beginning of the poem more explicitly make use of patterns of sound and rhythm to achieve their effects:

> Goats chewing almond seeds
> daub their sweat into the pale blue wall;
> they <u>scamper</u> from the <u>congregation com</u>ing
>
> in a wave of perfumes and too much cologne,
> in casual brights and patent leather,
> <u>bibles tucked</u> like <u>swords</u> under their <u>arms</u>. (I, i, ll. 1-6, my emphasis)

Here there is a nice echo of the way the unstressed syllables in the phrase "scam<u>per from the</u> congregation" speed up both the scampering goats, as in turn do the unstressed syllables in "under their" hasten the approach of the eager congregation. One can note, too, in the second stanza quoted, how the rhythmically balanced antitheses of the first two lines (wave of perfumes/ too much cologne; casual brights/ patent leather) catch the ambivalence between respectability and display, and lead into the "bibles tucked like swords" as a gesture that mixes a declaration of faith and a fashion statement. There are other occasions where *Prophets* makes use of rhetorical figures, such as anaphora; for instance in the sequence of lines that begins: "But how can I watch my grandmother/ transported like this into the congregation,/ hymning her lament, and not see her ululating near the river…" (VI, i, ll. 37-48). Here the poet, drawing a comparison between Clarice and his grandmother (one of whom was Ghanaian), laments Clarice's denial of her Africanness, repeating the phrase "and not see/ not see" over the next four stanzas in rising emphasis.

In other stanzas we can note how Dawes varies the four-stress line to meaningful effect. For instance, in the stanza:

> thumping with the wave-rock of the dip and sweet fall-back of
> dancehall and gravel-voiced djs proclaiming
> the new sound, the new prophecy of slackness. (III, i, ll. 10-12)

the five-stress, fourteen-syllable first line points to the rolling out of the DJ's line, such as in Shabba Ranks' "Mr Loverman" with its sixteen-syllable first line ("Well, if a loving you looking for you buck upon the right man").[2]

Another, but different, echoing of a musical effect comes at the beginning of Chapter XVI, *It Is the Cause*, introducing the first of the apparitions who inhabit Thalbot – the ghostly simulacrum of the ska trombonist Don Drummond. Here there is an effective imitation of the off-beat syncopations that transformed African American R & B into the Jamaican form of ska music, and in the clusters of stressed consonant blends (ch, sc, sl) and the plosives of "bowed"/ "bobbed" an echoing of the energies of the dance:

> The first visitation came riding the flapping
> coat tails of a ska syncopations, and the
> rudies with their dawtas in mini skirts
>
> and helmet heads smelling of the singe of the iron,
> chopped scissor-slashes between their legs,
> bowed, bobbed, grinned through the sweat, (XVI, i, ll. 1-6)

I have noted that the major effect Dawes achieves with the frequency of enjambment in his tercets (quite often across from one stanza to another) is the forward motion of the narrative line. On occasion, the line break and a less obvious running-on can create a different effect, where expectation is not fulfilled. For instance, in stanzas describing Thalbot as the madman/ warrior squatting on Old Hope Road, there is an enjambement:

> like a maroon on a raid into a redcoat camp
> with his machete slick and sticky
>
> with the crystallising syrup of cane juice (V, ii, ll. 25-29)

But here, the line break and the complete phrase of "machete slick and sticky" encourage us to pause, with the thought carried from the "red" of the first line that the machete is sticky with blood. This is an expectation anti-heroically undermined across the stanza break, confirming Thalbot as a figure located between pathos and absurdity.

In a poem with many bravura excellences, for me, three in particular stand out, and two of these merit further comment here. There is the brilliant *mise-en-scène* where Last Night is confessing his sexual shame to Clarice in her kitchen whilst she is preparing food; there is the passage where (with something of a nod to the climactic sermon Hurston writes for John Pearson in *Jonah's Gourd Vine* (see above, pp. 60-61) Clarice and her church celebrate the vanquishing of the heathen; and there is the tour-de-force of the description of Thalbot's (alias Jonah's) breakneck descent (Chapter XXIII, vi) down Mount Diablo, as the captive of the drunk, stoned coach driver. In each, patterns of sound and rhythm reinforce meaning. For instance, in the Last Night/ Clarice episode, look at how the sound patterns of Clarice's culinary responses speak her feelings in response to Last Night's confession:

> Clarice, domestic confessor of the wayward,
> cuts the heads of skellions with quick
>
> taps of the blade on the formica counter. (IX, i, ll. 5-7)

It is not only the implied metaphor of what else Clarice might consider cutting off, but the way the stresses on the consonants (quick, taps, blade, formica, counter) echo the hard, abrupt sounds of the chopping knife. Compare that to Clarice's second response:

> Clarice scoops the chopped
> vegetables in her shining hands, green and orange
> with slick wet tomatoes, and spills them
>
> into the exploding dutch-pot oil (IX, i, ll. 13-16)

Here the cluster of sibilants (scoops, vegetables, shining, slick, tomatoes, spills) prepares for what we know will be their sound in the oil of the dutch pot, and prepares the move from symbolic action to direct action. Then, in the utterance of a *steups*, comes an appropriately symbolic culinary closure, where the sound of the woman and the popping oil echo each other:

> Clarice turns away from the saltfish fritters
> and slaps him peppers and onion across the face...
> [...]
> She marches away with dramatic hissing teeth,
> The oil still popping in the dutch pot. (IX, i, ll. 52-57)

Another of the dramatic high-points comes when Dawes' verse matches the oral drama of the church service, at the moment of the mission's victory at Annotto Bay:

> Returned from the dense mist of St. Thomas in the East,
> returned intact from the stronghold of Satan
> and his minions of falling lights, returned unbroken,

> ...returned triumphant, let the church say amen.
> Returned with song: Can I get a witness!
> Returned with feet still skipping: Glory!
>
> Returned with captivity captive: Yes!
> With the chains of degradation broken asunder: Uhuh!
> With the faith intact despite the perilous way!
>
> Returned with a song of triumph on the lips!
> Returned with a song of victory on the lips!
> Returned, returned, returned! (XXII, v, ll. 1-12)

Here the verse enacts not only the language of spiritual triumph (Satan, captivity captive, chains broken, faith intact, psalmist's skipping feet), but also the call-and-response between preacher and congregation (Can I get a witness?, Glory! Yes!). Beyond this, in the repeated rhythms of "returned from", "returned with", rising to the "Uhuh!", and the "Returned, returned, returned!" there is an enactment of the action of "labouring" or "trumping" (see the summary for Chapter XXII), when the worshippers stamp, bend forward at the waist and groan ("Uhuh!") in a movement that brings on hyperventilation and access to the transcendence of possession and speaking in tongues.[3]

I think the reader can safely be left to see how the effects of Thalbot's plunge downhill are achieved, but one further moment in the poem is worth noting, when in a supremely self-reflexive and metatextual way, the poet (like Alexander Pope in "An Essay on Criticism" [1711] demonstrating his mastery of poetic effects[4]) ends the passage in Chapter XXIV (*Speaking for the First Time*). Here, supposedly, Clarice is speaking for herself, but manifestly in the poet's most overtly poetic voice. Clarice declares her joy in falling from spiritual grace into the joys of the erotic, but I think readers will recognise that the stanzas in fact provide the young poet with the opportunity to demonstrate what, as a poet, he has been up to. Clarice's words end in a rush of sibilants (note the pun), guttural consonants and vowels engaging in onomatopoeic display. We only briefly wonder just whose exhilaration the stanzas celebrate:

> "for my mouth explodes at the rush of sound,
> words tumbling forth in the thick smell of earthly
> truths, tongue running wildly, shaping words,
>
> flowering in the new sun. Falling thus, the lewd sibilants,
> the orgasmic gutturals, the round voluptuous vowels:
> myth falling, myth falling. It is exhilarating!" (XXIV, ll. 55-60)

3. Tropes and Imagery

As noted above, *Prophets* is a poem as much shaped by its lyric and thematic impulses as it is by narrative, and the narrative itself is often far from linear. Yet one has a strong sense that the poem as a whole achieves both a density and an organic unity. It does this through patterns of imagery that thread throughout the poem, and the repetition, in different contexts, of key tropes. Here, three examples are explored: the trope of the filmic, the trope of madness and the imagery of birds and flight. There are others, such as the trope of the trick and the trickster, moments of "interim" and the imagery of Pentecostal flames. Each functions as a structurally organising device and as an indication of the poem's deepest concerns.

i. Film and the tricks of construction

It is in the poem's concern with the ambivalent relationship between the trick and the trickster (discussed above, pp. 20-21) that the exploration of film as a trope in the poem becomes most pertinent. Film as artefact and filming and editing as processes with multiple options provide both analogical narrative devices and metatextual metaphors for the construction of *Prophets* as a poem that explores the intersections between the "trick" as the miraculous, the breach in fixed appearances (or what Dawes, quoting Bob Marley, would go on to call "natural mysticism") and the trick as manufactured illusion. Film, of course, created the illusion of reality through its movement through the projector at 24 frames per minute, a point made very explicitly in Chapter XV, *Legion* – the chapter where Dawes places the ambivalent idea of the trick at the centre of the poem.

Beyond this episode, the trope of the filmic enters and identifies the poem's structure. There is the play between *mise-en-scène* (for instance the carefully set-up scene between Clarice and Last Night in her kitchen, discussed above) and *montage* (for instance the jump-cuts that connect different stages in the narrative). The prologue itself works like the opening title sequence of a film by bringing together the main elements of the poem as a whole: the involvement of the poet's younger self and the tension between different possible versions of the prophetess's fall. *Introit*, where the empty space of the church is seen before the arrival of the congregation, employs the device of the *tracking shot* of the active camera moving around the still space, as it also does in Chapter XIII, *Sunday Morning*.[5]. There are scenes of both flash-forward and flashback, respectively in Chapter I, *Introit*, and Chapter VIII, *The Changing of the Guard*. In the first, there is an anticipation of the arrival of Clarice and the saints for the service, and in the latter, a return in time to the point when the church buys the grand St Andrew's house and installs Clarice as caretaker. Other chapters, such as X, *Hermit*, flash back further in time to reveal Clarice's wounded social origins. Montage is also used as an economical narrative device; for instance the progress of Last Night from his shelter into Clarice's church is managed through a series of jump-cuts. We see him first taking shelter in the empty cricket pavilion on campus (IV, i), hearing the competing sounds of ragamuffin (even sound behaves cinematically, "dollying through/ the craggy bramble") and worship, and we next see him stumbling into the church service (IV, ii) where he is slain by the spirit, and Clarice is smitten by him. Throughout *Prophets* there are foreground and background scenes that work on the principle of parallel montage. In Part One, the attention is mainly focused on Clarice and her church with the figure of Thalbot, her prophetic rival, intercut in the background. In Part Three, Thalbot's activities are the foreground and Clarice and the church are in the background. In the very first section of Chapter I, there is a neat example of what screen-writers call "Chekhov's gun": the locating of an image in an early scene that later proves significant. This is when Clarice and her motorcade pass "the madman's shrine on Hope Road" and fail to stop to cast out his demons, as in true obedience to Christ's teachings they ought to have done. They are more concerned with the impression their arrival at the service will make. The madman, we soon learn, is Thalbot and his subsequent role in Clarice's fall indicates that this was a failure of care with bad consequences. And if in cinematic structure *Prophets* rather more resembles an "art" film than a Hollywood blockbuster, it does not neglect to use, on occasions, the devices of popular television. For instance, Chapter II, *In a Shady Cloister Mew'd*, offers a *mise-en-scène* of Clarice sitting at her dressing table, alternatively watching television and staring into her mirror as she applies face cream. It is in the mirror, in a neat piece of narrative compression, that she has a vision of Thalbot in the guise of the madman, Legion, from the narrative of Jesus and the Gadarene swine. It is in the deconstruction of this narrative in Chapter XV, *Legion*, where even the most inattentive reader should be alerted to the filmic as a trope threaded through the poem – and also see that Dawes is engaged in a daring interrogation of the rhetoric of biblical narrative. The story, indeed, portrays Jesus as something of a trickster figure, for what could be a better demonstration of his powers than the hurtling pigs? The episode also points to the regular mechanics of the Pentecostal service, the demonstration of conviction and sanctification through healing miracles and the act of speaking in tongues. It also operates as a metatextual device for the poem as a whole, exposing the figure of the manipulating (and perhaps manipulative) *auteur* who constructs this narrative as an illusory reality for purposes of his own, only hinted at in the prologue and in the final chapter. The episode perhaps, too, works in a counter-revelatory way, by showing how easy it is to ironise the miraculous. This is Dawes at his most daring, because what he does in *Legion* would undoubtedly be seen as offensively profane by the "true believer".

What the filmic trope points to is not just how the poem itself is a constructed narrative, but also how, metaphorically, the filmic points to the similarly constructed nature of the Bible. Whilst Romantic criticism has long led us to regard the poem as the outpouring of the individual imagination (tempered by the shaping of craft), for the literalist believer, the Bible is the outpouring of God's word, filtered though it may be through the words of His various prophetic and apostolic amanuenses and translators. The perception of the Bible as a text written and edited for persuasive purposes is, of course, far from a new one, but it is powerful in the context of the poem.

ii. Madness

There are at least thirty separate references to madness in *Prophets*. Madmen (and they are almost all men, except the woman whom Clarice converts at the Annotto Bay mission, whom Last Night "visions" with "eight spirits in her twisted soul" (XXI, ii, l. 29), or the stoned sisters whose "minds slip slowly, unchecked./ They have not spoken for an hour" (XXI, i, ll. 17-18)) are a very visible part of the Kingston scenery. There are the "slow-breathing madmen" at the crossroads(III, ii, l. 3), the squatting madman downtown on Harbour Street who "shits his last meal with heartfelt reluctance/ before the patient mongrel" (III, iii, ll. 14-16), and the madmen in Parade Square who "have marked their spots/ in balding patches along the lawns" (XIV, i, ll. 8-9). The mad are the recipients of society's casual cruelties, whether victims of the doctors at the Bellevue asylum who "perform casual experiments,/ opening the gates of the patients' brains" (XXII, ii, ll. 7-8), or of the gunmen who "practice marksmanship on the dizzy madmen", or the whores who take out their resentment by pissing or spitting on "the madmen's drooping heads" (XXII, ii, ll. 14-15, 16-17).

Madness is an epithet applied both to the city ("the spastic madness of Nineveh" (XXII, iv, l. 36)) and to the behaviour of individuals otherwise regarded as sane, like Last Night, as preacherman, who after "sinning" with Clarice, "howled/and ran like a madman into the sea" (XXI, iii, ll. 4-5), and is seen by Thalbot "rolling like a madman in the water", desperate to purify himself. Beyond these generalised images, *Prophets* brings the focus close up to the temporary insanity of three of the four artistic apparitions who inhabit Thalbot, to Thalbot himself and to the biblical figure of Legion, the madman whose evil spirits are cast out into the unfortunate Gadarene swine. Beyond the specific descriptions of people or behaviours as mad, there are the uses of psychiatric terminology to describe literary strategies such as "the lazy path of literary schizophrenia", and descriptions of behaviours (Clarice's denial of her genetic Africanness) which have become so naturalised in the society that no one would dream of identifying it as any kind of madness, but which the poem presents in such a way that it is difficult not to see her denial as profoundly disturbed, self-alienated behaviour.

Of course, all this raises the question about what *Prophets* means by madness, and what its prevalence as a trope is saying in the poem. As a discursive commonplace, it is very obviously a slippery word, and one whose definition enters into the power relations of social determination. British colonial governments were no less prone than the Soviet Union at its most repressive to label their dissidents as mad and incarcerate them in psychiatric hospitals. Leonard Smith's *Insanity, Race and Colonialism: Managing Mental Disorder in the Post-Emancipation Caribbean 1838-1914* (2014) makes it clear that whilst many of those incarcerated – black, brown or white – were suffering from recognisable psychoses – mania, delusions, depressive illnesses – which had reached a level of social disability that made family-based care was impossible, there were others, black Jamaicans in the main, who expressed their psychic distress in hostility to white and high-brown Jamaicans to the level where the authorities felt the need to take them off the streets. *Prophets* reminds of this institutional context in the lines when Thalbot, inhabited by the spirit of the Don (Drummond) is "carried away like Bedward/ to the fluid calmness of injections/ the white walls and bed" (XVII, ii, l. 4). Bedward, as the notes to these lines spell out in more detail, was the revivalist preacher and prophet, Alexander Bedward, who, several times in his career, was incarcerated as a lunatic – the fate also of Leonard Howell and Claudius Henry, noted earlier.

But the colonial authorities were not the only social force with the power to define (and punish) those who opposed them as mad. When Thalbot threatens Last Night and Clarice with exposure, Clarice has a theological explanation for Thalbot's accusations, an hypocritically theocratic rationale for why he is evidently not one of the chosen:

"...Fallen, fallen!" laments Clarice.

"For the brilliance of blanketed miracles, secrets of the Almighty,
like the ark of the covenant and the sanctified mint of prophecy,
can blind the unchosen one, strike him dead if he sees.

Truths fed to the uninitiated sour and form ulcers.
How then could he see the ritual coupling of angels
on the black sand and not go blind with madness?" (XXII, vi, ll. 12-16)

Last Night's' expulsion of Thalbot from the community of the faithful is altogether blunter: "... He rises and curses// Thalbot's inconsistency and disobedience, declares him/ mad..." (XXII, xi, ll. 18-20).

From this it becomes clear that there are several competing frameworks for locating the meaning of madness in the poem. These include one concerned with social order, one concerned with rational anxieties about how people envision and perceive the world they exist in, and one that locates madness within a religious/biblical framework. Each of these has its own explanatory basis. I think, too, the Dawes wants to locate the pressures towards madness in history, and this is discussed further below.

To expand on the frameworks mentioned above, we might see the *official* framework as having both overt and hidden dimensions. The fate of figures such as Bedward and Claudius Henry show the two orders in collision. Both Bedward and Henry can be seen as expressing what Erna Brodber, in her preface to *Obeah and Other Powers: The Politics of Caribbean Religion and Healing* (2012) calls "ancestral anger", where within the context of a religious, African-Christian sense of a divinely intended justice, these prophets (invested as they were in the logic of the popular cultural world of dreams and visions, of mystical powers) challenge the wound of slavery that was still manifest in the economic and cultural exclusion of the black Jamaican majority. The colonial authorities, overtly responding to the expression of visions and mystical powers, incarcerated on the grounds of lunacy, as a way of concealing their real purpose, which was to behead movements with significant popular black followings and divert attention from their social and political claims for justice. Whilst paying lip-service to what was claimed in the earlier 20th century as a rationalistic-medical framework, it is clear that such colonial views were, in reality, deeply embedded in racist, non-scientific concepts of the Black/African psyche. In Leonard Smith's account of the Jamaican asylum (2014), it is evident that such 19th century founders of the asylum regime as Thomas Allen (who was lauded for bringing order to what was previously chaotic) based his practice on profoundly racist premises. Allen complained, for instance, that the asylum was forced to house an incurable class of "brutal negroes whose natural mental position is so low, as to justify their being irresponsible and of unsound mind".[6]

As indicated above (pp. 35-36), Clarice's church bases its understanding of personal psychology, including manifestations of madness, on what can be found in the Bible. Here *Prophets* focuses on two essential texts – and also references that element of Old Testament prophecy where, in George Rosen's words, "the Hebrew for 'to behave like a prophet' can also be rendered as 'to rave', 'to act like one beside himself', or 'to behave in an uncontrolled manner'"[7] – all aspects of Thalbot's behaviour. The two crucial texts include the narrative of the healing miracle when Jesus casts out evil spirits from the madman called Legion, and also the words of Jesus, quoted by Matthew (12: 43) which warn that if a house has been swept clean of evil spirits, there's nothing to stop the wandering spirit, who finds nowhere else to occupy, coming back and bringing "seven other spirits more wicked than himself…" Jesus's words were no doubt consistent with the psychology of madness of his day, particularly regarding the physical reality of evil spirits, though biblical commentary suggests that his words were chiefly an attack on formulaic religious orthodoxy, observance without animation by the holy ghost – a putting down of the Pharisees who had challenged him for doing healing work on the sabbath. But the equation of possession by evil spirits and madness is certainly central to the understanding of Clarice's church. When Last Night is taken up to the healing baptismal river to be born again:

> …they chastise his sin
> of a foul mouth, and then cast out the lingering spirits,
> the childhood deprivations, the shameful acts,
>
> the perversions of his corrupt mind;
> and he feels the violent escape of demons
> through a tidy round hole in his skull.
>
> They fly through the ficus berry leaves
> and he screams at their going;
> his body now deflated, void, vulnerable. (IX, ii, ll. 16-24)

His sin "of a foul mouth" is actually no more than his recounting of what the woman he has run away from demands of him (see notes to Chapter IX, *Confessional*); his shameful acts relate to the masturbation he confesses to Clarice; and if there are any "perversions of his corrupt mind", these can only be his misogyny and distaste for sexual desire – particularly in a woman – and these remain an approved part of his later ecclesiastical persona. As in the filmic deconstruction of the Gadarene episode, *Prophets* treats the church's interpretation of what constitutes insanity with ironies of both overt and implicit kinds. This is not to say that the poem denies the reality of belief in the psychic experience that its sufferers characterise as possession by evil spirits. The description of the Rastafarian woman captured for God by Clarice presents a powerfully persuasive image of that kind of belief:

> Seeing, she is drinking in, gulping, her visions unleashed;
> her tight neck flexes in quick spasms, as her head,
> sweat clean, but unruly like the patches of a mangy bitch,
>
> bobs and weaves, evading the jabs of the evil one.
> She is skipping to the thump and syncopation of hymnals;
> tongues of fire come flaming from her opened mouth. (XXII, ii, ll. 13-18)

What Dawes does do, though, is use the idea of the emptying out of one wandering spirit and occupation by several others as a neat narrative device to enable him to reflect on the nature and fate of artistic contributions to Jamaican society, in particular the fate of an iconic musician and three important Jamaican writers to a world that neither politics nor religion can rescue from its Ninevite state of war. This comes after Thalbot, like Last Night, arrives at Clarice's church and likewise falls smitten by the spirit. In his case, "Clarice prophesies into his panting body./ The sisters gather and clean Thalbot's/ body of residual spirits, the froth// of spit from his mouth and the grime / on his face…" (XVI, i, ll. 49-52).

Thereafter, Thalbot offers vacant possession to the four apparitions, the Jamaican artistic figures, all of whom have suffered some form of psychosis in the pursuit of their art. As one quits Thalbot, another enters.

We should also note that, as Kelly Baker Josephs' insightful critical monograph, *Disturbers of the Peace* (2013), demonstrates very cogently (but not always unchallengeably), *Prophets'* treatment of madness also takes place within the framework of the corpus of Caribbean writing (though she looks only at fiction and therefore does not mention *Prophets*). From Crazy Bow in Claude McKay's *Banana Bottom* (1933) to Mad Mary in Zadie Smith's *White Teeth* (2000), Joseph shows that the trope of madness and the figure of the mad person has had a powerful and prominent presence in Caribbean writing, as dominant a trope, she claims – somewhat less plausibly, I think – as race or gender. As noted in my earlier discussion of the literary hinterland to Dawes' treatment of the prophet figure (see above pp. 54-64), this is territory that Dawes was very much aware of, as his discussions of such figures in *Natural Mysticism* (1999) makes plain. One of the temptations that I think Josephs' study sometimes falls into is romanticising the nature of madness, as somehow a necessary condition (a phrase she draws from Sylvia Wynter's *The Hills of Hebron*) for challenging the dominant and apparently unchangeable European-imposed social order inherited from plantation society and its denigration of black skins and African-Creole cultural practices. As my discussion of that novel tried to show (pp. 54-64), this is not an analysis that either a more balanced reading of the novel or Sylvia Wynter's own subsequent self-criticisms really supports, but Josephs' thesis helps to make clear how *Prophets* rejects that romantic temptation. In Dawes' view, as expressed in the poem, madness is a condition of suffering, a condition that disables. When Thalbot is mad, he makes no connection to the world. When he is sane, as he sometimes is, his perceptions are shrewd and insightful.

All this indicates that, for Kwame Dawes, the cluster of behaviours, attitudes, ways of perceiving for which madness is an inexact but useful word, plays an important part in what he sees and what he wants to say about contemporary Jamaica. It is a matter close to home, as the later poetry collection *Impossible Flying* (2007) makes clear, in exploring the anguish of mental illness in his own family. It is perhaps from this experience that *Prophets* absolutely refuses to romanticise madness as any kind of creative strategy. The physical images associated with madness in the poem are stark; they point to incapacity, to disintegration, to a state of being locked away from quotidian human engagement, as in the account of Thalbot "padlocked, yale-locked, combination-locked/ by his cage of insanity" (V, i, ll. 4-5), or the image of the fourth apparition, the harrowed poet whose "mouth drools; his eyes do not see; his tongue/ uncertain of itself, drags, and sometimes he snaps// at the flies like a mongrel..." (XX, iv, ll. 14-16). These are the images of someone who has seen the inside of Ward 21 at the UWI Hospital (see the poems "Ward" and "Casting Out Demons" (*Impossible Flying*, pp. 36-39)).[8]

But *Prophets* has more to say about madness beyond the frameworks of social order, religious control and the literary corpus, indeed in aspects of the perception of reality that tend not to be seen as really mad at all, because the society as a whole lives in a state of denial. Indeed, the more I have thought about *Prophets*, the more it seems to be saying that Jamaicans (and other Caribbean people) continue to live with the after effects of historical trauma.

I think it is worthwhile here to survey the published views of professional Caribbean psychiatrists on the nature of psychosis in the region and the beginnings of academic study of the actual history of its treatment. Clearly, psychosis is a universal human phenomena, though it can take culturally specific forms,[9] but there are obvious aspects of Caribbean history that psychiatrists such as Frederick Hickling and others, in the very useful collection of essays, *Perspectives in Caribbean Psychology* (2008) argue have created the pressures out of which psychoses come. Similarly, Leonard Smith's *Insanity, Race and Colonialism* makes it clear that the effects of slavery in destroying the contexts of social, cultural and family life in which the African person had existed before enslavement, and the new contexts of powerlessness and bodily abuse, did not end with emancipation. It seems, indeed, a wonder of black survival in the Caribbean that those who were driven to madness were such a minority. Clearly, some individuals are more prone to suffering the disabling behaviours and ways of seeing the world that tend to be diagnosed as psychotic.[10] Nevertheless, it is impossible to ignore the impact of centuries of slavery and colonial rule, the long-continuing denigration of the Black/African body, mind and culture that arose from that denial of self-ownership, or social death, in Orlando Patterson's words,[11] as being powerful causal factors in the creation of madness in the Caribbean.

It is not necessary to cite the appalling brutalities recorded in the anti-slavery tracts, or the obscenities of power revealed in the Thistlewood papers to recognise the nature of slavery's trauma. It is there in the careful, cool documentation of "social death" in Orlando Patterson's *A Sociology of Slavery*; in the daily struggles merely to ensure bodily survival documented in Vincent Brown's brilliant historical study, *The Reaper's Garden: Death and Power in the World of Atlantic Slavery* (2008),[12] or the work of Randy M. Brown, *Surviving Slavery in the British Caribbean* (2017), which though based on records from Guyanese Demerara brings us closer to the daily consciousness of enslaved people throughout the region.[13] All these raise the question: can post-slavery trauma be a reality, productive of forms of psychosis, that persist into the present? Some of the work on Jewish holocaust survivors suggests strongly that psychological trauma can be passed down through the generations.[14] Frederick Hickling and others have argued that, for instance, styles of parenting (the use of sometimes brutal physical punishments) and attitudes to self-identity (Fanonian self-contempt) have their roots in the experience of slavery and post-slavery and have become culturally embedded and passed on from generation to generation.[15]

Perhaps the most considered social-scientific attempts to come to grips with the nature of the continuing trauma of history is to be found in the work of Erna Brodber. In her study, *The Second Generation of Freemen in Jamaica, 1907-1944* (2004), Brodber identifies an undercurrent of historic rage and anger persisting amongst the feelings of those Jamaicans who reached adulthood at the dawn of Jamaica's first moves towards limited self-government in 1944.

Some, unnamed spear-carriers in Dawes' poem, appear to be living the trauma without necessarily reflecting on it, but living it nevertheless in their bodies. Others, like Clarice, deny that history and what it has done to them; a few, like Thalbot, are all too aware of that history and are driven mad by it. The signal is given early in the poem, in the imagery describing the students' Guild Hall in which both the hedonism of the dance and the transcendence of the church service are seen as emerging from the belly of the slave ship. If this kind of history is blocked in many amnesiac Jamaican minds, it is certainly not in Dawes', as is revealed in a number of key poems in *Progeny of Air* (for instance "The New Crop Arrives", "Excursion to Port Royal" and "Talisman"); in the poems of *Requiem* (1996), which is explicitly framed by the continuing necessity of healing slavery's wounds;[16] and in the focus on wounded memories in *Wisteria* (2006) – a focus that continues into his most recent collections of *Wheels* (2011) and *City of Bones* (2017).

In *Prophets*, Brodber's "rage" is expressed in Thalbot's passionate desire to overturn the residues of the past of slavery and colonialism, and this entirely legitimate desire induces psychosis in Thalbot precisely because all around him he sees a denial of this reality. More generally in Thalbot's characterisation, the psychosis he manifests can be described as a state of extreme instability of the person. His multiple personalities – political informer, pseudo-dread, penitent, madman, prophet – are images in the poem of the historical pressures he cannot control. Thalbot's instability is also, it seems to me, is representative of a wider social and cultural instability. It is tracked in the shifts from colonial, to "socialist", to "free-market" social personas, as well as in the evidently unstable personal transformations in the church – the death of the "old man" and the birth of the new "born-again" saint – and subsequent falls from grace. The different trajectories of Last Night, the student "I", as well as Thalbot, all point to the hazardous fluidity of personal identity in the poem.

But if *Prophets* has a profound sense of the traumas that lie heavily on its world, it also suggests sources of healing. This includes the constant dialogue with the Africa which survives bodily in the genes and in creolised cultural expression, though these resources have to be freed from the weight of racist, colonial categorisation – such as the naming of the religious practice of Pukkumina as "Pocomania", the little madness of possession. But history, in Dawes' poem, is not merely one of trauma, but also a record of stoic survival and Creole inventiveness – legacies that are revealed in the genius for constant renewal, of versions galore, and the joyful, if sometimes confused, attempts to achieve a spiritual transcendence that is expressive of his characters' deepest cultural instincts.

iii: Birds, Flight (and falling)

The trope of flight and the imagery of birds provide one of the most prominent connective tissues of *Prophets*, making links to the biblical, folkloric, literary and quotidian imaginaries the poem draws on. Flight and the totemic image of the bird provide the key metaphors to describe Clarice, and the implicit directionality of flight is used metatextually to describe the ambition of the poem – as well as being a useful narrative device (an analogy to the jump-cut), to transfer characters, in imagination at least, from one location to another. This is seen in the episode where the poem moves Clarice, "flown over the foothills", in dream from her new surroundings in Castleberry's old house to revisit the yard of poverty and abuse of her childhood, and how she "returns in flight, her tongue now trimmed/ to King James' metaphors" (X, ii, l. 2 & 45). As an image, flight signifies both the distance Clarice has travelled and, with the pun on flight as escape, how rapidly (though not completely) she has left behind the Afrocentric Rastafarian world of her father for a biblically literalist Christianity.

The trope of flight is part, too, of the poem's dialogue with other texts,

here in particular the presence of flight as a central trope in Toni Morrison's
Song of Solomon (see the discussion above, pp. 69-70). Through that
resonance, flight enters into *Prophets*' focus on both the visible and hidden
presence of Africa in Jamaican mentalities. It makes a connection to the past
"before the slaves had Africa ripped / from their dreamings and heaven
flights" (I, l. 37) – an allusion to the powerful folk-belief that, provided they
avoided salt in their diet, escaping slaves could fly back to Africa (see the
notes to these lines, p. 115). In *Prophets*, this trope is chiefly connected to
the last book in the poem, *Flight*, and the journey of the anonymous
prophetess, over Africa to the USA. The connection of this contemporary
flight to the historical folk-belief is signalled in the image of the woman's
preparation for the journey: "My watertight goatskin satchel will carry/
smooth stones, cooling pebbles for under my tongue" (XXVIII, i, l. 11), but
it is also a flight that is in dialogue with Walcott's *Omeros* and the dreaming
journey of Achille (see pp. 51-52 above) in insisting on a connection that
is not to "this museum of broken dreams", but to the Africa of the present.

The trope of flight connects, specifically, to the presence of birds. There
is the allusion to Toni Morrison's *Sula* and the plague of robins in the
episode when Clarice's slaying of Thalbot in the spirit (XVI, ll. 44-45) is
associated with "crows who dive nose first / into the Liguanea plains", "a
rain of crows from the sky". This is seen by the witnessing congregation as
an omen of Clarice's spiritual power, but the image works ironically since,
by this stage, the reader knows that Clarice's "totem" is the bird, so that the
omen applies, more threateningly, to the prophetess herself, and predicts
the imagery later in the book describing her downfall. Here the poem
makes use of the quotidian repositories of ideas about birds – their actual
presence in the Jamaican sky and the way that the flight of birds generates
images of transcendence and the physicality of both power and vulnerabil-
ity. For instance, when Last Night is being baptised by immersion in the
river, "his soul [is] revived by the turning dove", but there is also the
presence of the "hawk [that] screams / over the Blue Mountains" (IX, ii, ll.
34-35), contrary images of peace and war.

Flight – inevitably involving the idea of rising and falling – takes one of
the dominant metaphors of Christian eschatology – ascent to heaven,
descent to hell – as an image that the poem ultimately reverses. It does so
both in the poem's own metatextual imagery and in the totemic images of
Clarice as a bird. In the prologue, to construct an image worthy of his
prophetess, the poet offers his "leaping metaphors" and introduces her in
the lines, "I know now that she did have wings, / brilliant multicoloured
plumes / that lifted her above the squalor and muck" (ll. 61-63). It is an
image that connects to how Clarice sees her declining, decrepit father,
once, too, a seer, now "his feathers drooping, tattered at the ends, / some
broken at the quill: his wings, his // dull filthy wings" (X, ii, ll. 64-67). But

though Clarice has made an escape from "the filthy caves of Wareika", it is to another kind of prison. This is signalled in the epigraph to Chapter II, *In a Shady Cloister Mew'd*, where (as the note unpacking this line shows, see pp. 119-120) the image is one of the imprisoned hunting bird and of the nunnery's denial of sexuality. This is echoed in the image of Clarice's "caged mind", which "cracking on the quiet, trembles" at the sight of Last Night's redemption (IV, ii, l. 38). The significance of the image is reinforced by its repetition in her own later self-justification: "But they always knew my secret fantasies/ in the pink and powder of my jewelled cage" (XXIV, l. 47). The specific imagery of Clarice as bird continues in the biblical imagery of Thalbot's imagining of himself as a contemporary Elijah, taking refuge from the revenge of Jezebel in the desert, where Elijah is fed by the ravens who bring him "bread and flesh in the morning, and bread and flesh in the evening" (see the note on pp. 252-253). However, such are Thalbot's misogynistic feelings towards Clarice that "When the charred raven comes with meat in its beak,/ slanting against the sun, Thalbot stones it/ and the thud sends it sudden down to the rock" (XXIII, xv, ll. 1-3). But this fate for Clarice is only in Thalbot's mind, and the last part of the poem, moving from poetic epic to myth, begins to reverse the signifiers of flight and falling.

The movement begins with Clarice declaring "Then I will fly – for it is flying – above the squalor of the journey" (XXII, viii, l. 30), continuing in Chapter XXIV in the mode of a Pirandellian character admitting that if she were to speak frankly, of some of the shameful truths she knows about the church, and about herself, her words would "shatter/ the brittle wing-bones of a myth" that the author is trying to create for her. But then she decides: "But the air is too thin here at the gate of heaven", and she will discard the visa to salvation because it demands the denial of her full sexual being, and she will accept a rapid descent:

"So now, I fall, giving myself up for dead
and not giving a damn who goes down with me.
Now broken, my wings limping, I gladly fall..."

Then the poem reverses the valences of rising and falling as Clarice is imagined amongst the "thick smell of earthly / truths" to cry out:

"... Falling thus, the lewd sibilants,
the orgasmic gutturals, the round voluptuous vowels:
myth falling, myth falling. It is exhilarating!"

SIX: ALLUSIVENESS IN PROPHETS

Prophets is the work of a writer who had already achieved a signal, distinctive voice. As a poem, it dramatises a deeply personal and fruitfully conflicted vision; in its structure there is not a chapter that doesn't bear the mark of a daring literary imagination; in its texture there is not a line that doesn't sound like Kwame Dawes. Yet, as the notes to the text will show, few lines go by without some allusion to an existing literary text, in particular to the Bible.

Just to get some sense of proportion, there are over fifty allusions to other literary texts, from Homer to Anthony McNeill; there are over twenty allusions to reggae lyrics, as well as many references to reggae artists and pop-cultural phenomena; overwhelmingly, there are one hundred and thirty-six allusions to verses in the Bible, including eight episodes that go beyond allusion into forms of versioning.

These bald facts tell us little. What tells us more is that, of the literary allusions, almost half are to other Caribbean writers, with Walcott – not unexpectedly, given the poem's relationship to *Omeros* – being the most frequent, followed by Lorna Goodison. This reinforces Dawes' comment, noted above (p. 48) that what he has taken from Walcott is "the permission to indulge in the richness of language and the grandness of poetic ambition". There is also one powerful allusion to a Kamau Brathwaite poem; he is undoubtedly also one of *Prophets'* progenitors, but one whose influence is less directly manifest in the poem's texture. Whilst the Dawes of *Prophets* is closer in cultural terms to Brathwaite than to Walcott – elsewhere Dawes makes a respectful acknowledgement of Brathwaite's championship of the African presence in Caribbean culture and his pioneering use of the aesthetics of jazz as a forerunner of his own reggae aesthetics[1] – I think that, on the one hand, Dawes did not see Brathwaite's current experiments with visual form as being a direction he wished to pursue,[2] and that, on the other, he found in Walcott the voice he wanted to challenge. There is also a single but pertinent allusion to the pioneering Jamaican poet of the modern voice, George Campbell, which indicates something further of Dawes' sense of heritage. As one would expect, there are references to the work of those who become the apparitions who inhabit Thalbot – Roger Mais, John Hearne and Anthony McNeill – as well as allusions to the novels of Zora Neale Hurston, Alice Walker and Toni Morrison discussed above (pp. 63-72).

Beyond the Caribbean, with nods to Homer and the poets from the Anglo tradition that one knows Dawes admires – Yeats, Eliot, and Hopkins – the most significant literary allusions are to Shakespeare, some of which are discussed below as allusions which tend to the oblique and which demand unpacking, but which point to how particular episodes should be read. There are important allusions to *A Midsummer Night's Dream*, *Othello* and *The Tempest*, with more passing references to *Macbeth*, *Anthony and Cleopatra* and *Julius Caesar*. One must take these as signals of Dawes' ambition that *Prophets* be seen as both an intensely Caribbean work, and also one that has some connection with the old-world Western literary tradition to which by education and cultural location all Caribbean writers are heirs.

The allusions to reggae tend to fall into two categories: those from roots reggae that sing in a prophetic voice and are deeply Bible inflected, including songs by Israel Vibration, Peter Tosh (particularly in language), Culture, Big Youth, Max Romeo, and of course Bob Marley, whose songs make up a quarter of the lyrics alluded to. Whilst these are instrumentals without lyrics, there are several nods to the titles of Don Drummond tracks that point to the Rastafarian turn in Jamaican music. The other references are to the songs of 1980s' dancehall. These point to the era of hedonism, guntalk and sexualised dancing, including songs by Ini Kamoze, Mad Cobra and others, and the naming of dancehall stars such as Shabba Ranks and Supercat. These song references signal the shift from the era of the prophetic protest of roots reggae to the era of free-market, every-man-for-himself that forms the social and political context of the poem.

Readers will find identifications and explanations for all the biblical allusions in the Notes and Summaries section, but an overview of how Dawes' uses them gives indications of what he is up to in the poem. The sources can be grouped into six areas. There are a significant number from Genesis, and other early books of the Bible that give what can be called "origin" stories, such as Noah and the flood, Jacob's ladder, the tower of Babel, Jacob and Esau, Abraham and Isaac, and Lot and his daughters. There are the narratives of Jewish exile such as Joseph and Potiphar's wife, Daniel, Nebuchadnezzar and the pointing finger, Moses and the tablets and the divided Red Sea. There are the David narratives, including David and Bathsheba and David dancing before the Lord, key texts that reveal the Bible's sometimes puzzling morality and the presence or absence of God's favour. There is an extended reference to the Song of Solomon (or Song of Songs) to which Clarice turns in justification of her womanly sexual desires. These biblical allusions can be seen as fulfilling a number of functions. They take the place of Greek mythology as foundational narratives in a tradition with particular meaning to the Caribbean, and perhaps, more than anything, they are the stories that even the most perfunctory

Jamaican churchgoer would have been brought up on, some of which provide stock allusions in roots reggae. Of this group, the stories of Lot, of Joseph and Potiphar's wife, the Song of Solomon and of David and Bathsheba are expanded beyond allusion into versions of different kinds.

The second, and unsurprisingly largest group of allusions are drawn from the prophetic books, with multiple references to Isaiah, Nahum, Job, Hosea, Jeremiah, Ezekiel, Joshua, Elijah and Jonah. These are the references that comment on the contemporary state of Kingston as a wicked Nineveh and provide a background to the kind of prophet Thalbot takes himself to be, touching on the narrow line between inspiration and madness and the undeniable tendency towards misogyny in many of these Old Testament figures. Of these prophetic books, two are given more extensive versioning treatment: the narratives of Elijah and Jezebel and, most expansively, the Book of Jonah.

Thirdly, there are several allusions to the Psalms, which focus on the themes of the psalmist's sense of persecution, his quarrels with God and, sometimes, moments of joy.

The fourth group of biblical narratives are those drawn from the four gospels. Some of these are analogous to the core stories of the Old Testament as being fundamental to the essentials of the Christian tradition and distinguishing features of faith: the nativity, the crucifixion and the resurrection. There are passages that relate to the consequences of belief and unbelief, and the fate of each group in the metaphor of sheep and goats, and the rapture that will divide believers and unbelievers on the day of judgement. The largest group of gospel narratives relate to Jesus' miracles, since healing and the miraculous are at the heart of the practice and the belief system of Clarice's church. Besides Lazarus and the crippled man who walks again, the most extensive treatment is given to the narrative of Jesus casting out the demons from the man known as Legion and their passage into the Gadarene swine. This narrative, as noted above, also provides, along with Jesus's thesis on the topic, the most extensive resource for exploring the theme of madness in the poem, with particular reference to Thalbot. It also, of course, provides the crucial plot device of explaining how the four artistic apparitions come to inhabit him.

The fifth group of allusions relate to the books that narrate the trials and progress of the early church and the letters of guidance sent to the scattered Christian flocks, such as Philippians, Corinthians, Ephesians and Peter. These are the books that, in many ways, are most pertinent to the church at the heart of this poem. As noted above, the saints of Clarice's church see themselves as being in the same beleaguered situation as the persecuted early Christians, and, in particular, take the sermons on being born again, on the necessary death of the sinful "old man" and the birth of the new saint, as being the essence of their Christian purpose. As a Charismatic/Pentecostalist church, it is not surprising that the imagery of tongues of fire and rushing mighty winds from Acts 2 threads its way through the poem (see the notes on p. 130, 164 and 165).

The final source of allusion is drawn from the Book of Revelation and from the apocalyptic prophecies in the Book of Isaiah, in particular the imageries of the dragon and the Great Beast that accompany Thalbot's torment as a defeated prophet hiding out on the Edgeware coast. These allusions have powerful resonance in Jamaica where strands of millenarianism have a vibrant life in some of the independent black churches and in some strands of Rastafarianism.[3]

So, there is nothing accidental about Dawes' choice of biblical allusions, and whilst this survey does no more than provide the context for discussing *how* Dawes uses allusion in the poem, it is the role of allusion as a poetic device that places the relationship between writer and reader at the heart of the discussion – and reveals most about *Prophets* as a poem – that this commentary now turns to.

The starting point must be a recognition, following Christopher Ricks, that whilst we may primarily think of allusion as a form of metaphor[4] – comparing two unlike things for their likeness – there is also a degree of metonymic use in *Prophets*, by which I mean using allusive references as a part for the whole, as direct, motivated signs of the beliefs and inner states of characters. The church's preachers and saints not only use the words and narratives of the Bible to interpret their world, or as a rhetoric of conviction, but see themselves as actors in those same narratives, as members of a church no less elect, no less threatened, no less living in the imminence of apocalypse and judgement than the members of the early Christian church. They are no less a chosen people than the Jews of the Old Testament, no less part of a narrative of divine promise that finds the salvation of Christian times forecast in the narratives of the written past. It is also a church within a culture that readily acknowledges the power and reality of the prophetic, albeit, as discussed above, taking rather different Old and New Testament forms.

Whatever the text referenced, sacred or secular, the allusiveness of *Prophets* works at a number of levels and at different poles of implicitness and explicitness. Allusion's most surface (but not superficial) manifestation works at the level of textual enrichment, of investing the verse of the poem with often witty and apt phrases that – in the way that poets have always done – display a learning and skilfulness in their deployment that signals the writer's acknowledgement of the literary past he or she has inherited and is in dialogue with. Such allusiveness also creates a potential pact between writer and reader. For example, the description of the church brothers on their way to service, carrying "bibles tucked like swords under their arms" works as a simile without needing any awareness on the reader's part that an allusion has been made. As it stands, the image tells us something about how the brothers present themselves to the world. To know that the line alludes to Ephesians 6: 17 – "Take the helmet of salvation and the sword of the Spirit, which is the word of God" – engages writer and reader in a deepened appreciation of the appropriateness of the simile and encourages a more multi-levelled reading. It tells us that, in obedience to this injunction, these Bibles are very definitely carried to be seen; it suggests further that the brothers are very probably familiar with this verse itself; and it offers a not unaffectionate irony in pointing to the distance between the self-image of heroic soldiery encompassed by the hosts of Satan, and the Sunday morning of the actual scene. No doubt the brothers look a little absurd to the more cynical of the students on the University campus whose Guild Hall the church has hired.

Sometimes, allusion may be just a matter of the writer coming across a phrase in another text that seems apposite – even if the meanings in the source and here in *Prophets* are not really comparable. There's the use of the phrase "injured coast" from a Paul Simon song that aptly describes Last Night's flight from his sexually demanding woman (see p. 134). Sometimes the allusion is made in tribute to one of Dawes' poetic masters, such as the ironic description of Ras Pedro's "dull filthy wings" as a reversal of Manley Hopkins' "ah! bright wings" in his poem "God's Grandeur". The same kind of honouring goes on in the allusions to Alice Walker's *The Color Purple* (see the note to the phrase "The wind breaking through my open mouth" (XXIII, vi, l. 66) below on p. 245-246), or to Toni Morrison's plague of robins in *Sula*. Allusions of this kind work at a textual level even if the reader does not recognise them. Sometimes the allusion is even more private and not really part of publicly accessible knowledge, such as a line describing the whereabouts of the second of Thalbot's haunting apparitions as "the spirit stays off the coast". Only friends and acquaintances of Dawes would have recognised this as a dig at the poet Wayne Brown (then still alive, the author of the collection *On the Coast* (1973)) who had once told Dawes to burn his poems as valueless.[5]

At a second level, allusion deepens the socio-cultural ground within which the characters of the poem operate – and it can do so with rich ambivalence. At one level, the saints of the church really do speak in this Bible-quoting way, waging their battles against a sinful, sometimes demonic world. But as in any human institution, the poem notes how the language of the saints can become a device for wielding power and influence within the church and as a mask that covers the less noble human passions of envy and the desire for wealth and privilege. *Prophets* rarely suggests that such uses of biblical reference are consciously hypocritical or Machiavellian, but it does suggest at times a lack of self-knowledge, such as in the episode where the "sybil mother" couches her anguish that she has not managed to obtain a green card to the USA (whilst others much less deserving have) in terms of God's will, that "the Lord has kept me here". The reference is to Philippians 1: 23-24 where Paul or Timothy tells his followers "I am torn between the two: I desire to depart and be with Christ, which is better by far, but it is necessary for you that I remain in the body". The allusion is part of a passage that is rich with biblical quotation (see the notes to Chapter III, ii, pp. 129-130), words which suggest the sybil mother's confusion between the desire to get to heaven and the desire to get to the USA. The allusion points to the element of self-deception in this "daughter of Zion", seemingly unaware how comically hypocritical the real pain behind her protestations of sanctity make her sound.

The third way that *Prophets* uses allusion is in adapting "familiar" narratives from the Bible to point to similarities between present and past. This may take the form, most obviously, of rewriting a biblical narrative in contemporary terms, as in the adaptation of the story of Lot and the Angels to describe the CIA's attempted rescue of Thalbot from Kingston, where the register of the telling is consciously un-biblical. By contrast, the narrative of Thalbot/Jonah's journey to Kingston to expose Clarice and Last Night moves between contemporary and biblical registers. At the simplest level, these adaptations are virtuoso performances for the pleasure of the reader, though the Thalbot/Jonah story moves in both directions. We see Thalbot as delusional, dressing up his pique and misogyny in biblical terms as Jonah and as Elijah in conflict with Jezebel; but we also begin to wonder if these revered prophets in the Old Testament weren't rather like Thalbot in their human pettiness. The pleasure also comes in the wonderful re-enactment of Jonah's voyage to Nineveh in Thalbot's journey from the hills down into Kingston, with its metaphoric resonances between his descent into the green sea of ferns and Jonah's plunge below the sea in the belly of the fish. At this level, Dawes engages in the Olympian sport of retelling, practised by such illustrious forbears as Ovid, Virgil, Dante, Shakespeare and through to Joyce and Walcott. This is the art of making it new. But there is more to it than this, because the allusion also points in another direction. The retelling of the story is also very much a part of the reggae tradition Kwame Dawes grew up on and celebrates in *Natural Mysticism*. In the early 1960s Lloyd Briscoe had a ska song "Jonah (the Master)" (Island 45) which begins "Jonah, Jonah where are you going to?/ Jonah, Jonah where are you going to?/ I'm going to Nineveh to warn the nation". Israel Vibration's "If You Do Bad" also retells God's command to Jonah to go to Nineveh. There is no obvious doubling of places as in *Prophets*, but the way Israel Vibration's song addresses Jonah, as if he were someone around in the present, implies this: "Jah sent Jonah to Nineveh to warn the people/ To tell them to change from their evil and tricky ways/

Jonah knew what the men were like, so he didn't want to go. He decided to turn and go the other way// Jonah, where are you going?/ You were sent to Nineveh to warn the people." This strategy in prophetic reggae, where the original story is retold with a contemporary resonance, is also present in Keith Hudson's "Jonah" on *Rasta Communication* (Joint International, 1978), which berates the half-hearted prophet who ducks his mission: "From the bottom of the sea, I seek equality for me/ Now Jonah Jonah Jonah, come out now/ And see me, you know me better, come on!/ Come on and change me, ooh, teach me."[6] How much the Jonah story is part of the Jamaican popular consciousness is further revealed in a recent interview with the roots singer I Kong (nephew of the Chinese Jamaican producer Lesley Kong) who said, explaining his long absence from the scene, after his successful album, *The Way It Is* (1976): "I was like Jonah who was sent to Nineveh to warn and Jonah ran away and they put Jonah in the belly of the whale. I was like that. I ran away from His work."[7]

At this level, even if the reader has only a very vague idea of the original narrative, the allusion works, though deeper knowledge of the details of the particular narrative reinforces the pleasure and awareness of the skill the poet has employed.

In the case of the references to the incestuous relationship between Lot and his daughters, used allusively in the narrative of Clarice's childhood sexual abuse by her father, Ras Pedro, the Bible narrative complicates our reading of the account, since in the Bible it is Lot's daughters who initiate the incest (after Lot's wife has become a pillar of salt) in order to continue the family line. Obviously, whether the reader knows the Lot and his daughters narrative affects how the episode is read.

But neither the use of allusion nor the process of adaptation, given that both in the end depend on reader knowledge, is without risks. It is not just that the reader has to recognise that it *is* an allusion, but in some instances also needs to be prepared to pursue the quoted, alluded phrase beyond its surface to its context and meaning within its source text. This is asking for more than a recognition of textual facility, an aptness of phrase. In some instances the full meaning of the relationship between alluding text and alluded matter only becomes clear with that more extensive knowledge. For instance, it is very clear that the epigraph at the beginning of Chapter II (*In a Shady Cloister Mew'd*) is a direct quotation. On the surface we may take it to refer to the dark and amiably ghost-ridden house that Clarice occupies. On the surface, even if we recognise the epigraph as coming from *A Midsummer Night's Dream*, this still fits the interpretation that Clarice is being rewarded by her church with the privilege of residence in this grand, albeit decaying house. It is a huge social step upwards from poor beginnings. What is actually happening only becomes clear if we understand the precise meaning of "mew'd" and the quoted phrase's context in the play.

"Mew'd" signifies the notion of confinement, from its original meaning of a mews, the place where birds captured for falconry were forcibly confined (literally while they were moulting). This is the sense in which Shakespeare uses the word both in the lines quoted and in *The Taming of the Shrew* where Baptista is asked, "What, will you mew her up?"; it is explicit in the words of Theseus in *A Midsummer Night's Dream* where he is warning Hermia that unless she accepts Demetrius as a husband, she will be shut up and denied all sexual pleasures, like a virgin nun. In other words, the epigraph is really telling the reader not only that the senior brothers of the church are keeping Clarice captive, but also that this is because they have suspicions about her sexual desires. The epigraph also introduces the imagery of birds and flight that is attached to Clarice as her totemic image. The question must be: is this a casual piece of poetic risk taking or is its opacity a deliberate offer to the complicit, ideal reader about what will be revealed about Clarice later in the poem?

It is probable, for instance, that far fewer readers know the narrative of Lot's flight from Sodom with the assistance of the visiting angels than the story of Jonah, making the adaptation much riskier as a version, because it needs recognition to make its effect. Not only does its deliberately hard-boiled style depend for its point on recognising the contrast with the King James style of the original, but the unwary reader might well be puzzled about what angels might be doing in extracting Thalbot from his house in Kingston. The realisation that agents from the CIA share at least some similarities with angels in the Old Testament – at least with respect to their ability to appear and disappear with practised ease – is a witty analogy that makes it clear how much allusiveness is a joint game between writer and reader.

The same could be said of the allusion from the Book of Nahum that is the epigraph for Chapter III, *Who Will Mourn for Her?*, where only a knowledge of the prophet's bloodthirsty warnings about the fate of Nineveh makes full sense, for instance, of the imagery of the city as a whore who "lifts her skirts" – alluding to Nahum's image of the city as a harlot whose skirts "I will discover upon thy face" (see notes, pp. 124-125).

Sometimes part of the allusion may be reasonably well known, but its precise resonance dependent on non-literary knowledge. One brilliantly condensed allusion brings together the ancient classics, Dawes' reading of Toni Morrison and a popular-cultural detail from 1980s' Jamaica. It comes at a point where *Prophets* is bewailing present times, but offering hope in the constant return of the rebellious Jamaican spirit through the survival (despite unfashionability) of conscious reggae legends such as Big Youth in these days of slackness and guntalk. Dawes writes of such figures as "emerging yet again from the asphalt/ with their magic teeth and split lips" (V, iv, ll. 11-12). Here the allusion references not only the legend of

Cadmus and the dragon's teeth, a similar allusion to one used in Toni Morrison's *Song of Solomon*, but also the fact that Big Youth boasted a mouth of diamond-studded teeth (see notes, p. 139).

One further example further illustrates the way allusions can point in different directions. It comes in the image of the raven that Thalbot stones away when he is re-enacting the prophet Elijah's quarrel with Jezebel.

> When the charred raven comes with meat in its beak,
> slanting against the sun, Thalbot stones it
> and the thud sends it sudden down to the rock. (XXII, xv, ll. 1-3)

This alludes to the Book of Kings and the ravens that God sends to feed Elijah when he is hiding in the desert, in flight from Ahab and Jezebel: "And the ravens brought him bread and flesh in the morning..." (1 Kings 16: 6). But this is a "charred raven", and as I have expanded in the notes (pp. 252-253), there are probable further allusions to poems by Wordsworth McAndrew and Ted Hughes, both of which tell of a bird's Promethian flight to the sun and its punishment by scorching. Here the image suggests, in Thalbot's mind, that Clarice has over-reached herself and fallen from grace. Further, in the contrast with Elijah's presumed gratitude to the ravens who feed him, the image very obviously points to Thalbot's deeply conflicted and voyeuristic sexual feelings about Clarice after he witnesses the lovemaking on the beach. Then the image of the fallen, stoned-down bird connects – again in Thalbot's mind – to a further falling, that of Jezebel who, when Ahab gets God's message and she doesn't, is cast from the walls of the palace and consumed by dogs:

> ...Thalbot hears

> Clarice's panting like bloody Jezebel calling him down
> to the rocks. The mongrels catch the scent
> of death while she is falling from the wall. (XXII, xv, ll. 8-11)

However, there is an irony here, since we know that Clarice's fall from favour in the church is nothing like as fatal as Thalbot would like to imagine. We are led to read the allusion to the Jezebel narrative as reflecting both Thalbot's warped imagination and the elements of misogyny in Jamaican culture (and, by implication, the strength of Jamaican women). Justin Hinds' song "Carry Go Bring Come" ("You're going from town to town making disturbances/ It's time you stopped doing those things, you old Jezebel") is a very specific reference here, but it is part of a much wider referencing of the Bible and the wickedness of women, as in Bob Marley and the Wailers' "Adam and Eve": "Any anywhere you go/ Woman is the root of all evil..."

This discussion has pointed to some of the ways in which *Prophets* is engaged with biblical allusion. But what is this referencing trying to achieve and what does the poem gain from it?

One answer is that biblical allusion contributes to the truthfulness of the poem as an exact portrayal of a society deeply enmeshed, at personal and popular cultural levels, with the Bible. As Linton Kwesi Johnson writes:

> The King James Bible is not just a holy book in Jamaica. It is an important aspect of the very fabric of Jamaican oral culture. Used with dexterity and wit, biblical sayings are very powerful tools in the rhetoric of everyday discourse, and a rich repository of metaphor, simile, aphorism and imagery.[8]

But more intrinsic to the drama of the poem, these allusions and versions work as metaphors that are vehicles for the poem's inner conflict between scepticism and a desire for faith.

Marilyn Robinson in her essay "Book of Books"[9] makes a distinction that is useful here: "In our strange cultural moment it is necessary to make a distinction between religious propaganda and religious thought, the second of these being an attempt to do some sort of justice to the rich difficulties present in the tradition." This is helpful because it is between these two poles that the poem's approach to the texture and narratives of the Bible is positioned. For the church at the centre of the poem, the Bible is quite literally true, an infallible guide to belief, behaviour and destiny. For the church, quoting the Bible is sincere propaganda, the means to conviction. For Dawes, I think, the approach to the Bible in the poem (including his willingness to follow the poem's independent logic) is a form of religious thought, and this includes asking uncomfortable questions about the construction of the Bible itself. Does it, too, fall into the territory of religious propaganda? These are no doubt uncomfortable questions for a poet who is sincere believer in salvation through the incarnation of God in Christ, who doesn't, I think, feel that the universe makes sense unless there is some divine teleological purpose at work in it. Curiously, whilst it is in the gospels of the New Testament that one suspects Dawes' faith is rooted, it is these narratives that are subjected to the greatest degree of irony. Conversely, whilst it is clear that the God of the Old Testament is frequently capricious, vindictive and manipulative, and his prophets deeply flawed as human beings, it is in these Old Testament stories that one most senses an appreciation of the Bible as a richly unstable text, open to a sense of the mystery of existence.

This is the implication that lurks allusively behind the quotation made by Clarice when she is crowing about her triumph in converting the heathen of Annotto Bay. She cries out, "she who has ears to hear, let her hear" (XXII, iv, l. 1). This is a slight variation on Jesus's words to the crowd he is teaching through parables, such as the parable of the sower of seeds.[10] Both Mark 4: 9 and Matthew 11: 15 have "He that hath ears to hear, let him hear." On the surface, this may appear only a slightly hubristic borrowing of Christ's words in the heat of her triumph. Clarice's misquotation, in the light of what we have learnt of the poem's allusive strategies, should alert us to consider the wider context of these words. Here the problem is that Mark and Matthew offer different, indeed seemingly opposite versions. The disciples ask Jesus what the parables mean. Mark seems to be saying that the parables are told despite, or even because, the multitude will fail to understand them ("all these things are done in parables: That seeing they may see, and not perceive; and hearing they may hear, and not understand; lest at any time they should be converted, and their sins should be forgiven them" (4: 11-12)). The implication seems to be that true believers are open to the holy spirit and don't need these kinds of persuasive stories – a version of salvation that seems narrow and exclusive. Matthew offers a more palatable version, that parables are told because the multitude would not understand the gospel presented in any other form ("Therefore speak I to them in parables: because they seeing see not; and hearing they hear not, neither do they understand" (13: 13). As a close reader of the Bible, Dawes would know that the matter of interpreting parables is complex and far more open and uncertain than the way Clarice quotes Jesus's words. She speaks as if it is the obvious and incontrovertible proof that, as the converter of the infidels, she must have God's favour. It is one of the points where Dawes' use of allusion is much more double-edged than it seems, critical of the way religious mystery has been reduced to magical thought and propaganda.

CONCLUSION

In many respects, *Prophets* is an anti-epic. If we think of the endings to the great epics of antiquity, or to a contemporary Caribbean epic such as *Omeros*, in their relationship to the nation, to the future and to the virtues of literature, they almost always arrive at a place of rest in which the future stands open in possibility and literature has vindicated its position. Homer has brought Odysseus home, ready to fight another day and the Greeks, if battered, can commemorate a victory. Virgil's Aeneas can look towards the transformation of defeated Trojans into imperial Romans. V.S. Reid's *New Day* (1949) looks with at least cautious optimism towards a brighter Jamaican future with its destiny in its own hands[1] and, as we have seen, Derek Walcott brings his Odyssean self home, enacts the healing of the breech between Europe and Africa, and contemplates a new beginning for St Lucia as an independent nation. Each of these epic texts (Homer's at least implicitly) sets out to demonstrate the central role of the literary imagination in the making of the new nation, or in Virgil's case, the glory of Augustus and the Roman Empire. Reid makes his Aeneas in the shape of his nationalist hero, N.W. Manley; Walcott dares to believe that his work can speak for his people.

How different *Prophets* is. Its two protagonists have ended in mutual defeat: exile in Clarice's case, wounded silence in Thalbot's. Far from coming home, Dawes writes from American exile and his avatar prophetess is also leaving his island. Not least, the poem ends with a distinctly pessimistic valuation of itself as a poem. Even in relationship to what has gone before, his need to turn back to "the old songs, Marley's call/ from the darkness", he can say no more than that:

> ...the leaves of the slim

> volume of verse, this quartet, this clandestine fantasy, this hope
> for the power of earth-makers, stone breakers,
> rustled insignificantly and impotently like a poem. (XXVII, ll. 15-18)

Moreover, *Prophets'* dramatisation of the four artistic apparitions who inhabit Thalbot, who ought to represent the past heights of Jamaican literary and musical achievement, tell stories that end variously in madness, self-destructive behaviour and early death. These are prophets utterly without honour in their nation, or at best honoured (like Don Drummond) by only a fragment of it, and recognised as deeply flawed.

If Homer and Virgil have portrayed their gods as capricious and frequently at odds with their human heroes, their epics end with some kind of rapprochement. Athena finally helps Odysseus to find safe harbour, whilst Venus protects Aeneas in his battle with Turnus and his mission to found a new civilisation. In *Prophets*, the narrating "I" and his God remain at loggerheads. The poet, in his song, has lamented "like a spoilt child" and confesses:

I write these poems with trepidation,
as if this tantrum might bring down the wrath
of the Almighty. (XXVIII, v, ll. 19-21)

And what of the future of the nation? Much of *Prophets* portrays a nation that seems to have said farewell to its most hopeful days. Indeed, if one takes the poem at its word, one must wonder at times if the Kingston that Dawes portrays can survive, if it, as a modern Nineveh, isn't bound to collapse under the pressure of its violent conflicts.

All this is true, and one expects a postmodern epic to be open-ended. *Prophets* more than fulfils that refusal of closure or a comfortable perspective towards the future. But yet, despair is not the feeling that reading *Prophets* generates. What one takes away from the poem is a zestfulness, an energy, a delight in its own inventiveness. As Clarice proclaims: "myth falling, myth falling. It is exhilarating!"

With the hindsight of twenty-three years, *Prophets* is a work that can be seen as having a crucial role in the paradigm shift in Caribbean writing that Kamau Brathwaite pioneered and named as the CR, the cultural revolution.[2] It stands in a distinctly critical relationship to what had gone before, and – irrespective of whether such authors acknowledge its influence – one can see *Prophets* as a text that created a space for the writing of authors such as Kei Miller, Vladimir Lucien, Ishion Hutchinson, Marcia Douglas and others who, in recent years, have been exploring aspects of Caribbean spirituality with empathetic inwardness. Of course, Dawes' work has its own literary ancestry in constructing a treaty between the voices of Walcott and Brathwaite, and one can see similar directions in the poetry of Lorna Goodison and in the fiction of Erna Brodber. What Dawes achieves in *Prophets* is the creation of an epic poem richly infused from two overlapping areas of Jamaican popular culture: Bible narratives as a nativised element in the Jamaican imaginary, and the language and world view of Jamaican popular music. He recognises that the language and narratives of the Bible are deeply embedded in Jamaican sayings, in social conduct and in the discourse of religious practice. In this way he goes beyond acknowledging the Bible as the scriptural basis of Christian belief. He finds inspiration in the oral styles and the lyrics of reggae (and in the Rastafarian influenced ska of Don Drummond), particularly in the "roots", conscious reggae represented by musicians such as Bob Marley, Burning Spear (Winston Rodney) and Lee Scratch Perry. In bringing these elements together in a work of refined poetic imagination and skill, he offers something that was new and, I believe, deserving of a long-lasting and prominent place in the canon of Caribbean writing.

NOTES AND SUMMARIES

EPIGRAPH

…but it was something to have at least a choice of nightmares:
This quotation from Joseph Conrad's *Heart of Darkness* (1960 [1899],
p. 75) relates to the choice Marlow makes between attaching himself
to the individual and open barbarity of Kurtz or to the hypocrisy of
the equally exploitative company, which masks its barbarity behind
the veneer of bureaucratic order. What Conrad meant by "it was
something… at least" has been endlessly debated. But what clues does
this epigraph offer to a reading of *Prophets*? Most obviously it speaks
to the choice between the nightmare of colonialism and the disordered
state of post-colonial Jamaica at the time of the poem's writing, a generation
after independence in 1962. *Prophets* ducks nothing in its portrayal of
a society riven by political corruption and violence, gangsterism, drug
wars, human rights abuses, and vast inequalities of wealth and poverty;
that remains shaped by the race and colour hierarchies bequeathed by
slavery. The epigraph implies that independence at least offers choices,
however nightmarish. The quotation also connects to the theme of
madness in *Prophets*, since Marlow has come to the conclusion that
Kurtz is mad. Beyond that, other choices that *Prophets* explores include
those between staying or leaving Jamaica, and between the bloodless
order of those churches whose cultural heritage is European (see Chapter
XXVIII, iii) and the kind of charismatic evangelical church that provides
the poem's setting, but where there is a narrow line between the miraculous
and the fraudulent.

PROLOGUE

Summary

The prologue works in a metatextual way to introduce the themes of
the poem as a whole. It engages with the relationship between imagination
and "truth". On the one hand the poet claims freedom for his imagination
– the leaping metaphors which introduce the trope of flight – in
constructing the drama of the prophetess's rise and fall, and, on the
other hand, he admits the responsible desire to uncover whatever may
have been the "truth" of the experience. It confesses the poet's personal
investment in the shaping of the poem, as a broken, guilt-ridden and
confused young man who finds solace in the kindness of the prophetess
and her church. But it also expresses a drive to understand the trajectory
of a personal disappointment, the implication that there has been some
"sleight-of-hand" involved, that things experienced (the miracles, perhaps)
were not as they seemed. The prologue also introduces the theme of
gender in the poem, the acknowledgement that this is a poem about a
woman – both respected and lusted after – written by a man. In this
there is both a confession of desire – and at points in the poem there
are undoubtedly eroticisations of the female body as seen or imagined
from a male perspective – and the self-reflexive admission of this
temptation, to "reach for her tarnished flesh" and "dare to imagine
her coupling" (ll. 44, 46).

The prologue also implies some element of classic *bildungsroman* in the
relationship between the older reflective writer located at a distance of both
time and place (here, in this barren city of silence in the USA) and a
younger, experiencing self. But if there is an heuristic motivation, the
prologue insists on it being an aesthetic, artistic one, where the poem
discovers its own logic and "shapes its own peculiar metaphors".

The prologue also works like the opening title sequence of a film (see the
discussion above, pp. 80-82) in offering flash-forwards to scenes that we
expect to be developed: the actual role of the experiencing "I" in the church
and the elaboration of what is evidently a story of sexual indiscretion, and
some accounting of how "this daughter of holiness" comes to fall "so
impossibly hard" from grace.

The challenge the prologue sets for the poem is whether it can convince
the reader that, despite that fall, his prophetess can really fly above "the
squalor and muck". But the prologue also expresses its own enigma and
ambivalence in time. It declares itself as a beginning, a declaration of intent
("to write her"); as about something that has happened with its flash-
forwards ("I know now"); as something that may or may not have happened
(remembering, dreaming, imagining), or is in process ("I am seeking clues").

Notes

construct enigma (l. 1): Since an enigma is generally something that exists that cannot be readily explained, to say that the poem constructs an enigma is a declaration of the poem's location somewhere between memory and the artifice of invention.

secure as a victim (ll. 9-10): See Kwame Dawes' story, "The Clearing" in *A Place to Hide* (2003, pp. 231-237) and the episode in his novel, *Bivouac* (2010, pp. 36ff,), where the quasi-autobiographical figure of Ferron runs away to luxuriate in his misery.

which made her prophesy my need (l. 15): How she does this is given fuller treatment in the way Last Night's problem is diagnosed (IV, ii, l. 8-17). The generosity and intimacy of the offer of help is also suggested in the way Last Night is treated in Chapter IX. The use of the word *prophesy* in this context introduces the first of the two kinds of prophecy that run through the poem. Both are concerned with bringing to light something hidden from general awareness – this is the prophet's gift. Later we encounter the more generally Old Testament use of prophecy associated with Thalbot; this kind makes predictive warnings about what will happen to Jamaican society if it continues to behave as it is doing, a fate to which the society is apparently blind. In the kind of prophecy in action here, the signs observed are more individual – Clarice's ability to uncover hidden motivations and the gap between what people claim and the truth.

my constant indiscretions (l. 21): The indiscretions referenced here echo those suggested in poems about masturbation and youthful sexual experiment in *Progeny of Air* (1994) such as "Newcomer" and "Off the Mark".

who fell/ so impossibly hard into the thighs// of unbelievers (l. 23-25): A complex metaphor that implies, as a flash-forward, that Clarice's future lies outside the church, that sexual desire is involved (her own) and that there has been some breach of trust. Throughout the poem, thighs are a frequent metonym for desire. Clarice feels "the looseness in her thighs" (II, i. l. 25); the eyes of Castleberry "gentle on her thigh" (II, i, l. 63); reference is made to "her sweaty thighs" (IV, ii, l. 32), "her thigh catches the light" – in Last Night's vision (VII, i, l. 21); she leaves her door ajar "like parted thighs" (XI, ii, l. 23); and when she herself speaks she talks of "revealing the muscle and flesh of my thighs" (XXIV, i, l. 41). In the Bible there are several references to the swearing of a promise by placing a hand on the thigh (Genesis 24: 2; 24: 9) which perhaps suggests ironically that there has been some breach of promise.

translates itself (l. 26): The poem uses the word both in the sense that any act of writing has the imperfection of translation – what Dawes describes in a slightly later poem "Shook Foil" (*Shook Foil* (1997), p. 41) when he writes "How quickly the grandeur fades into a poem" – and also in the sense of "transported", as the King James Version (KJV) uses the word to describe how the prophet Enoch is "translated that he should not see death" (Hebrews 11: 5).

my squalid indiscretions (l. 34): A distinctly masturbatory image (see lines 44-46) for what the writing of the poem has involved – as if it involves a breach of confidence in revealing to the world the flaws in a church where, for a time, he found "the sure path of the daily guidance of the spirit".

Here in this barren city of silence (l. 43): As the final chapter (XXVIII) charts, the avatar for the poet, the unnamed prophetess, leaves Jamaica, and speaks from the context of Sumter, South Carolina – the journey Dawes himself made in 1992. Why the city is described as barren is explained in Chapter XXVIII, iii, when, for instance, the prophetess, who speaks as "I", attacks the "sterile sermons" of the orthodox white churches.

dare to imagine her coupling (l. 46): A flash-forward to Chapter XXI, iii, and the admission that this is an event fictively imagined, and therefore even more of a betrayal.

a ladder in the clouds (l. 55): Seeing Clarice, as if she is an angel, in an allusion to Genesis 28: 10-14 where Jacob sees a ladder "set up on the earth, and the top of it reached heaven; and behold, the angels of God were ascending and descending on it". Quite a number of Pentecostal churches in the USA are named "Jacob's Ladder Church".

PART ONE

CHAPTER I
Introit

Summary

"Introit" introduces the empty space before the Sunday morning service at the University of the West Indies (UWI) Guild meeting hall, occupied only by goats (the holy sheep are just arriving). Clarice, at Castleberry's old house, is getting ready for the service, consulting her visions before being collected by the church "brothers", the senior males. Whilst Clarice has the spiritual gift, this is a church where the chain of command from God to man to woman is an article of faith. The chapter introduces several themes: the clash between the secular and the sacred; the temptations of the flesh that must be resisted; the trope of flight; and the paralleling of two kinds of journeys – spiritual and economic – that Clarice has made out of poverty on the strength of her prophetic gifts. The need to clean out the hall from the previous night's dance is ironically linked to the casting out of demons, and there's a flash-forward to the presence of Thalbot, Clarice's future rival, as a madman on Hope Road. This is a scene-setting episode that tracks cinematically around the empty space, observing the irony of two kinds of abandonment: one, the alcohol and ganja-fuelled pleasures of the previous night's student dance and the other of the spiritual transport of the service to come, but suggesting that both arise from the same history – the same arrival on the slave ship.

Notes

Introit: The psalm or antiphon sung by the priest as he/she approaches the altar, an antiphon expects a response from the congregation – here both an analogy for this first chapter as an entry point in the poem's structure, and an allusion to the African-centric call-and-response dynamic between preacher and congregation in the service to come.

Casual brights (l. 5): A term no longer used to describe colourful but respectable clothing.

patent leather (l. 5): Plastic-coated leather shoes with a glossy, shiny finish – a somewhat dandified but old-fashioned item of formal wear.

Bibles tucked like swords under their arms (l. 6): This refers to

Ephesians 6: 17: "Take the helmet of salvation and the sword of the Spirit, which is the word of God." This is not just an apt allusion that works in a metaphorical way, but a truth about the self-perception of these members of the congregation, who are almost certainly familiar with this text, and see themselves as fulfilling its injunction to be Christ's soldiers. It is an image that is also used by Sylvia Wynter in *The Hills of Hebron* where the Prophet Moses "took the Bible in his hands, like a sword" (p. 180) when he goes to confront the Rev. Brooke over the girl the white clergyman has made pregnant.

A saint (l. 11): As a saved, born-again Charismatic/Pentecostalist, Clarice *is* a saint – one who has attained spiritual perfection – which includes her chastity.

The journey… beyond the wall (l. 15): As becomes clear (in Chapter X, ii) Clarice has made both a spiritual and social journey from the humblest beginnings "beyond the wall". This alludes to back o'wall, the Rastafarian squatters' settlement in West Kingston that became Tivoli Gardens in the 1960s. See Chapter X, *Hermit*, for Clarice's breach from her father and her escape from an incestuously abusive relationship. As woman with aspirations of social success, it is a past ("Head forward") she wants to forget.

Her mantle of importance is her light (l. 20): A neat pun on a mantle as a cloak, and a gas mantle as the source of (spiritual) light.

the slick "off-the-wharfs" cars (l. 21): This signals the prosperity of at least some of the churchgoers; these are expensive new imported cars, the result of the liberalisation of imports in the neo-liberal capitalist 1980s. In 1985, less than 2% of Jamaicans owned cars; around 42,000 cars in a population of 2.5 million.

flail them with revelations of their straying minds (l. 28): This introduces the source of Clarice's particular prophetic power – her ability to read the minds of her congregation, particularly their sexual temptations. "Flail" comes from the action of winnowing corn from chaff – a frequent metaphor for separating the saved from the damned. The English Standard version has the prophet Enoch declaring (Judges 8: 7), "I will flail your flesh with the thorns of the wilderness and with briers."

Kingston's satellite suburbs (l. 30): The area of huge housing growth in outer Kingston from the 1960s onwards – generally middle-income areas.

leaning tombstone of the Castleberrys (l. 33): The church has bought the house of an old white Jamaican family (see VIII, i & ii) in St Andrew, the parish surrounding Kingston, once the housing area of the light-skinned, upper-middle class. Castleberry (whose ghost appears later) references but is not a portrait of a figure such as H.D. Carberry (1921-89), a lawyer who rose to be a judge in the court of appeal, whose poems as a young man were collected posthumously in *It Takes a Mighty Fire* (1995) but were originally published in *Focus* in the 1940s, the literary journal edited by Edna Manley. Carberry was one of a group of white/light-brown Jamaicans like Philip Sherlock and M.G. Smith who, as ardent nationalists, discovered the people. Carberry writes of "The beauty of my people/And the beauty of the land" (??). Castleberry is not Carberry, but the name echoes, and aspects of the latter's actual existence are drawn on to signify the kind of man Castleberry is, and to signal another element of social change. Castleberry's offspring have abandoned Jamaica; he is part of an older, now disappearing Kingston; his witness to the unity of all Jamaicans has become less persuasive in a society of widening social divisions that has been discovering its actual blackness.

their dreamings and heaven flights (l. 37): This alludes to the belief of some enslaved Africans that they could fly back to Guinea, provided they did not eat salt, which was of course a staple of slave foods such as the salt cod imported from Newfoundland. The motif of flight appears throughout the poem and concludes it. See the discussion of the trope and the discussion of what *Prophets* drew from the example of Toni Morrison's *Song of Solomon* (1977) in the critical commentary (pp. 69-70, 90). See also Lorna McDaniel, "The Flying Africans: Extent and Strength of the Myth in the Americas" (1990).

seeing Clarice like that (l. 41): She is standing in the "spill of shade and light" with her "curve of breast" – one of the many moments when the erotic challenges the spiritual.

the antennae of steel and babel metal of the madman's/ shrine on Hope Road (l. 48): A flash-forward (see Chapter V) to the presence of Thalbot, the rival prophet who is squatting in the newly built "monolith" of the Sovereign Centre shopping mall – the "babylon mansion" that signifies to Thalbot the hubris of commerce challenging God in the image of the tower of Babel – a reference to Genesis 11: 1-9, where God punishes the builders of the tower for presuming to reach heaven under their own efforts. God confuses the tongues of the builders, who up to that point have spoken a single language, so they can no longer communicate and they are scattered over the earth. The Babel reference also notes that the generally low-rise buildings of old Kingston are being replaced by high-rise towers.

red daze (l. 49): Thalbot is a heavy ganja user. As the group Israel Vibration sang in "Red Eyes" on the album *Forever* (1991): "My eyes are red/ I can feel it from this crop of callie herb / slappin' in my head."

"Stop for the casting out of demons" (l. 50): This is one of the functions of the Pentecostal service; here there's a failure to minister to Thalbot's distress. This introduces the motif of madness, and the narrative of the Gadarene swine, that recurs the poem. See p. 121 below for a discussion, and see also the critical commentary (pp. 82-88) on the significance of the trope of madness in the poem.

ii

The Guild Building (l. 5): The hall of the students' union building on the Mona Campus, site of Saturday night dances and Sunday morning service. The contrasts between the secular and sacred are obvious, but there are also resemblances. Both involve joyfulness, exuberance and dance; the phrase "rocks its own lamentations" points in both directions, to the reggae played at the student dance and to congregational worship. The meeting points between sacred and secular connect, for instance, in a Bob Marley song such as "One Drop" (*Survival*, 1979) with a title that refers to the dance rhythms of reggae and a lyric that refers to the dreadness of the Book of Revelation: "It dread, dread. For hunger (dread, dread) and starvation /(dread, dread, dread, dread), /Lamentation (dread dread), /But read it in Revelation (dread, dread, dread, dread): / You'll find your redemption". Part of the under-story of *Prophets* is that despite the antagonism of the Charismatic/Pentecostal churches to secular Jamaican culture, and to Rastafarianism in particular (regarded as a pagan idolatry), all come out of the hold of the same "old slaver", bearing the same imprints of Africa. All have their "intoxications" (whether Red Stripe, ganja or the holy spirit).

The use of the Guild building also signals how new a church this is – too new to have a church building of their own – though no doubt the Castleberry residence awaits conversion.

renk (l. 5): A patwa version of rank, as in foul-smelling.

Red Stripe (l. 6): A popular brand of Jamaican lager.

liberation of the encumbered souls (l. 8): This is a densely compacted image that links several things: the fug of the meeting hall after the student dance is compared to the squalor of the hold of the slave ship. This has to be cleansed by the churchgoers before the service. Further, the process of spiritual sanctification expected from the morning service is linked to the decanting of enslaved Africans from the slave ship onto Jamaican soil. In the church service, "encumbered souls" are freed from the sinful body (the "drifting carcass"), just as the slave ship becomes a carcass when emptied of the human lives brought to Jamaica. The connection is that for the church, an unsaved person is a slave to sin. This image points to the common origins of both hedonistic students and pious churchgoers. Both of their forebears emerged from the hold of the slave ship. In the case of the disembarking Africans, the word "liberation" is used ironically, since they were certainly not being freed.

rites of carnival (l. 9): A reference to the religious origins of carnival (*carne vale* – farewell to flesh) in the ritual of feasting before the meatless penance of Lent, the season of fasting before Easter.

The goats bleat their remembrances (l. 18): They bewail their lost/ eaten brethren, of course, and no doubt their metaphorical fate when they will be divided from the faithful sheep and suffer damnation. (See Matthew 25: 31: "He will put the sheep on his right and the goats on his left".) Serious as it is, *Prophets* is full of such joking ironies.

hallelujah chorus (l. 19): The antiphonal call and response of hallelujahs at the church service (and the name of the most famous piece from Handel's baroque oratorio, *The Messiah* (1742) as well as the Bunny Wailer penned "Hallelujah Time" which appeared on the Bob Marley and the Wailer's album, *Burning* (1973)).

the sweep of prophecies (l. 20): The image of the broom is a popular one for spiritual cleansing. See Isaiah 14: 23 ("'I will sweep it [Babylon] with the broom of destruction,' declares the Lord of hosts").

scream (l. 23): The worshippers cry out in the excitement of possession by the holy spirit.

pyres of sacrifice (l. 27): An ironic contrast to the actual sacrifice of animals performed by some African-centred religious groups (and by the Old Testament Jews), the former of which Clarice's church would regard as idolatrous.

Clarice sirens the gathering (l. 30): An ironic pun on the prophetess's clarion call to prayer and the seductiveness of the sirens who tempted Ulysses in Book 12 of *The Odyssey*, ll. 165ff, where he puts wax in the ears of his crew to prevent them from hearing the sirens, and makes the crew tie him to the mast of his ship so he can hear but not follow his attraction. By contrast, when Clarice later tempts Last Night, there's no wax for his ears or restricting bonds that keep him from temptation.

CHAPTER II
In a Shady Cloister Mew'd

Summary

The scene takes place in Castleberry's old house and portrays an almost
affectionate relationship between Clarice and the old ghost. It's a scene
that establishes both the passing of the old Jamaica and the sensuality
that Clarice struggles to contain.

In this episode we are introduced to the nature of Clarice's dreaming
prophecies and to the multiple layers of presentation that will characterise
Prophets as a whole. There is, for instance: the concrete physicality of
Clarice in front of her mirror putting on skin-lightening cream; the entry
into the poem of the biblical narrative of the Gadarene swine and the
healing of Legion (which relates to the Thalbot figure bypassed on the way
to service); the blurring in Clarice's mind between a popular TV pro-
gramme and biblical narrative; the gothic fantasy of the ghost of Castleberry
and the way in which all these elements feed into and arise from Clarice's
repressed sexuality and the blurring of the spiritual and the sensual in her
mind: "Clarice seines from this bounty of her dreaming – /[…]/ the voice
of her saviour breaking the erotic twilight" (II, i, ll. 58, 64)

In this chapter, Dawes engages with the relationship between the erotic
and the spiritual. Can Clarice's sexual longings (denied by, repressed by her
church) really be sublimated into the spiritual? The narrative of her fall later
in the poem suggests that for the church there can be no such sublimation,
though for Clarice, as an individual woman, it can be imagined.

We may note how, in time sequence, chapter VIII, *The Changing of the
Guard*, recapitulates and actually precedes what happens here. This scene,
narrated in the present continuous tense, points to it as a lyric, not linked
to any specific moment in time, just as throughout the poem there are flash-
forwards and flashbacks that disrupt linearity.

Notes

In a Shady Cloister Mew'd: This is a deeply ironic epigraph from *A
Midsummer Night's Dream* (Act 1, Scene 1, ll. 70-73), which does much
more than locate Clarice in Castleberry's old house, since the quotation
concerns Theseus's warning to Hermia about what will happen to her
if she refuses to marry Demetrius. He asks her whether she could bear
to "endure the livery of a nun,/ For aye to be in shady cloister mew'd,/
To live a barren sister all your life,/ Chanting faint hymns to the cold,
fruitless moon". He goes on to tell her, "But earthlier happy is the

rose distilled/ Than that which, withering on the virgin thorn,/ Grows, lives, and dies in single blessedness" (ll. 76-78). The epigraph presages a scene that reinforces the images of Clarice's repressed sexuality and goes to the heart of her predicament as a sensual woman of whom, as a saint, absolute chastity is expected.

This epigraph also continues the tropes of flight and birds connected to Clarice (the "wings" and "brilliant multicoloured plumes" (Prologue, ll. 61-62). "Mew'd" refers to the mews, the building in which birds captured for falconry were confined whilst they were moulting. Here she is a captive bird, denied flight. Since she is one of the strong, sensuous women who contributes to the portrayal of Clarice, Dawes may also be remembering the description of Janie by Teacake in Zora Neale Hurston's *Their Eyes Were Watching God* (1986 [1937]) when he speaks of her as being like "underneath uh dove's wing next tuh mah face" (p. 157).

Castleberry's horny ghost (l. 2): The reference figure of Carberry was known as a quiet, retiring man. Here, the fictional Castleberry's "look, no touching" locates him far away from the predatory sexual power of the white master of historical fact.

She does not/ turn him out into the abyss (l. 13): A generosity that presages Clarice's kindness to Last Night (VII, i) and to the broken student (Prologue, ll. 18-21). But this is far from how a good saint should respond; the ghost should be seen as a demon, which it is her Christian duty to cast out.

Hawaii Five O (l. 25): This was a popular American TV programme (CBS 1968-1980), a police procedural set in Hawaii, involving a white-led team with Hawaiian underlings, brought together to deal with unrest on the island. The image that attracts Clarice is from the closing credits. Note the not very subtle but quite funny sexual double-entendres (humping, dipping, withdrawing, horning, ejaculate) and the echo of the Guinness spilt in the Guild building in "the boys sweat brown". Later, the TV image merges with Clarice's vision of the madman and the Gadarene episode, discussed below, and an even more explicit image of her sexual longing, as she "stands waiting for their coming with the froth/ and white of the sea against the black sand at her feet" (l. 57).

Ponds (l. 31): Whether Clarice is using Ponds' Vanishing cream (designed to reduce the glow of oil in the skin), or Ponds White Beauty Cream (a skin lightener) it is clear what effect Clarice desires ("Her face is white"). This contrasts sharply with the other vision she sees in the mirror, of the Christ with the "thick, dipped-in-burnt-sienna lips", the kind of Rastafarian image of Christ, "the pastoral dread", as was being painted by such artists as Ralph Campbell's (1921-1985) *Ecce Homo* (1955) or Osmond Watson's (1934-2005) *Malachi the Prophet* and *Peace and Love* – very different images from Clarice's blue-eyed Jesus (for these paintings see *Jamaica Journal*, Vol. 2, Nos. 2&3, 1983). See also Chapter VI, *Denial*: "her bleeding Christ has crystal blue eyes" (i, l. 12).

Gadarenes (l. 40): In Luke 8: 26-39, Christ casts out spirits from the man who calls himself Legion (because his occupying spirits are many), which then rush into a herd of swine who cast themselves into the sea. This is a flash-forward to the more extended and cynically deconstructed treatment in Chapter XV, *Legion*. Here, the image is in Clarice's prophetic mirror (a cinematic device Dawes uses several times) and we deduce that the vagrant madman is Thalbot. We may note that in her dreaming, Thalbot is healed of his madness; in the "actuality" of the saints' drive to church, he is ignored. As fitting the reverie in her "fertile mind", which draws as much from TV viewing as from the Bible, there is a blending of different generic elements in the description: the garlic of the popular gothic horror movie, the manacles drawn from the history of slavery, as well as the images drawn from the iconography of Jamaican art.

pastoral dread (l. 47): Jesus as a Rastafarian good shepherd. A reference to the literary genre of pastoral, first found in ancient Greek literature, which even then romanticised the simple life of the shepherd as looking back to the golden age when people lived in harmony with nature – a Rastafarian ideal.

the chop of the sea (l. 50): One can forgive a young poet such a terrible pun! It reminds, though, that *Prophets* has many elements of humour. See the introduction (pp. 47-48) for a discussion of verbal play as one of the elements drawn from the example of Walcott's *Omeros*.

the scarless wound of a miracle (l. 55): As the sea closes over the drowned pigs, it leaves no sign of the turmoil of their entry.

seines from this bounty of her dreaming... breaking the erotic twilight (l. 58): This makes a series of Walcott allusions. Firstly, to one of Walcott's favourite images of fishermen throwing seine nets in the surf, here attached to Clarice catching what is at this stage an uncomfortable mixing of the sacred and the erotic. Secondly, to the erotic search for the white goddess in *Dream on Monkey Mountain*. Thirdly, to the essay preface to this play: "What the Twilight Says:

An Overture". Walcott's *The Bounty* was not published until 1997, so that verbal connection is probably fortuitous. Dawes may also be remembering an image from Zora Neale Hurston's *Their Eyes Were Watching God* (1986 [1937]), where Janie "pulled in her horizon like a great fish-net" (p. 286).

the clutter of potent seed (l. 69): An image that connects to the lines in Chapter III, iii, l. 3ff, when the source of the ideological and cultural imperialism afflicting Jamaica is seen as "The poisoned heaven's sudden curse / blows from Newark's phallic white towers / spewing their toxic sperm into the fertile sky", making a connection between private and public effects, and suggesting that Clarice's sexual restlessness comes from both within and without.

The dank smell of black earth and turning worms (l. 70): A gothic *memento mori*, such as is found in one of the verse ballads of M.G. Lewis's *The Monk*: "The worms, They crept in, and the worms, They crept out,/ And sported his eyes and his temples about" (2008 [1796], p. 315). This is a "gather ye rosebuds while ye may" moment for Clarice.

the vessel, so alive with longings (l. 76): An ambivalent image that speaks both of Clarice's sexual and spiritual longings. In the Pentecostalist church, the pure, virgin, woman's body is a vessel waiting to be filled up with the spirit (cf. Austin-Broos, *Jamaica Genesis*, pp. 146-151). But to be "vacant like this" is also to be in a state of vulnerability. On the one hand, she is open to visions, but she is also open to sexual temptations. The poem suggests that for Clarice "vacancy" comes to feel like a kind of barrenness.

Distilled of the dross (l. 80): A nice pun based on the metaphor of distilling potable spirits that relates variously to the poet's ambition (to create a aesthetically realised poem from the raw experience), to the poem's theme (how the spiritual can rise from the sensuously profane) and to Clarice's practice as a prophetess who carefully manages her public persona in order to control her flock (for her own benefit).

The turmoil of midnight cats (l. 83): An image that flashes forward to the moment on the beach (XXI, iii); the fact that Clarice does not shut out such sounds is another indication of her longings.

On her bedpost perches the spirit – no ghost (l. 89): It may be a holy spirit, and not a demonic one, but the image recalls Fuselli's famous Gothic painting *The Nightmare* (1781) of the incubus squatting on the dreaming woman – an image that connects to the erotic charge of Clarice's "smack of lips, then swallows".

He feeds her tiny morsels of potage (l. 91): This is a reference both to Genesis 25: 34: "Then Jacob gave Esau some bread and potage" in return for his birthright, and also to Hebrews 12: 16, where the early Christian recipients of the epistle are warned: "Lest there be any fornicator, or profane person, as Esau, who for a morsel of meat sold his birthright." The image suggests Clarice's temptation to want both spirit (the birthright) and the flesh (the potage).

CHAPTER III
Who will Mourn for Her?

Summary

In this chapter, the view pans out to give a wider (and deeper) perspective in time and space. It locates Kingston geographically (shielded from the north by Cuba and the Palisadoes spit of land), and in both contemporary history and biblical narrative. In the latter, Kingston is the sinful Babylonian city of Nineveh, awaiting, as the prophet Nahum hopes, the Lord's wrathful punishment. In the present, as the critical commentary above, pp. 26-29 outlines, the poem catches the city at the point where the dreams of socialist decolonisation under Michael Manley's PNP (People's National Party) had been defeated by the International Monetary Fund's (IMF) imposition of structural adjustment (forced privatisation and the cutting of welfare provision); by some CIA interference on the side of the conservative opposition; and by internal dissension within the PNP and popular disenchantment. As a result, the JLP (Jamaica Labour Party) under Edward Seaga has returned to power with its neo-liberal free market economics and pro Ronald Reagan politics. The commercial bourgeoisie is once more on the rise, and the poor have taken refuge in the hedonism of the dancehall or the street corner preacher's promise of heaven. In *Prophets* these two tendencies are only superficially opposites. The gravel-voiced DJs and the mawga sermoniser employ similar styles, and even the faithful confuse the self-sacrificing route to heaven with the gaining of a green card to escape to the materially rich heaven of the USA.

    This chapter contextualises the fate of the messages Clarice and Thalbot have to offer. Faith in Manley's reaching out to working-class black Jamaica through reggae, rasta and images of African pride has evaporated; the socialist true believer have gone to ground or become infidels. The middle-class in places like Beverly Hills have resumed their pursuit of conspicuous consumption, and politics has been corrupted by the alliance between "visionless" politicians and the ghetto enforcers ("rubbing 'risto shoulders/ with the muck and blood of the ghetto"). The award of public building contracts to party supporters and turning a blind eye to the business of drug-trafficking has become the norm. In this context, Clarice's message of individual salvation has ready listeners; Thalbot's radical social message meets deaf ears.

Notes

Who Will Mourn for Her: The epigraph is taken from the Book of Nahum, which we might at first take to refer to Clarice, but the "her" is Nineveh, the Babylonian city in the throes of war. The Book of Nahum is an oracular poem prophesying – wishing for – the sack of Nineveh where: "the chariots shall rage in the streets" (2: 4), "the sword shall devour the young lions" (2: 13) and "there is none end of their corpses" (3: 3). Nineveh is, of course, Kingston, in the decade of mass political killings when in the nine months preceding the 1980 general elections, 844 Jamaicans were killed, over a third in one Kingston political constituency (*Jamaica Observer*, 30 October, 2012). As Nahum laments: "Woe to the bloody city! It is full of lies and robbery: the prey departeth not." Nahum is also the denouncer of Nineveh's sexual slackness, "the whoredoms of the well-favoured harlot, the mistress of witchcrafts" (3: 4), and threatens to "discover thy skirts upon thy face, and I will shew the nations thy nakedness, and the kingdoms thy shame", a theme that connects to the "batty-riders ... in the lewd light"; it is an image referred to more explicitly in section iii of this chapter. The reference also points to the horrified, but entranced, obsession of some Old Testament prophets with sex.

the harmattan (l. 2): The wind that carries dust from West Africa to the Caribbean. See Kamau Brathwaite's essay, "The African Presence in Caribbean Literature" (*Roots*, 1993, pp. 191-192) versions of the essay first published in 1970-73, where he writes how, "by an obscure miracle or connection, this arab's nomad wind, cracker of fante wood a thousand miles away, did not die on the sea-shore of west africa, its continental limit; it drifted on, reaching the new world archipelago to create our drought, imposing an african season on the caribbean sea. and it was on these winds too, and in this season, that the slave ships came from guinea, bearing my ancestors to this other land..."

the restless spirit of abandoned slaves (l. 3): A reference to the fact that sick, enslaved Africans on-board ship were cast over the side to drown, and in the instance of the slave ship *Zong* (1781), one third of the Africans were thrown overboard in order to make an insurance claim because they were worth more as lost cargo than live people. This is the subject of J.M.W. Turner's famous painting, *Slave Ship: Slavers Throwing Overboard the Dead and Dying* (1840). It is also the starting point of David Dabydeen's long poem, *Turner*, published in 1995, the same year as *Prophets*.

guarded by the wall of first defence (l. 7): This is the Palisadoes, the spit of land that shelters Kingston. The "decoy" alludes to the fact that before the fall of the Soviet Union, the USA of Reagan in the 1980s was hotly interested in combatting signs of resistance in its claimed back yard (Grenada in 1983). Cuba, though, was still the main target of US hostility, and the rapprochement between Michael Manley's PNP and Cuba in the late 1970s was one of the excuses for CIA interference in Jamaican affairs and its assistance in arming the opposition pro-capitalist JLP's political enforcers. However, by the time in which *Prophets* is set, the Soviet Union had fallen and Jamaica was in the neo-liberal era of the JLP's Edward Seaga ("with the pragmatics of finding the right price every time"), so Cuba's significance is only geographic.

Cuba's agnostic bravado (l. 8): As a communist and hence non-religious state, and still in the forefront to US imperialism.

dip and sweet fall-back (l. 10): A dance movement named in the folk song "Dip and Fall Back" ("My advice there is nothing nice/ Like dip and fall back") – see Olive Lewin, *Rock It Come Over* (2001), p. 109); it is also referred to in Justin Hinds' and Patra's songs of the same name (the former on the Wolf label 7 inch, 1977; the latter on the album, *Scent of Attraction*, 1995). The term is also a reference to the nickname given to a Jamaican dish in which the eater would dip boiled green bananas in the Run Down, a dish of salt mackerel stewed in coconut milk.

gravel-voiced djs (l. 11): Hear, for instance, Shabba Ranks, Buju Banton and Bounty Killer. The deep-voiced, gruff, ultra-masculine style is part of the context of a period of explicit reference to gun violence, macho bravado, sexual boasting and often by a virulent homophobia. (Note, in Jamaica, DJs were not, as elsewhere, the players of disks (this was the role of the "selector") but the artists who sang, chanted, rapped, toasted over the backing tracks, the dub plates.)

prophecy of slackness (l. 12): This references the turn of reggae to the style known as dancehall, with sexually explicit lyrics such as sung by Shabba Ranks and Yellowman – though it's worth noting that "slackness" was always part of earlier folkstyles, such as mento. Carolyn Cooper in *Sound Clash: Jamaican Dancehall Culture at Large* (2004) has defended the genre of dancehall from dismissal as merely lewd and misogynist by demonstrating both a range of actual artist philosophies within the genre and a continuing commitment to do at least one of the things prophets have always done: to tell a nation about itself and its flaws.

airy crotches (l. 13): The style of loose baggy trousers where the crotch line was often halfway to the knees.

grind (l. 15): As in wine and grine – dancing where the man and the woman press their crotches into each other and simulate at least one element of the sex act. This was not a new phenomena, as is shown in Prince Buster's song "Wine and Grine", on his Fab label (1968), which ends: "She'll love you when you wine and grine/ Just take it steady all the time/ She want a ruff, ruff stroker/ She want a cool, cool stroker".

batty-riders (l. 16): Short-short shorts worn by women at the dancehall to expose the buttocks (batty).

Beverly Hills (l. 18): One of the new, affluent upper-middle class housing areas north of Kingston.

skank (l. 20): This plays on the double meaning of the word, referring both to the characteristic dance of reggae – body bending forward, knees raised, arms extended – and to "skank", to deceive or trick someone. It is a pun that Bob Marley employs in his track, "Top Ranking" ("top ranking, top ranking,/ are you skanking?", on *Survival*, 1979)

politricksters (l. 21): A Jamaican blend word that dates back at least to the 1960s. At the "Smile Jamaica" concert in 1976, Bob Marley is reported to have declared that his performance was not related to any "politricks". See Midnight Raver <blog/2014/12/marley-smile-jamaica>.

'risto shoulders (l. 22): A reference to "aristocratic", up-town politicians' involvement with the ghetto dons who distributed favours and ensured votes from their garrison communities. Also, one of the brief dance fads of the eighties was a move called "shoulder move", which generated a long-lived rhythm of that name (Jah Thomas, "Shoulder Move", 1983).

every Christ is fixing a tidy nest up in the sky (l. 24): An allusion to the involvement of some of the new churches in the corrupt politics of the time, and of the tendency of some of the American-influenced evangelical churches to equate godliness with prosperity (the "prosperity gospel"), that investment in prayers and tithing (contributions to the church) would bring material rewards. Conversely, poverty was seen as a merited sign of God's disfavour. The words also allude to the equation between heaven and getting a green card to the USA (see section ii of this chapter).

the scent of the hull (l. 26): An obvious allusion to the slave ship and the despair that for the poorest Jamaicans little has changed, though the predators are different ("a new evolution of nature"), a vision that covers both neo-colonial politicians and preachers on the make (the gulls) preying on the worms, the crawlers. It is an image that suggests a familiarity with Ted Hughes' eponymous Crow (*Crow*, 1971), and one that surfaces in Dawes' own earlier poem "Sex Sells Annette" in *Progeny of Air* (1994, pp. 92-96), which has the lines: "The soldier crab was naked/ when Annette captured his home.// She didn't kill him, just plucked him out and tossed him/ brandishing his claws like a fist full of knives/ in the swallowing black sand."

ii

the crossroads (l. 1): Kingston's intersection at Halfway Tree that roughly divides the haves of the city from the have-nots.

chuckle at the spectacle (l. 3): As ubiquitous observers, the mad men are familiar with the preacher's "tricks".

crown and anchor board (l. 5): A gambling game with dice, like the three-card monte, a classic street confidence trick, a hustle to catch the gullible. A metaphor that suggests the credulous are being invited to invest their hard-won dollars (as a contribution to the preacher) in the hope of gaining heaven, or God's assistance in getting a green card, "a visa for the soul".

haremed sisters (l. 7): The preacherman often had an attendant group of women – with the implication here of sexual predation, as made explicit in the fictional portraits of such "shepherds" as Moses Barton in Sylvia Wynter's *The Hills of Hebron* (1962) and Shepherd John in Orlando Patterson's *The Children of Sisyphus* (1964).

to come home, come home… (l. 9): The words of an evangelical hymn "Ye who are weary, come home, home etc."; this is an ironic reference because the followers' dearest wish is for a green card to escape Jamaica.

the mawga sermoniser (l. 10): The scrawniness (mawga / meagre) of the street-corner preacher indicates his lack of success in gaining contributions.

The testimonies (l. 13): As in old-style advertising, these are testimonials from those who have got visas that the Lord has helped them. *Prophets* catches Jamaican Pentecostalism at the point of moving from a concern only with the spirit and an austere abnegation of worldly things, to seeing God and the church as an ally in getting the things of the world (see Malcolm Calley, *God's People: West Indian Pentecostal Sects in England* (1965), pp. 136-137).

the Lord has kept me here (l. 18): A reference to Philippians 1: 23-24 where either Paul or Timothy (the text is not clear) tells his followers: "I am torn between the two: I desire to depart [i.e. die] and be with Christ, which is better by far, but it is more necessary for you that I remain in the body" – a source that reinforces the sense of hubris and hypocrisy of the prophesying "sybil mother". One may note the distinctly cynical view of fundamentalist mentalities in this section of the poem, but also the brilliant way Dawes embeds the voice of this self-deceiving woman ("this dawta of Zion"), incredulous that the wicked prosper and the saintly are held back, in the rhythms of the verse and the solipsistic repetition of "me".

Is not one somebody me pray over an anoint with oil... on Oxford Street (ll. 23-24): A reference both to Isaiah 61: 3 ("to bestow on them a crown of beauty/ instead of ashes/ the oil of gladness/ instead of mourning") and the fact that Oxford Street, off Spanish Town Road, is the site of Kingston Public Hospital where one would undoubtedly find sick people, whom the woman has anointed. Anointing with olive oil is part of the ministry of some evangelical Pentecostals, but condemned by other evangelical churches as often merely an excuse for moneymaking.

I see the glory, Hallelujah (l. 26): From the "Battle Hymn of the Republic" – an ironic reference to the conflation of heaven and the USA.

stink a dem ole neaga (l. 28): A respectful nod to Edward Baugh's classic poem "Nigger Sweat" – about the crowds waiting for USA visas, which begins "No disrespect, mi boss/ just honest nigger sweat". This poem was first published in *A Tale of the Rainforest* (1988) and can be found in *Black Sand: New and Selected Poems* (2013), pp. 126-127.

red-eye (l. 37): Envious.

whatever arrows the Lord sen my way (l. 38): These are both the arrows of the Lord's deliverance (2 Kings 13: 17-19) and of Job's persecution ("The arrows of the Almighty are in me..." (Job 6: 4)).

him nah go give me more dan what/ I can bear (ll. 39-40): She refers to 1 Corinthians 10: 13 ("...And God is faithful; he will not let you be tempted beyond what you can bear. But when you are tempted, he will also provide a way out so that you can endure it").

Tongues like fire in the place (l. 41): This is a reference both to the Pentecostal moment in Acts 2: 3 ("They saw what seemed to be tongues of fire that separated and came to rest on each of them") which gives the apostles the ability to speak in the tongues of the gentiles, and to the heightened point in the church assembly when worshippers begin speaking in tongues.

this chastisement is hotter (l. 43): This is a reference to Hosea 10: 10 ("When it is my desire I will chastise them") and to Revelation 3: 19 ("Those whom I love, I reprove and discipline, therefore be zealous and repent"). The reference is both realistic and intertextual in a literary way. The woman would know and refer to these texts.

iii

the poison of heaven (l. 1): The right-wing propaganda from Reagan's USA (heaven as in the previous section).

Newark's phallic white towers (l. 2): The radio and TV towers that broadcast the gospel of prosperity and the glories of consumer USA to a receptive Jamaica. The "she" is the sky over Nineveh, imaged as the harlot of Nahum whose skirts "I will discover upon thy face". (In other words, exposing in Nahum's censorious eyes the shame of her private parts.) The verses also echo back to the scene (II, ii, ll. 25-69) of Clarice in front of the TV, "the clutter of potent seed spilling like this// to germinate in her fertile mind" – the images that begin to merge with her genuine spiritual revelations. The underlying image is of the sky as a woman being impregnated by the toxic sperm blowing over from Newark's phallic towers. Because toxic, there is no healthy embryo, but an early miscarriage when the sky rains down menstrual blood ("Her rain of gaudy wetness" (II, iii, l. 9)).

The natives cough up blood and yellow phlegm (l. 10): Because they have swallowed the blood from the aborting sky; also an image of the tubercular illnesses of the poor.

Morgan's deck (l. 12): The kind of name that might be given to a tourist hotel bar – after the pirate Henry Morgan of Port Royal (c. 1635-

1688), who was appointed Jamaica's Lieutenant Governor – an appropriately freebooting icon for the current period whom Peter Tosh references in his song, "Can't Blame the Youth" ("You teach the youths about the pirate Morgan,/ And you say he was a very great man..." (Intel Diplo label, 1972)).

Harbour Street (l. 14): Formerly a commercial area, but at the time of the poem's setting, one of the poorest areas of urban dereliction down by the sea in south Kingston.

the patient mongrel: See the note on dogs as invariably a negative symbol in the Bible – and Jamaica (XXIII, i, l. 1; XXIII, iii, l. 2, and p. 220 below).

the squatting madman (l. 14): Who may indeed be Thalbot.

on the hills... white satellites (ll. 19-20): Unlike Trinidad, the hills in Jamaica are where the rich live, who, according to the poem, not only get their entertainments from the USA, but their values and political loyalties as well ("welcoming the swooping helicopters"), a reference perhaps to the support Caribbean elites gave to the US invasion of Grenada. Thus the "white satellites" are both the actual dishes and the light-skinned elites who were ideological satellites of the USA.

with a satchel of visas (l. 24): This alludes to the economic support that Prime Minister Edward Seaga was able to mobilise from Ronald Reagan's USA in return for ending ties with Cuba, supporting the invasion of Grenada and enthusiastically embracing the gospel of neo-liberal capitalism. In return, there was a relaxation of the IMF's conditions for credit, and a relaxation of the conditions for gaining entry visas to the USA. See Ronald Libby, "The United States and Jamaica: Playing the American Card" (1990). Between 1980 and 1990, 213,805 Jamaicans travelled to the USA, 9% of the population. See also Alejandra Bronfman, *On the Move: The Caribbean since 1989* (2007).

fly Dixie high (l. 25): This is not the Stars and Stripes, but the Confederate flag of the southern states, once committed to holding on to slavery.

Note the stump; our feet are impressed in it still (l. 28): A series of complex punning double images pointing in the direction both of those who did the selling and those who were sold. The stump is literally the block on which the auctioneer stood to sell slaves; it may also allude to the fact that amputations of legs and arms were used as reprisals

against runaway slaves; and "on the stump" refers back to the electioneering
'risto politicians. "Impressed" puns on the double meaning of still being
moulded by the ordering of society bequeathed from slavery and of
being press-ganged – of slaves taken against their will. See Kwame Dawes'
poem "Talisman" (*Progeny of Air*, pp. 36-40) where a history lesson on
slavery ("… stands the whiteman, slave man,/ bossman, whipman, chop-
their-hands-off-// when-they-run-man") emotionally divides the class,
reminding the black class members that their white classmates, the
children of the Pennants, Issas, Alexanders and De Lissers, the "ultimate
merchants" are still those with privilege, who remain economically
powerful in Jamaican society.

old mould, now new world order (l. 29): Those who knew what
imperialism and colonialism meant were not fooled by such renamings
as globalism and the new world order.

the feet of the descending prophet (l. 32): This is a reference to
Isaiah 52: 7 ("How beautiful on the mountains are the feet of those
who bring good news") – an ironic flash-forward to the scenes where
Thalbot reluctantly descends the mountains to bring God's warning
to Nineveh/ Kingston. In this scene we are offered images of Thalbot
both as madman and as bonafide prophet, images that are only seemingly
incompatible. The prophet hesitates because he senses the times have
changed and the people have become increasingly unresponsive to his
message.

CHAPTER IV
This Day of Aborted Beginnings

Summary

Chapter IV introduces and brings the character of Last Night into the action. We may deduce him as an alternative version of the "I", the student self of the narrator (see the Prologue) who is similarly broken. We learn the source of Last Night's brokenness – his fear of the termagant, sexually voracious (in patwa, a teggereg) woman, Thelma. We witness his seeking refuge in the church service and his "slaying" by the spirit. We also note how Clarice is emotionally smitten by Last Night, who goes on to play a significant role in *Prophets*. See Chapters IX, XI and XXI, where we see his rapid rise in the church as the preacher with whom Clarice "sins".

Notes

i

ragamuffin sounds (l. 3): The sounds of ragga or post-reggae dancehall music. Throughout the chapter, the account of the service plays on the competing sacred and secular sounds and their ironic similarities of heightened emotion.

The Mona valley (l. 4): Where the University is situated.

dollying through … (l. 4): The verb "to dolly" in Jamaican English refers to the act of moving skilfully through a crowded field in person or in or on a vehicle (a bicycle, motorbike or car) by swaying to and fro to avoid collision. The term may well derive from the use of that term in the cinema industry. So here we also find a verbal alert to the presence of cinematic imagery (even though here for sound) throughout *Prophets*. A dolly was a tracking shot in the days when the camera was on "dolly tracks" moving forward towards or away from the focal point.

Last Night (l. 10): The nicknaming of persons is a familiar Jamaican/ Caribbean phenomena. In this instance, the reference is to the colour of Last Night's skin, i.e., "'Im so black 'im look like last night". See "Otherwise Known As", Lance Nenton talking to Charles Hyatt, *Jamaica Observer*, 1 November 2014.

pippy wash (l. 11): A wash is the Jamaican term for a drink made with fresh limes and brown sugar.

clawing cheese (l. 16): In Jamaican, "clawing" (cf. cloying) is an adjective that describes the persistent and uncomfortable stickiness and sweetness of certain foods (like the mix, in this case, of doughy sweet buns and inexpensive heavily processed canned cheese) in the throat. The term is often used as a metaphor to describe a person whose manner achieves a similar effect on one's sensibilities. Compare Ben Jonson's *The Alchemist* (1610) where Face instructs Drugger: "You must eat no cheese [...] it breeds melancholy and that breeds worms" (Act III, Scene 4).

hardo (l. 17): A dense, hard-dough bread.

hoods (l. 20): Jamaican patwa for the erect penis (hood/wood).

ii

poor t'ing (l. 4): Elsewhere a "poor-me-one" or to be "poor-thing-fied", i.e. self-pitying.

How far you think/ you can run from the Lord (ll. 8-9): Clarice paraphrases Psalm 139: 7, "Whither shall I flee from thy presence". Here we have the essence of Clarice's power, her particular brand of prophecy with its shrewd understanding of the human heart.

Slain like this (l. 23): Such slayings of the spirit (he falls to the floor as a sign of repentance) are the stuff of the evangelical Charismatic promise.

the flight to some injured coast... multiplication of self (ll. 25-26): The first phrase is borrowed from a Paul Simon song "The Coast (Work-in-Progress)" on *The Rhythm of the Saints* album (1990): "Summer skies and stars are falling/ All along the injured coast". The second phrase relates to Last Night's desire to procreate in his own image – though clearly only with a woman who respects his fragile male ego. See, too, Kwame Dawes' *Jacko Jacobus* (1996), the narrative of another prophet and founder of a nation, whose destiny is "...to be the stud you are, grind your seed deep, howl, howl, for all you/ are worth, then sleep and perhaps dream of glory" (p. 13).

her caged mind (l. 38): A reference back to the image of Clarice as the "mew'd" falcon (epigraph to Chapter II).

CHAPTER V
Sovereign City

Summary

Chapter V introduces us to the complex persona of Thalbot: street madman, would-be CIA agent, and future warner man who has been ejected from his old refuge on Hope Road and is squatting in the new shopping mall, built in its place. In Thalbot, Dawes explores a different model of prophecy from that we have seen in Clarice. He is an Old Testament prophet whose role is to cry woe on the corruption of the times, to warn of the wrath to come. But he is also an intensely Jamaican figure, the inheritor of the long tradition of public prophet-figures, as well as street-preaching warner women and men. Unlike Clarice, with her susceptibility to American soaps and lightening cream, Thalbot is militantly black with a radical view of Jamaican history, a stance that, as the critical commentary above outlines (pp. 38-44), puts him in the tradition of such political/religious prophets of blackness as Alexander Bedward, Leonard Howell and Claudius Henry.

Notes

Sovereign City: At the time of the writing of *Prophets*, this new shopping mall, built in the 1980s on Hope Road, is a sign of the triumph of American-style commerce in the new era. It was built on the site of a mock Tudor-style house and the old post office – both colonial relics. Dawes reflects on the irony of its naming, in an era when genuine sovereignty appeared to be an illusion.

Thalbot: In *Prophets*, Thalbot is a version of "Legion", the principal character of the Gadarene swine episode in Luke's gospel (cf. p. 121). Like Legion, Thalbot has multiple personas. The factual "truth" of the fictional Thalbot as just such a multiple character has some reality in some well-attested conversions in Jamaica – for instance, of a JLP gunman (who might well have been an actual or would-be secret agent for the CIA), a ghetto enforcer with several murders to his credit, who was reprieved from prison and became a well-respected pastor.

Again, as the critical commentary explores, prophecy and madness have both biblical and Jamaican interpenetrations, whether actual or as defined by the state. The prophet and pioneer of a militant black sensibility, Alexander Bedward, for instance, was incarcerated in the Bellevue mental hospital by the colonial government following his declaration that he was going to fly, but moreso because he was building a working class following.

As in most places, nakedness is almost invariably taken as a sign of street madness in Jamaica, though Isaiah is supposed to have walked around naked, preaching, for over three years. ("Then the Lord said, 'Just as my servant Isaiah has gone stripped and barefoot for three years, as a sign and portent against Egypt and Cush...'" Isaiah 20: 3). As discussed in the introduction, Dawes handles the interconnections between madness, spirituality and resistance quite differently from earlier Caribbean authors (see above, pp. 54-58), ranging from the comic treatments in Naipaul's *Miguel Street* ("Man-Man") and Selvon's Brackley in *The Lonely Londoners*, the more noble treatment of Taffy in Earl Lovelace's *The Wine of Astonishment* and most complexly in Jean "Binta" Breeze's poem "The Madwoman". There is also Prince Buster's song "Madness", which suggests a certain ambivalence of attitude: "Madness, madness, they call it madness / Well if this is madness / Then I know I'm filled with gladness".

gutter mud and motor oil (l. 9): Note the contrasts between Thalbot and Clarice. She is seen whitening her face, whilst Thalbot is making himself blacker. She is attempting to suppress signs of her awakening sexuality, whilst Thalbot's sexuality is one *only* of display. As the women note: "What a waste..."

ii

This section works as a flashback to explain how Thalbot comes to inhabit the Sovereign Centre.

The jaded pink mansion (l. 2): This was one of the derelict old colonial buildings on Hope Road that civic groups attempted to rescue, but which were part of the loss of old Kingston to the modernity of shopping malls like the Sovereign Centre. Thalbot is forced to make the transition from old world to new. This is another contrast with Clarice who takes possession of Castleberry's grand house as its caretaker, whilst Thalbot is evicted from his refuge.

the Institute (l. 26): The Institute of Jamaica (where Dawes' father, the writer Neville Dawes, had been director until the JLP government came to power and sacked him as a committed Marxist socialist). No doubt the white Jamaicanised English dread refers to some actual person.

like a maroon on a raid (l. 38): A reference to the Maroon wars fought in the 1730s (and a second war in 1795) against the British redcoat army. Maroon (runaway) resistance forced a treaty that ceded a degree of independence to those who lived in Accompong, Trelawny Town, Moore Town, Scott's Pass and Nanny Town. The point is that Thalbot locates his prophecy in episodes of resistance in Jamaican history – unlike Clarice whose inspiration is from the USA. However, unlike the Maroons' machetes, no doubt covered in redcoat blood, Thalbot's machete is only coated in sugarcane juice. For the history of the Maroons, see Mavis C. Campbell, *The Maroons of Jamaica: A History of Resistance, Collaboration and Betrayal* (1988).

iii

Malcolm X (l. 6): The film made by Spike Lee and starring Denzel Washington was on release in Jamaica in 1992.

Sovereign? (l. 14): Another lament over the loss of sovereignty, the result of the abandonment by the JLP of the Manley programme of decolonisation, to become a virtual satellite of the USA.

mint and jasmine public toilets (l. 18): I.e. the bushes.

would-be secret agent (l. 22): See Chapter XIV (*The Making of a Prophet*) for a flashback that locates Thalbot's history as would-be agent of the CIA some time before his current fall into street madness. At this current stage of the poem, as a fierce critic of Sovereign City, which he bewails as a neo-colonialist imposition, Thalbot has evidently regretted his CIA affiliations (in fact we see him turning his back on the chance to leave for the USA in Chapter XIV, v) to become a memorialist of the cruelties and injustices of Jamaica's slave and colonial past. His mission is one that, on the surface at least, fails – he is the perennial outsider. Clarice, by contrast, sets her back on the past, but is inhabited by it more than she ever realises.

slavemaster castle (l. 25): The jaded pink mansion on Hope Road, demolished to make way for the Sovereign Centre.

naked as any Kojo (l. 26): I.e. as an African man, his West African (Akan) name (born on Monday) is an index of Thalbot's blackness. One of Dawes' brothers is a Kojo and Dawes has written about the prejudices he himself encountered in Jamaica as an African as late as the 1970s in poems such as "On Being Unka's Brother" from *Progeny of Air* (1994) and in *A Far Cry from Plymouth Rock* (2007), pp. 65-72. The reference is, of course, also to the Maroon chief, Captain Cudjoe, whose successful guerilla war with the British ended with a treaty that recognised the Maroons as an independent entity in Jamaica.

shithouse imperialist/bloodsucking monstrosity (l. 32): A homage, perhaps, to the late great reggae artist Peter Tosh and his excoriation of the Babylon "shitstem", here represented by this "new Babylon mansion".

temple to the gospel/ of the dollar (ll. 46-47): See above to "every Christ is fixing a tidy nest up in the sky": and the televangelists' prosperity gospel preaching that having faith, speaking God's word and making donations to the church will bring prosperity. Oral Roberts (1918-2009), a Pentecostal televangelist, is perhaps the best-known proponent. He accumulated great personal wealth until the sexual and financial scandals affecting other notorious televangelists impacted on donations and he had to sell his holiday homes and three of his Mercedes (Wikipedia). See Christopher Reed, "Oral Roberts Obituary", *The Guardian*, 15 December 2009, online.

toy-general outfit (l. 55): The quasi-military uniform of the "guardy" or security guard.

iv

Matilda's corner (l. 2): The corner of Hope Road and Old Hope Road.

yet another voice, wailing in the wilderness (l. 7): This references Jeremiah 9: 10 ("I will weep for the mountains and wail for the wilderness pastures"), and Matthew 3: 3 ("A voice of one calling in the desert,/ Prepare the way for the Lord") and probably the reggae group Culture's song, "I'm alone in the wilderness" (*Two Sevens Clash*, 1977). It's worth noting the deliberate ambivalence of tone in this section: the elements of cynicism ("plies his trade", "spawns its prophets in plenty", "curious/ to see what two-headed monstrosity", "the market is glutted with sybils and clarices", "the spectacle of verbal acrobatics and scandal") and the elements of recognition of something more profound ("magic teeth", "songs of redemption on their lips"). This is the cool dismissive tone of the rationalist, the observer of the actuality of scandal and pretence, who yet as a believer recognises this ground as the source of prophetic artists such as Don Drummond, Big Youth and Marley, who see behind the "verbal acrobatics" and the "curve of the words" that Kingston/ Nineveh refuses to hear.

Don D or the Yout' (l. 10): Don Drummond (1932-1969) was the brilliant but troubled jazz and ska trombonist who murdered his girlfriend and died in Bellevue psychiatric hospital. He appears as the model for one of the artistic figures driven to madness by the complexities of Jamaican life in Chapter XVII (*It is the Cause: Bellevue Ska*). See the further notes for that chapter (pp. 184-194). Big Youth (1949–) was another musical pioneer, whose album *Screaming Target* (1973) set the pace for the chanting DJ style with conscious, Rastafarian-influenced lyrics.

Emerging yet again... with their magic teeth and split lips (l. 11-12): Big Youth's conscious lyrics went out of fashion in the 1980s of dancehall gangsta and slackness, but he had a renewed success in the 1990s and spawned a new generation of conscious artists. Big Youth is well known for his impressive mouthful of jewel-studded teeth. The "magic teeth" also references the teeth Cadmus sows from the dragon he has killed – which spring up as armed warriors – the return of the rebel spirit. Whilst no doubt dating from much earlier Greek oral sources, the best-known version is in Ovid's *Metamorphoses*, Book III, ll. 95-114. It is also a sentence that may have been remembered from Toni Morrison's *Song of Solomon*, where Corinthians hears men talking in a room and wonders "If perhaps it was a secret hour in which men rose like giants from dragon's teeth" (1995 [1977]), p. 221.

like shepherd in the fields (l. 14): This references Luke 2: 8: "And there were in the same country shepherds abiding in the field, keeping watch over their flock by night", to whom the angel brings news of the coming birth of Jesus.

cauls on his heads (l. 17): To be born with a caul (amniotic sac) was to be blessed with second sight. The double-headedness connects to the long history of miraculous/monstrous appearances in the wilder shores of millenarian prophecy, such as Mary Toft (1701-1763) who claimed to have given birth to rabbits, or Joanna Southcott (1750-1814), a prophetess with an estimated 100,000 followers, who announced she was pregnant at the age of sixty-four and would deliver the new messiah (see James Hopkins, *A Woman to Deliver the People* (2014)).

Jobs and Nahums (l. 19): Job was the righteous man of the Bible whom God tests with multiple afflictions. Nahum is the prophet wishing for the destruction of Nineveh (see above, Chapter III, Epigraph).

songs of redemption on his lips (l. 18): A reference to Bob Marley's "Redemption Song" (*Uprising*, 1980).

sybils and clarices (l. 20): A nice self-referential joke. Sybils – the oracular prophetesses of ancient Greece.

verbal acrobatics (l. 23): See the essay by Kei Miller, once a preacher in training at the same kind of church featured in *Prophets*, on the moment he realised he was listening to the patterns of rhetoric rather than the message of the sermon ("Riffing of Religion", *Writing Down the Vision* (2013), p. 139ff).

CHAPTER VI
Denial

Summary

In this chapter, the "I" voice of the narrator takes further the exploration of his multi-levelled relationship to the figure of Clarice – as a woman known through experience, as a fictionalised character and as figure of myth whose self-deceiving denials of her blackness and Africanness will be restored to truth through the power of poetry to soar above sordid realities. Again, Clarice's contrasts with Thalbot are emphasised. Whilst he accentuates his Africanness, she denies hers – her skin, her hair, her body and her speech – and reveals her colonialised mentality in thinking it sacrilegious to imagine Christ as other than having "crystal blue eyes" – all this despite the Jamaican Africanness of the way she sways to the bassline and batters the tambourine during the service.

Here, the "I" enters the poem in several manifestations: as the poet/writer who reveals his metatextual shaping of the poem; as the biographical person, "Kwame Dawes", the writer with African connections, who uses elements of his family story in the poem (see Chapter XI, *Infidelity*); and as a quasi-autobiographical character in the action, the broken student who reveals himself in the prologue. We should remember, of course, that the "autobiographical" elements are as much part of the fiction of the poem as any other element.

In the second section of the chapter, the poet announces he will reverse the outcomes (exit to Toronto) that Clarice supposedly desires (and may have achieved after her fall from grace), though he also acknowledges that his imaginative action of placing her in Africa is a nostalgic dream, the creation of myth.

Notes

i

denial three times over (l. 2): This refers to Peter's denial of Christ at the time of the crucifixion when he is asked three times if he knows Jesus. It is recorded in all the gospels. Matthew 26: 75 has: "And Peter remembered the word of Jesus, which said unto him, Before the cock crow, thou shalt deny me thrice. And he went out, and wept bitterly."

King James' syntax (l. 10): The Elizabethan language and grammar of the King James Bible of 1611, rather than Jamaican patwa.

Crystal blue eyes (l. 12): The image of the blond, blue-eyed Jesus seems to have emerged in the 19th century, but reached popular consciousness through the famous blond Jesus of Warner Sallman of 1935, probably the most widely reproduced painting in the 20th century, and the inspiration for Hollywood Jesuses such Jeffrey Hunter in *King of Kings* (1961) and Robert Powell in *Jesus of Nazareth* (1977).

Water-walker (l. 14): See Matthew 14: 25-26: "And in the fourth watch of the night Jesus went unto them, walking on the sea. And when the disciples saw him walking on the sea, they were troubled, saying, It is a spirit; and they cried out for fear."

clad in whiter-than-snow… (l. 14): An allusion that points to the hymns that equate whiteness with spiritual purity: "Wash me in the blood of the lamb, / and I shall be whiter than snow…" – an I.D. Sankey hymn in the Church Mission Hymnal.

seamless expensive threads (l. 15): A paraphrase of John 19: 23. "When the soldiers crucified Jesus, they took his clothes, dividing them into four shares, one for each of them, with the undergarment remaining. The garment was seamless, woven in one piece from top to bottom." Clarice, echoing some of the ideas propagated by prosperity doctrine preachers in the 1990s (cf. Rev. Creflo Dollar and Bishop Jonathan Alvarado), reads this as an indication that saints should not be denied some of the good things in life, since Jesus, himself, was evidently wealthy enough to own an expensive garment.

the noble missionaries… being stewed in groundnut paste (l. 36): This is precisely the kind of racist image of white evangelical propaganda that the calypsonian Sparrow satirised and turned on its head in "Congo Man" (1965), with its refrain: "I never eat white meat yet".

How can I watch my grandmother (l. 37): Dawes' maternal grandmother was a Fante, Ghanaian woman, Amelia Clarke, herself a committed Pentecostal Christian.

Ululating (l. 39): The high-pitched trilling sound made by (mainly) grieving women in Africa and the Middle East, amongst other places.

Elmina suburb (l. 44): The fort in Ghana that was the centre of the Akan, Gold Coast slave trade.

bones grope blindly for missing joints (l. 45): This refers to the punishment mutilations of the enslaved Africans, using the words of Ezekiel 37: 7: "And as I was prophesying, there was a noise, a rattling sound, and the bones came together, bone to bone…" – an image that becomes part of the iconography of resurrecting souls at the end of world. It is an image Dawes returns to in a recent poetry collection, *City of Bones* (2017). The allusion is also a cinematic one, to the 1963 film *Jason and the Argonauts*, well known for the famous "battle of the skeletons" scene. Like most classic films of Hollywood of the 1930s, 40s, 50s and 60s, this film was aired on television in Jamaica in the 1970s and 80s.

still St Thomas soil, black Maroon mother (l. 55): St Thomas in the East, a preponderantly rural parish, was noted as one of the places where African survivals were strong (see Chapter XXII, *The Saints Return Triumphant*). St Thomas is the parish in which the Morant Bay rebellion took place in 1865. For Maroons see note above (pp. 136-137).

ii

kente (l. 1): Interwoven cloth, made of strips of fabric by the Akan of Ghana, once the cloth of royalty and ceremony, which Clarice would reject as an attempt to make her look pagan.

Toronto's blue sterility (l. 5): See Kwame Dawes' earlier poem "Prime Minister Reunites with his Mother" in *Progeny of Air*, pp. 84-89, where a black Jamaican woman who has migrated to Toronto is found working for white people, "clearing their shit, emptying out their piss-pans/ […] mothering their wayward children".

whispered conferences (l. 15): A neat relocation to Africa, but essentially a continuation of Clarice's role as the confidant of Last Night and "I", the broken student.

the one who comes from the lofty rock face (l. 16): I.e., the Lord. This references Isaiah 2: 2: "And it shall come to pass in the last days, that the mountain of the Lord's house shall be established in the top of the mountains, and shall be exalted above the hills; and all nations shall flow unto it."

symphony of gunshots (l. 21): The line looks forward to Clarice's fall from grace, her expulsion from the church and from her room at Castleberry's. It implies that she has returned to the ghetto from which she rose (see Chapter XXIII, xv). It is also a reminder of the prophet Nahum's images of war-torn Nineveh.

CHAPTER VII
The Old Man

Summary

Clarice has rescued Last Night from his homelessness and spiritual crisis and taken him home. There she torments him with Bible verses, revelations of her prophetic knowledge of his lusts and sexual misdemeanours, and tantalising glimpses of her forbidden flesh. The episode is full of punning double-entendres between the innocent and the sexual: references to Clarice "still wet"; "the powdered cleft"; Last Night daring not think of "her private stepping out of her wet panties"; and his fleeing to his "hole in the east" when she sends him packing for the erection she has caused.

Notes

The Old Man (Epigraph): This refers to the unregenerate man not yet reborn to holiness (and a colloquial term for the penis). The source is Ephesians 4: 22-24: "That ye put off concerning the former conversation the old man, which is corrupt according to deceitful lusts,/ And be renewed in the spirit of your mind; And that ye put on the new man, which after God is created righteousness and true holiness." Also, Colossians 3: 9: "Do not lie to each other, since you have taken off your old self with its practices and have put on the new self…"

casual in her yellow nightdress (l. 3): As we discover, not casual at all, and not at all the behaviour of a chaste prophetess.

blue-balled (l. 25): Allegedly a state caused by prolonged sexual arousal without ejaculation.

… to cool the burning of his flesh… (l. 31): An allusion to Corinthians 7: 9: "…for it is better to marry than to burn with passion…"

to be buried once and for all at the river (l. 33): Baptism through total immersion in the river will enact and thus symbolise the "burial" of the dead "old man" and the spiritual rebirth/ resurrection of the "new man" (but see IX, ii, and pp. 149-150 below).

CHAPTER VIII
Changing the Guard

Summary

The chapter is a flashback to the moment when Clarice first takes up
residence in the house the church has bought from Castleberry's heirs,
after his death and before their return flight to Toronto. The chapter
portrays a world of white privilege that has largely gone (from Kingston
at least), with its houseful of servants (now to be called helpers) and
the European style of décor. The chapter returns to Clarice's easy
cohabitation with Castleberry's ghost and her first vanquishing of Thalbot
who has temporarily squatted in the empty house. The chapter gives
a different view of Clarice as the "smiling, sly-eyed woman" who
understands the body language ("the cutting eye") of the departing
helpers all too well.

Notes

i

opaque crystals (l. 13): A sign of the decay of age.

**the sun bathers are paler now, casual on the// Myrtle Bank pool
deck** (ll. 12-13): This is an ironic comment on the reversal between
the now sunlight-bleached painting and the actuality that the skins at
the once fashionable hotel are now much darker. The Myrtle Bank
once operated a colour bar, until it was breached in 1948 by a black
Jamaican journalist, Evon Blake (1906-1988), who leaped into the whites-
only pool. See <nlj.gov.jm/biographies/evon-blake-1906-1988>.

griffins (l. 18): Mythical creatures with the body of a lion and the
head and wings of an eagle.

potent sorrel (l. 26): The red Christmas drink made with dried hibiscus
flowers, no doubt laced with rum.

bombay tree (l. 29): A type of mango.

new age church of middle-class believers: This is no doubt how
Castleberry's now Canadian heirs see the church. The church itself
would be horrified, seeing new ageism as a mishmash of pagan nonsense,

or as one pastor, Dr David R. Reagan, writes on the internet: "a convoluted theology straight from the pit of hell", or as "spiritual pornography"! <christinprophecy.org/articles/the-new-age-church/>.

helpers (l. 36): The Manley government of the 1970s decreed that servants be called helpers.

ii

Barbican's foothills (l. 11): The area to the north of Sovereign City, a rapidly growing area of poor housing in the middle of long-standing middle-class suburbia. Barbican Road runs off Hope Road.

He fell into a pot of ferns (l. 25): A joke perhaps on John Keats' "Isabella or the Pot of Basil", in which the pot also contains the body of a dead man, Isabella's lover, murdered by her brothers.

Dovecot's lonely slopes (l. 27): The cemetery in Kingston 10, on the far side of Spanish Town from Kingston, towards Guanaboa Vale.

Toronto (l. 28): This is no doubt a family that was part of the white flight out of Jamaica in the 1970s, with only the now deceased Castleberry, a patriot of the old school, remaining.

iii

the exact count is nine days (l. 2): This refers to the nine nights of the wake, with its clear origins in West African custom, which as a Charismatic/Pentecostalist Clarice ought to abhor as a pagan rite, but which she instinctively follows.

his nakedness a weapon (l. 17): See Chapter V, i. It is symptomatic that Clarice is entirely unimpressed.

dulcimena (l. 19): A hard cardboard suitcase that signals the poverty from which Clarice is rising.

It is her laugh now that drives him sane (l. 28): Compare *Introit* i, where Clarice, on her way to the service, ignores her spiritual task of casting out Thalbot's demons. Ironically, of course, it is being driven to sanity that puts Thalbot on the path to exposing Clarice's sin.

iv

he will be soundly cast out (l. 6): As a ghost, Castleberry must be regarded as a malign spirit; it is her Christian duty to exorcise his presence, but as we note (Chapter II, i) she does not do this, perhaps enjoying Castleberry's eyes on her nakedness.

CHAPTER IX
Confessional

Summary

The chapter advances the growing sexual tension between Clarice and Last Night, as he takes his turn in tormenting her with his stories of his former partner's sexual boldness in talking "nasty about what she want a man fe do her", in contrast, of course, to Clarice's tortured indirections of longing. The counterpoint between Last Night's increasingly explicit confessions and Clarice's responses made through the vegetables she is chopping, or the uneasy shuffling of her feet, is wittily and vividly done, as the rhythms of the verse catch the action to perfection. The church looks to provide a solution by advancing Last Night's river baptism into being born again as a new man, vanquishing the "old man" of lust – but they also more practically recommend that the two should not meet in seclusion "after this cleansing", and her clasping of his chilled hand indicates the necessity for this prohibition.

Notes

i

My damning fantasy, what cling to my brain/ like bloodstain (l. 1): An echo of several lines in *Macbeth* that bring together bloodstained hands, fantasy, a "false creation/ proceeding from the heat-oppressed brain".

skellions (l. 6): Jamaican name for scallions, a vegetable resembling a large spring onion.

dutch-pot (l. 16): The archetypal utensil of Jamaican cuisine, a creole version of the casserole pot.

Maxi Priest (l. 18): Black British singer of Jamaican descent, born Max Alfred Elliott (1961-) a leading exponent of reggae-fusion Lovers Rock. His best known album, *Bonafide* (1990), contains his hit, "Close to You". It is quite possibly this the radio is playing. If this was the case, the first line of the song, "She was a Jezebel, this burstin' queen/ Livin' like a bad sweet dream", is more than ironically apposite. See Chapter XVII, i, l. 44; and XXIII, xv, l. 9. In any case, you would not listen to Maxi Priest if you wanted to cool the sexual tension.

the bogle (l. 19): A sensuous, pelvis-swaying dance popular in 1980s' Jamaican dancehall (q.v. the butterfly) named after a DJ (Gerald Levy, 1964-2005) who called himself Mr Bogle. The dance's name also alludes to the Jamaican National Hero, Paul Bogle, who was an African deacon who led the Morant Bay Rebellion/ Uprising – a nice example of the capacity of Jamaican popular culture to merge the serious with the frivolous.

batty bang out (l. 22): Her backside is accentuated by her "batty-riders" (shorts). "Bang", here, suggests a protrusion, as in "bang belly" for a pregnant woman or a child suffering from malnutrition.

pure slackness (l. 31): A witty oxymoron – slackness (talking dirty) being anything but pure.

she bruk with a piece of shouting/ like she vex with me (l. 45): Dawes comments wittily on a certain kind of Jamaican masculinity that doesn't go for woman on top, or can't cope with the idea that her orgasm might not have too much to do with him.

me abuse myself (l. 51): If sexual purity is demanded of Charismatic/ Pentecostal women, men are certainly forbidden masturbation, seen as a major sin – though whether Sister Clarice's slap is doctrinal or expresses a jealous sense that he has been unfaithful to her is left ambiguous, like her "hips swaying with too much accent".

ii

they chastise his sin... and he feels the violent escape of demons/ through a tidy round hole in the skull (ll. 16-21): The model of a Pentecostal act of purification before baptism, and one that connects to the ur-narrative of the Gadarene swine. However, as in the case of Thalbot (see Chapter XVI, ll. 48-64) the very act of emptying out ("his body now deflated, void, vulnerable") makes Last Night as open to occupation by other lingering spirits as by the holy spirit. This is the gist of Jesus's warning to the Pharisees as reported in St Matthew's gospel (12: 43-45) which is used as the epigraph for Part Two ("When the unclean spirit has gone out of a person, it wades through waterless regions looking for a resting place, but finds none. Then it says, 'I will return to the house from which I came.' It finds it empty, swept, and put in order. Then it goes and brings along seven other spirits more evil than itself, and they enter and live there; and the last state of the

person is worse than the first. So it will be also with this evil generation.")
This is part of a riposte to the Jewish priests who are trying to trip up
Jesus and condemn him for performing miracles on the sabbath. Jesus's
retort is directed at the Pharisees as punctilious keepers of orthodox
order (as in the image of the swept house) but who, if they are not
filled with the holy ghost, are not immune to occupation by evil spirits,
as manifest in their attempts to trip Jesus up. This warning connects
to Last Night's sanctity which is meant to be secured by his total immersion
in the river. The fact that it stains his white robes brown looks ironic.

In Part 2, Chapters XIV, XV, XVII-IXX, Jesus's warning becomes the
narrative device for setting up Thalbot's possession by the four apparitions.

the hawk screams / over the Blue Mountains (l. 35): This image
connects to Clarice as the "mew'd" bird of prey now freed. As noted
in the introduction, the adjacent images of peace ("his soul revived by
the turning dove") and war (the hawk) indicate an ambivalent outcome.
This is probably also an act of homage to the poet's father, Neville
Dawes, with the images in his poetry of "the drunk hawks and worse"
("Acceptance") and "the hawks dip/ wing-tipped diving" ("Fugue"),
both collected in *Fugue and other Writings* (2012).

this Nineveh of their undoing (l. 38): This makes the point that
even this church is not immune to the corrupting environment of 1980s'
Kingston.

CHAPTER X
Hermit

Summary

This chapter takes us in a flashback to Clarice's past as the daughter of Ras Pedro, a Rastafarian musician and "failed" prophet. He is a precursor in the poem to the sequence of artist figures who inhabit Thalbot. Ras Pedro has struggled unsuccessfully with the commercial imperatives of changing fashion that rapidly consign musical artists to the scrap heap. He is a forgotten man living in what was formerly a dynamic cultural encampment, now a free fire zone for gangs and the police. The chapter also offers a back story to Clarice's social motivations, suggesting an element of self-conflict in her sexuality as a result of the incestuous abuse she has suffered, and the origins of her gift for prophecy. Here, as elsewhere, Dawes uses the cinematic device of visual images drawn from a character's memory and imagination, but the narrative also draws on the archetype of a biblical story – the narrative of the incestuous relationship between Lot (the escapee from Sodom) and his daughters, a narrative that suggests an ambiguity concerning Clarice's role in that relationship. Her journey back to her father is one of the dreaming imagination. There will be no return to her father's world in Wareika, though she carries more of it within her than she can ever admit.

Notes

i

the filthy caves of Wareika (l. 1): Wareika Hill, south east of Kingston and to the south of the Long Mountain range, was the site of a famous Rastafarian encampment, most closely associated with Count Ossie (aka Oswald Williams, 1926-1976), a master drummer and pioneer of the infusion of Rastafarian rhythms into what became reggae. The 1960 Jamaican hit record, "Oh Carolina", made by the Folkes Brothers and produced by Prince Buster, featured Count Ossie and his troupe of drummers. (The song was also recorded by Shaggy in 1993.) Count Ossie was the founder of the group, The Mystic Revelations of Rastafari, whose three albums – with their mix of chanting, narrative, Rastafarian hymns and free-form jazz – *Grounation* (1973), *Tales from Mozambique* (1975) and *Man from Higher Heights* (1983) are all still available. It should be stressed that though *Prophets* alludes to features of Count Ossie's life (which was cut short by a road accident), the figure of Ras Pedro is a wholly fictitious character, particularly with respect to the incestuous relationship with Clarice. In *Prophets*, the point of the episode is twofold: to provide a back-story for Clarice and to reinforce the picture of how regrettably, in some respects, times have changed. According to the accounts of Verene Reckord ("Rastafarian Music – An Introductory Study", 1977) and the eye witness of Douglas R.A. Mack ("The Camps", in *Babylon to Rastafari*, 1999), the camp set up in the early 1950s was a vibrant place of musical invention, with a community centre on Glasspole Street which, according to Mack, by the 1970s had become a place of pilgrimage for other musicians and everyone "from university intellectuals and handcart pushers". As the chapter indicates, by the 80s and 90s, Count Ossie was dead and his spiritual reggae out of fashion. The chapter observes the detritus of the back-to-Africa dream. Wareika Hill had become the territory of renegade armed gangs and their warfare with the militarised police; its vibrancy as a centre of musical culture had long gone.

not Arawak bones/ not hieroglyphs (l. 2): Wareika Hill was one of the sites where Taino artefacts and statuary were found. See Lesley-Gail Atkinson, *The Earliest Inhabitants: The Dynamics of the Jamaican Taino* (2006). One of the papers notes that the Wareika site is one of those difficult to access because it is in "a socially volatile area" (p. 36).

the Emperor's mounted army (l. 2): This imagines Rastafarian iconography showing the Emperor Haile Selassie resisting the Italian invasion of 1935-36. Whilst the image shows the white dead, the reality was that Ethiopian resistance fell under Italian military superiority (including the use of poison gas and dum-dum bullets); the Emperor was forced into exile in England, and a period of Italian colonial occupation followed.

chillum bubbling (l. 10): This is the ceremonial Rastafarian pipe for smoking ganja, as brought by Indian indentured labourers to Jamaica (though "bubbling" suggests this was a "chalice", a pipe with a water chamber to cool the smoke).

Ras Pedro (l. 11): As noted, he is a wholly fictitious character, but in addition to Count Ossie, elements of other actual persons have gone into locating this figure in the Jamaican landscape. In its Spanish flavour, the name echoes that of Rico Rodriguez (1934-2015), master trombonist who came from Cuba to Jamaica, who did once live in the Wareika encampment (and made a brilliant African-centric instrumental reggae album called *The Man from Wareika* (1977)). However, in the identification of Ras Pedro as a drummer and pioneer of the Rastafarian turn in reggae, the reference relates more closely to Count Ossie (see above).

sucks in his daily dreams and revelation (l. 14): These come via the strong sensi (sensimilla, see the note to ii, l. 53, below) in his chillum; smoking ganja is a sacrament, a parallel with Clarice's engagement with the spirit in church.

the posses in hiding (l. 16): This might include the Hot Stepper Posse (which had affiliations to the PNP), which in the JLP era of the poem was being hunted down by the armed police. See, for instance, Laurie Gunst, *Born Fi' Dead: A Journey Through the Yardie Underworld* (2003).

package pieces of pork for a joke (l. 17): An insult, because for a Rastafarian pork is unclean.

a fragrant offering to Satan (ll. 22-23): Although animal sacrifices were part of Jewish rite (see Leviticus 16), for Christian evangelicals they had been made unnecessary by the crucifixion, and their place in, for instance, Kumina rite was regarded as idolatrous and Satanic by Clarice's church. See the note to Chapter I, ii, l. 27.

shitty of Nineveh (l. 25): A neat combination of biblical resonance and Rastafarian wordplay.

rapid digital / bass-lines (l. 28): An allusion to the computer-driven techno-reggae pioneered by Wayne Smith (1965-2014) and the producer King Jammie, such as the track "Under Mi Sleng Teng", made using a Cassio keyboard (1985, collected on the album *King Jammie, A Man and His Music, Vol. 2: Computer Style* (1991)) that for a time drove acoustic session musicians out of the studios by using drum machines and synthesisers.

abomination (l. 29): A much-used term in the Bible (with 152 occurrences according to the Pentecostal United Church of God: < https://www.ucg.org/bible-study-tools/bible-questions-and-answers/what-is-an-abomination>), meaning something that is deeply offensive to God, something that crosses a taboo.

scotch bonnets [...] like red sentries (l. 31): A simile that draws on Jamaican botany (the fiery red peppers) and Jamaican history (the red-coated British soldiery who provided target practice for the Maroons).

he asks Jah for mercy (ll. 33-34): Jah is the shortened form of Jehovah in the King James Bible (see Psalm 68: 4), but Ras Pedro, like most Rastafarians, uses it to refer to His Imperial Majesty, Haile Selassie.

their horns/ piled in the broken shack (ll. 35): This is an image that links the biblical image of ram's horn trumpets at the battle of Jericho (Joshua 6: 1-27); horns (i.e. trumpets and trombones) as featured in the heavy classic roots reggae of Count Ossie and Burning Spear; and the goats that once provided skins to make Rastafarian drums – now all gone.

thirty exercise books and still growing (ll. 37-38): This is perhaps a sideways glance at the voluminous and highly idiosyncratic writings (mimeographed poems and tracts) of the nomadic Rastafarian artist Ras Dizzy (1932-2008) such as *A Prince Who is a Pauper* (1973) and *Rastafarians Society Watchman* (nd).

Queen of whores (l. 42): This is the Queen of England, Elizabeth II, as the archetype of Babylonian power, who came to open the new stadium built in Independence Park in 1966 for the Empire and Commonwealth Games. Ras Pedro draws on the Book of Revelation 17: 4-5: "And the woman was arrayed in purple and scarlet colour, and decked with gold and precious stones and pearls, having a golden cup in her hand full of abominations and filthiness of her fornication: And upon her forehead was a name written, mystery, Babylon the Great, the mother of harlots and abominations of the earth." Hear, too, the Heptones' song "Mistry Babylon" (Black Ark, 1977).

Bellevue (l. 45): The Kingston psychiatric hospital. See also Chapter XVII.

ii

sacrificial goats (l. 4): They gave their skins in willing sacrifice to be made into drums for praising Jah.

She saw Lot drunk and naked// his black snake nodding on his thigh./ Having seen, she was taken: (l. 6): In Genesis 19: 30-38, after his escape from Sodom, Lot dwells in a cave in the mountains with his two daughters, who make him drunk on wine "that we may preserve seed of our father", and lie with him in his drunkenness. Both conceive a child by him. Lot's wife had been turned into a pillar of salt in the departure from Sodom. There is a deliberate ambivalence here, in the last clause. As contemporary readers, we inevitably see Ras Pedro as criminal in abusing his daughter, but in the biblical narrative on which the passage is based, it is the daughters who engineer Lot's drunkenness and the incest, evidently with a degree of divine approval. At the least, reading the phrase in the double sense of "taken" (a sexual act against the woman's will/ to be attracted to something) makes sense of Clarice's apparent sense of complicity when she declares herself "delinquent and whore".

Clarice (l. 10): I.e she who has been gifted with the *clear eyes* of foresight.

fantastic designs from tattered fabric (l. 13): A description that could be of the kente cloth in which the poet would like to clothe Clarice. See Chapter VI (*Denial*) ii, l. 1.

strange tongues without prompting (l. 19): This implies an absolute genuineness of prophetic inspiration, whereas to some extent the speaking in tongues of the Pentecostal services involves choreographed moves towards the moment of glossolalia, and the suspicion that, for some at least, it is a self-willed, conscious (or even faked) activity.

Channel One Studios (l. 22): One of the essential recording studios (on Maxfield Avenue) of classic reggae and a record label of that name. Founded by Joseph (JoJo) Hookim, it opened in 1972 and pioneered the then most up-to-date recording facilities with a 16-track recorder. Its characteristic "Rockers" sound was an updating that remained true to the reggae essentials of socially conscious music. The label's house band was the Revolutionaries, locating it as part of the radical Michael Manley era. The studio closed in the early 1990s.

chant grounations (l. 24): From a grounding, a Rastafarian reasoning session, to be conducted sitting down, and hence close to the soil, though the "chant" suggests the ritual repetition of established truths. The phrase references both Count Ossie's album of that name, and Walter Rodney's famous book *The Groundings With My Brothers* (1969), based on his time at UWI before his expulsion by the Shearer government.

sucking caviar, champagne and custom-built spliffs (l. 29): For a time in the late 1980s, the centre of gravity of reggae production moved to the USA, with labels such as VP. More money came to artists, but some of the true consciousness moved out. See Kwame Dawes' poem "Meeting" in *Shook Foil: A Collection of Reggae Poems* (1997), where he writes of an encounter (possibly with the Wailers) in a New York hotel, and sees the "buffalo soldiers who have found/ a subtle marrying of yard with show-biz affluence" (p. 49).

a smalls of gratitude (l. 30): I.e. begging for small change, as in "Beg you a smalls".

righteous skirt (l. 31): As a Rastafarian woman, this would be modestly long.

cook ital (l. 32): This is to cook in the Rastafarian way, vegetarian (v/ital food) without salt.

constructs a new past (l. 34): A neat joke concerning the biblical narrative in which Lot's wife is turned into a pillar of salt.

she declares herself delinquent and whore (l. 43): This is the kind of language used in Jamaican child protection acts (Kwame Dawes' mother was a senior social worker), but an indication here both of Clarice's self-determination and her feeling of complicity in the incest.

her tongue now trimmed (l. 44): See the description in Chapter VI (*Betrayal*), i, l. 6-7: "Africa clogs thick in her tongue/ now twisting around King James' syntax" for the sense in which, for Clarice, though there has been social advance, there has been a reduction of possibility.

his future is written (l. 48): As an idolater, there is no saving her father from his inexorable journey to hell.

this interim (l. 49): A phrase that is used quite frequently in *Prophets* as indicating an empty moment, a limbo between times, a period of stasis. It is perhaps a homage to Neville Dawes' novel, *Interim* (1978), which imagines a revolutionary Jamaica and its defeat. See the "romantic interim" of Chapter XIII (*Sunday Morning*), l. 47.

Sensi (l. 53): Sensimilla, ganja bud from the female plant that hasn't been fertilised by the male, therefore seedless and strong.

discarded branch gathering dust (l. 55): See, too, the description of Thalbot's "branch" (Chapter V (*Sovereign City*), i, l. 10) – a play on the patwa name for penis as hood or wood.

another life caught in the/ bramble (ll. 59-60): A reference to Genesis 22: 13 when Abraham is saved from having to sacrifice his son Isaac: "And Abraham lifted up his eyes, and beheld behind him a ram caught in the thicket by his horns. And Abraham went and took the ram, and offered him up for burnt offering in the stead of his son [Isaac]." In this instance, it is Ras Pedro who is the caught ram. He thinks there is no sacrifice he can make that will induce Jah's blessings. Rastafarians were divided on animal sacrifice. Whilst the Ethiopian Orthodox church practised sacrifice, most Jamaican Rastas opposed it, since it was a practice connected to the more directly African-centric (Kongo and Orisha) groups such as Kumina, and also by practitioners of obeah, whom they also vehemently opposed.

his feathers drooping... dull filthy wings (ll. 64-67): This is an image that looks forward prophetically to how Thalbot imagines the downfall of Clarice in Chapter XXIII, xv, as the charred raven he has stoned to her death, whose "silver-black feathers/ flutter slightly in the breeze". The phrase also alludes ironically to Gerard Manley Hopkins' poem, "God's Grandeur" (1877): "Because the Holy Ghost over the bent/ World broods with warm breast and with ah! bright wings" (Gerard Manley Hopkins, *Poems and Prose,* p. 27). This is a poem Kwame Dawes returns to in his poem, "Shook Foil", in *Shook Foil* (1997), pp. 40-41. It is probably also an allusion to Gabriel Garcia Marquez' well-known magical realist short story "A Very Old Man with Enormous Wings" (1955) first published in English in *Leaf Storm and other Stories* (1972), pp. 105-112.

no Nile silver and blue to barge down (ll. 70-71): This is a loose allusion to the description of Cleopatra in *Anthony and Cleopatra,* Act II, scene II ("The barge she sat in, like a burnish'd throne,/ Burned on the water..."), an allusion also taken up by Derek Walcott in his play *A Branch of the Blue Nile* (1986).

the broken prophet (l. 81): As a prophet, Ras Pedro is broken because his vision of Africa can never be restored to reality. The phrase is also an allusion to the biblical commentaries that describe Elijah as the broken prophet (1 Kings 19: 2-3), who though victorious over the idolators of Baal, runs away when he is threatened by Jezebel with the same fate ("Then Jezebel sent a messenger unto Elijah, saying, So let the gods do to me, and more also, if I make not thy life as the life of one of them (i.e. the defeated Baalites) by tomorrow about this time./ And when he saw that, he arose, and went for his life, and came to Beersheba..."). Whilst Ras Pedro is rejected and surpassed by his daughter, she is later compared to Jezebel by Thalbot in XXIII, xv. Similarly, Hosea is described as "the brokenhearted prophet" because he feels abandoned by Israel.

CHAPTER XI
Infidelity

Summary

Last Night, still prohibited from being alone with Clarice (which they evidently ignore), has obtained a job as a janitor at an unnamed museum closely resembling the Institute of Jamaica, which as a youth Kwame Dawes would have been familiar with since his father was its director for almost a decade. The scene moves in several directions. It connects to Last Night's sexual frustration and his fanciful attraction to a wooden sculpture of an African woman, and to Clarice's jealous response to his confession of imaginary infidelity; it connects to the theme of Africa and the theme of infidelity to the African origins of the majority of Jamaicans; and it inserts Dawes's own family history into the narrative. The Baptist missionaries in the chapter make reference to Dawes' own grandparents who spent many years in Nigeria as teachers under the sponsorship of the British Colonial Office and several missionary societies. We note that whilst Last Night dusts the artefacts "without much regard/ for the disturbance of the spirits", he is nevertheless drawn to kiss the sculpted Masai woman and is "Transported for an instant to the outskirts of her village", though he ultimately resists this moment of poetic revelation by "praying like mad". This is about as far as Dawes will go in *Prophets* towards imagining that the breach with Africa can be healed. This particular piece of art is one that Dawes says has been in his family since the early 1970s when it was gifted to his family by an artist from Tanzania. (Information supplied by Kwame Dawes.)

Notes

i

is stored in crates and mothballs (l. 6): An apt image for the general distancing of Africa in the Jamaican psyche.

her cyclops eye, following him (l. 16): I.e. a single eye, as that of the cyclops Polyphemus with whom Odysseus fought in Homer's *Odyssey* (Book 9). Last Night, of course, guiltily imagines it is Clarice's eye observing him. (See summary above.)

Baptist missionaries (l. 20): Levi Augustus Dawes (died 1943) and Laura Ada Dawes (née Mills) worked in Nigeria as teachers sponsored by missionary societies and the British Colonial Office between circa 1911 and 1927, returning from time to time to Jamaica. There was also a great uncle, James, who went to Sierra Leone as a missionary, where he died in 1913. L.A.S. Dawes is recorded, for instance, as giving a talk on the progress of agriculture in Africa in his natal village, Sturge Town, in the rural and hilly part of St Ann. (It was named after the Baptist missionary Joseph Sturge. Founded in 1839, it was one of the earliest post-slavery free villages in Jamaica.) Kwame Dawes' father (Neville) and uncle (Winston) and aunts (Flo and Laura) were born in Warri, Nigeria, and were noted as returning to Jamaica in the *Gleaner* shipping news of 28 September 1927. (Information supplied by Kwame Dawes.)

like evidence of their travail with the heathen (l. 21): Whilst as Christian missionaries they would undoubtedly have regarded unconverted Africans as heathens, unlike the contemporary Pentecostal churches, the Baptist Dawes family always saw themselves as African Jamaicans.

Some obi's cherished protection (l. 24): An obeahman's talisman – like a Jamaican *gazung-fet* – but now used as a paperweight.

African-nosed (l. 26): A Kwame Dawes joke against himself. As he writes in a blog post: "in all the images I have seen of the grand ones [the grandparents], this lump of glorious clay seems impervious to the invasion of other genes" ("Are We Related?" 19 February 2013).

the harmattan of Sahara's season of dispersal (l. 39): See the note to Chapter III, i, l. 2. Here, though, the image is less one of connection but of entropic dispersal, a reminder that what the wind brings is dust, which is the fate of the African artefacts.

Transported for an instant to the outskirts of her village (l. 49): See the notes to Chapter VI (*Denial*), i. ll. 37ff., where the poet wishfully places Clarice in an African village. The suggestion that Last Night is drawn to make the same connection (with the statue as proxy for Clarice) is an instance of the fluidity of characterisation discussed in the summary for Chapter XV.

ii

spinning leaves (l. 2): Reading the tea leaves at the bottom of the cup. The ancient art of tasseography had evidently reached Jamaica.

sanctified by a sudden hallelujah (l. 10): The reader will have to decide how sincere or how hypocritical Clarice is being in displaying her quasi-wifely suspicions of Last Night's symbolic infidelity.

Them waiting, / always waiting... to come seckle dem conniving ways in (ll. 12-15): Clarice expresses the Pentecostal psychological theory of spiritual possession, of seeing Last Night as an empty vessel who has been swept clean of sin, but who is not yet filled up with sanctity, not yet a saint, and therefore vulnerable to invasion by malign conniving spirits, emissaries of the devil.

the pink and yellow / of her forbidden room (l. 21): See the later trope connecting Clarice with coral and seashells (Chapter XXI, *The Priest and the Prophetess Sin*, iii, ll. 11-13: "She slept in coral and shell/ and woke to the yellow/ of Annotto Bay").

in her temple/ with her satchel of penance and her chastisement (l. 26): A sly sexual double-entendre. What Clarice really wants Last Night to bring to her temple is his balls (satchel/scrotum) and cock (chastisement/wood/penis). Another instance of *Prophets'* fun with sex and sanctity despite the seriousness of its themes.

CHAPTER XII
The Fear of Prophecy

Summary

The chapter returns to the figure of the "I", the broken student who, in the prologue, inserts himself into the narrative as the recipient, like Last Night, of Clarice's support and generosity. In this episode, the narrator is terrified that what he thinks are his sexual misdemeanours will be exposed by Clarice, with her unerring eye for such hidden secrets. When they are not, he is profoundly grateful. Whilst the narrative does not say this, the reader knows that Clarice has her own secrets to hide. It is an episode balanced between confession (the weeping, the repentance) and a degree of questioning of the theatre of the church, which in this instance appears to be going through the motions ("sluggish worship time", "cacophony"), no doubt because of Clarice's preoccupations. As a chapter, it plays with the ironies of the roles of the omniscient author and the limited point of view of the experiencing, quasi-autobiographical "I".

Notes

the thing with the mango (l. 2): Which, in leaving its juice behind on the moustache, also points to the source of the maddening scent of sex.

Eden's infamous fig (l. 4): There has long been the theory that the forbidden fruit in the garden of Eden was not in fact the apple but the fig. Given the way that the cut inside of the fig has a fleshy resemblance to the inside of the vulva, then the knowledge of sex would appear to be a crucial aspect of what Eve introduces Adam to, which explains, perhaps, the myth of shame and the covering fig leaves.

Joseph leaving his manhood... Potiphar's wife (l. 7): This is a reference to the episode in the narrative of the Jewish exile in Egypt when Joseph (of the coat of many colours) is sexually entrapped by the wife of Potiphar, in whose house Joseph is a trusted steward. See Genesis 39: 6-18:

> And she caught him by his garment, saying, Lie with me: and he left his garment in her hand, and fled, and got him out./ And it came to pass, when she saw that he had left his garment in her hand, and was fled forth, / That she called unto the men of her house, and spake unto

them, saying, See, he hath brought in an Hebrew unto us to mock us; he came in unto me to lie with me, and I cried with a loud voice: / And it came to pass, when he heard that I lifted up my voice and cried, that he left his garment with me, and fled, and got him out.

Just as Joseph's coat is used as evidence of his guilt, so the student fears that the smell of sex on his moustache will betray him. This is a serious matter, since not only is extramarital sex strictly forbidden by the church (and the Potiphar story hints that Jennifer may be someone else's wife), but he and Jennifer have also evidently been enjoying oral sex – which is quite taboo for some religious Jamaicans.

as if to psyche her out (l. 19): An example of the playful ambiguity between the roles of "autobiographical" young man and poet as omniscient author. The young man cannot have known what is in Clarice's mind, though the poet who invents her private life does. This playfulness is deepened when we read Clarice's recollection of the scene in Chapter XXVI (*The Perks of Prophecy*), confirming that she has known just what was in the young man's mind.

my// fantasy, flaming with its startling detail? (l. 25): See the previous note. Here, the play with limited point of view and omniscience is even more ironically metatextual. What the experiencing "I" confesses – his sexual fantasies about Clarice – becomes part of the constructed narrative of the poem, just as Clarice's encounter with Last Night on the beach in Chapter XXI (*The Priest and the Prophetess Sin*) relates back to the prologue where the poet confesses to daring "to imagine her coupling/ in the blackness of the beach" (*Prologue*, ll. 46-47). We may note, too, how the phrase connects to Last Night's "My damning fantasy, what cling to my brain" (Chapter IX, i, l. 1), and to the sexual fantasies Clarice has as she watches the *Hawaii Five O* canoeists on television. In *Prophets*, characters are both distinct and sometimes fluidly interchangeable.

CHAPTER XIII
Sunday Morning

Summary

This chapter continues the previous one and returns to and expands Chapter I (*Introit*) in its focus on the memories of the "I" who is both a participant – a "bildungsroman" character in the narrative – and the poet/narrator who is outside it, revealing, at times, a metatextual hand, his writerly choices in making the poem. Here, he is the former student remembering in intimate visual and aural detail aspects of the campus with a fond but realistic eye for elements of both beauty and imperfection. This chapter looks forward to the closing chapters of *Prophets* in the way it functions as a lyric poem exploring the tension between beauty and squalor (bougainvillea and sulphur – with its whiff of hell), between images of spiritual liberation (the butterflies) and psychic imprisonment (the bamboo strangled by plaits of barbed wire). It returns to the "I's" experience of being both an intimate part of the service and its somewhat ironic observer, in the way that descriptions touch on both the ethereal ("the sermon flames its tongue of deliverance") and the corporeal of the "fanning flurry" of overheated worshippers and their grunts of possession and release as they hyperventilate to bring on the visions of spiritual possession. Above all, *Sunday Morning* enacts the inner conflict between the observing, creating poet and the would-be born-again believer. It does this in the way this chapter, structured like a lyric poem, creates metaphorical analogies between the observed natural scene outside the church and the rituals of the church service within it. There are the multiple images of *tongues*, connecting flowers, the glossolaliac tongues of the worshippers and the flames of Pentecost. The trees look like" starved acolytes" (l. 34), raising their branches in the same way as the worshippers lift their arms. The chapter records a crisis of commitment. Members of the congregation are quick to note the young man's "wandering eye" as a sign of loss of faith: "they think I have died inside/ unfeeling to the prophecy coming like the wind" (ll. 49-50). This lyric is an important clue to reading ambivalence as central to the whole narrative of *Prophets*. There is the experience described as a romantic interim; the oxymoron of the "life-giving bubble of indulgence" and the poem's return to the remembered experience in the last line: "I am saved again without a shot being fired". In many respects, this chapter is the most pivotal in *Prophets*, particularly when it is read, as it can be, as a work of spiritual autobiography.

Notes

tongues of yellow and speckled blood (ll. 1-2): This begins the sequence of tongue images: the wind that licks the shak-shak pods; the sermon which "flames its tongue of deliverance"; and the speaking in tongues (l. 41). These images reveal below their surface, variously, references to the blood of crucifixion, the fires of hell, the fiery tongues of Pentecost, and the rushing mighty wind that brings those tongues.

shak-shak pods (l. 11): The long seed-pods of the flamboyant tree, which rattle when dry.

chemical bottles, old film (l. 23): Possibly the remembered debris of some kind of photographic studio around the Guild Hall, but also a connection to the filmic trope of Chapter XV.

gungu vines (l. 24): A climbing shrub, *Cajanus Cajun*, source of pigeon or gungu peas.

coolie-plum trees (l. 31): A form of crab-apple, *Ziziphus Mauritania*, with brownish orange fruit, known as dunks elsewhere in the region.

overrun with butterflies (l. 35): The butterfly is a common image for the soul, as an image of transformation (see Marina Warner, *Fantastic Metamorphoses, Other Worlds* (2002, pp. 79-93). The image is carried forward into line 52, with its contrast between the spiritual and the very earthly (the cow shit). But see also the "women butterflying on the beach" (Chapter XXIII, viii, l. 24). In the conjunction of the butterflies and the fertility of the flowering/fruiting trees, Dawes is perhaps remembering/ alluding to the key passage early in Zora Neale Hurston's *Their Eyes Were Watching God* (1986 [1937]) when Janie has a vision of what love might be like: "She saw a dust-bearing bee sink into the sanctum of a bloom; the thousand sister-calyxes arch to meet the love embrace and ecstatic shiver of a tree from root to tiniest branch creaming in every blossom and frothing with delight" (p. 24). This merging of the erotic, the natural and the sacred (the sanctum) connects closely to the situation of the distracted student, torn between the pleasures of eros and saving his soul.

David from the wilderness (l. 44): This references the future King David when he is in flight from King Saul, who wants to kill him because he is jealous of David's military prowess. The reference is to 1 Samuel 23: 14 and David's seven years' of wandering, before his triumphal entry into kingship: "And David abode in the wilderness in strong holds, and remained in a mountain in the wilderness of Ziph. And Saul sought him every day, but God delivered him not into his hand." Here the allusion makes an ambivalent reflection on what the "I" gains from this moment of reverie. Is it an ironic take on the student's self-indulgent way of seeing himself as a lost soul in the wilderness, or does he indeed gain some moment of spiritual grace?

glowing for my indulgence (l. 45): A doubly ambivalent phrase. We have to ask: Is he glowing with spiritual radiance, or blushing with embarrassment? Is it the self-indulgence that Ephesians 2: 3 warns against ("indulging the desires of the flesh and of the mind [that makes the indulgent] by nature children of wrath"), or is it an indulgence in the sense of being granted some spiritual grace?

This romantic interim (l. 47): The phrase connects to and contrasts with the use of the word interim in reference to Ras Pedro's interim (Chapter X, ii, l. 50). There, "this interim is redundant; nothing new will come…". Here the interim is much more productive. It is a "romantic" interim in the sense, I think, of those Wordsworthian "spots of time", as in *The Prelude*, Book 12, ll. 208-10: "There are in our existence spots of time, / That with distinct pre-eminence retain / A renovating virtue…"

the voice of prophecy coming like the wind (l. 50): A reference once more to the New Testament narrative of Pentecost: "And suddenly there came a sound from heaven as of a rushing mighty wind, and it filled all the house where they were sitting. And there appeared unto them cloven tongues like as of fire, and it sat upon each of them" (Acts 2: 2-3).

The bright red blood… in the crystal decanter (l. 51): This is the communion wine for the eucharist service, and another image of the tension between spiritual mystery (the wine as Christ's blood) and the physical reality of the Wincarnis tonic wine that is used as its symbol.

the precious glass-bowl silence (l. 55): This condensed image expresses the sense of pushing back the intrusive, distracting noises of battered tambourines and the congregation speaking in tongues, to create a space in which something precious comes ("the life-giving bubble of indulgence"). There is, too, a visual resonance between the images of glass-bowl and bubble. But the glass-bowl image also suggests that his distraction is being observed by the congregation (as if he is in a goldfish bowl, lacking any privacy). Dawes is alluding to a passage in

Kamau Brathwaite's poem "Jah" (*Islands*, 1969): "and we float, high up over the sighs of the city,/ like fish in a gold water world// we float round and round/ in the bright bubbled bowl/ without hope of hook,/ of the fisherman's tugging-in root;" (p. 4).

I am saved again without a shot being fired (l. 57): At one level this refers to the previous episode where the student expresses his relief that his sexual adventurings have not been exposed by Clarice's prophetic vision; and more deeply, but tentatively, it expresses the feeling that there *has* been a moment of grace (he has been "saved" though in a different sense from the way the church uses the word) and though he may well have been "unfeeling to the prophecy coming like the wind", he has been reached by the (quiet?) voice that "carries clear over water". Since there is no water (river or sea) mentioned in the chapter, then we may assume that the water is allegorical, as in the "well of water springing up to eternal life" in John 4: 14, or the voice of Jesus walking on the sea who says to the alarmed disciples: "But straightway Jesus spake unto them, saying, Be of good cheer; it is I; be not afraid" (Matthew 4: 14).

PART TWO

CHAPTER XIV
The Making of a Prophet

Summary

This chapter goes back in time and to the narrative mode, to explain how Thalbot came to be the homeless madman expelled from the house being demolished in Hope Road and sent packing from the Castleberry's house by Clarice. The first section of the chapter again locates the narrative in the Kingston of the 1980s-1990s, an interim of decolonising energies burnt out, and sovereignty abandoned in obeisance to neo-liberal globalisation. The second section enlarges on the social and cultural manifestations of this era – its hedonism, the slackness of dancehall music, the prevalence of cocaine, prostitution, political corruption and the selling of the memory of Bob Marley as a piece of prime real estate. The third section concerns the position of Thalbot in this new world order, following the collapse of the Soviet Union. As the political loyalties of Jamaica become less crucial to US interests, what becomes more concerning to the USA is the spread of criminal activity into their imperial heartland. The relaxation of conditions for obtaining a visa to the USA, one of the rewards Ronald Reagan gave Edward Seaga for his loyalty, has the unintended consequence of giving entry to members of the criminal posses, as well as to the majority of immigrants seeking to better themselves in more legal ways. In Kingston, the once quasi-political gangs have got out of hand and now have their own criminal/entrepreneurial agendas. Some, when things get hot, take their organisations and criminal skills to the USA.

In a witty play on the narrative of the angels who help Lot escape from the wicked city of Sodom, the CIA (the angels who come from heaven/the USA) have come to give free passage to Thalbot to the USA, in return for information on the gangs. He, described as a fake Rasta, has evidently played some quasi-political role in the past. He is on the point of departure when the appeal of heaven dwindles and he thinks about what he will miss in Jamaica. Meantime his house has been burnt down in reprisal for his assumed informing, and, homeless, he loses his mind and becomes the madman we encounter at the beginning of the poem.

Notes

When an evil spirit [...] put in order (Epigraph): See the note to Chapter IX, ii, l. 20. This is Matthew quoting Jesus's words.

Parade, Parade Square: A park in downtown Kingston, on the site of former military parade grounds, properly St William Grant Park (in honour of a black Garveyite trade unionist of the 1930s), formerly Victoria Park – another sign of historical change in Kingston.

lignum vitae (l. 1): The national tree of Jamaica (*Guiacum Officinale*), with blue flowers, hard wood, all of whose parts serve medicinal purposes.

Gillespie-like (l. 12): A reference to the African American jazz trumpeter Dizzy Gillespie (1917-1993) who was famed for his elastic cheeks, which swelled like a ball when he was playing. Since the statue of Queen Victoria was moved at Independence in 1962 from its then prominent position, this is a Gillespie with deflated cheeks.

Marcus (l. 16): This is Marcus Garvey (1987-1940), the Jamaican prophet of Pan-Africanism, an inspirer of Rastafarianism with his message of return to Africa (though he strongly disapproved of Rastafarianism's earliest manifestations), who took his Universal Negro Improvement Association from Jamaica to the USA, where, at its peak, it claimed four million members. A prophet without honour in Jamaica during his lifetime, Garvey was finally made a Jamaican National Hero in 1969. His statue as a hero of Jamaica stands in Parade Square, but his message of African/ Black empowerment, as the verse suggests, goes ignored in the free-market 1990s.

ii

Who fa pum-pum, this is, Cabbie? (l. 13): Who is going to get my sex? (pum-pum=vagina).

rockus (l. 17): Raucous.

Knutsford Boulevard (ll. 18-19): An area of hotels and embassies in New Kingston near Emancipation Park.

Shabbas, Supercats, Cool Rulers (ll. 22-23): Shabba Ranks (1966—) is a dancehall DJ who was at the height of his fame in the mid 1980s, though his most popular album *Golden Touch* was released in 1990. By the mid 1990s he was out of fashion and dropped by his record company. Super Cat, an Indo-Jamaican with a "bad man", "don man" reputation, also known as Wild Apache (1963—) had many hits in the late 1980s with albums such as *Boops!* (1986). His career was given a boost by his version of "My Girl Josephine" on the film *Prêt-à-Porter* (1994), but for him, too, the 90s were a lean time. The Cool Ruler was Gregory Isaacs (1951-2010), one of the most popular singers of the 1970s and early 1980s with a mix of conscious songs and love songs. He was a founding father of lovers' rock (hear the album *Night Nurse*, 1982). Though Isaacs never really went out of style as an unparalleled singer of love songs, his career hit turbulence with crack cocaine addiction and prison sentences for drug-dealing and gun possession. He, too, was forced to earn a living in the Knutsford supper-clubs.

Payola (l. 25): The practice of giving bribes for favours – originally a scandal in the US recording industry where prominent radio DJ's took bribes from record labels to play their songs in the 1950s. According to Dennis Howard ("Payola in Jamaica: Illegal and unethical or standard practice", *Jamaica Observer*, 17 April, 2011), payola has been a major corrupting force between the record industry and Jamaican radio since the 1960s. No one has ever been prosecuted.

shared ideologies (l. 26): This references the neo-liberal, neo-conservative ideology of unfettered market forces and the downgrading of the role of the state in providing welfare services, as imposed by the IMF's structural adjustment programmes. These gave free reign to commercial elites and hit the poor.

bush jackets (l. 29): The style of heavyweight shirt, sometimes called the Kariba suit, elsewhere known as the shirt-jac, worn tie-less by the more radical Caribbean politicians as a sign of their decolonisation from wearing the formal shirt, suit jacket and tie of colonial propriety. After the defeat of the Michael Manley government, suits and ties returned.

"And *I* will feel alright" (ll. 40-41): A phrase from the Bob Marley song "One Love" (*Exodus*, 1977): "Let's get together and I will feel alright", used as an allusion to the cynical marketisation of Marley's memory.

Restoration Kingston (l. 42): A witty and ironic comparison between the post-revolutionary 1980s in Jamaica and the restoration of the monarchy after the end of the republican Commonwealth in England in 1660. In Jamaica, when the conservative JLP returned to power, some of the "ancient regime" whites returned, after the white and middle-class flight to the USA (as royalist nobles returned to England), and free-market capitalism took over from the quasi-socialist experiments ("socialist puritanism") of the first Michael Manley PNP government. In 17th-century England, the "Restoration", portrayed in most popular historical versions as a period of licence – sexual and cultural – after the puritanism of the Commonwealth, saw the return of aristocracy and wit (in the theatre of Dryden, Wycherly, Vanbrugh and Congreve), and the release of mercantile energies. The comparison is perhaps ironic in that only in the licence of cocaine and slackness and the opportunities for a small, politically favoured elite to make money does the comparison really hold good. Thereafter, the English "Restoration" settled into the constitutional compromise of the "Glorious Revolution" of 1689 and the taming of monarchical power. Dawes sees Kingston in the moment of licence before 1689.

shocking-out (l. 46): This refers to a sensually abandoned, body-shaking style of dancing, and to an Ini Kamoze (1957—) dancehall song on the album of that name, released by Ras Records in 1988.

boops (l. 48): A sugar daddy, usually an older man who "keeps" a younger woman. The boops weeps because in the new commercial climate, where women can market sex on their own behalf, they no longer need their keepers.

is pum-pum rule the world now (l. 51): A reference to the prominence of outspoken women DJs like Lady Saw (Marion Hall, 1972—), with her songs like "Life without Dick" (on *Raw: The Best of Lady Saw*, 1998).

flex out (l. 52): An allusion to Wild Cobra's 1992 song "Flex" from *Hard to Wet, Easy to Dry*, and the line: "Girl flex, time to have sex."

Dancehall gone Grammy and all (l. 54): As the centre of production moved to the USA, bringing some artists major financial rewards and show biz awards (the Grammy from the US Recording Academy), the cost of this crossover to a wider American and international market was perhaps most felt in the loss of the direct connection between Jamaican artists and Jamaican listeners in dialogue about Jamaican concerns. The 1994 Grammy for the Inner Circle album *Bad Boys* illustrates the process nicely. Once this had been Jacob Miller's backing band. Under Miller, the band sang "conscious", Rastafarian-influenced reggae. After Miller died in a car crash in 1980, the band moved to the USA and produced anodyne reggae fusion (with MOR pop and rock influences).

iii

Two angels with briefcases (l. 1): This episode is constructed around the narrative of Lot's dramatic flight from Sodom (Genesis 19) at the behest of two angels who tell him to flee the city because it will be destroyed. The biblical episode explains why, after their father offers them as sacrifice, to save the arses of the visiting angels, Thalbot's daughters are so keen to see the back of him:

> "And there came two angels to Sodom at even; and Lot sat in the gate of Sodom: and Lot seeing them rose up to meet them; and he bowed himself with his face toward the ground;/ And he said, Behold now, my lords, turn in, I pray you, into your servant's house, and tarry all night, and wash your feet, and ye shall rise up early, and go on your ways. And they said, Nay; but we will abide in the street all night./ And he pressed upon them greatly; and they turned in unto him, and entered into his house; and he made them a feast, and did bake unleavened bread, and they did eat./ But before they lay down, the men of the city, even the men of Sodom, compassed the house round, both old and young, all the people from every quarter:/ And they called unto Lot, and said unto him, Where are the men which came in to thee this night? Bring them out unto us, that we may know them./ And Lot went out at the door unto them, and shut the door after him,/ And said, I pray you, brethren, do not so wickedly./ Behold now, I have two daughters which have not known man; let me, I pray you, bring them out unto you, and do ye to them as is good in your eyes: only unto these men do nothing; for therefore came they under the shadow of my roof./ And they said, Stand back. And they said again, This one fellow came in to sojourn, and he will needs be a judge: now will we deal worse with thee, than with them. And they pressed sore upon the man, even Lot, and came near to break the door./ But the men put forth their hand, and pulled Lot into the house to them, and shut to the door./ And they smote the men that were at the door of the house with blindness, both small and great: so that they wearied themselves to find the door."

The references to **"angels... heaven"** is also a continuation of the confusion of the churchgoers described in Chapter III, ii, ll. 18-19 between seeking salvation and seeking a green card for right of entry to the more immediate heaven of the USA. There is, of course, the near pun between angels and agents (of the CIA) whose capacity for turning up unexpectedly rather resembles the reported behaviour of angels in the Bible.

heaven had been infiltrated (l. 6): As noted above, when the Jamaican state declared war on the posses who had got out of political control, a good many yardies found their way into the USA.

The Haitians (l. 10): Many refugee Haitians fled from the Duvalier dictatorships (father and son, both USA supported) in the 1970s, and then more fled from the military repression following the overthrow of the democratically elected president, Jean-Bertrand Aristide, in 1991. In their attempts to get into the USA, some were held at Guantanamo Bay (Cuba) as a successor to Ellis Island in New York Bay where generations of immigrants were, until 1954, held in transit, or prior to expulsion.

purgatory (l. 11): Guantanamo Bay is described as being the place of limbo between reaching heaven (entry to the USA) and hell (expulsion back to Haiti) – also as a place which is neither really American or Cuban.

Satan now a friend (l. 17): With the fall of the Soviet Union, one part of Reagan's axis of evil had gone, and the new Russian plutocracy were very evidently the most enthusiastic kind of capitalists.

wearing back their whites robes (l. 24): The image of the Ku Klux Klan, signifying the anti-immigrant mood of the USA.

the Jacob ladder (l. 28): These CIA angels entered Jamaica more discreetly than the angels who descended on a ladder from heaven to the dreaming Jacob. (Genesis 28:12: "And he dreamed, and behold a ladder set up on the earth, and the top of it reached to heaven: and behold the angels of God ascending and descending on it.")

not an invasion (l. 31): Unlike the invasion of Grenada, subversion of regimes the USA disapproved of could come in more indirect and hidden ways.

Pseudo-dread (l. 34): Thalbot is Legion (see Chapter II, l. 40) a man of many personas, a would-be informer, vagrant, prophet, and here fake Rastafarian.

milk and honey (l. 39): There are countless verses in the Bible that promise the Jewish people a land flowing with milk and honey, provided they obey God's word: "So I have come down to deliver them from the power of the Egyptians, and to bring them up from that land to a good and spacious land, to a land flowing with milk and honey..." (Exodus 3: 3).

this satellite of hell (l. 50): I.e. Cuba.

get a touch of the smart attack (l. 51): This was the kind of phrase the US military used during the 1990-91 Gulf war to persuade the media and public that their attacks had "pinpoint" accuracy because the bombs were so smart. This lie was then covered by the phrase "collateral damage".

like the rapture (l. 53): This refers to the belief amongst some Christian evangelicals that just before the apocalyptic "last days" come, true Christian believers (of their particular sect) will suddenly be seized (rapt) from earth and taken to heaven. The belief draws on Matthew 24: 40-41: "Two men will be in the field; one will be taken and the other left. Two women will be grinding with a hand mill; one will be taken and the other left."

sodomise their little rarse / right there and then (l. 74): An accurate translation in Jamaican patwa of what the men who hang around outside Lot's house have in mind when they ask Lot to send out his two visitors "that we may know them" (this is, after all, Sodom) and why in the biblical narrative Lot is presented as in some respects virtuous in proposing to send out his daughters instead.

one wave of the hand (l. 80): Like the angels in Genesis, the CIA men smite the posse with blindness – perhaps in these days using mace.

iv

Palisadoes (l. 1): The spit of land on the way from Kingston to the Norman Manley Airport.

v

burnt husk of his home (l. 6): No doubt payback from the "serious fellows" for acting as an informer.

Thalbot's spirit took in the voices of ghosts (l. 10): This is a flash-forward to the episodes where Thalbot is invaded by the spirits of characters who draw on aspects of the public personas of Don Drummond (see Chapter XVII), Roger Mais (XVIII), John Hearne (XIX) and Anthony McNeill (XX), the first a musician, the rest writers, all portrayed as images of the beleaguered and suffering artist in Jamaica. How these spirits come to invade Thalbot is predicted in the epigraph for Part

Two, taken from Matthew 12: 43 quoting Jesus's words on the opportunistic behaviour of wandering spirits (see the note to IX, ii, l. 20). Thalbot, having been emptied out of one persona (the would-be secret agent), offers vacant possession to others.

"I have heard them in the dead of night, coming" (l. 18): Whilst presented as a quotation that sounds like T.S. Eliot, I cannot track down any specific allusion, and Kwame Dawes himself can throw no light on the subject.

the vine shelter (l. 21): This refers to both the ruined house of Chapter V, ii and the vine/gourd (Chapter XXIII, xiv) under which Thalbot, as prophet, later takes refuge (see notes for that chapter).

his death-in-life in the whale's belly (l. 29): A reference forward to the Jonah figure Thalbot becomes in Chapter XXIII.

CHAPTER XV
Legion

Summary

At almost exactly the halfway point in *Prophets*, this chapter comes as
an interlude that draws attention to the various metatextual elements
in the poem: its dub version use of several biblical narratives (Legion,
Lot and the Angels, Jonah and the big fish, Elijah and Jezebel); the
referencing of the aesthetics of film that runs through the whole poem;
and the points at which the writer shows his hand as the "dub-organiser".
In Jamaicanising and deconstructing in cinematic terms the narrative
drawn from Luke, which gives an account of Jesus' casting-out of demons
from Legion and the demons' flight into a herd of pigs (the Gadarene
swine – see the note to Chapter II, I, l. 40) for the source), Dawes
writes his most daring (and, one suspects, in the eyes of some Christians,
sacrilegious) exploration of the tension expressed in the poem between
a yearning for belief in the miraculous at the heart of Christianity, and
the suspicion of theatre, even elements of tricksterism (see the critical
commentary, pp. 20-21), in the Charismatic/ Pentecostal church of
prophecy that is the principal milieu of the poem. Here Dawes takes
a narrative written as proof of Christ's divinity and subjects it to a version
that has Judas tastelessly debating the rights of pigs and the waste of
good pork, with interjections from some cynical movie-maker on the
best way to manipulate the audience's emotions through the use of
various cinematic devices. It is worth noting that Dawes' version is
not the first flippant treatment of the episode. In *The Merchant of Venice*
(1605), Shylock refuses Bassanio's invitation to dinner by saying: "Yes,
to smell pork; to eat of the habitation which your prophet the Nazarite
conjured the devil into" (Act 1, scene 3, ll. 33-35).

As elsewhere, the treatment of the Gadarene episode points in several
directions. The casting-out of spirits is, of course, central to the mission of
Clarice's church, and the psychology of Jesus's theory of the opportunistic
behaviour of malign wandering spirits is very much part of the church's
belief system. The focus on madness and the figure of "Legion" connects
in narrative terms to Thalbot and his multiple personas, but it also connects
to the more general fluidity of characterisation in the poem as a whole – the
way that the boundaries between "I", Last Night, Thalbot and Clarice are
quite permeable with respect to the themes of the poem. This is also part
of what the poem has to say about the instability of the person in Jamaica
at the time of its setting. The church itself is focused on the breaking down
and remaking of persons (the driving out of the "old man" and the born-
again new person); there is the fractured "I" of the student who is torn

between belief and doubt; the condition of Jamaicans stretched between the old selves of colonialism and the new selves of post-independence, and, specifically in the poem, between the conscious, justice-seeking selves of the revolutionary 1970s and the hedonistic, self-seeking selves of the new world order.

The position of the chapter is also metatextual in the sense that it invites the reader to participate in the deconstruction of a well-known narrative and focus on the constructed character of the poem itself – the choices made about narrative sequencing (its syntagmatic arrangement), and the decisions made at each point along that sequence (its paradigmatic choices) concerning, for instance, the choice of tone (elevated, ironic, cynical, uncertain) and the rhetorical devices the poem employs. The chapter also invites us to think about the poem's biblical sources. For a fundamentalist church, the narratives of the Bible are literal, gospel truth. The use of such references and versions in *Prophets* adds somewhat cynical insights to a more generally historicised awareness that the narratives in the Bible have been written, edited and collected with specific ideological goals – to present to the Jewish people their destiny as God's chosen; to persuade later readers of the Bible that Jesus's divinity has been foretold in the Old Testament, and that the miracles he performs provide proof that he is indeed the messiah. Yet, what *Legion* wants to suggest is that somewhere, within all the artifice, there is a miracle of some kind.

Notes

Legion: The episode in Luke (8: 26-33) is as follows:

> And they arrived at the country of the Gadarenes, which is over against Galilee./ And when he went forth to land, there met him out of the city a certain man, which had devils long time, and ware no clothes, neither abode in any house, but in the tombs./ When he saw Jesus, he cried out, and fell down before him, and with a loud voice said, What have I to do with thee, Jesus, thou Son of God most high? I beseech thee, torment me not./ (For he had commanded the unclean spirit to come out of the man. For oftentimes it had caught him: and he was kept bound with chains and in fetters; and he brake the bands, and was driven of the devil into the wilderness.)/ And Jesus asked him, saying, What is thy name? And he said, Legion: because many devils were entered into him./
>
> And they besought him that he would not command them to go out into the deep./ And there was there an herd of many swine feeding on the mountain: and they besought him that he would suffer them to enter into them. And he suffered them./ Then went the devils out of the man, and entered into the swine: and the herd ran violently down a steep place into the lake, and were choked.

mise en scène (l. 2): This means literally "to put on the stage", but here is used to describe the composition of the film set, the props, background lighting, the position of the actors and their movements (i.e. the aspects of film-making that are prior either to camera movements or the cutting and rejoining of film (this is pre-digital film-making) that takes place in the editing suite.

Pragmatic Judas (l. 2): In John 12: 4-6, Judas is picked out as a pragmatist when Mary Magdalen anoints Jesus's feet in the days before the crucifixion: "Then took Mary a pound of ointment of spikenard, very costly, and anointed the feet of Jesus, and wiped his feet with her hair: and the house was filled with the odour of the ointment." Judas objects and says, "Why was not this ointment sold for three hundred pence, and given to the poor?"

jerked (l. 6): The Jamaican way of cooking pork that goes back to the earliest Maroons of the 17th century, involving dry spicing, use of hot peppers and, originally, cooking over pit fires.

kosher miracle (l. 14): A gently offensive play on the meanings of kosher as "genuine" and as sacred to the Jews.

close in tight (l. 16): The close-up of camera movement or lens-adjustment to focus on small details, seeming to bring the object closer to the viewer.

Cut (l. 19): This is usually made in the editing process, to first select some segment of action, for instance, and then to juxtapose (in montage – literally the joining of one strip of film to another) one image with another, or one unit of action with another.

Trent-like councils (l. 18): The Councils of Trent (1545-1563) were the major deliberations when the Roman Catholic church established all the essentials of Catholic dogma in opposition to the Protestant reformation – i.e. this is as big a debate as can be imagined. On the practice and furore over the whitening of a blue-eyed Jesus in Hollywood films see the note to Chapter VI, i, l. 12.

zoom in (l. 22): This is a rapid camera movement that gives the viewer the illusion that it is they who are coming closer to the subject – a different effect from close-up where the image is brought closer to the viewer.

surround sound (ll. 25-26): This was first used in a Disney film of 1940, but was common in movie theatres from the 1970s onwards, with loudspeakers in the cinema surrounding the audience to give the illusion of moving sound or of the audience being in the middle of the action.

zombied theatre (l. 26): The viewers have had their independent judgements taken away by manipulative filmic effects, just as in its original sense a zombi was someone whose soul had been stolen so that they became an unresisting slave to his/her master.

pan now (l. 26): This involves moving the camera, usually on the horizontal plane, to either follow a moving object or to move across a still subject – as an alternative to making a movement by cutting and montage in the editing process. Fast panning blurs the image, giving the illusion of speed.

pigs... hogs... swine (l. 35): A reminder of the way the word choice manipulates our attitude to the referent.

handheld and unstable (ll. 47-48): Usually movie cameras are on stable mountings – in the old days on tracks – to ensure a jerk-free movement and a stable image. Using a hand-held camera, as part of the aesthetic of *cinema vérité*, is designed to give the illusion of immediate witness, or, as a cliché of horror movies, to suggest the disturbed and unevenly moving visual point-of-view of a frightened character.

SPCA (l. 51): This is the American Society for Prevention of Cruelty to Animals – though it was actually American Humane who established the code for the use of animals in films.

a stampede camera (l. 53): This was the kind of camera movement made famous by John Ford in *Stage Coach* (1939) where viewers are placed as if they are underneath the hooves of the stagecoach horses.

voice-over (l. 64): The non-narrative (non-diegetic) use of commentary on the action of the film, from outside the action. Used in classic films such as *Citizen Kane*, and as a technique of first-person narration in many detective *filmes noires*.

parting shot (l. 78): The often stable, middle-distance scene that viewers are left with when the action ends and before the final credits come up.

chopper shot (l. 87): Literally (or as if) shot from a helicopter, a shot that accentuates the fact that it is the point of vision that is moving and looking down – the kind of shot, used with such great elan, in Wim Wenders' *Wings of Desire* (1987).

golden ribbons... greying sky (l. 86): A reminder of how easy it is to manipulate mood through lighting and lens effects.

the steady-cam (l. 88): This is free-moving like the handheld camera shot, but made with stabilising technology that isolates the movement of the operator from the camera. First introduced in 1975.

CHAPTER XVI
Communion

Summary

This chapter returns us to the church for the Sunday morning service. It is a special service, a first Sunday, where communion is celebrated with breaking of bread and drinking of wine as symbolic of the body and blood of Christ. As a first Sunday, it is also marked by the arrival of worshippers from a sister church located in the countryside – a realistic portrayal of the kind of visiting fellowship such churches practised. Clarice's reputation as a prophet has no doubt spread and the chapter emphasises, again, that though she may deny it, Clarice is African-Jamaican through and through. As a plot element, the chapter prepares for the sequence of the chapters after XXI when Clarice's church go on a mission, making the journey out of Kingston to Annotto Bay on the north coast to bring salvation to the people there. Most importantly, though, for the plot, the chapter brings Clarice and Thalbot together, when he stumbles into the church and, for a time, finds support and healing at her hands.

Notes

first Sunday (l. 1): The first Sunday of the month; the celebration of communion in most Charismatic/Pentecostalist churches was not a weekly event.

the grey metal table (l. 1): A contrast to the elaborately dressed altars with rich cloth and gold or brass candlesticks of the Catholic and Anglican churches.

Wincarnis (l. 4): A sweet British tonic wine (it contained herbs – and at one time meat extract) fortified with spirits for long keeping, which was once popular in Jamaica. This is the communion wine symbolising the blood of Christ.

Hardo (hard-dough) (l. 4): A dense country bread, almost with the appearance of being unleavened, and therefore appropriate for communion, here symbolising the body of Christ.

three kings and two queens (l. 7): These are the "saints" from the sister church (like the three kings/magi who attend Christ's birth, but now with women in attendance).

pink and blue gabardine suits (l. 8): An indication of the visitors' unsophisticated country origins.

Antiphonal (l. 10): Call and response style.

the cup of salvation (l. 13): The cup containing the communion wine. See the note to line 9.

The blood that gives me strength (l. 17): This comes from the popular 1970s' hymn written by African American gospel singer, Andrea Crouch: "The blood that Jesus shed for me/ Way back in Calvary/ The blood that gives me strength/ From day to day/ It will never lose its power."

pastries of the loafer and chalice (l. 22): I.e. the communion plate for wafers, and metal chalice for communion wine of the Anglican and Catholic churches. These are delicate and refined in comparison to the images of yam mounds and heavy tumblers of a church that consciously rejects what it would see as the vanity and corruption of the established churches.

Warieka marl pits (l. 24): This is where Clarice grew up. See Chapter X. Marl is silty, clay soil, rich in carbonates, so it is dug out and widely used in agriculture as a form of lime.

lignum vitae (l. 24): The national tree of Jamaica. See the note to Chapter XIV, i, l.1.

mahoe (l. 26): Also a national tree of Jamaica (*Hibiscus Elatus*). The blue mahoe has flowers that change from yellow to deep red as it matures.

supple broken neck (l. 28): Because her Bible is opened so often at so many different places, in order to track down the relevant verse for quotation, its spine has been broken and become flexible.

now cutting through bone, marrow… (l. 30): This refers to Hebrews 4: 12: "For the word of God is living and active. Sharper than any double-edged sword, it penetrates even to dividing soul and spirit, joints and marrow…" The passage comes from an epistle insisting on the sanctity of the Sabbath, the urgency of repentance and the fate of those who hear the gospel and ignore it and neglect to observe the Sabbath. It is a favourite saying of the righteous, as in James Baldwin's *The Amen Corner*, where Sister Boxer warns that "The truth is a two-edged sword" (p. 70).

the word resurrecting Lazarus (l. 31): This references one of the central miracles in the life of Christ, the resurrection of Lazarus, dead in his tomb for four days (John 11: 1-44) until Jesus "cried with a loud voice, Lazarus, come forth./ And he that was dead came forth…".

The stone moving (l. 32): This relates to the time after Christ is taken down from the cross and buried in a tomb. When the two Marys visit the tomb the following day, it is empty, and in Matthew's version (28: 2 ff.) an angel is sitting on it, and he explains that Jesus is risen: "And, behold, there was a great earthquake: for the angel of the Lord descended from heaven, and came and rolled back the stone from the door, and sat upon it." It also references the African Jamaican spiritual, "Mother the great stone got to move/ Mother the great stone, stone of Babylon,/ Mother the great stone got to move…". The song has also long been associated with both the traditional African religions of Jamaica (African Zion) and Rastafarian hymnology. Some Pentecostal churches also perform this song during worship. See also Lorna Goodison's poem, "Mother the Great Stone Got to Move" (*Selected Poems*, 1993, p. 138).

this wind and fire (l. 35): The Pentecostal moment when the disciples receive the gift of tongues. See note to Chapter XIII, l. 50.

in the interim, in this lull/ between the spoken word and incarnation (ll. 36-37): In the service, this is the moment between the end of Clarice's prophesying and the point where the communion is celebrated in the words recorded in Matthew (26: 26): "This is my body…" It is a reference to the words of John 1: 14, which recount the movement from God's promise ("In the beginning was the Word"), to the point where Jesus takes on human form to fulfil that promise: "And the Word was made flesh, and dwelt among us, (and we beheld his glory, the glory as of the only begotten of the Father,) full of grace and truth."

drifting like a wind-borne newspaper (l. 39): On the surface this is an image of Thalbot as rubbish carried in whatever direction his madness takes him, but it is also an allusion to the mysterious way the spirit moves from John 3: 8: "The wind bloweth where it listeth, and thou hearest the sound thereof, but canst not tell whence it cometh, and whither it goeth: so is every one that is born of the Spirit."

Clarice points her finger to the dizzy / crows who dive nose first (ll. 44-45) and **the rain of crows from the sky** (l. 56): These are the vulturine johncrows (*Cathartes aura*) which hover high above the ground and dive down for carrion. They are Jamaican birds of ill omen, harbingers of death, ambiguously imaging Thalbot's fall and the death of the "old man" (qv, pp. 89, 95, 144) as he is cleansed of the residual malign spirits that have inhabited him. But when Clarice weeps and sees the rain of crows from the sky, does she see something more ominous, that relates to herself? It is an image that connects to and contrasts with the image of Clarice as the "mew'd" bird (the epigraph to Chapter II), her "caged" mind (IV, ii, l. 38), and later to the "charred raven [that] comes with meat in its beak" that Thalbot imagines he stones to the ground (Chapter XXIII, xv, l. 1) – all images of confinement, whilst this is an ambivalent image of freedom and falling. These supernatural and magical realist moments also echo intentionally the scene of the plague of robins that marks the return of Sula to Medallion after her long and controversial absence in Toni Morrison's novel, *Sula* (2004 [1973], pp. 89-90), which Kwame Dawes told me he was reading at the time of writing *Prophets*. Sula arrives back with a bad reputation, so that the fall of the robins is seen by the townspeople as an ominous warning. Since Clarice's later treatment of Thalbot (see Chapter XXIII, xi) is the most shameful of her actions, the association with Sula hints at a side of Clarice not so far seen, echoing the way Morrison displays Sula's coldness of heart in condemning her mother, Eva, to abandonment in an old people's home.

Thalbot falls (l. 48): As, of course, Last Night also did, the sure sign that he has been smitten by the spirit.

CHAPTER XVII
It is the Cause (Bellevue Ska)

Summary

Having been cleansed of malign spirits, Thalbot is now an empty vessel, with a vacancy for any other wandering spirits looking for a home. In this and the following three chapters, he is inhabited by the spirits of four iconic Jamaican artists, all of whom have been deeply troubled persons, afflicted both by their own inner demons and by the race and class structures and the Philistinism of Jamaican society. In these episodes, the poem explores the alternative inspirations of art and religion. It also reflects on issues of gender largely absent from the concerns of these artists in their time. On the one hand, there is the art-excluding religious practice of the Charismatics, on the other the attempts by these artists – one musician and three writers – to address truths about themselves and their society. Whilst each ultimately arrives at a point of failure, there is an elegiac quality about these episodes that commemorates their struggles.

For the "I" of *Prophets*, these are the existential choices he faces as a would-be writer and man of faith. As noted above, there is the moment in Chapter XIII (*Sunday Morning*) when the writer and would-be "saint" come into conflict when his poetic "wandering eye" takes in the landscape and pushes back from his consciousness the religious ardour of the congregation (see the summary and the notes for line 44 onwards).

The reflections on gender are more implicit in the sense that the reader must make the connections, but these are not hard to see. It is not just that these are men who, in the end, fail, but they fail in particularly gendered ways. The first, in attempting to assert control over the woman he loves, kills her when she resists. The second lives a life of bohemian public display in ways that were only available to men. The third behaves in a rashly provocative way that appears to be a manifestation of male pride. The fourth engages in forms of self-destructive risk-taking that seem more common amongst men than women. That is the analysis the reader is invited to make, and to see the comparisons between all the male figures in the poem and Clarice. Both Last Night and Thalbot are putty in her hands, and if, like the apparitions, Clarice suffers a defeat of a kind, it is in the cause of ascending to her completer womanhood. As is noted in Chapter XIV: "For is pum-pum rule the world now" (XIV, ii, ll. 51). Elsewhere in his writing (*Natural Mysticism* (1990) pp. 84, 230-235), Dawes shows a keen awareness that the 1980s were the time when women writers such as Lorna Goodison, Olive Senior, Erna Brodber and Dionne Brand made their triumphant entry into Caribbean writing to tell a different story.

In structure, this and the next three chapters resemble the way in which Dawes interrupts the narrative of his next narrative poem, *Jacko Jacobus* (1996), with a group of lyric poems about reggae musicians such as Winston Rodney (Burning Spear), Lee Scratch Perry and Sister Patra, seen as trickster figures for their attempts/ ability to hold together the gifts of prophecy with the commerce of earning a living from reggae. As such, these figures comment on the ambivalent, multiplicitous nature of the quasi-divine trickster figure and provide alternatives to the archetype of Jacko, the dub version of the prophet Jacob as told in Genesis 25, who founds the nation of Israel (Genesis 35) on the basis of the trick he plays on his father to steal his older brother, Esau's birthright.

The chapters that portray the four apparitions who possess Thalbot do a number of things. They deepen the historical focus of the narrative since their individual stories take us back to the 1940s. They reinforce our awareness that, along with everything else, the poem is a rich repository of the changing ways Jamaicans have expressed themselves through styles of movement, dress, dance, music, the reception of popular films, food and drug habits. Above all, they offer an ambivalent commentary on the very existence of the poem itself. Can it possibly hope to achieve more than the instances of sometimes heroic but flawed failure that these artistic ghosts provide? Whilst these portrayals of artistic, human failures sometimes appear quite harsh, they must be read in the context of what the poet has to say about himself – both as the broken young man who seeks solace from Clarice and her church, and as the writer who, in the last chapter, *Flight* (XXVIII), confesses that "This song has lamented like a spoilt child" (v, ll. 16).

Whilst none of the four artists is named in the poem, their identities would be very obvious to any Jamaican reader, so they are named here, with the absolute proviso that we recognise that these are fictive characters whose portrayals aim at aesthetic and thematic truths, not biographical ones. They are based on the public narratives about these figures, the gossip, myths, opinions, cautionary tales (and sometimes reality) that it was possible to hear around Kingston. These are figures where resemblances are intended as aids to plausibility, but where quasi-biographical portrayal makes no attempt to avoid variance with what factually based research would reveal. Where differences are noted between what is factual and what is in the poem, this is not to reprove Dawes for getting his facts wrong, but to emphasise the fictitivity of the detail. The other point to make is that in these four episodes, the actor is neither the referenced figure, nor Thalbot, but the hybrid creation of their flowing together, after the moment of inhabitation. There are moments, for instance, when Thalbot finds himself enacting Drummond, misreading the blast of horns, "the impatient expletives as applause;/ the rotten fruit, bouquets of roses" (XVII, i, ll. 68-69), when he returns to his old madman's game of directing the

Kingston traffic. Sometimes one element surprises the other, when the second apparition (referencing Roger Mais) is surprised to find that he now (as a pale-skinned man) enjoys the sun, but is puzzled to be thrown out of an upmarket jazz club (because he is now in the body of a black vagrant), whilst Thalbot is curious about why he has suddenly developed epicurean tastes in food.

The first of the episodes focuses on the tragic figure of Don Drummond (1932-1969), a superb jazz trombonist and one of the pioneers of ska, of Rastafarian and black consciousness in Jamaican music, some of the best of whose music can be found on the Treasure Isle *Memorial Album* and the Studio One *Best of Don Drummond*. But Drummond was also an unstable man whose conflicted relationship with his lover, a rumba dancer, ends in her murder at his hands and his incarceration and early death in the Bellevue psychiatric hospital. As indicated by the chapter title, "It is the cause", the narrative of Drummond's act of murder is read through the prism of Shakespeare's *Othello*. This invites us to recognise the class and racial dimensions of Drummond's tragedy: he was black, from a very poor family, raised by the nuns of the famous Alpha Boys' School, whilst his girlfriend, Anita "Marguerita" Mahfood, was light-skinned, from a fairly well-to-do Lebanese family.

Part i of Chapter XVII locates Drummond in two dimensions. Firstly, as the founding figure of so much of what has been vibrant, Afro-centric and prophetic in Jamaican popular culture (see the notes to Lee "Scratch" Perry – eccentric genius of the Black Ark studio, Queenie and Kumina (p. 189)). Secondly, the poem locates Drummond in a line of biblical prophet figures (David, Joseph and Elijah) who all very nearly came to grief at the hands of women, generally someone else's wife, sometimes innocently as in the case of Joseph and Elijah, sometimes as a result of succumbing to their desires as in the case of David. Here, in the parodic versions of the stories being told here, the chapter touches on the deeply rooted strain of misogyny in Jamaican popular art, such as when Bob Marley and the Wailers sing in "Adam and Eve" that "Woman is the root of all evil" and a group like the Heptones combine ethereal harmonies with disturbingly misogynistic lyrics such as in "I've Got the Handle" where the group sing, "So don't try to fight me, girl / 'cause you'll need first aid". Don Drummond is thus not only another prophet who falls, and a man whose desire to control "his" woman brings tragedy, but a figure whose actions have cultural resonance.

At the end of this first section, Drummond's ghost finds its way into Thalbot ("the spirit of Don the horn man reinvents itself/ in Thalbot" (ll. 79-80), a possession that takes place twenty years after Drummond's death. In part ii, Thalbot acts out his possession by Drummond until, in a repetition of history, he is carried away in a police van to the asylum.

Notes

It is the cause (Chapter subtitle): This is a very brief quotation from *Othello* (1604) Act V, Scene ii, when Othello enters Desdemona's bedchamber after he has been persuaded of her infidelity by Iago and the trickery of the planted handkerchief. As he enters, he says: "It is the cause, it is the cause, my soul,—/ Let me not name it to you, you chaste stars!—/ It is the cause. Yet I'll not shed her blood;/ Nor scar that whiter skin of hers than snow,/ And smooth as monumental alabaster./ Yet she must die, else she'll betray more men." The issues of jealousy and infidelity undoubtedly enter the Drummond story, since Anita Mahfood was married to someone else and there is some evidence that it was her decision to go out to dance against Drummond's wishes that provoked his murderous rage. Anita Mahfood's whiteness against Drummond's blackness is picked up in the last line of the chapter in reference to her "porcelain belly", which, of course, alludes to Shakespeare's Desdemona's "alabaster skin".

It is possible here that *Prophets* comes to *Othello* via two earlier allusions to the play in Caribbean poetry, which Dawes would have undoubtedly known. In Kamau Brathwaite's "All God's Chillun" in *Rights of Passage* (1967), the Uncle Tom figure is urged to "... bus'/ the crinoline off the white woman,// man, be the black buttin' ram/ that she makes you/ an' let's get to hell out'a Pharoah's land!" (*Rights of Passage*, 1973, p. 20). This, in its turn, is almost certainly a response to Derek Walcott's slightly earlier and differently disturbing poem, "Goats and Monkeys", from *The Castaway and Other Poems* (1965, pp. 27-28), which begins with the *Othello* epigraph "...even now, an old black ram/ is tupping your white ewe". The poem continues in the vein of Walcott's "A Far Cry from Africa", with Africa "a vast sidling shadow", and the Moor in the classical image of a horned monster, or the contemporary white and fearful image of Black Power: "was not his racial, panther-black revenge/ pulsing her chamber with raw musk..." (p. 27). Whilst Walcott's poem pulls back from what it seems to be implying, with the conclusion that the beast is "no more monstrous for being black", it nevertheless declares that: "Virgin and ape, maid and malevolent Moor,/ their immoral coupling still halves our world" (p. 28). Kwame Dawes' treatment of this *Othello* allusion is altogether more balanced in its contemporary treatment of the play's dynamics of sex and race, and certainly far from the tone of hysteria in Walcott's poem or the implicit misogyny of the counter voice in Brathwaite's poem who is urging the respectful Uncle Tom to fight back against white privilege by any means necessary – though we should not assume that the urging voice is the poet's.

Love is Earth's mission/ despite the massed dead (Epigraph): This comes from Anthony McNeill's poem, "A Wreath for the Suicide Heart", first collected in *Chinese Lanterns from the Blue Child* (1996, p. 17). The poem touches on the theme of love and disaster that encompasses Drummond and Mahfood, and Clarice and Last Night: "Somebody is hanging:/ a logwood tree/ laden with blossoms/ in a deep wood./ The body stirs left/ in the wind; If the wind could send/ its miracle breath/ back to that person,/ I tell you it would./ Love is Earth's mission/ despite the massed dead./ On the night of the hanging /the Autumn moon bled."

ska syncopations (l. 2): Jazz-inflected dance music that emerged in Jamaica in the late 1950s, a fusion of Jamaican folk styles such as mento with New Orleans rhythm and blues. It became ska when the rhythm changed to syncopation by a heavy emphasis on the off-beat. Drummond was the preeminent composer of original ska melodies when he played with the premier ska band, the Skatalites. Other leaders of ska bands included Prince Buster, Tommy McCook and Roland Alphonso.

rudies (l. 3): The rude boys, the creators of the rebellious youth culture that grew out of ska and the dancehall (which were sometimes dangerous places), that grew out of rapid urbanisation, unemployment and poverty in Kingston from the early 1960s on. As the subject of "moral panics" by the Jamaican middle class, the rudies parallel the teddy boys and later mods and rockers in the UK or motorbike gangs in the USA. A whole swathe of reggae songs addressed the rudies, either in support of their frustrated energies or condemnatory of their role in dancehall violence. See Garth White, "Rudie Oh Rudie" (1965) and the Trojan compilation CD, *Rudies All Around* (TRL 322, 1993) which offers a powerful cultural history as well as many brilliant songs.

helmet heads... singe of the iron (l. 4): A nice observation of how much the style of dancehall dress culture had changed. Photographs of the 1950s and early 1960s show young women with short, straightened hair (the singe of the iron) and skirts with slits up the front – but decorous in comparison to the batty-riders of later days.

bowed; bobbed (l. 6): The characteristic movement of ska dancing, caught in the jaundiced, middle-class perceptions of Alexander Blackman in Orlando Patterson's novel, *An Absence of Ruins* (2012 [1967]). Looking with the eye of an alien anthropologist at his own people, Blackman records:

their bodies bent from the waist, their torsos bobbing up and down in
an agile, repetitive bowing: necks stretching in and out like irate turkeys,
hands alternating between their thighs and their chins like panting long-
distance runners. Yet, despite the awkward angularity of their movements,
despite the appearance of an excessive display of energy, an innate sense
of rhythm seemed to smooth over everything making the dance something
beautiful to watch. Its vulgarity mocking itself, this ska, a droll, defiant
beautification of clumsiness. (p. 42)

eyes blazing like midnight riders (l. 7): A reference to Bob Marley's
song "Midnight Ravers" on *Catch a Fire* (1973): "I see ten thousand
warriors,/ And they are riding without horses…". Marley quite probably
refers to the Book of Revelation where John sees the figure of one
"like the son of man", whose eyes were like "blazing fire" (Revelation
1: 14).

blast of Django's gunfire (ll. 8-9): Django is the hero of Sergio
Corbucci's spaghetti Western of that name (1966) with Franco Nero
in the title role, very popular in Jamaica as indicated by Lee Perry's
instrumental album, *Return of Django* (Trojan, 1969).

Yallahs (l. 11): A coastal town in St Thomas Parish.

body of Queenie (l. 12): Queenie was Imogene Kennedy (c. 1920-
1998, born in St Thomas), a spiritual leader of the Kumina religion, a
faith brought by Kongo (Congolese) indentured labourers to Jamaica
in the 19th century. An interview with Queenie provided Kamau Brathwaite
with the epigraph and title for his trilogy, *The Arrivants* (1973): "Well,
muh ol' arrivance… is from Africa… That's muh ol' arrivants family…".
See James Early, "The 'Re-communalization' of a Jamaican Kumina
Drum" (2014).

Takoradi, Lome (l. 13): The first is in the western region of Ghana,
from where many enslaved Africans would have originated. Lome in
Togo lay between the slave-trading nations of Ashanti and Dahomey,
and was a disproportionate source of enslavement. It was also a centre
for Vodun practice, another connection with the Caribbean. Queenie's
spirit therefore goes back to origins. Dawes' maternal grandfather lived
in the city of Lome for much of his life, and Dawes as a child spent
several summers there with his family in the 1960s.

spray the rum … around the pole (l. 14): I.e. to offer libations to
the ancestors; the centre pole (the *poto mitan*) is common to most of
the Caribbean's African-centred religions – Orisha, Vodun, Santeria,

as well as Kumina – as the lightning rod to call down the gods. See Chapter XXI, ii, l. 11ff where Clarice is shown to have this power.

the ghost with cauled eyes (l. 16): Drummond was reputed to have been born with a caul – a sign of second sight. See Lorna Goodison's verse in her poem, "For Don Drummond", in *Tamarind Season* (1980): "Dem say him born/ with a caul,/ a not-quite-opaque/ white veil / through which he visioned/ only he knew." See also the note to Chapter V, iv, l. 17.

green vision of Addis Ababa (l. 16): This alludes to two of Drummond's compositions, "Green Island" and "Addis Ababa" (both Studio One, 1965) and to Drummond's Rastafarian sympathies.

Anita, the rumba queen (l. 23): Anita Mahfood (c. 1944-1965) was Drummond's inseparable lover in a relationship that was reported as tempestuous. She was, though, married to another man, a Honduran boxer. She was what was termed in those days an "exotic dancer", specialising in the "rumba" as a staple of nightclub performances. Cuba formerly offered, with its casinos and gambling, probably the richest pickings on the entertainment circuit, until the Cuban revolution of 1959.

Batista's Cuba (l. 24): Fulgencio Batista (1901-1973) was the corrupt, USA-supported Cuban dictator who was overthrown by the Cuban revolution.

Oh prophet, how can you see through// this haze? wails David... ghost of the Hittite... (ll. 30-31): David is the first of three prophet figures – followed by Joseph and Elijah – who see in Don D a fellow prophet and step forward to warn him that women and prophecy don't mix. The problem is that none of the warning stories, told in deliberately parodic versions, is quite true, so it is perhaps unsurprising that the prophetic trombonist ignores their warnings.

David, speaking of the smokey fug of the club through which Don D is staring at Anita, offers a cautionary Bible story about the dangers of seducing other men's wives. This is his story of his affair with Bathsheba, the wife of Uriah the Hittite. From his roof, he sees her bathing; as king, he sends for her, makes love to her (how willing she is is not disclosed) and makes her pregnant. David then sends for Uriah, who is away at war, and tries to get him to go home to make love to his wife (to cover up his adultery). Uriah, a righteous man, does not do this even when David makes him drunk. David then arranges with his military commander, Joab, that

Uriah should be left in a place of battle where he is likely to be killed. In punishment, God causes David's son with Bathsheba to die (2 Samuel 12: 18-20) – though David's second son with her, Solomon, evidently has God's approval. 2 Samuel 11: 2-18, 26-27 tells the story thus:

> And it came to pass in an eveningtide, that David arose from off his bed, and walked upon the roof of the king's house: and from the roof he saw a woman washing herself; and the woman was very beautiful to look upon./ And David sent and enquired after the woman. And one said, Is not this Bathsheba, the daughter of Eliam, the wife of Uriah the Hittite?/ And David sent messengers, and took her; and she came in unto him, and he lay with her; for she was purified from her uncleanness: and she returned unto her house./ And the woman conceived, and sent and told David, and said, I am with child./ And David sent to Joab, saying, Send me Uriah the Hittite. And Joab sent Uriah to David./ And when Uriah was come unto him [...] David said to Uriah, Go down to thy house, and wash thy feet. [...] But Uriah slept at the door of the king's house with all the servants of his lord, and went not down to his house. / [...] David said unto Uriah, Camest thou not from thy journey? why then didst thou not go down unto thine house?/ And Uriah said unto David, The ark, and Israel, and Judah, abide in tents; and my lord Joab, and the servants of my lord, are encamped in the open fields; shall I then go into mine house, to eat and to drink, and to lie with my wife? As thou livest, and as thy soul liveth, I will not do this thing./ And David said to Uriah, Tarry here to day also, and to morrow I will let thee depart. [...] And it came to pass in the morning, that David wrote a letter to Joab, and sent it by the hand of Uriah./ And he wrote in the letter, saying, Set ye Uriah in the forefront of the hottest battle, and retire ye from him, that he may be smitten, and die./ And it came to pass, when Joab observed the city, that he assigned Uriah unto a place where he knew that valiant men were./ And the men of the city went out, and fought with Joab: and there fell some of the people of the servants of David; and Uriah the Hittite died also./ Then Joab sent and told David all the things concerning the war [...] And when the wife of Uriah heard that Uriah her husband was dead, she mourned for her husband./ And when the mourning was past, David sent and fetched her to his house, and she became his wife, and bare him a son. But the thing that David had done displeased the Lord."

However, it is only after the first son dies and the prophet Nathan points out to David the reasons for God's displeasure that he expresses mild remorse. The details of the "wail" and the ghost of Uriah returning to torment David's conscience are inventions. David, in short, gets away with his crimes.

Bathsheba shed her skin (l. 35): I.e. she is bathing, naked. But of course it is her clothes she sheds, not her skin – a nudge to the reader to be wary of the story offered.

tampered testicles (l. 39): This references another story of a prophet's ill-luck with a woman. Joseph is put in an invidious position when the Egyptian Potiphar's wife takes a fancy to him and tries to take him to her bed. As the note for Chapter XII (ll. 7) indicates, what is here is an imaginative parody of the actual biblical version. There is nothing to suggest that Potiphar's wife gets anywhere near Joseph's testicles, and the "frisky righteous butt" is more the musical (*Joseph and the Amazing Technicolor Dreamcoat*, 1968) than the Bible.

"Don't do it!" says Elijah… (l. 43): This is a parody version of the travails of the Prophet Elijah with Jezebel, the wife of Ahab, who has seduced her husband's people to follow the false gods of Baal. After Elijah slays all the followers of Baal, Jezebel sets out for vengeance on Elijah who has to flee for his life into the desert (1 Kings 19: 1-3). There is no hint in the original that Elijah lusts after Jezebel – far from it!

Jezebel, whose flesh nourishes the dogs… (ll. 44-45): After Ahab becomes reconvinced that Jehovah is the only true god, Jezebel is thrown to her death from the palace walls and is eaten by dogs, so only her skull remains (2 Kings 9: 3-37). This is in fulfilment of God's word: "And also concerning Jezebel the Lord says: 'Dogs will devour Jezebel by the wall of Jezree'". This is a narrative connected elsewhere in the poem to Clarice and Thalbot. See notes to Chapter XXIII, xxii and xv, passim.

new jazz from the Alpha…(l. 51): This references the origins of Drummond's schooling in music at the Alpha Boys' School on South Camp Road, Kingston, an orphanage that also took in troubled boys. It was run by nuns who gave the boys an intensive musical schooling so that they could earn their livings in this way. Many of Jamaica's jazz and reggae instrumentalists came through this school.

the Cosmic (l. 57): Another reference to Don Drummond, also known as Don Cosmic, the title of one of his tunes on the Studio 1 label (c. 1960) and collected on the CD, *In Memory of Don Drummond*.

he guides the traffic (l. 64): This is Thalbot, smartened up by the church after his slaying by the spirit, but now inhabited by Drummond's apparition, who is directing the traffic like a bandleader directing his band.

after the secret burial… after the natty dreads capture the

tombstone (ll. 73-74): This refers to the attempt of some Rastafarians to seize the body of Don Drummond because they objected strongly to the fact that he had been buried according to Roman Catholic rites (the Alpha Boys' School was run by Catholic nuns). The incident also echoes a famous Don Drummond title, "The Reburial", which celebrates the return of the remains of Marcus Garvey from England to Jamaica and his reburial in Heroes Park in 1964.

kete (l. x): A high-sounding small repeater drum used in Rastafarian music.

ii

carried away like Bedward (l. 4): Alexander Bedward (c. 1859-1930) was a revivalist preacher who grew out of the Native Baptist church and attracted many followers to August Town. He was a crucial link between Paul Bogle, the executed leader of the 1865 Morant Bay rebellion, and Marcus Garvey. He preached a militant Christianity that was both anti-colonial and urged the cause of black pride. He was charged with sedition but sent to the mental asylum. On his release his support grew until he told his followers he could fly and they could fly to heaven, and began to claim that he was a reincarnation of Jesus. He was again incarcerated in the asylum until his death. Bedward is one of the subjects of Kei Miller's novel, *August Town* (2016).

"You pray tonight, Anita?" (l. 8): This is Thalbot speaking, in the spirit of Drummond, alluding again to Othello's speech as he enters Desdemona's bed chamber. See the note to the title of this chapter, above.

iii

The boys sprint in the interim (l. 1): Presumably the rudie fans of Don Drummond, the generation abandoned by its prophets.

smoky jolly buses (l. 2): These were the buses once run by the Jamaican Omnibus Service, who promoted the buses as Jolly Joseph's. During the first Michael Manley government the buses were nationalised, but as the economy worsened and investment in maintaining the service declined, breakdowns were frequent. The service was wound up by Edward Seaga's JLP government, to be taken over by privately run mini-vans and "robots". Kingston now operates a urban public transit system called Kingston Transit. The reference signals that this scene is happening in the past.

searches for its old vomit (l. 6): A reference to Proverbs 26: 11: "As a dog returneth to his vomit, so a fool returneth to his folly." A reflection that perhaps Jamaica has not learnt enough from the intervening years. Dawes might also have remembered the use of this proverb in James Baldwin's *The Amen Corner* where Sister Moore and Sister Boxer are fighting a battle conducted through "true" proverbs: "the dog is turned to his own vomit again and the sow that was washed to her wallowing in the mire" (p. 85).

Anita's wounds, like Caesar's/ sing their arias (l. 10): This refers to Shakespeare's *Julius Caesar* (Act 3, Scene 1, ll. 259-262) where Anthony, after the assassination of Caesar says: "Over thy wounds do I now prophecy–/ Which like dumb mouths, do ope their ruby lips,/ To beg the voice and utterance of my tongue". Dawes makes the point that whilst Drummond has been celebrated as an iconic figure, in a misogynistic climate his victim has tended to disappear as a person in her own right, though recently, in 2013, Mahfood was honoured by the University of Technology, Jamaica for her contribution to Jamaican music (*Jamaican Observer*, 31 March, 2013). There is in fact one Mahfood song on the *Don Drummond Memorial Album*, the haunting "Woman a Come".

CHAPTER XVIII
On the Road to Emmaus

Summary

The second spirit who inhabits Thalbot is very recognisably based on the public persona of the Jamaican novelist Roger Mais (1905-1955), author of the classic novels, *The Hills Were Joyful Together*, *Brother Man* and *Black Lightning* (all published in this sequence between 1952-1954). Prior to this, Mais had self-published two collections of short stories in the 1940s (*And Most of All Man* and *Face and Other Stories*), and wrote many verse plays, only one of which, *George William Gordon*, was published. Significantly, this play is about an estate-owning but radical mulatto who allied himself with Paul Bogle and the native Baptists and was vindictively hung on the slenderest evidence for alleged complicity in the Morant Bay rebellion of 1865. Mais was himself a light-skinned man, born into a fairly prosperous rural middle-class family. He admitted to having gone to Kingston to offer his services to the colonial militia to help put down the black working-class rebellion of 1938, but had a Damascene conversion to the cause of the poor and thereafter, for a time, threw in his lot with the nationalist People's National Party (PNP) led by Norman Manley and became part of the artistic intelligentsia around Edna Manley and the publication of the occasional literary journal, *Focus*. This, after the pioneering writing of Claude McKay (1889-1948) in the second and third decades of the 20th century, contained the first real expressions of a modernising literary culture in nationalist Jamaica.

In 1944, Mais was sentenced to two years in prison for sedition, for writing an article entitled "Now We Know" for the radical newspaper, *Public Opinion*. The article was blisteringly critical of Winston Churchill's hypocrisy in calling on the colonies to support the British war effort in the cause of freedom, whilst making it clear that Britain had no intention of releasing its hold on its colonial empire. However, it seems evident that in the postwar period, Mais' hopes for the possibilities of radical decolonisation in Jamaica were much diminished by the election of the populist conservative Alexander Bustamante and the Jamaica Labour Party in the 1944 elections, and by the turn towards street warfare between supporters of the two main political parties. In around 1951, Mais wrote another manifesto, "Why I love and leave Jamaica", which recounted how he had been spat at on the street in an incident which he read as an instance of wholly unjustifiable class animosity against himself as a self-evidently light-skinned, middle-class man by a poor black Jamaican. The Mais of this time who emerges from the papers deposited with the University of the West Indies archives suggests a much more conflicted man, whose touchstone had become "Art" and a lifestyle of bohemian privilege in place of his earlier, more radical, enthusiasms. Thereafter, Mais spent several years in France and England, only returning to Jamaica in 1955 when he discovered that he was mortally ill with cancer. He died soon after his return.

Nevertheless, Mais remains a significant Jamaican writer. *The Hills Were Joyful Together* is an incisive portrait of Jamaica on the cusp of modernity, and its focus on the historically embedded propensity for violence of both the Jamaican state and those who refuse to accept their poverty is important, in a disturbingly prophetic way. *Brother Man* remains current as the first genuinely sympathetic portrayal of a Rastafarian, who becomes a Christ-like figure in Mais' turn towards religious allegory. (Dawes' musical *One Love: A Dubaretta*, which opened at the Lyrical Hammersmith in 2006, is a reggae vershan of Mais' *Brother Man*). *Black Lightning* is not only Mais's most artistically realised novel, but an early exploration of the responsibilities of the artist in Jamaican society and a brave, if sometimes disguised, account of love between two men.

Mais' significance as the second of the wandering spirits in *Prophets* is located in the themes of the artist's relevance to, and vexed relationship with, the nation, and in Mais' case to his ambivalent relationship to the African majority of the Jamaican population. There is also his movement away from the political kingdom to religious allegory, and this locates him as an important precursor of the themes explored in *Prophets*, and to Kwame Dawes' personal deliberations about what kind of writer he wanted to be. In his unpublished essay, "A Brief Autobiography of an Ex-Playwright", Dawes records that "all my work was deeply religious and sometimes quite evangelical in its polemics. This was by design. I was then a very devout university Christian and I was committed to speaking of the cosmology of Christianity through drama." Mais is thus an important witness in exploring whether this kind of dual loyalty was possible – to religion and literary art.

Again, as I argue above (pp. 185-186), whilst the second spirit draws on what was known about Mais, it is not a biographical portrait, but a fictive exploration of a particular kind of problematic artistic relationship to Jamaica. It draws on Dawes' reading of Mais' fiction, and his reservations about some of the positions Mais adopted – such as the somewhat self-indulgent, self-dramatising streak in Mais's writing and public persona that presented himself as a sacrificial victim of Jamaican society – as well as a sympathetic awareness that the pressures that drove Mais from Jamaica in the 1940s were not so different from those that took Dawes away from Jamaica to the USA in 1992, when hoped-for employment opportunities in Jamaica did not materialise.

Notes

On the road to Emmaus: A reference to Luke 24: 13-32, which narrates how Cleopas and another disciple fail to recognise the risen Jesus on the road a day or so after the crucifixion, though they do so later when they invite the encountered stranger home to eat with them. The whole passage in the King James Version goes thus:

> And, behold, two of them went that same day to a village called Emmaus, which was from Jerusalem about threescore furlongs./ And they talked together of all these things which had happened./ And it came to pass, that, while they communed together and reasoned, Jesus himself drew near, and went with them./ But their eyes were holden that they should not know him./ And he said unto them, What manner of communications are these that ye have one to another, as ye walk, and are sad?/ And the one of them, whose name was Cleopas, answering said unto him, Art thou only a stranger in Jerusalem, and hast not known the things which are come to pass there in these days?/ And he said unto them, What things? And they said unto him, Concerning Jesus of Nazareth, which was a prophet mighty in deed and word before God and all the people:/ And how the chief priests and our rulers delivered him to be condemned to death, and have crucified him./ But we trusted that it had been he which should have redeemed Israel: and beside all this, today is the third day since these things were done./ Yea, and certain women also of our company made us astonished, which were early at the sepulchre; / And when they found not his body, they came, saying, that they had also seen a vision of angels, which said that he was alive./ And certain of them which were with us went to the sepulchre, and found it even so as the women had said: but him they saw not./ Then he said unto them, O fools, and slow of heart to believe all that the prophets have spoken:/ Ought not Christ to have suffered these things, and to enter into his glory?/ And beginning at Moses and all the prophets, he expounded unto them in all the scriptures the things concerning himself./ And they drew nigh unto the village, whither they went: and he made as though he would have gone further./ But they constrained him, saying, Abide with us: for it is toward evening, and the day is far spent. And he went in to tarry with them./ And it came to pass, as he sat at meat with them, he took bread, and blessed it, and brake, and gave to them./ And their eyes were opened, and they knew him; and he vanished out of their sight./ And they said one to another, Did not our heart burn within us, while he talked with us by the way, and while he opened to us the scriptures?

The reading of Mais's career through this passage from Luke speaks of the prophet who is not, and certainly thinks he is not, recognised or honoured in his own country. And though there is no doubt that Dawes regards Mais as a writer of importance, the use of the epigraph has a degree of irony in that Mais was inclined to present himself ("in typical melodramatic fashion") in a somewhat self-aggrandising way as a prophet with a divine mission. The road to Emmaus also, perhaps, suggests Mais's journey away from the political kingdom of the one-time seditionary to the author who roots his work in Christian allegory: John Powers as the Christ-like figure of *Brother Man* and Jake as a Samson figure afflicted with spiritual blindness in *Black Lightning*. Whilst Dawes' portrayal of the second apparition may be seen as critical of Mais' sense of self-importance, this doesn't, of course, negate the general point of the epigraph: that Jamaica fails to recognise its prophets until they are safely dead.

There is here, also, an allusion to T.S. Eliot's *The Waste Land* which is marked by Eliot's wilful "misdirection" in a note referring to the Shackleton Antarctic expedition (p. 79) when his lines point much more obviously to the Bible: "Who is the third who walks always beside you?/ When I count, there are only you and I together/ But when I look ahead up the white road/ There is always another one walking beside you/ Gliding wrapt in a brown mantle, hooded/ I do not know whether a man or a woman/ —But who is that on the other side of you?" (*The Complete Poems and Plays*, p. 73).

The second apparition (l. 1): Perhaps an echo of W.B. Yeats' poem, "The Apparitions" (*Collected Poems*, p. 386), which begins: "Because there is safety in derision/ I talked about an apparition" – though Yeats has fifteen apparitions to Dawes' four.

bearing promise of land in their beaks (l. 6): This refers to the doves in the story of Noah who return to the ark with evidence that dry land has been found: "And the dove came in to him in the evening; and, lo, in her mouth was an olive leaf pluckt off: so Noah knew that the waters were abated from off the earth" (Genesis 8: 11). In this instance, they are Caribbean birds, the white, long-necked egrets (*Egretta thula*).

his cancerous eye and muddy skin (l. 7): As noted above, Mais returned to Jamaica mortally ill with stomach cancer.

pale of the belly (ll. 9-10): Unlike Thalbot, who is black, the second apparition is, like Mais, a light-skinned man.

cultured things like cafes and wine at meals (l. 11): Mais was returning to Jamaica after fairly lengthy stays in France and London, where he evidently enjoyed playing the free-spirited bohemian. This image of Mais comes from the brief article by his friend John Hearne, "Roger Mais: A Personal Memoir", *Bim* (1955).

perpetual cigarette (l. 12): There is an iconic photographs of Mais with a cigarette drooping from his lips. A murder clue because the cigarettes possibly contributed to his cancer.

Sweet on Greek classic structures (l. 14): Mais wrote several pastiche "classical" Greek dramas such as *Apollo in Delos* and *Atalanta at Calydon* (both 1950) and his play "George William Gordon: A Historical Play in 14 Scenes" (published in *A Time and a Season: Eight Caribbean Plays*, ed. Errol Hill (Trinidad: UWI Extramural Studies Unit, 1976, but written in the 1940s), makes use of a Greek tragedy-style chorus. Karina Williamson reports how in an early draft of the play, the section of the chorus beginning "Black man" was originally titled "The Backward Brother" (online, "Re-inventing Jamaican History: Roger Mais and George William Gordon" (2002).

Achilles, Christ and Jason (l. 15): Christ is the John Power character in *Brother Man*; Achilles is more probably a sideways look at Derek Walcott's *Omeros* and his St Lucian fisherman character Achille. Jason is the leader of the Argonauts in their quest for the golden fleece. To the best of my knowledge, no Jason analogue appears in Caribbean writing until the searching character of that name in Geoffrey Philp's novel, *Benjamin, My Son* (2003).

his calling was a bolt from the blue (l. 17): As noted above, Mais was a member of the comfortable middle class who was about to volunteer to join the state militia to protect the status quo from black insurrection. He reported his sudden awareness of the desperate economic state of the black urban working class and turned away.

a three o three (l. 21): the rifle and bullet of standard British Empire issue, dating from the 1890s.

he did go blind for a minute (l. 23): An allusion to Saul/ Paul's conversion on the road to Damascus, where the persecutor of Christians becomes the early church's foremost apostle – though Paul's blindness is rather more extensive: "For three days he was blind, and did not eat or drink anything." This is part of the narrative of Acts 9: 3-9 where "a light from heaven flashed round him. He fell to the ground and heard a voice say…"

the lazy path of literary schizophrenia (l. 24): Playing on the idea of channelling other voices than one's own, Dawes alludes to the archetypal position of the writer in the Caribbean, who through origins and/or education is structurally part of the middle class, but who attempts to speak for the poor and the working class *without reflecting* on his own privileged position. Mais appears to have suffered a particularly acute version of this condition. It was not, though, an inevitable condition of writerly psychology. For instance, George Lamming addresses directly the discrepancy that access to education has created between himself as a writer and his character, Powell, with the powerful insertion of an authorial confession (Author's Note) that disrupts the narrative of his novel, *Season of Adventure* (1960, p. 330-332).

his return is unheralded (l. 25): This refers to the spirit's purely imagined second coming and his inhabitation of the again vacant Thalbot who is on the quayside begging for money ("transacting a smalls") from an old friend.

the change in tastes... (l. 30): The scattered biographical details of Mais' life record instances of a man who was very willing to borrow from friends to maintain a comfortably bohemian lifestyle.

his inexplicable eviction from the premises (l. 34): The second apparition inhabiting Thalbot is seemingly unaware that he looks like a vagrant black man trying to enter an up-town club with an exclusive door-entry policy.

At last the sun seems welcome on his skin. Nigger like this... (l. 35): This also alludes to the fact that Thalbot is black, whilst Mais was of the near-white middle class.

lives his fantasy (l. 38): This is the transformation of the pale apparition into the black and naked prophet (the form in which the reader has so far met Thalbot). This refers back to the phrase about literary schizophrenia. At last, the writer who has ventriloquised the urban poor has become the figure his fiction attempted to speak for.

"O city/ of desolate lanes..." (l. 42): A reference to Mais's novel *Brother Man* ("the tongues in the lanes clack-clack almost continuously" (p. 7)), and perhaps an echo of Eliot's images of urban desolation in *The Waste Land*.

barefooted/ and dignified as well-trained messiahs (ll. 44-45): It is evident that, in even in Thalbot's skin, the apparition gilds what he sees. Kingston's street prophets rarely appear so dignified and restrained.

embrace me now, I have returned renewed (l. 45): Returning in the 1980s, in the guise of a black man, the apparition inhabiting Thalbot hopes for a better reception than the historic Mais received, but as he discovers, revolution is now out of fashion.

but how casual they all seem about this treasure/ in their midst (l. 48): The apparition agrees with the thesis expressed in Kwame Dawes' then soon to be published monograph, *Natural Mysticism: Towards a New Reggae Aesthetic* (1999), which argues for reggae (with its "rooting of memory" in the enslaved past) as an uniquely national and post-colonial form and notes the way that the Caribbean middle class (including the literary middle class) failed to see how important reggae was as a form that created an authentic postcolonial aesthetic in its combination of the prophetic, the sensuous, the political and the spiritual.

prophecy [...] from the Bible (l. 49): As the critical commentary (see pp. 31, 40, 43, 94-95, 98-99) outlines, there is a substantial body of reggae steeped in quotation or allusion to biblical prophecy.

blind Tiresias (l. 50): This is the blind prophet, who spends seven years in a woman's body, who appears in *The Odyssey* and in many ancient Greek tragedies, and of course in Eliot's *The Waste Land* as the figure who "...sat by Thebes below the wall/ and walked among the lowest of the dead" (p. 69). In the context of the bodily transformations of this episode of *Prophets*, this is a particularly apt allusion. The blindness connects to Jake in Mais's *Black Lightning*, and the prophesying to the swine and mongrels alludes, perhaps, to the figure of Brother Solomon, the conflicted Rastafarian leader in Orlando Patterson's *The Children of Sisyphus* (1967), who deceives his dungle-dwelling followers with a promise of return to Africa.

Readers of Dawes' work will note that allusions to blindness abound, no doubt because of his own concerns with issues of sight directly related to his own struggles with eyesight and the history of blindness in his family.

the novels sell well these days (l. 52): Mais's *Brother Man* was republished in the Heinemann Caribbean Writers series in 1974 – no doubt because it was on the Caribbean schools examination book list.

giggle at the quaintness of his fantasies in prose (l. 54): One of the flaws of Mais's novels that most critics would agree on is his inability to portray man/woman love relationships in a plausibly realistic way (a sexism in his work that Dawes addressed in an essay, "Violence and Patriarchy: Male Domination in Roger Mais's *Brother Man*" (1994). There is also, at several points in Mais's work, a slightly titillating fascination with S&M expressions of sexuality, for instance, John Powers' quasi-martyrdom includes his being urinated on by an old woman. The other significant flaw is his failure to represent urban Jamaican patwa in an effective way.

the women seem tougher... they do not go mad in the streets... (l. 55): An allusion to the fact that in Mais's first two novels, leading women characters go mad in spectacular ways. In *The Hills are Joyful Together*, Rema goes mad and commits suicide by fire; in *Brother Man*, Cordelia experiences a similar breakdown and Girlie goes mad after stabbing the vicious Papacita.

New Day, new day (l. 60): An ironic allusion to V.S. Reid's novel, *New Day* (1949), which attempted to see the coming of a new Jamaica in the modest constitutional changes that brought adult suffrage in 1944. The Jamaica of the 1980s and 90s is undoubtedly a new day, but not such as Reid hoped or imagined.

He will talk it (l. 63): We are still in the era of dub poetry, but at a point of diminishing returns from the height of its radicalism and popularity of the 1970s.

sawdust in the new air (l. 64): I.e. in the post-revolutionary 1980s and 90s, the revolutionary dub poem is no longer a living thing. There is, perhaps, also a witty allusion to the majesty of Thalbot's "branch", his "wood" that so much impressed the passing women – now mere sawdust!

rising masses and swinging sickles (l. 65): A reference to songs such as Max Romeo's "Revelation Time" from back in 1975, with its lines: "Wedge up your hammer!/ Sharpen up your sickle!/ Revelation time" (collected on the 1978 album, later the CD, *Open the Iron Gate*).

the Castros, Gorbachevs, the Munroes (l. 68): These are all examples of the changing times of old revolutionaries after the fall of the Soviet Union. Castro lost the support Cuba had once enjoyed from the USSR's purchase of their sugar and Cuba entered a period of stagnation. Mikhail Gorbachev (1931—) was, of course, the last (reformist) "communist" leader of the Soviet Union, before his replacement by the pro-capitalist Boris Yeltsin. Trevor Munroe (1944—), a UWI-based sociologist, was the political leader of the Marxist-Leninist Worker's Party of Jamaica (WPJ). Although the WPJ's membership was never very large, its relationship with the left wing of the PNP and its support for the PNP in the 1980 elections was used as the excuse for an hysterical anti-communist campaign alleging that the WPJ was putting Jamaica in Moscow's hands. The WPJ disbanded in 1992 following the collapse of the Soviet Union. Thereafter Munroe became a social democrat and joined the PNP.

fish play tunnel games with old bones (l. 71): In Mais's *The Hills Were Joyful Together*, there are interspersed passages of poetic prose that have the general purpose of trying to distance in time and space the novel's claustrophobic social realist narrative set variously in an impoverished yard and the prison in Kingston, to transmute its realism into a more remote and timeless kind of art. One such passage begins: "The sea is an old man babbling his dreams" and it includes images of submerged bones under the sea where "the shin-bone pipes hollow requiems" – a reference to the bones of the myriad enslaved persons who drowned or whose bodies were thrown into the sea during the Middle Passage.

carved into art (l. 74): Mais moved away from a radical political position and realist aesthetics towards religious allegory and an art which is not bound by time or place.

long discarded poems (l. 77): Mais was a poet in his earliest days. Some were published in *Focus*.

they part ways (l. 84): I.e. Thalbot and the second apparition.

The spirit stays off the coast (l. 90): Quite possibly a dig at the poetry of Wayne Brown (1944-2009). His collection, *On the Coast* (1973) was criticised in some quarters as derivative of Walcott's poetry (see the further notes below) and Dawes himself had reasons not to look on Brown too kindly after the latter told him to burn his poetry. (See "A Brief Autobiography of an Ex-Playwright".)

it is too late for old prophecies (l. 91): Whilst Jamaican schoolchildren might be studying *Brother Man*, the religiously inspired (quasi-Rastafarian) social revolution that John Powers represents is long out of fashion.

...twist and tangle of sea grape trees (l. 95): These are images that, like the reference to a "green night" (l. 80) above, suggest that this is now the era when those who had been uncomfortable with the rhetoric of radical blackness, were able to find in the poetry of Derek Walcott (albeit through a narrow reading of Walcott's work) a vision in which the politics of race and social revolution are either not present or are, at the most, oblique. Walcott's first collection published outside the Caribbean was *In a Green Night* (1962); *Sea Grapes* came in 1976.

The spirit watches the seines curve... coming up empty (l. 96): The thrown nets (seines) of the fisherman standing in the sea. Another Walcottian image. "The Schooner *Flight*" has the verse: "and there, on that last stretch of sand,/ on a beach bare of all but light,/ dark hands start pulling in the seine/ of the dark sea, deep, deep inland" (*The Star-Apple Kingdom* (1979, p. 10). And in *Omeros* (1990) Achille says to Philoctete: "... no/ African ever hurled his wide seine at the bay// by which he was born with such beauty" (p. 233).

his vacated carcass (l. 102): Thalbot is now an empty vessel again, ready for a fresh inhabitation.

CHAPTER XIX
Equinox

Summary

The third apparition, whose separated spirit inhabits the vacancy in Thalbot after the departure of the second, the Roger Mais figure of the previous chapter, will be obvious to most older Jamaicans as a fictionalised portrait of the novelist and journalist, John Hearne (1926-1994). Like Mais, Hearne was a "white" or "red" Jamaican, the world of whose earlier novels, set in the imaginary island of Cayuna, is preponderantly that of the light-skinned middle and upper class, and, indeed, of the old planter elite. Hearne was unquestionably Jamaica's finest novelist of the 1950s and 60s, but both he and the world he wrote about came increasingly to be seen as irrelevant to the Jamaica of the 1970s that was painfully coming to terms with its majority blackness and the creolised African cultural heritage of its lower classes. Whilst Mais wrote predominantly, in his published fiction, about working-class black Jamaicans, his early death saved him from having to confront this changed world in any political sense. Hearne, by contrast, who wrote predominantly about elite, brown Jamaica, did attempt, at first, to engage politically with the new world, at one time being an enthusiastic supporter and journalistic writer on behalf of the PNP under the leadership of Michael Manley, whom he served as an advisor. In colour and class, Hearne and Manley belonged to the same social elite, both being also old boys of Jamaica College. But when the PNP espoused democratic socialism, established friendly relations with Cuba and sections of the party adopted the rhetoric and iconography of Black Power, Hearne evidently regarded this as a betrayal and switched sides. This was in a period when many members of the white and brown middle class took fright and abandoned Jamaica. For his change of mind and now virulently anti-PNP journalism, Hearne suffered a severe beating at the hands of PNP thugs when he unwisely attended a PNP rally. By the time of the 1980 election, he was writing a rabidly and sometimes quite hysterically anti-communist column in the conservative *Gleaner*, in support of the JLP. He wrote for instance that if Jamaicans didn't vote against the PNP, "they will never again have a chance to vote a governing party out of power... our homes may be taken", that the PNP would institute a "tyranny more certain and more efficient than that of the slave-master in plantation days" (*Daily Gleaner* 5 October 1980).

Thereafter (and before this period as well), his career shows a pattern of departures and returns to Jamaica, attempts to live off his record as an admired novelist through writer-residencies abroad, and returns when these proved financially and personally disappointing. As his daughter, Shivaun Hearne reveals in her painfully honest memoir, *John Hearne: Life and Fiction, A Critical Biographical Study*, John Hearne collapsed psychologically under these pressures and disappointments, began drinking heavily, suffered a stroke at an early age and lived out his sixties as an invalid, prematurely aged.

For *Prophets*, the figure of Hearne, whom Dawes encountered when Hearne taught for a time at UWI Mona, is another example of the complexity and pain of being a writer in Jamaica, of having to deal with the pressures and minefields of race, the Philistinism of much of the middle class and the virulence and violence of the politics of the 1970s and 1980s. The third apparition is acknowledged as unquestionably a writer of major talent (whose work warrants revisiting today, sixty years after it was written). He, like the second apparition, suffers the fate of the writer in a society that does not value its talent, who is destined, all too soon, to become a literary footnote. But the figure of the third apparition is not seen as blameless: he is charged with a too-comfortable acceptance of the privileges of his class and a too-easy admission of mild guilt over that privilege. Again, it's important to recognise the fictivity of the third apparition, based though it is on what was really no more than gossip (amongst the literati) in Kingston. Indeed, Dawes changes some actual biographical details (where Hearne's breakdown took place, for instance) to emphasise that what he writes is fiction.

Notes

Equinox (Chapter title): This is the time, twice a year, when the sun intersects the celestial equator (an imaginary projection of the terrestrial equator into space), when day and night are of equal length; so a point of in-betweenness, an "interim", which is where the poem sees the third apparition as located, somewhere between the old colonial world and the new – and unable to make the transition. The chapter itself comes at around the halfway point in the structure of *Prophets*. The title is also an allusion to Hearne's novel of 1959, *The Autumn Equinox*.

Charleston (l. 2): This is a fictive detail. Hearne never seems to have visited Charleston, South Carolina (unlike Kwame Dawes). In the mid-1980s, Hearne did leave Jamaica in pursuit of a series of writer-in-residence posts, mainly in Canada. It was on his return from Fredericton, New Brunswick, that he suffered a psychological collapse and was hospitalised. This, too, is the second imagined replaying of a previous event.

gabardine bush-jacket suit (l. 7): The uniform of a supporter of Michael Manley's modernising social-democratic nationalism, which the apparition has discarded.

the scars... still tender (ll. 8-9): As a one-time supporter of Michael Manley, who then became a harsh critic of his socialist turn, John Hearne was severely beaten by PNP thugs when he, some thought provocatively, showed up at a party rally in 1977 (Shivaun Hearne, *John Hearne's Life and Fiction*, pp. 71-72). This eerily echoes the incident in Hearne's first novel, *Voices Under the Window* (1955), in which the main character, Mark Latimer, a "red" Jamaican, who shares a good deal of Hearne's biography, is attending a political rally when he is hacked by a machete-carrying black demonstrator who mistakes him, as a near white, for one of the enemy. Latimer spends the novel dying and remembering his life.

drunk red nigger (l. 12): Hearne was a Jamaican white (he would have been black in the USA), who like many Jamaican whites also had African ancestry. A red man – a man of mixed race, like Shabine, the hero of Derek Walcott's poem, "The Schooner *Flight*" from *The Star-Apple Kingdom* (1979), who says, "I'm just a red nigger who love the sea". See above his daughter's acknowledgement that Hearne had a serious problem with alcohol.

Ward Twenty-One (l. 19): The psychiatric ward of the University Hospital of the West Indies – a connection, of course, to the first apparition, the Don Drummond figure, though he was incarcerated in the much grimmer Bellevue Hospital.

this poor West Indian... coconut tree splendour (ll. 22-23): The contrasting images locate the apparition in the gap between self-perception and the perceptions of others. For the American or Canadian universities, he is literally this poor West Indian looking to earn a little money as a writer-in-residence on the basis of a fading literary reputation, whilst the reference to "coconut tree splendour" alludes to Hearne's celebration of what he saw as the vanishing qualities of estate life in his Cayuna novels, a life of graceful pleasures and rich personal relationships amongst the bourgeoisie. Others, such as Sylvia Wynter ("We Must Learn to Sit Down Together and Talk About a Little Culture" (1969)), read Hearne's novels as an evasion of the social injustice and history of past oppression on which the gracious life of such estate was founded. See, for instance, Hearne's portrayal of the planter character, Nicholas Stacey in *The Autumn Equinox*, a celebration of a lifestyle that put him severely at odds with a spirit of decolonisation.

the insignificance of his return (l. 27): Hearne had been born in Canada, but with no real reputation as a writer there, crying "Home, Home" means nothing.

drooping head and shuffling gait (l. 32): The images in this and the following lines – the "stroke", the "tattered hat" – are a sad and recognisable portrait of a man familiar around Kingston in the 1980s, who, after the stroke, had aged rapidly. Whilst still alive, he has already become an apparition, the spirit gone.

The soul, long returned to the Gordon Town/hills (l. 40): We are to imagine that the bodily "Hearne" and his wandering spirit separate at Charleston, that the spirit makes its way to Gordon Town (in semi-rural St Andrew, not so far from Kingston) before it encounters the now vacant Thalbot, after the abortive entries into the cows and goat.

the self-righteousness... the insufferable posturing... his denials of the poor at the gate (l. 46): This is the inhabited Thalbot reflecting self-critically on his previous life. This is, of course, Dawes' critique of the Hearne of the Cayuna novels, whom he has elsewhere recognised as a fine novelist and writer of elegant prose, but an author who never manages to do more than express his unease over the privilege of his position without breaking from it. The "poor at the gate" alludes to Hearne's first novel, *Stranger at the Gate* (1956) and to Luke 16: 19-20: "There was a certain rich man, which was clothed in purple and fine linen, and fared sumptuously every day: And there was a certain beggar named Lazarus, which was laid at his gate, full of sores..." There is also an allusion to the parable of the wedding feast in Luke 14: 15-24, where a certain man invites the well-to-do to a supper and all find excuses not to come. The man instructs his servant: "Go out quickly into the streets and lanes of the city, and bring in hither the poor, and the maimed, and the halt, and the blind [...] For I say unto you, That none of those men which were bidden shall taste of my supper."

The turn to self-criticism perhaps reflects on the changes in perspective suggested by Hearne's last novel, *The Sure Salvation* (1981). See the note to "I wrote of the slaves and drivers" (p. 210) below. For Kwame Dawes' more sympathetic account of John Hearne as man and writer, see his introduction to the Peepal Tree/ Calabash reissue of *Voices Under the Window* (2005).

wronged helper conquered by the worm (l. 49): This makes the point that the dead, exploited servants (now euphemised as helpers) of the rich will derive no satisfaction at all from mere expressions of guilty conscience, or the platitude of death as the great leveller. It is also an allusion to Poe's poem, "The Conqueror Worm" with the lines, "…the play is the tragedy,/ And its hero the conqueror worm".

rotting colonial castles (l. 52): This is an allusion to Derek Walcott's poem, "Ruins of a Great House" (*In a Green Night*, p. 20) with its line, "Some slave is rotting in this manorial lake" and its conclusion, "All in compassion ends…", a comforting bypassing of the fact that the inheritors of the master and the inheritors of the slave still occupy vastly different and unequal worlds – a charge of complicity with that privileged world that the poem lays against Hearne's Cayuna novels (as well as against Walcott).

he recalls… (l. 55): This is the elderly, retired figure who recalls the old days of privilege rather than the hazards of negotiating blackness and the calls for social justice in the new post-colonial world.

Myrtle Bank (l. 57): The hotel in Kingston once patronised, exclusively, by the white elite. See the note to Chapter VIII (*The Changing of the Guard*), ll. 12-13.

Negril (l. 58): A resort of choice for the elite, on the west coast, before it more recently became a popular tourist destination.

Melbourne Park (l. 60): Formerly the home of the Melbourne Cricket Club in Kingston, formed in 1892, and though not a club of the expatriate white elite, in its origins, a club of the relatively privileged.

Caribbean Voices (l. 62): A reference to the BBC programme produced by Henry Swanzy between 1945-1958 that gave exposure and income to the exodus of Caribbean writers to London (Selvon, Salkey, V.S. Naipaul, George Lamming et al). Hearne was also in London between 1952-1956, but was only a minor contributor to the programme.

at the uniform (l. 66): Hearne served in the RAF in England between 1944-1947, an experience drawn on in his first novel, *Voices under the Window* (2005 [1955]).

the whores, the crude gentility of cockney lovemaking (l. 67): This alludes to the London passages of *Voices under the Window* (1955).

the pleasures of the old colonial class (ll. 71-72): As, for instance, propounded by Nicholas Stacey in *The Autumn Equinox*.

ii

ites (l. 6): The red of the tam (knitted hat) the young reporter wears.

I wrote of the slaves and drivers (l. 13): Hearne's last novel, *The Sure Salvation* (1981), written twenty years after the Cayuna novels, is set on a slave ship and presents a notably darker, less gilded view of the Jamaican past and its continuing impact on the present.

I had a black lover (l. 15): As does Mark Latimer, the white (red) hero of Hearne's first novel, *Voices under the Window*. It is an aspect of the unquestioning masculinities of the four apparitions that this third one imagines the young female reporter will be impressed by this claim.

iii

We (l. 1): Note that this is the voice of the poet as narrator, not the student character, who is speaking as "we Jamaicans".

Rhodes Scholars (l. 2): The now controversial award named after the imperialist Cecil Rhodes (see the "Rhodes Must Fall" campaign that began in Capetown, South Africa, and then went to Oxford University). Several distinguished Jamaicans such as Stuart Hall, Rex Nettleford, Mervyn Morris and Trevor Munroe received the award.

nailed-down intellectuals (l. 3): *Prophets* reflects on how Jamaica is forever at risk of losing its creative energies either through emigration (the "holy" Green card) or through tying down its intellectuals through the bureaucratic demands of university administration. Sylvia Wynter wrote an important essay, "We Must Learn to Sit Down Together and Talk About a Little Culture…" (1968/69) that starts with the observation that, whilst UWI was providing some berths for "nailed-down intellectuals", the Caribbean's writers were generally forced to leave.

the words that remain in the trees (l. 8): This is a neatly ambivalent phrase: on the one hand it is an image that indicates the presence of words that haven't yet made it onto paper and been published (wood/ trees as the source of paper) and as such are condemned to become clichéd and sour through verbal repetition; on the other hand, it is an image that alludes to the tree as the common site for affixing notices in the Caribbean, which become yellowed by time and increasingly ignored. This is the fate of the third apparition.

CHAPTER XX
Requiem for the Harrowed Poet

Summary

The portrayal of the fourth, final, apparition is different in several respects from those of the first three. They, as the notes to the previous chapters indicate, are fictionalised portrayals that draw on the known public personas of the unmistakeable figures of Don Drummond, Roger Mais and John Hearne. If there is a persona that the fourth apparition draws on, it is the very definitely legendary ("All this we heard like a rumour whispered"), as opposed to the actual biographical figure of the Jamaican poet, Anthony McNeill (1941-1996). McNeill was an extraordinary talent who, like his fellow writer apparitions, suffered from the indifference of all but a handful of his fellow Jamaican poets and almost universal puzzlement over his avant-garde aesthetics. McNeill also had a self-destructive streak that shortened his life through drug and alcohol abuse; and it is these often mythical narratives of self-destructiveness and their apparent consequence in silencing the poet that the chapter focuses on.

In the 1970s, McNeill published three collections that were well received, particularly by other poets, but in the following decade he published no complete collection. *Hello, UnGod* was published by a small U S Press in 1971; *Reel from the "Life Movie"* was published under Kamau Brathwaite's editorship of Savacou Press in 1972; and the Institute of Jamaica, under the editorship of Kwame Dawes's father, Neville Dawes, published his *Credences at the Altar of Cloud* in a beautiful edition in 1979. Though intensely involved with all aspects of Jamaican culture (his poems about Rastafarian figures in *Reel from the "Life Movie"* have been widely anthologised), McNeill's work relates much more closely to the New World American modernist tradition (from William Carlos Williams through to W.S. Merwin) than to the British tradition out of which most Caribbean poetry has come; it was far more modernist and experimental than that of any writer of his time, with the exception of Kamau Brathwaite, and McNeill was even, perhaps, an influence on the latter. There were aspects of Jamaica's discovery of its blackness and the vibrancy of its popular reggae culture with which he was deeply in tune, but he never allowed himself to be confined by the slogans of radical politics or cultural nationalism. One of McNeill's heroes was William Blake, and there is a sense in which he seemed to contrive (in the sheer volume and strangeness of some of his writing) to make his work as unpublishable as Blake's – and out of the same kind of estrangement with the times he lived in.

The apparition who inhabits Thalbot in this chapter is not the McNeill who wrote those outstanding collections, but the legendary figure who seems to have disappeared from public view at some point in the 1980s, with stories (who knows of what reliability) emerging from time to time that pointed to mental disintegration. The chapter is given the title of a requiem, but as the last stanza indicates, "no requiem for the poet [...]/just this quiet dozing and sleepwalking". McNeill was indeed still alive at the time of *Prophets'* writing and publication, but appeared to have fallen into terminal silence.

In the space of this absence, what the fourth apparition exemplifies is a typology of self-destructive failure, a type that was, sadly, too well known in Jamaica in the 1980s and early 90s, much of it connected with the plague of cocaine and crack addiction that destroyed the lives of a number of artists and public figures during this period. Here the chapter is less interested in the actual historical figure of McNeill and more in writing a Jeremiad about what Jamaica does to its brightest and best talents – and a lamentation concerning the streak of self-destructiveness that spread into the ranks of the gifted. As Barry Chevannes notes in an essay on "Crime and Drug-Related issues in Jamaica" (2001), whilst the ghetto dons controlled the trade, it was the "uptown professional and moneyed classes" who were the principal buyers.

Unlike the narratives of the previous inhabitations of Thalbot by the first three apparitions, there is no point at which we see the occupation taking place and there are no points of friction between host and uninvited guest. From the start we must suppose that the "he" of the chapter is already a fusion between the two.

An afterword on McNeill

At his death in 1996, McNeill left behind over twenty completed collections of poetry (which Peepal Tree Press is committed to publishing).

Before his death, McNeill put together his posthumous collection, which won the 1995 Jamaica National Literary Award, *Chinese Lanterns from the Blue Child*. Peepal Tree published this collection in 1998. Now, a new generation of writers is discovering his work and drawing inspiration from it.

Notes

Requiem for the Harrowed Poet (Subtitle): Perhaps Dawes was recollecting the title of one of Edgar Mittelholzer's Kaywana novels, *The Harrowing of Hubertus* (1954), an account of spiritual and psychological suffering. Literally, harrowing describes the action of the harrow, breaking up soil to a fine tilth after it has been ploughed. Dawes was possibly also playing on the sound echoes between "harrowed" and "hallowed".

i

Unhinged like this… the croaking lizards set up camp (ll. 1-9): These three verses merge the spiritually vacant figure of Thalbot with the image of the harrowed poet. The setting of a beach connects to Thalbot's situation at the end of Chapter XVIII (ll. 90ff) after his parting from the second apparition, when he is described as "spent / and void on the black beach// he languishes in the fishbones and guts / […] left by the fishermen". (We don't see when Thalbot and the third apparition part.) But the images of the apparently abandoned hut in which the "he"/ Thalbot is sheltering also suggest the situation of the silenced poet: "unhinged", "the soundless mouth", "the eyes boarded up", and the stench of the refrigerator horribly suggests the idea of someone rotting from within.

croaking lizard (l. 9): Actually a gekko, named for the loud sound they make at nights. With pads on their feet they can walk upside down on ceilings. (See Olive Senior, *Encyclopaedia of Jamaican Heritage*, p. 291.) Here a noisy contrast to the poet's silent mouth.

ii

He stands on Old Hope Road (l. 1): Thalbot as poet is back on his favourite street. The transformation of the wooden branch of Thalbot's penis into a chunk of tractor tyre indicates the merger of the two figures.

reams of paper in his fists (l. 5): McNeill, in legend, was famed for taking around reams of poems to his friends, and abandoning them at their homes. (In reality, his many unpublished collections were carefully organised and in good shape, with carbon-papered duplicates.)

a transport careening towards Nine Miles and the fabulous Heartease (l. 9): An image of blighted creativity. The lorry is moving towards the village in St Ann where Bob Marley was born. Heartease is a village in St Thomas and also the title of Lorna Goodison's third collection of poetry, published in 1988. The harrowed poet is stuck where he is and only the sheets of his poems – and perhaps his poetic gift – are flying away. In Lorna Goodison's three poems of that name, Heartease is fabulous because it is a place of the imagination, just around the corner, and never quite reached, but also a place that people don't know they are already standing in, a place of possibility whose directions could be pointed to by "singers and musicians" called out "by their hidden holy names" (*Heartease*, pp. 32-39).

The anthologists… mapping his fall from grace (ll. 14-21): An observation that some of the interest in the harrowed poet's work was less drawn by its integral merits than by the myths of his damaged public persona – and the possibility of making a parasitical career out of writing about it.

iii

the sting of pinewood and candles (l. 3): As if a coffin is being fashioned and a wake for the dead being held.

strangers in black (l. 4): These are evidently premature mourners, since the poet is not yet dead. We may deduce from the feeble singing, that these are not members of Clarice's church, but members of the polite middle class.

iv

immaculate like the conception (l. 1): I.e. like the Virgin Mary, who at her birth was freed from original sin because she would be the future bearer of Jesus – though one suspects that the poem probably refers to the misconception that the phrase applies to the virgin birth. The Immaculate Conception High School is one of the top high schools for girls in Jamaica, where McNeill taught in 1990, though the suggestion of misdemeanour is fictional.

Michaelangelo's David dipped in tar and grime (l. 3): Photographs of the young McNeill indicate that, like Michaelangelo's sculpture of David (1501-1504), he was an uncommonly good-looking man. The tar and grime take us back to Thalbot in Chapter V, i, where he is toning his skin with "gutter mud and motor oil".

reciting Hopkins (l. 6): Perhaps the harrowed poet was an enthusiast for the poetry of Gerard Manley Hopkins. Kwame Dawes certainly was, as *Shook Foil* indicates.

the ungodding of ungod (l. 8): This is an allusion to one of the repeated figures of McNeill's poetry, Ungod, a version of William Blake's Nobodaddy, Blake's satire on the figure of the jealous, vengeful Old Testament God, and in this case a no god.

Mary would have to be ten years old! (l. 13): A cynical comment on the oldest in years at which the harrowed poet thinks a virgin could be found in Jamaica. Another instance of the misogyny of these figures.

whiskey breath through the classroom (l. 11): The story went that McNeill had an unfortunate and brief period as a school teacher.

v

the ward (l. 4): Like the first and third apparitions, the fourth spent some time hospitalised in a psychiatric ward.

old prolific way (l. 6): McNeill, during the 1980s wrote, as he said, sometimes in a trance. It is possible that a good number of the twenty or so unpublished collections were written in a single year.

The poems are all reruns (l. 7): In McNeill's work there are poems that are repeated from one collection to another, but in strikingly different contexts – "all reruns" is poetic licence.

CHAPTER XXI
The Preacher and the Prophetess Sin

Summary

This chapter resumes the narrative focus on Clarice and Last Night and their church some time (weeks? months?) after they were last encountered in Chapters XII and XIII. In the interim, it is evident that Last Night, after his conversion in Chapter IV and his river baptism in Chapter IX, has risen rapidly in the church. This kind of progress is very possible in a church where members may be "born again" into sainthood through such external signs as being struck down by the holy spirit (literally falling to the ground), sincere and very public confession and contrition for past sins, baptism by immersion, the gifts of apt biblical quotation and speaking in tongues. Whilst it is not revealed immediately to the reader, Last Night has a new identity as the preacher who arrives to join Clarice in the mission the Kingston church has taken to the resort of Annotto Bay on Jamaica's north coast. It is evident, too, that despite their separation at the behest of the church elders, their attraction, particularly on Clarice's part, is far from dead. This and the next chapter represent both the high point of Clarice's spiritual triumph, and also the moment at which her fall from grace in the church becomes inevitable when the scandal of her "sin" on the beach becomes known. We see Clarice and the Preacher/Last Night responding to the event very differently: he in an agony of guilt, she in defiance.

Their action is read through three Bible narratives with very different implied attitudes and outcomes: a revisiting of the story of David and Bathsheba; the fate of Jezebel; and The Song of Solomon. The first two narratives point to the double standards and misogyny that contribute to Clarice's downfall. In this and the next chapter, *Prophets* probes the complexities of Clarice's character and her mission. The poem asks: why can she not have both spiritual transcendence and sexual fulfilment? Yet the narrative also suggests that there is an element of hubris, of recklessness in her behaviour, particularly in the institutional context of the church that has provided her with such a rapid rise in her personal fortunes.

Thalbot does not appear again until Chapter XXIII, but it becomes evident at that point that he, also a convert to the church (see the end of Chapter XVI, ll. 39ff), has also been present at Annotto Bay and has witnessed what happened on the beach.

Even more than in the scenes that took place on the Mona campus (see Chapter I, ii), the poem brings the spiritual yearnings of the worshippers into the same space as dancehall slackness at its most dissolute. Annotto Bay is presented as a place of stoned revellers, lewd DJs and sexually provocative dancers. It defines everything in the world of the flesh the church stands against, but the juxtaposition reminds the reader that worshippers, weed-smokers and dancers all seek some transport out of the limiting circumstances of their daily lives.

There is also a quizzical eye cast on how secure Last Night's passage into righteousness can really be, given the rapidity of his conversion and what we know about his sexual hang-ups.

This chapter returns to a cinematic style, the camera constantly searching for detail in colour and in action, to provide a vivid documentary of the times.

Notes

i

weed-infested buoys (ll. 7-8): This is, of course, a double, ingenious and suitably maritime and ganja-oriented pun for a seaside resort, playing on the patwa version of boys (bwoys).

tams (l. 8): These are the knitted hats designed to hold and cover a Rastafarian's locks (probably a shortening of the Scottish tam-o-shanter).

bogle (l. 10): A dance, see the note for Chapter IX, l. 19.

butterfly (l. 11): A sensual dance involving the movement of the knees in and out laterally, like the wings of a butterfly, throwing sexual emphasis on the pelvis. See also Chapter XIII, l. 35 where actual butterflies are both a source of distraction and symbols of the soul.

Supercat (l. 12): A dancehall star. See the note for Chapter XIV, ii, l. 22.

Shabba (l. 13): A dancehall star. See the note for Chapter XIV, ii, l. 22.

Flex! (l. 13): To show off. This refers to a song by Mad Cobra: "Love how the gal dem flex" (from the album *Hard to Wet, Easy to Dry*, 1992).

Dragon stouts (l. 16): A strong (7.5% vol.) and sweet Jamaican dark beer.

preacherman (l. 19): A naming that alludes to the popular image of the glib preacher on the make with a weakness for women, as in the "sweet-talkin son of a preacherman" of Dusty Springfield's song (*Dusty in Memphis*, 1969), or the Papa who was a rolling stone who, in the Temptations' song of that name (1972)," talks about saving souls" while "stealin in the name of the Lord"; or the 1971 film *Preacherman* about just such a character. A more nuanced portrait of such a figure, inspired and poetic in speech, but an inveterate womaniser, is Zora Neale Hurston's John Pearson in *Jonah's Gourd Vine* (1934).

handmaidens of the Lord (l. 22): A very ironic reference to the stoned dancers using Mary's words of agreement to the Angel Gabriel when he comes to tell her that she has been chosen as the virgin mother of Jesus. (Luke 1: 38: "And Mary said, Behold the handmaid of the Lord…") It is one of the most sacred moments in the New Testament.

close like the Red Sea (l. 24): This is a reference to Exodus 14: 1-31, when Moses, leading the Israelites out of slavery from Egypt, persuades God to part the Red Sea and then close it again on the pursuing Egyptians: "And the waters returned, and covered the chariots, and the horsemen, and all the host of Pharaoh that came into the sea after them; there remained not so much as one of them" (14: 28). Seeing the "handmaidens", whom tribes have passed through, in this way reveals not only that the preacher (Last Night) has sex on his mind, but also perhaps the temptation in the church to confuse what is desired with reality.

ii

red, gold and blue triangular flag (l. 6): A Christian flag where red stands for the salvation of the soul, gold for baptism in the holy ghost and blue for divine healing. Ironically, these, too, have been borrowed from the Afro-centric Revival churches opposed by Clarice's. (See Barry Chevannes, "Revivalism: A Disappearing Religion" (1978, pp. 1-17.)

pole in the balm yard (l. 11): An image that locates Clarice in the space between the dancehall (the huge sound-systems (speakers) pumping out ragga music) courtesy of the JPS electricity supply, and the Africa of the centre pole (the *poto mitan* in Haitian Vodun) where the electricity that connects the earth and heavens is divine. The balm yard is a place of healing in Kumina and Revival (see, for instance, Erna Brodber's novel, *Myal* (1988)). This is another of the areas of activity that connects Clarice's church to the very African-centric Revivalist churches that the mission has come to vanquish. Their similarities are something

Clarice's church would vehemently deny. Dawes points in the poem to what is irrepressible in the African roots of Jamaican popular cultural and religious expression. Africa is the referent of the "soil of ages".

God to man to woman (l. 19): This command is core to the gendered theocracy of churches such as Clarice's, though as Diane Austin-Broos observes in *Jamaica Genesis: Religion and the Politics of Moral Order* (1997), the reality of gender power in such churches is far more ambivalent than the official doctrine (see pp. 126-130). Whilst Clarice's style of dress signifies her modest deference to the preacher, as does her secondary role in warming up the congregation for his entry, it is clear that it is her preaching that wins the converts – and it is not, of course, how she treats him on the beach.

the curiosity of a crowd gathering around/ a swelling corpse (l. 21): An indication that many present are there out of idle curiosity, hoping to see the spectacle of people abandoning their bodily restraints in a state of spiritual possession.

O fallen idolatrous town (l. 22): This is a reference to Deuteronomy 13: 12-18, to the city of the Canaanites who, having followed false prophets, innocent and guilty alike, will be slaughtered: "Thou shalt surely smite the inhabitants of that city with the edge of the sword, destroying it utterly, and all that *is* therein, and the cattle thereof, with the edge of the sword." Clarice's church has evidently come to Annotto Bay *because* it is a place where the Revival churches such as the African Methodist Episcopal Zion church persist, churches that Clarice's church regards as idolatrous. What is portrayed in this and the next chapter gives a condensed version of the contrary fortunes of the American-oriented Pentecostalists and the Revival churches, the latter of which, according to Barry Chevannes' paper "Revivalism: A Disappearing Religion", suffered absorption into the former. See the critical commentary, pp. 32-38.

a dashiki and bandana (l. 26): The woman's dress suggests something of a mix between Revivalism and more modern links to Africa. The uniform of Revivalism was generally white linen garments, sometimes worn with coloured sashes. The dashiki is traditionally a male garment, and that she is wearing it suggests that her attire is an improvised Africanist stance, which was not unusual in Jamaica at the time. In other words, the outfit betrays a connection to Rastafarianism, whilst her red eyes suggest indulgence in either ganja or rum, and her "jigging" to "the bass and drum from the rumshop" to more contemporary dancehall pleasures. Whether Revival, Rastafarian or dancehall, she represents the idolaters that the mission has come to root out.

the whites (l. 27): Over proof and crude white rum, as used as libations in Pukkumina ceremonies – rites abhorrent to Charismatics and Pentecostalists as pagan.

eight spirits in her twisted soul (l. 29): This is a reference to Luke 8: 2 where Jesus is healing the sick: "And certain women, which had been healed of evil spirits and infirmities: Mary called Magdalene, out of whom went seven devils". The preacherman will go one better with eight.

iii

coupled like dogs (l. 2): The metaphoric and actual presence of dogs throughout *Prophets* (see: III, iii, l. 14; XVII, iii, ll. 44-45; iv, l. 20; XXII, vi, l. 11; XXIII, xv, l. 9) generally signifies something dire in the situation of the people involved. This resonates with a range of both biblical and Jamaican allusions, in almost all of which dogs have a bad press as creatures with disgusting habits ("As a dog returneth to his vomit..." (Proverbs 26: 11)); associated with uncontrolled sexuality ("An me shame like a dog with me something still / a stan up sameway", as Last Night confesses, IX, i, l. 50); or outcast creatures, eaters of carrion and feeders on corpses of those who have fallen in battle or who, like Jezebel (see note to Chapter XXIII, xv, l. 9), have suffered God's punishment.

sucked her teeth (ll. 9-10): A *cheupse*, the ultimate sound of a Jamaican woman's disgust. Subordinate Clarice may now be in the church, but she has not forgotten the days when she dangled Last Night in sexual torment in her house.

She slept in coral and shell (l. 11): This is the second association of Clarice with coral and shell. In Chapter VII, ii, l. 21, it is the "pink and yellow of her/ forbidden room", and see the more extensive note below for section iv, l. 35.

avocado and ackee... coconut oil (l. 21): As unctuous, rich foods, eating these is a sign of Clarice's sexual contentment, as opposed to Last Night's uncomfortable guilt.

iv

hymns of rejoicing (l. 6): The mission may be going well, but Clarice clearly, and hubristically, feels she has achieved another kind of victory.

ignited with revival... fallen at the altar (ll. 7-8): Revival here is used in the sense of the missions of conversion, conducted from the time of the 18th-century Methodists such as John Wesley onwards. At such missions, sinners are drawn to repent and often display their contrition and possession by the holy spirit by falling to the ground. The fact that the same word describes both what Clarice's church has come to do, and the Jamaican Revival churches that the mission has come to vanquish, indicates their blurring in reality.

Bathsheba (l. 16): Another reference to the wife of Uriah the Hittite whom King David seduces (see note to Chapter XVII, l. 36). Here the reference signals how the preacher searches the Bible for ways to soften his sense of guilt. Whilst David's and Bathsheba's first child dies as a divine punishment, David himself manifestly gets away with his adultery and proxy murder of Uriah – as Last Night hopes to get away with his indiscretion.

mongrel scavenging for bones (l. 20): An intrusive image that, by contrast, links Clarice with the fate of Jezebel, whose body is eaten by dogs (see note to Chapter XVII, l. 47).

swoop off the mountains (l. 29): An image of God's chosen people triumphant as the Israelites swoop down on the Philistines, and on Edom and the Ammonites: "But they shall fly upon the shoulders of the Philistines toward the west; they shall spoil them of the east together: they shall lay their hand upon Edom and Moab; and the children of Ammon shall obey them" (Isaiah 11: 14).

the word is being birthed in his heart (l. 30): An allusion to 1 Peter 1: 23: "Being born again, not of corruptible seed, but of incorruptible, by the word of God."

her ministry of shells (l. 35): This refers back to the image of Clarice on the previous night when she "sleeps in coral and shell" (iii, l. 11). It also alludes to Botticelli's painting, *The Birth of Venus*, in which the goddess of love rises naked out of a shell, just as – as the following chapter will develop – Clarice rises into her erotic selfhood. Much later in the poem, in Chapter XXIII, xiv, ll. 21-22, Thalbot, the abandoned prophet, shows how betrayed he feels by Clarice when he "patterns the sea bed with a landscape/ of pink-blue shells and smooth pebbles. // This is his mocking shrine". As Mercea Eliade writes, the shell has an ancient connection with female sexuality:

> Oysters, sea-shells, the snail and the pearl figure constantly in aquatic cosmology as well as sexual symbolism. They all participate, indeed, in the sacred powers that are concentrated in Waters, in the Moon and in Woman; they are, moreover, emblems of these forces for a variety of reasons – the resemblance between the marine shell and the genital organs of woman... (*Images and Symbols: Studies in Religious Symbolism*, 1961, p. 125).

The image of women and waters is picked up in the next chapter.

The preacherman looks to the hills (1. 48): He echoes the abandoned psalmist of Psalm 121: 1 who asks: "I lift up my eyes to the hills – from whence cometh my help?" The absence of wind is the absence of the Pentecostal spirit.

CHAPTER XXII
The Saints Return Triumphant

Summary

The true believers of the church (the saints) return from their mission to convert the idolatrous members of the Revival sects, practitioners of magic and Rastafarians. They bring back their converts as trophies to the mission compound and there is much rejoicing amongst the faithful – and an engrossing spectacle for onlookers. The chapter continues the focus on Clarice's and Last Night's continuing differences of response to the mission's triumph and their sexual encounter on the beach. He is guilt-ridden and, at first, cannot believe that as a sinner he can have anything to do with the conversions he is being praised for. In part, he genuinely believes he has been sinful, but remembering his problems with Thelma, the woman who can "talk / nasty about what she want a man fe do her" (Chapter IX), it is also clear that he has more personal hang-ups about sex. Only when the church service rises to a crescendo of spiritual upliftment and physical abandon is he able to shake off his doubts about his role in the mission's triumph.

The chapter further explores the ironies that underlie the church's mission against the idolatrous, because whilst they would deny any resemblance, the poem suggests that Clarice's church is deeply immersed in the same Afro-centric, bodily engagement with reaching spiritual transcendence. Whilst the Charismatics, in their Bible-rooted convictions, have no doubts about their fundamental difference, as true Christians, from those they regard as heathen, some of those they convert and the onlookers to the mission see matters differently. They interpret the church's (Clarice's) spiritual powers within the context of a creolised African belief system, and conclude that Clarice's triumph is down to her superior magical powers. In other words, they see her as an obeah woman. In truth, Clarice herself engages in the same kind of magical thinking when she convinces herself she must have God's forgiveness/ approval for her "sin" because of her success in making converts, and because, thus far, she has evaded any bad consequences for her actions.

Above all, the poem demonstrates the shared identity between victors and vanquished in section v, where the rhythms of the verse mimic the sound patterns of "labouring" (trumping) as the worshippers stamp, bend forward at the waist and groan ("Uhuh!") in a movement that brings on hyperventilation as the gateway to spirit possession. This, too, is a spiritual technique that has migrated from the Revival groups to become part of Jamaicanised Charismatic worship.

In part vi of the chapter, we learn of Thalbot's fate: that he has been present at the Annotto Bay mission, but that after his salvation and purification from evil spirits, he has descended into "the old madness" and has fled the scene around the mission to the seashore where we next meet him in Chapter XXIII. Clarice publicly accounts for his fall as a sign that God has not chosen him for redemption, though the narrative suggests that his madness has more to do with what he has witnessed on the beach.

The most important elements of the chapter, in parts vii and viii, focus on the central drama of *Prophets*, which is the conflict (which she triumphantly resolves to her own satisfaction) between the erotic and the spiritual in Clarice's rise and fall. Here, Clarice's narrative is filtered through a reading of the Song of Solomon (or Song of Songs), the poem's most important biblical text for arguing the common identity of the erotic and the spiritual as aspects of the transcendent. This is one of those points in the narrative where *Prophets* becomes most openly metatextual, in revealing the voice of the poet speaking quite explicitly on behalf of Clarice, in ways that she (as a matter of sociological realism) could not speak for herself. Here she becomes the figure of "constructed myth", rather than the prophetess encountered in "reality". But whilst this is a point at which the poem/poet speaks for Clarice and her desires, it also has to acknowledge that she is destined to fall foul of her church's restrictive and fearful attitudes to sexuality – the cause of her fall.

The last section of this chapter moves from resonances with the Song of Solomon to allusions to Shakespeare's *The Tempest*. Like Prospero, who with the aid of Ariel confuses the memories of those he shipwrecks on his island, Clarice would like to be able to use her powers to wipe Thalbot's memories of what he has seen on the beach. Like Prospero at the end of *The Tempest*, at this point Clarice must also give up her magic, her prophetic gift ("the hubris of her swelling visions" (XXII, ix, l. 15) and its rewards ("the saints gather at her door" (l. 17). As she passes into the complex state of her full humanity, no longer contemplating "absolutes; / the dialectics of good versus evil" (ll. 13-14), the poem leaves us with a more mysterious sense of being: "God is in heaven. Silent. The winds lift and move" (l. 18).

Notes

i

The Saints Return Triumphant. The title connects to the fourfold idea of the church as the church triumphant, the church militant, the church penitent, and the church expectant. The church triumphant signifies the congregation of saints who have experienced the beatific vision of salvation. The title also refers to the end-time that the early church believed was soon to come, as in Thessalonians 3: 13: "To the end he may stablish your hearts unblameable in holiness before God, even our Father, at the coming of our Lord Jesus Christ with all his saints." These are the three states of the Catholic Church as recorded in its Catechism. See Philip Kosloski, "The Visible Church on earth is only one part of a much larger reality", *Aleteia*, online (2017).

the children of perdition: This is about as bad a phrase as a Christian can use to name the damned. It makes reference to Chapter 17 of the gospel of St John, which records Jesus's conversation with God, telling God that he has completed his work on earth, and that he has left behind his disciples to carry on his mission. Jesus asks God to treat the disciples as being as much at one with God as he himself is. The specific reference is in verse 12 ("While I was with them in the world, I kept them in thy name: those that thou gavest me I have kept, and none of them is lost, but the son of perdition; that the scripture might be fulfilled"). The son of perdition is, of course, Judas Iscariot, the disciple who betrays Jesus to the Romans for thirty pieces of silver (Matthew 26: 15). This is an important text for a church like Clarice's, that sees itself as being the inheritor of the disciples, those who are the saved and whose duty is to convert others, in sharp contradistinction to those destined for the perdition of hell. In this passage (ll. 2-8), the children of perdition (the idolators the mission has come to save) are pictured as the Jewish people being brought out of slavery in Egypt and rescued from their idolatry by Clarice, as Moses rescued the Jews from the idolatry of the golden calf that Aaron had made in disobedience to God's instructions (Exodus 32: 1). They will then reach the promised land ("this fertile land of salvation") after passing through the divided Red Sea ("the parting of the waters"). See also the note to Chapter XXI, l. 24.

good tidings (l. 12): Famously, the words of the angel to the shepherds with the news of Christ's birth: "And the angel said unto them, Fear not: for, behold, I bring you good tidings of great joy, which shall be to all people" (Luke 2: 10).

displayed like the spoils of war (l. 14): Another echo of the church triumphant, since the Latin word *triumphans* refers to the imperial Roman victory parades, when they brought back conquered people as captives to be sold as slaves.

freshly heaved from black water of St Thomas in the East (ll. 15-16): This is a witty reference to Matthew 4: 19, when he reports Jesus saying to the disciples, "Follow me, and I will make you fishers of men." The allusion is of course continued in the image of the saved, like landed fish, "mouths still gasping for air".

How the mighty have fallen (l. 16): A reference to Samuel 1: 19, where David laments the slaying of Saul and Jonathan: "A gazelle lies slain on your heights, Israel. How the mighty have fallen."

ii

puss eyes (l. 2): She has eyes like a cat's, but there is also a pun on pussy, the tool of her trade.

a gig unleashed (l. 4): She's whirling round like a spinning top; a "gig" is the old and now obsolete (in British English) word, which has survived in Jamaican English.

the thrashing floor (l. 6): Originally, literally, the floor of the barn where wheat was threshed with a flail, dividing the wheat grain from the chaff, but widely used as a metaphor in the Bible to signify a place of lamentations and the place where the saved and unsaved are separated. In some Caribbean evangelical and Revival churches, there is a place in the church designated as the threshing floor on which the repentant would lie to bewail their sins. In the first sense of a place of lamentation, see Genesis 50: 10-11: "they came to the threshing floor of Atad... they lamented there with a very great and sorrowful lamentation", or Isaiah 21: 10: "O my threshed people, and my afflicted of the threshing floor". In the second sense of separating the saved from the damned, see Matthew 3: 12: "His winnowing fork in his hand, and he will thoroughly clear his threshing floor, and he will gather the wheat into his barn, but will burn up the chaff with unquenchable fire."

nyah queen (l. 7): This is an abbreviation for Nyabinghi, one of the earliest and most African-oriented of Rastafarian groups, who took their inspiration for wearing uncut, matted or braided dreadlocks from photographs (c. 1930s) of Nyabinghi "cult" members fighting colonial rule in Uganda. See Barry Chevannes, *Rastafari: Roots and Ideology* (1994, p. 43).

the twitch in her tight jaw (l. 10): The powers that hold Sandra, the Rasta woman, are a far from willing to give up their conquest, and in the eyes of the congregation she is still fighting her way out of the devil's clutches, "evading the jabs of the evil one."

Broad-mouthed (l. 19): This signifies both the woman's outspokenness and her African appearance.

sprinkled her dust at the feet of God's messenger (ll. 19-20): Merle, the obeah woman, attempts to use magic to defeat the missionaries, a kind of reversal of the advice that Matthew gives to gospel proselytisers: "And whosoever shall not receive you, nor hear your words, when ye depart out of that house or city, shake off the dust of your feet." (Matthew 10: 14). There is also an echo of the scene in *The Color Purple* where Celie curses Mr ——— and "A dust devil flew up on the porch between us, fill my mouth with dirt. The dirt say, Anything you do to me, already done to you" (1983, p. 176).

invisible zombies/ to hurl stones (ll. 20-21): Used in the original Caribbean/ African sense of a dead person brought back to life, whose soul has been stolen, who becomes the slave of his or her possessor. This is conflated with the popular belief in the presence of invisible duppies who are responsible for poltergeist activities, principally the apparently otherwise inexplicable throwing of stones onto the tin roofs of houses. But see the previous chapter where "The zinc roofs are strewn with bricks, stones, and twigs / tossed there by boys stoning the mango trees" (XXI, iv, ll. 10-11).

croaking lizard (l. 24): See note to Chapter XX, i, l. 9. The reference to Merle's power over men connects her with Clarice in important ways. They find an affinity that pushes against patriarchal structures, though Clarice is only just beginning to recognise this. It is a power that rests in the authority of their personalities and the spiritual energies each can summon. There is also something of Toni Morrison's Sula in Merle.

her satchel of plagues and pestilence (l. 26): This is an image that conflates Merle with Pandora and the box of plagues she opens, and the ten plagues (from water into blood and frogs, to the death of the first-born) that God inflicts on Egypt to persuade the Pharoah to release the Israelites from slavery. (See Exodus, 7: 14ff, 7: 25 ff, 8: 16 ff, 9: 1-12, 10: 1-29).

giddy with this new reckoning (l. 28): Merle, the obeah woman, perceives that she has been defeated by someone with superior powers, and that allying herself with Clarice will not only restore her position but strengthen her powers – a suggestion that, though there has been a victory and a defeat, the framework within which Merle and many of the onlookers interpret what has happened is resolutely Afro-centric, that Clarice is in fact a superior obeah woman.

iii

the encounter on Mount Sinai (l. 2): Clarice has the same look of triumph that Moses had when he came down from Mount Sinai with the tablets (the Ten Commandments): "…that Moses wist not that the skin of his face shone while he talked with him" (Exodus 34: 29). Moses covers his face with a veil when he comes before the Israelites. Clarice, we suspect, is not only much more aware of how she looks, but is keen to display her heavenly glow.

undulating trophies (l. 5): The converts are dancing and jumping up and down with the spirit.

he who has eyes, let him see (l. 6): References, loosely, Mark 8: 18, though the actual words may be Sigmund Freud's.

iv

she who has ears to hear, let her hear (l. 1): Matthew 11: 15 has "He that hath ears to hear, let him hear". See the critical commentary (pp. 102-103) for a more detailed discussion of the actual complexity of the way this allusion is being used – to signify that the ways of God are more complex and mysterious than Clarice supposes. The shift in gender is also part of the wider questioning of gendered power dynamics in the poem.

David before Michal (l. 5): This refers to the sarcastic, disapproving comment of Michal, the daughter of Saul, and David's then wife, when David dances naked before the Lord as a sign of his triumph in bringing the ark of the covenant back to Jerusalem – an episode that occurs before the David and Bathsheba narrative. The passage begins: "Then David returned to bless his household. And Michal the daughter of Saul came out to meet David, and said, How glorious was the King of Israel today, who uncovered himself today in the eyes of the handmaids of his servants, as one of the vain fellows shamelessly uncovereth himself." In this instance, God is evidently on David's side, since he punishes Michal with a lifetime's barrenness. Whilst the idea of dancing naked might trouble Clarice's church, no doubt the narrative would be interpreted as Michal's just punishment for disrespecting her husband (2 Samuel 6: 20).

the maidens of God (l. 4): Unlike Michal's maidservants, the stoned girls on the beach with the Dragon stouts (Chapter XXI, i, l. 16) are evidently enjoying the spectacle of the church brothers dancing in their tight clothes.

the babble of unknown tongues (l. 8): A reference both to the congregation speaking in tongues (glossolalia) and to the tower of Babel. See note to Chapter I, l. 48.

v

St Thomas in the East (l. 1): A preponderantly rural parish, the location of Morant Bay and the rebellion of 1865; a parish of deeply embedded Afro-Jamaican survivals such as the religious practice of Kumina, which Clarice's church regards as satanic.

minions of falling lights (l. 3): I.e. Lucifer. See Luke 10: 18: "I saw Satan falling like lightning from heaven".

Can I get a witness? (l. 5): A commonplace of the black American church (alluded to in the song of that title performed by both Marvin Gaye and Stevie Wonder) where the speaker testifies about her/ his religious experience and then calls, "Can I get a witness?", meaning "can anyone else speak to and confirm the truth of this experience". In these moments, the poem reveals, with some irony, the increased influence of American culture on the Jamaican culture through the medium of the evangelical churches.

Returned with feet still skipping (l. 6): This comes from Psalm 29: 6: "He maketh them also to skip like a calf; Lebanon and Sirion like a young unicorn."

Returned with captivity captive (l. 8): This comes from Ephesians 4: 8: "...when he ascended on high, he led captivity captive and gave gifts unto men." This is a passage subject to varied interpretations and translations, but probably here interpreted as Jesus coming back from death (captivity) with a personified death as a captive, through his sacrificial death on the cross and subsequent resurrection.

Her tears soften her path like scattered roses (l. 18): A lovely line, with perhaps an echo of The Message Bible's translation of Psalm 65: 11: "scatter rose petals down your paths" (1993), or Dante Gabriel Rossetti's "The Blessed Damozel": "Her robe, ungirt from clasp to hem, / No wrought flowers did adorn/ But a white rose of Mary's gift…"

vi

the earth rebirthing (l. 3): An allusion to Revelation 21: 1: "And I saw a new heaven and a new earth: for the first heaven and the first earth were passed away; and there was no more sea."

Thalbot's descent into the old madness (l. 6): Thalbot has been cleansed of his spirits (see Chapter XVI, *Communion*, l. 48ff.), but left vacant for fresh possession (as by the four apparitions in Chapters XVII to XX). This time he is possessed by the spirits of Jonah and Elijah.

cleaned like this, the demons have returned seven-fold (ll. 7-8): Another reference to Jesus' warning on the return of wandering spirits. See note to IX, ii, ll. 16-21: This repeated invasion is how Clarice interprets Thalbot's further fall to the congregation, ensuring that the story he tells about what he has seen is dismissed as madness. If he has indeed claimed to have seen the coupling of angels on the beach, then in his unsanctified state this will inevitably blind and madden him.

water-bellied whores (l. 9): A suggestion that these women are sickly and dropsical, but also pointing to the fact they are performing the "water pumpy" dance in which the dancer simulates the action of a water pump, an image which also prepares for the connection made between water and female sexuality. As Clarice says later, "I am woman, I am blood, I am water" and speaks of her "watery arrivals".

beaching his broken soul on some stone-hearted mongrel (l. 11): A parody of the narrative of the Gadarene swine (see notes to II, l. 40, and to Chapter XV), and another association between dogs and the spiritual lower depths.

the ark of the covenant (l. 14): The holy of holies of the Israelites, the huge chest built to God's prescription (Exodus 25: 10-22) that contains the stone tablets on which the Ten Commandments are written. When the ark falls into the wrong hands (as the Philistines at one time capture it in battle) bad things happen to them, including plagues of haemorrhoids and boils – i.e. the ulcers: "But the hand of the Lord was heavy upon them of Ashdod, and he destroyed them, and smote them with emerods" (1 Samuel 5: 6).

sanctified mint of prophecy (l. 14): Like a new (mint) coin, the light of prophecy is too bright for those destined for damnation.

How then could he see the ritual coupling of angels... (l. 17): In almost all biblical accounts, angels are images of sexlessness, and certainly not supposed to be coupling on the beach – a scene where there was no element, though Clarice might like to pretend otherwise, of ritual. There is, however, a puzzling passage in Genesis 6 (pre Noah) in which angels or "Sons of God" are said to have slept with "daughters of humans" – a circumstance that leads directly to God's frustration with humans and his decision to bring about the flood. If Thalbot is thinking of this episode, then it provides another reason for his distress.

vii

broken-faced saints (l. 1): I.e. Last Night, the man Clarice loves, whom she saved from dereliction, but who is now displaying the agony of guilt on his face. The phrase acutely catches one of the vulnerabilities of the followers of this church. Unlike most other denominations, for whom godliness is always something to be worked towards, and never regarded as something humanly achievable in life, for this church there is the burden of maintaining absolute saintliness following the believer's rebirth into the spirit. This, the poem wonders, might well be an hubristic ambition. Untarnished saintliness is always vulnerable to human temptations through time, so the image of the "broken-faced saints" can be read as describing painted sacred ikons cracked by the passage of time.

the indiscretions of the believers (l. 5): This is, of course, dangerous territory for Clarice. She has made her reputation as a prophetess by exposing, during the church service, the hidden (mainly sexual) indiscretions of members of the congregation and the subsequent counselling sessions she evidently undertakes. The fact that she has committed her own "indiscretion" is hardly likely to be forgiven by those she has exposed. It also suggests she has used her prophetic gifts in a self-serving way.

cutting the bone and marrow / of closeted secrets (ll. 6-7): Another reference to Hebrews 4: 12: "For the word of God is living and active, and sharper than any two-edged sword, piercing even to dividing asunder of soul and spirit, and of the joints and marrow, and is a discerner of the thoughts and intents of the heart." A discerner of the heart is precisely what Clarice has been.

dart in blasts of fire from my trembling hands (l. 9): As if the pointing finger that Clarice directs towards the sinful has been directed by God. See the prologue where the poet reports: "She is the prophetess/ whose finger, pointed, stirred bumps// in my flesh" (ll. 6-8). Clarice no doubt sees her finger like the one that writes on the wall at Belshazzar's feast ("like the bloody cipher of his finger" – see the note to XXVII, l. 6).

this constant flow/ of milk from my swelling breasts (ll. 13-14): Clarice compares herself to Jerusalem as the promised holy place for the Israelites, where, as Isaiah promises, "…ye may suck and be satisfied with the breasts of her consolations; that ye may milk out, and be delighted with the abundance of her giving…" (Isaiah 66: 11). This recalls the earlier scene where "The brothers recite their verses to ward off/ the lust, seeing Clarice like that, her curve of breast". We may think here that Clarice makes a somewhat self-serving conflation of the spiritual and the orgasmic. The image of the nurturing breast also looks forward to the passage (section viii) that echoes the Song of Solomon, where the beloved is "comely as Jerusalem" (6: 3) and there are several encomiums to her breasts ("thy breasts shall be as clusters of the vine", 7: 8). It is also an image of Clarice's desire for a full womanhood beyond sexual denial.

viii

the sky winked at my writhing (l. 8): At first Clarice displays a perhaps predictable ambivalence between her self-confident justifications of her sexuality, and her attempts to excuse it as "the succumbing of my limbs to the nerves'/ attack", and her hope that God will let her off. But then in what follows, in channelling the Song of Solomon, she declares that "this coming of spasms on the black sand/ is nothing but a prayer given wings…". Though even here she wants to have it both ways, claiming, "my will usurped". It is here that the poem's approach to Clarice is at its richest. It asserts the desired unity of the spiritual and the sensual; it constructs a mythical image of Clarice that asserts her possibility; but at the same time it does not ignore her human flaws.

I am woman… (l. 10): From this point on, Clarice either quotes from or echoes the rhythms of the Song of Solomon (also known as the Song of Songs). In the Song, richly open to a multitude of interpretations, most notably as an allegory of the love between God and Israel or (in post-New Testament readings) between Christ as the bridegroom and the Christian church as bride. Read unallegorically, as it is here, with, as suggested in the critical commentary, the encouragement of Toni Morrison's *Song of Solomon*, it is a celebration of sexual love and the sensuality of the body, a dialogue between a male and a female voice.

I am blood, I am water (l. 10): Cf: Song of Solomon, 4: 15: "A fountain of gardens, a well of living waters, and streams from Lebanon." Also a daring echo of the account of the wound of Christ in John 19: 34: "But one of the soldiers with a spear pierced his side, and forthwith came there out blood and water."

cloister of miracles (l. 16): This is a reminder of the epigraph from Chapter II, from *A Midsummer Night's Dream*, "In a shady cloister mew'd", that introduces the theme of conflict between sexuality and spirituality, of the impossible deal that Clarice embraces, that as the prophetess working miracles of insight into others' indiscretions and spiritual needs and channeller of the holy spirit, she must deny her sexuality, like a nun in a cloister.

pluck her, tickle her (l. 19): This converts the musical metaphors of "I am the songs gathering [...] " around "tuned instruments" (also echoing Psalm 150: "Praise him upon the well-tuned cymbals") into the sequence of sexual metaphors that follow: "pluck her", "each caress on my tilting body ekes a parable", as if she is a guitar or lyre to be played by her lover.

I am comely, I am black (l. 22): The Song has: "I am black, but comely" (1: 5). What is here is a significant revision, since in the Song the singer wants to excuse her blackness because she has been in the sun. This is Clarice as "constructed myth", not the Clarice who used lightening cream. This echoes both one of the moral drives behind Morrison's *Song of Solomon* and the episode when, in that novel, Guitar tries to persuade Hagar that before she can love anyone unpossessively, she must learn to love herself, to see herself as black *and* comely, or in his words, a "pretty black-skinned girl" (p. 123).

my watery arrivals are testaments of ultimate love (ll. 22-23): Here Clarice affirms that her full womanhood, her blood, her tears and her orgasms – all these "waters" – represent her spiritual authenticity. She is affirming the kind of assured sexuality that eludes Last Night.

mere trompings before the possession (l. 26): Here the poem puns on the words "trumpery" (something showy but worthless) and "trumping", the action of worshippers stamping and bending to work themselves into a state of hyperventilation and receptivity to spirit possession (see the chapter summary above). In other words, just as the labouring of the worshippers is the prelude to divine possession, so the clumsiness and physicality of lovemaking is prelude to its transcendence in sexual joy.

Last Night vanished (l. 28): This connects to a repeated theme in the Song of Solomon of the disappearance of the male beloved. "By night on my bed I sought him whom my soul loveth: I sought him, but I found him not" (3: 1).

Then I will soar – for it is flying – above the squalor of the journey (l. 30): This is a flash-forward to one of the master tropes in *Prophets*. See especially Chapters XXIII, xv; XXIV, *Speaking for the First Time*; XXVIII, *Flight* and the prologue, all of which explore the tensions between flight and imprisonment, and lead to Chapter XXIV, where falling is recontextualised as flight. See, too, the critical commentary, pp. 89-92.

the visions of the triumphant gazelles (l. 31): Here Clarice sees her beloved in the metaphor that closes the Song: "…behold, he cometh, leaping upon the mountains, skipping upon the hills./ My beloved is like a roe or a young hart…" (2: 9).

ix

She gets them on the toilet seat sometimes (l. 2): The whole of the stanza, with the addition of "again", exactly repeats the stanza in Chapter II when Clarice has a vision of the story of Legion and the Gadarene swine, which at that point relates to Thalbot as street madman. Here, again using the neat filmic device of the prophetic mirror, *Prophets* manages to be in two places at once: seeing what her nemesis, the witnessing Thalbot ("his head filled with the secrets of her eternal damnation"), is up to.

She speaks the wind from the oceans (l. 6): Just as Prospero in *The Tempest* uses his magic to raise the storm to shipwreck his enemies, and has Ariel disorder the minds of the voyagers, so "Not a soul/ But felt a fever of the mad and play'd/ Some tricks of desperation" (Act 1 scene 1, ll. 209-211) and wipes clean at various times in the play the memories and consciousness of Miranda and Ferdinand, so Clarice attempts to use her powers to wipe Thalbot's memories – something, at this point, he himself wishes would happen.

the dialectics of good versus evil are now insignificant (l. 14): As there was for Prospero, there is a price. The woman who merely calculates for her own advantage, who can no longer live by the moral absolutes of the church if she is to protect her sexual self, must give up the magic "of her swelling visions".

The winds lift and move (l. 18): An echo of John 3: 8: "The wind bloweth where it listeth, and thou hearest the sound thereof, but canst not tell whence it cometh, and whither it goeth: so is every one that is born of the Spirit." Here the poem suggests a vision that is broader, both less comforting and less frightening, because it has abandoned the absolute certainty which, in their opposing ways, both Clarice and Thalbot have possessed, that God is intimately concerned with their individual fortunes.

PART THREE

CHAPTER XXIII
Thalbot and the Vine

Summary

This, the longest and most narrative-driven section of *Prophets* is a remarkable tour-de-force of wit, drama, and pathos, and brilliantly enactive verse (for instance in the description of the careering passage of the bus that swallows Thalbot and carries him to Kingston. Attention switches to what happens to Thalbot after he flees from the mission after witnessing the coupling of Clarice and Last Night on the beach. Except for what lies in Thalbot's memory, and in his imagination, in this chapter, we see only one more glimpse of the flesh-and-blood Clarice, when in section xi she persuades the church to disfellowship Thalbot (who she fears will confirm the rumours of her indiscretion) on the grounds that he is a reprobate, onanist and madman. At this point, the church members appear prepared to give her the benefit of the doubt concerning the rumours of her "sin", though, by the time we reach Chapter XXIV, it is evident that the church no longer believes her denials. However, because she knows too many embarrassing secrets about the sins of others, there is no public act of disfellowshipping, no dramatic casting-out from the church. Instead, influential brothers in the church obtain a visa for her departure to Canada, in return for her silence. This is the matter of Chapter XXIV, but it lies behind and casts an ironic eye on the present chapter's narrative focus on Thalbot. As the epigraph for Part Three suggests, the narrative casts Thalbot in the role of Jonah whom God tells to leave Joppa (Annotto Bay) and go to the wicked Babylonian city of Nineveh (Kingston) to warn the inhabitants of God's imminent wrath. Like Jonah, Thalbot is reluctant to go to Nineveh, knowing all too well the kind of ill treatment he can expect – seen as a madman preaching on the streets. Instead, like Jonah, who planned to flee instead to Tarshish by boat, Thalbot decides to catch a bus to Montego Bay. In a witty interplay between the narratives, like Jonah on the ship when a storm strikes it, Thalbot confesses himself to be the probable reason for the bus's mechanical problems, and though not quite cast overboard, he leaves the bus for Montego Bay (Tarshish), flounders around in the darkness of the country night, until he is graphically swallowed by a coach heading for Kingston (Nineveh). On the coach, Thalbot, locked in his misogynistic repulsion from the sexuality of women, is tormented by his memories of Clarice on the beach. He cannot accept that the same woman who performs miracles could also engage in sex with Last Night. We are reminded of the women in Chapter V, i, who observe the size of Thalbot's "branch" of a penis and bewail the waste.

In the Book of Jonah, Jonah enters Nineveh and prophesies that "Yet forty days and Nineveh shall be overthrown" (1: 3). This does not in fact happen because, from the king down, the inhabitants of Nineveh make a show of their repentance in sackcloth and ashes and fasting. In a very rare show of mercy, "God repented of the evil, that he had said he would do unto them; and he did not" (3: 10). This is not what Jonah expects, and "it displeased Jonah exceedingly, and he was very angry" (4: 1). He quarrels with God and goes off in a dudgeon to sulk. This encourages God to mystify him even more with some further torments, whilst doing nothing to punish the wicked Ninevites. All this is parallelled in Thalbot's arrival in the city.

But if in general Thalbot, as prophet, is something of a figure of ridicule, a confused victim lacking in prophetic authority, in section ix of this chapter, at the very moment when Clarice appears at her least honourable, when she curses Thalbot to save her skin, Thalbot displays a moment of wit and political astuteness when he recognises: "'If a liar and deceiver comes and says,/ 'I will prophesy for you plenty wine and beer,'/ he would be just the prophet for this people" (XXIII, ix, ll. 11-12).

In the final sections of the chapter, as the polymorphous figure he is, Thalbot ceases to enact Jonah and becomes Elijah, another prophet to whom God gives a hard time. It is at this point that Clarice re-enters the narrative, but only metaphorically, first as the raven that brings Elijah food in the desert, and then as a bird that plunges to its death (struck by a stone that Thalbot casts). This echoes Jezebel's fall from the walls of the city in the Elijah narrative and gives resonance to Thalbot's misogynistic conviction that the woman who once converted him is a Jezebel (see note below). As we learn in Chapter XXIV, this is mere wish fulfilment on Thalbot's part, since Clarice is on her way to the Canada (next door to heaven).

Notes

Thalbot and the Vine: This refers to the closing moments of the Jonah narrative where, seemingly feeling a little sorry for his sulking prophet, but really to teach him another lesson, "the Lord God prepared a gourd, and made it to come over Jonah, that it might be a shadow over his head. So Jonah was exceedingly glad of the gourd" (Jonah 4: 6). However, Jonah is still so disgusted with God's failure to punish the Ninevites that God, to teach him not to question his decisions, prepares a worm and the next day "it smote the gourd and it withered".

a tattered coat on their backs (l. 8): This is perhaps an echo of W.B. Yeats' "tattered coat upon a stick", in "Sailing to Byzantium" (*Collected Poems*, 1967, p. 217).

Avoid proper names, stick to pronouns… (ll. 10-11): This echoes the parodic, deconstructive style encountered in the film version of the Gadarene swine narrative in Chapter XV (*Legion*).

such as aspirates (l. 12): I.e., the sound "h" as in He.

eat grass (l. 18): As Daniel prophesies to Nebuchadnezzar: "they shall make thee to eat grass as oxen" (Daniel 4: 25). Nebuchadnezzar is the Babylonian tyrant under whose kingdom Israel falls. Daniel is one of the Jews taken to Babylon to serve the king, but with God's blessing he turns the tables on Babylon. He survives in the lions' den and in the fiery furnace; he interprets the writing hand at Belshazzar's feast and tells Nebuchadnezzar that his dreams prophesy the king's coming madness, when he will eat grass. The Daniel story is one of the most popular tropes of reggae songs, with its context of Babylonian exile, and its potential analogies for the wily and resourceful rastaman surviving the Jamaican Babylon. Hear, for instance, Prince Alla's "Daniel in the Lion's Den" (1978), Alpha and Omega's album of that name (1990), The Congo's "La La Bam Bam" (1977) and the Abyssinians' "Abendigo" (1976).

the brilliant impossible you have witnessed/ in the churchyard these last few nights (ll. 21-22): This refers to the conversion of so many sinners and idolaters and miracles of healing as witnessed in the previous chapter. But this, of course, is not what Thalbot carries in his head.

his own vicarious coming (l. 31): I.e. Thalbot masturbates, a sign of his conflicted attraction to Clarice, and a sin; onanism is almost as bad as extramarital sex in the eyes of the church.

cool and silent among the shell and coral (l. 37): Thalbot's suicidal thoughts echo the imagery surrounding Clarice: "she slept in coral and shell", (XXI, iii, l. 11); "her ministry of shells" (XXII, iv, l. 35), and, after the night on the beach, the mocking shrine he later builds for her of "pink-blue shells" (XXIII, xiv, l. 22). All these are signs of Thalbot's conflicted desires for Clarice.

midnight acolytes of worms / snake… (l. 42): A vision of hell in the most dispossessed areas of Kingston that recalls the descriptions of the Dungle in Orlando Patterson's *The Children of Sisyphus* (1964). In the Bible, worms are invariably associated with death and decay as in Micah 7: 17: "They shall lick the dust like a serpent, they shall move out of their holes like worms of the earth: they shall be afraid of the Lord our God, and shall fear because of thee."

their carelessly/ dropped defecation (ll. 45-46): This is in disobedience to the instruction of Deuteronomy 23: 13: "And thou shalt have a paddle upon thy weapon; and it shall be, when thou wilt ease thyself abroad, thou shalt dig therewith, and shalt turn back and cover that which cometh from thee".

ii

Bellevue (l. 1): This is the mental hospital. Though God has told Thalbot to speak "like a naked madman", Thalbot knows all too well how madmen are treated in Kingston, subject to the street violence of "stone throwers", "gunmen" and "whores". To be locked up in Bellevue would not be much better.

Seaview (l. 5): A derelict part of West Kingston, off Spanish Town Road.

casual experiments (l. 7): The performance of lobotomies and ECTs was common at Bellevue up to the 1970s and 1980s, though the scandalous mistreatment of the mentally ill is still a subject for media exposure. See Dr Alfred Dawes, "It is Madness How as a Society We Treat the Mentally Ill", *The Gleaner*, 5 October 2016. Online.

The broken vessel (l. 14): This alludes to Psalm 31: 12: "I am forgotten as a dead man out of mind: I am like a broken vessel."

Oh let the stones fall off the mountains (l. 19): This is a reference to Hosea 10: 8, where as a punishment for building idolatrous shrines, the prophet foretells: "The high places of Aven, the sins of Israel shall be destroyed: the thorn and thistles will grow over their altar. / Then they will say to the mountains, 'Cover us!' And to the hills, 'Fall on us'."

nyabinghi (l. 20): A Rastafarian. See the note to Chapter XXII, ii, l. 7.

renta-dreads (l. 20): Men who sells sex to tourist women at beach resorts, another instance of the passage from Rastafarian righteousness to commerce – though such (usually unemployed) young men were rarely more than rasta in dress style.

the Beast jerking... off (l. 26): This is the USA envisioned as the Beast of Revelation 13: "And they worshipped the dragon which gave power unto the beast: and they worshipped the beast, saying, Who is like unto the beast? who is able to make war with him?". The lines make reference once again to the connection between the wealthy Jamaican upper classes and right-wing elements in the USA. There is also a reference back to Newark's radio and tv stations pumping US propaganda over the Caribbean basin: "The poison of heaven's sudden curse/ blows from Newark's phallic white towers,/ spewing their toxic sperm into the fertile sky" (III, iii, ll. 1-3). This is the era of Ronald Reagan and US state-sponsored subversion of radical politics in the Caribbean and Central America, working hand-in-hand with the ultra-capitalist doctrines of the right-wing televangelists with their prosperity gospel. See note to Chapter III, l. 24.

This fire will leave the earth / black... (ll. 27-28): This is Thalbot's millenarian dream of a divine cleansing when the world ends. He perhaps thinks of the Epistle of St Peter: "But the heavens and the earth which are now preserved by the same word, are reserved for fire until the day of judgment and perdition of ungodly men" (2 Peter 3: 7).

For what right has a city/ to live again? (ll. 31-32): Like Jonah and Nineveh, Thalbot does not want to see Kingston saved – though he is given a personal motivation for this feeling, which we can only guess at in Jonah.

she with her proffered bottom (l. 35): A more explicit description of just what is meant by "they coupled like dogs", and thus all the more scandalous to Thalbot for not being missionary position (and another reason why the equally sexually squeamish Last Night runs into the sea to cleanse himself).

iii

Shabba and the Cat (l. 8): Dancehall stars. See notes for Chapter XIV, ii, ll. 22-23.

Cherished colly (l. 9): A reference to Collie weed, ganja, as in Lee Perry's song "Roast fish, Collie Weed and Corn Bread". Originally ganja was bought from the coolie (collie) man, from amongst the Indians who came to Jamaica as indentured labourers between 1845 and 1917.

synthetic bass lines (ll. 10-11): Computer-generated dancehall music (q.v. Wayne Smith's "Under Mi Sleng Teng") – no doubt anathema to a true rootsman like Kwame Dawes. See note to Chapter XV, i, l. 28.

watched like the sparrow (l. 18): In other words, being watched by God. From Luke 12: 6: "Are not five sparrows sold for two pennies? Yet not one of them is forgotten by God." Also the hymn, "His eye is on the Sparrow", written in 1905 by Civilla D. Martin: "I sing because I'm happy,/ I sing because I'm free/ For his eye is on the sparrow,/ and I know he watches me." There's also an allusion to this verse in Jimmy Cliff's song, "Keep Your Eyes on the Sparrow", a song about not being looked upon in the human world, having "a cloud that overshadows me/ blocks the light from my eyes..." The instruction of the chorus: "Somebody tell me to/ keep your eyes on the sparrow" is an instruction to himself to trust in God's oversight.

iv

Joppa (l. 1): I.e. Annotto Bay. Thalbot had presumably fled to somewhere on the coast, south of the resort.

and someone mentions a curse (l. 20): This relates to the point in the Jonah narrative when "The Lord sent a great wind into the sea... so the ship was like to be broken", and the seamen become suspicious of Jonah's presence and ask him, "Tell us, we pray thee, for whose cause this evil is upon us" (Jonah 1: 8).

the others search their past for a reason (l. 21): This parallels the point where the seamen (1: 7) say, "Come, let us cast lots, that we may know for whose cause this evil is upon us. So they cast lots, and the lots fell upon Jonah."

so Thalbot walks away (l. 31): This mirrors the point at which "they took up Jonah, and cast him forth into the sea: and the sea ceased from her raging" (1: 15).

v.

the hiss of a whale's breathing (l. 2): This parallels Jonah 1: 17: "Now the Lord had prepared a great fish to swallow up Jonah. And Jonah was in the belly of the fish for three days and three nights."

quart of whites (l. 6): This is a fearsome quantity (at least 70 cl) of over-proof white rum that the driver has drunk. For Thalbot, the ride down the hill must be almost as risky as Jonah's sojourn in the whale.

a cage of soldered iron for a crown (l. 8): Jamaican buses of this period had a luggage roof-rack that looked like a crown.

bear him west (ll. 20-21): Thalbot still wants to go west to Montego Bay (Tarshish), but is instead virtually kidnapped by the driver and taken to Kingston (Nineveh).

a jacked deer (l. 26): He is as if under the influence of drugs, as in "jacked up".

Mount Diablo (l. 49): A mountain peak (at 2455 ft) in St Catherine parish, halfway between the coast and Spanish Town.

scattered crushed callaloo leaves (ll. 50-51): All signs, with the green bananas and pepper seeds, that this is a country bus usually carrying market vendors to town.

The sermon in his belly sours (l. 66): As Thalbot nears Kingston, the idea of preaching to the wicked looks like an increasingly bad idea. This is an allusion to Revelation 10: 9-11: "And I went unto the angel, and said unto him, Give me the little book. And he said unto me, Take it, and eat it up; and it shall make thy belly bitter, but it shall be in thy mouth sweet as honey./ And I took the little book out of the angel's hand, and ate it up; and it was in my mouth sweet as honey: and as soon as I had eaten it, my belly was bitter./ And he said unto me, Thou must prophesy again before many peoples, and nations, and tongues, and kings."

vi

When trouble catch me, undress me, leave me bleeding by the roadside (l. 1): Thalbot pictures himself as the victim in the parable of the Good Samaritan (Luke 10: 25-37): "A certain man went down from Jerusalem to Jericho, and fell among thieves, which stripped him of his raiment, and wounded him, and departed, leaving him half dead" (10: 30). Thalbot's reflection reminds that this parable is about the mysterious sources of true charity, when pious Jewish priests pass by on the other side of the road, and the Samaritan, between whose nation and the Jews there was bitter hostility, takes care of the stranger.

The dead arising and the cripple gyrating (l. 9): Thalbot displays here his inability to accept that the healing miracles performed by Clarice at the mission service and the evidence of her sexual desires can exist in the same context. The miracles echo, of course, those performed by Jesus to raise Lazarus (John 11: 1-44, see notes to Chapter XVI, l. 31) and heal a crippled man (Matthew 9: 1-4): "And, behold, they brought to him a man sick of the palsy, lying on a bed: and Jesus seeing their faith said unto the sick of the palsy; Son, be of good cheer; thy sins be forgiven thee.[...] Arise, take up thy bed, and go unto thine house."

milking him, milking him (l. 13): An image of the violent taking of Last Night's seed that contrasts sharply with Clarice's image of herself as a giver, with "this constant flow / of milk from my swelling breasts". See note to Chapter XXII, vii, ll. 13-14. From Thalbot's perspective, there has been a loss of manhood. It is part of the poem's critique of the male prophet figure's misogynist insistence on having power over women, which echoes the way Moses Barton (in Sylvia Wynter's *The Hills of Hebron*) feels when he feels "compelled" to take Miss Kate: "Had this woman, like Delilah, come forward [...] to rob him of the secret of his strength, to draw out of him the substance that made him inviolable, the son of God" (p. 210). On his return home, Barton woke up his wife and "took her brutally".

when last you said your prayers, woman,/ when last you count your beads? (ll. 14-15): Thalbot again quotes Othello ("Have you prayed tonight, Desdemona" Act 5, Scene 2) and repeats the reference to "it is the cause, it is the cause" (Chapter XVII, ii) from that play. All this implies that Thalbot is still haunted by the sexual jealousy of the first apparition, the Don Drummond figure, when he kills his lover, Anita Mahfood.

the thin membrane of your drying sex (ll. 16-17): Thalbot's violently misogynistic objectification of Clarice's sexuality, the image of her as a virtual rapist ("milking him, milking him") goes to the heart of a kind of puritanism – obsessed with, but disgusted by sexuality – that

Prophets indicts as a deep flaw in the kind of church that Clarice leads. The image of the membrane picked at by the soldier crab (a wish for the drying up of her sexuality) works as a disgusted opposite to the imagery that connects Clarice to the erotic symbolism of seashells. It is an image that Dawes borrows from his own poem, "Sex Sells Annette", from *Progeny of Air* (1994) of a naked soldier crab's "delicate thin membrane" (p. 94).

It is the cause (l. 19): From *Othello*. See note to ll. 14-15 above.

duppy transport (l. 22): I.e. ghostly – as in the bus's sudden appearance in the night. Thalbot can't really believe he has been swallowed up by it.

Beckon me like a siren (l. 24): Another reference to Ulysses and the sirens. See note to Chapter I, ii, l. 30.

unclean lips and cankered eye (l. 29): The unclean lips come from Isaiah 6: 5: "Then said I, Woe is me! for I am undone; because I am a man of unclean lips, and I dwell in the midst of a people of unclean lips: for mine eyes have seen the King, the Lord of hosts." The cankered eye possibly relates to "And their word will eat as doth a canker" in 2 Timothy 2: 17.

who hear me cryin? (l. 30): Thalbot echoes the abandoned psalmist's cry (Psalm 27, verse 7): "Hear, O Lord, when I cry with my voice: have mercy also upon me, and answer me."

when you toss me into the current (l. 31): This is a neat merging of the narrative of Jonah thrown into the sea, and the journey downhill that Thalbot is making into the intense, fern-rich greenery of the route down from Mount Diablo, which parallels Jonah's words to God: "The waters compassed me about, even to the soul: the depth closed me round about, the weeds were wrapped about my head" (2: 5). The temptation to drown himself shows how despairing Thalbot is, in contrast to the moment when he resists the second apparition's suicidal impulse, when "drowning, drowning, they part ways" (XVIII, i, l. 84) and Thalbot "pops like a buoy to the surface". Now he feels "this pull to the edge / to the bosom of the sea where the gravel sand / and picking fish would cleanse all mortality / from his fallen flesh" (XXIII, i, ll. 32-36).

is dead a dead now! (l. 43): A comic play on the difference between patwa and standard, where to "dead" is also a verb, so in standard what

Thalbot is saying translates as "I am going to die, soon". As a character in Patterson's *The Children of Sisyphus* says, "Lawd, Mr. Solomon... ah goin dead now..." (p. 68). It echoes, perhaps the play on tense in Hamlet's "Horatio, I am dead" (Act V, scene 2, l. 333).

for what must follow this absence of faith? (ll. 43-44): Thalbot's question is one that is fundamental to the debate, to the elements of autobiographical enquiry, within *Prophets*.

Albert Pierrepoint (l. 46): He was a British hangman (1905-1992) who followed in the footsteps of his father and uncle in the trade and executed 435 condemned persons until he retired in 1956. Later he concluded that hanging was not a deterrent to murder.

the judgement of heaven/ done sound on the blast of this bus (ll. 48-49): The constant papping of the horn of the drunken, stoned driver as he careers down sharp bends makes Thalbot think of the last trump: "In a moment, in the twinkling of an eye, at the last trump: for the trumpet shall sound, and the dead shall be raised incorruptible, and we shall be changed" (Corinthians 15: 52).

a bungy gone crazy (l. 50): Instead of the neck-snapping jolt of the hangman's rope, Thalbot is amazed to find himself still alive and bouncing at the end of rubber rope after the vertiginous, breakneck plunge of the coach around yet another downwards bend.

Rio Cobre (l. 53): The major river that runs through Bog Walk via Spanish Town into Kingston Harbour.

who it was that bear me up,/ bring me forward still breathing? (ll. 58-59): An echo of the psalmist who cries: "He brought me up also out of an horrible pit, out of the miry clay, and set my feet upon a rock, and established my goings" (Psalm 40: 2).

The wind beating through my open mouth (ll. 64-65): This is the wind of God's inspiration (as in Job 33: 4: "The Spirit of God has made me, And the breath of the Almighty gives me life"). However, Thalbot, with a humility that Clarice lacks in her absolute certainty of being God's voice, is far less sure that what he thinks is the absolute truth. He will accept the relativity of the transaction because he can no longer credit the absoluteness of the miracle. It is also a line that echoes Celie in the cursing scene in *The Color Purple*. She is probably quoting the same biblical source when she says to Mr ———, "You better stop talking because all I'm telling you ain't coming just from me. Look like when I open my mouth the air rush in and shape words" (p. 176).

Yes, Father, see me here, flat... (l. 66): This echoes Jonah's quarrel with God about being left in Nineveh with no fire to come, even though he has done as instructed (i, l. 18).

viii

Marcus and the fat queen (l. 5): The statues of Marcus Garvey and Queen Victoria in Parade Gardens.

On the beach (l. 7): Thalbot is on the Edgewater beach of the sea coast of Portmore, across the bay from Kingston. See the note to x, l. 1.

limboing (l. 2): Originally a dance for exercise on the limited space of slave ships, now a beach entertainment for tourists; it involves leaning as far backwards as possible whilst still on one's feet, passing under a bar, shoulders almost to the ground.

Madonna brassieres (l. 5): The iconic Gaultier cone bras that the singer wore (as an outer garment) on her Blond Ambition tour of 1990.

bogling (l. 7): A dance. See note to Chapter IX, i, l. 19.

festival (l. 7): Fried cornbread dumplings, beach food often eaten with fish (such as snapper).

dutch pan (l. 8): A cooking pot. See note to Chapter IX, i, l. 16.

batty-riders (l. 11): Shorts. See note to Chapter III, i, l. 16.

pum-pum printers (l. 12): Shorts so tight they show of the shape and cleft of the vulva.

Supercat... coolie glow (l. 14): See note Chapter XIV, ii, ll. 22-23. Supercat is a DJ of Indo-Jamaican ethnicity, for which the popular but derogatory term was coolie. Coolie hair is straight black hair.

raggamuffin (l. 21): Post-reggae dancehall music. See note for Chapter IV, l. 3.

The wind falls (l. 22): The breath of the spirit leaves Thalbot. Clarice's curse/ excommunication, which comes in section xi, has evidently been effective.

ix

naked like this (l. 4): A sign amongst prophets of extreme lamentation. "And the Lord said, Like as my servant Isaiah hath walked naked and barefoot three years for a sign and wonder upon Egypt and upon Ethiopia…" (Isaiah 20: 3). In Jamaica, as elsewhere, nakedness on the street is taken as a sure sign of madness.

will howl like a jackal (l. 6): "Because of this I will weep and wail; I will go barefoot and naked. I will howl like a jackal and moan like an owl" (Micah 1: 8).

male guinep tree (ll. 7-8): Only the female tree bears fruit. The term man-guinep is used to jibe at men without children, as in Burro Banton's song, "Man-Guinep" (2006).

x.

Edgeware coast (l. 1): Part of Portmore, the land facing Kingston. The point is that Thalbot, in disobedience to God, isn't in Kingston proper. Shouting his prophetic warnings across the water (l. 15), where the smells travel faster than the sound, is obviously a pretty lame excuse for what he is supposed to be doing.

Palisadoes (l. 5): The spit of land that protects Kingston, where the airport is.

stinking dungle (l. 9): A blend word formed from dung hill/jungle, formerly a squatter encampment on a rubbish tip in West Kingston, the setting for Orlando Patterson's *The Children of Sisyphus*.

white lines his lip (l. 10): A discharge that is the result of vitamin deficiency and starvation, also known as white-corner mouth.

cactus… bramble… stony path (l. 18): These are all emblems of the aridity and spiritual desolation of Thalbot at his lowest ebb. It prefaces part xii where he enacts the desert sojourn of the desolate Elijah: "he himself went a day's journey into the wilderness. He came to a broom bush, sat down under it and prayed that he might die" (1 Kings 19: 3).

xi

The congregation (l. 1): The scene is back with Clarice and the church at Annotto Bay.

Clarice visions Thalbot (l. 7): The grammatical ambivalence of the phrase suggests a fabrication, that this isn't a vision that comes to her (as it did in Chapter II, l. 40ff), but that she invents an image of him masturbating in order to destroy his reputation, to prevent him bearing witness to her "sinning" with Last Night.

They deny the falsehood of the rumours (l. 21): This and announcing where Thalbot is to be found (knowing what some of the congregation will do to him) is surely the least admirable thing that Clarice does, and, in the moral economy of this poetic fiction, must be the act that most warrants her downfall in the world of reality as opposed to myth.

xii

I have spoken the prophecy like you asked me (l. 1): As Jonah, in a display of spectacular passive-aggressiveness, complains to God after God decides not to destroy Nineveh: "Therefore now, O Lord, take, I beseech thee, my life from me; for it is better for me to die than to live" (4: 3).

swinging his machete there in the Kishon Valley (l. 6): Thalbot metamorphoses from Jonah to Elijah who slays the idolators of Baal: "Elijah brought them down to the brook Kishon, and slew them there." (1 Kings 18: 40). In reality, Thalbot has taken a government work-creation job in the municipal park and is taking it out on the flowers.

A cloud small as a man's fist (l. 12): Another reference to Elijah and the sign that supposedly marks the end of the drought that is God's punishment on Ahab and Jezebel for their idolatry. ("And it came to pass at the seventh time, that he said, Behold, there ariseth a little cloud out of the sea, like a man's hand. And he said, Go up, say unto Ahab, Prepare thy chariot, and get thee down, that the rain stop thee not" (1 Kings 18: 44). Last Night and Clarice have become that wicked pair in Thalbot's embittered imagination.

It is the cause (l. 19): In repeating Othello's words as he enters Desdemona's bedchamber to murder her (see notes to Chapter XVII, Epigraph), Thalbot imagines he has killed Clarice amongst the flowers he has hacked down.

The broom tree: Such a tree as Elijah sits under. See the note to x, l. 10, above.

xiii

wind whipping its electric tail (l. 15): An image that suggests an apocalyptic dragon from the book of Revelation. This echoes 1 Kings 19: 11: "a great and strong wind rent the mountains, and brake in pieces the rocks before the Lord; but the Lord was not in the wind: and after the wind an earthquake; but the Lord was not in the earthquake". The image probably also references Hurricane Gilbert whose destructive path through Jamaica in 1988 (killing over 100 people) would still be fresh in Dawes' mind at the time of writing this poem. Dawes may also be remembering the climactic hurricane in Hurston's *Their Eyes Were Watching God*, also described as a beast: "The monstropolous beast had left his bed. The two hundred miles an hour wind had loosed his chains" (p. 239).

he howls into the wind, rejoicing (ll. 23-24): Thalbot thinks that the end of the world is nigh, and is glad for it.

Marcus Garvey Drive, Mandela Highway (l. 28): These are busy roads in central Kingston. Thalbot hopes the wind will turn inland and destroy the wicked city.

after so much fasting (l. 35): Elijah fasts for forty days and nights (1 Kings 18: 8).

whipping his tail (l. 36): A twist on line 15. God is giving Thalbot licks.

it tickles the tears of the kneeling onlookers (l. 39): We are back with Jonah and his disgust over God's mild treatment of the wicked Ninevites who repented just in time.

his arms spread, his eyes giving their last passion of tears (ll. 44-45): An indication, in the crucifixion image, that Thalbot belongs to the self-dramatising tendency of Caribbean prophets, at least as portrayed in the region's fiction. Staged self-crucifixions are fictionalised in Sam Selvon's Brackley in *The Lonely Londoners* (1956); Jan Carew's Prophet Jordan in *Black Midas* (1958); V.S. Naipaul's Man-Man in *Miguel Street* (1959); Ismith Khan's Manko in *The Crucifixion* (1987); Earl Lovelace's Taffy in *The Dragon Can't Dance* (1979); Andrew Salkey's Mother Johnson in *A Quality of Violence* (1959) and Sylvia Wynter's Moses Barton in *The Hills of Hebron* (1962).

just sits there lamely (l. 49): Like Jonah, Thalbot is puzzled by God's inaction.

xiv

the mesh of vine (l. 1): This is an edible gourd, not a grape vine.

Freshly growing, it shelters Thalbot's dazed body (l. 6): This summarises Jonah 4: 6: "And the Lord God prepared a gourd, and made it to come up over Jonah, that it might be a shadow over his head, to deliver him from his grief. So Jonah was exceeding glad of the gourd."

he eats without relish, grudgingly (l. 12): Both Jonah and Elijah declare to God that they want to die.

This is his mocking shrine (l. 22): Built as it is with pink-blue shells, the motif associated with Clarice (see notes to Chapter XXI, iv, l. 11), this is evidently a shrine to her – built in mock idolatry, and in defiance of God, as if to say to God, "Where is your power, if you can let things like this happen, you let Clarice thrive but punish me?"

now defiant artist – / to ungod (l. 22-23): Thalbot is still evidently hosting traces of the spirit of the fourth apparition. See note to Chapter XX, iv, l. 8.

the surreal of ladders (ll. 28): This is a reference to Jacob's ladder: "And he dreamed, and behold a ladder set up on the earth, and the top of it reached to heaven: and behold the angels of God ascending and descending on it" (Genesis 28: 12). Thalbot is looking for a sign from heaven.

Soon colonies of worms (l. 31): This refers to the Jonah narrative when God destroys the gourd ("But God prepared a worm when the morning rose the next day, and it smote the gourd that it withered" (Jonah 4: 7). The image conflates Thalbot's persistent disgust with sexuality with the biblical association, echoed in several places in *Prophets*, of worms with death.

this revelation (l. 34): Thalbot belatedly realises that God is a capricious joker and can do what he likes, irrespective of human ideas of right and wrong.

In Kingston's orange glow [...] The eye of cyclops in the dusk, winks (ll. 43-49): Here the poem seems to agree with Thalbot's assessment of God's remoteness and apparent unconcern with human affairs. This is the Jamaica in which, in 1992, 629 people were murdered and 646 people killed on the roads.

Kill me now! (l. 50): A dramatisation of Jonah's misery: "the sun beat upon the head of Jonah, that he fainted, and wished in himself to die, and said, It is better for me to die than to live" (Jonah 4: 8).

So soft is the hand… (l. 55): Here, perhaps, we hear the poet speaking. The words also echo what God says to Jonah: "And should not I spare Nineveh, that great city, wherein are more than six-score thousand persons that cannot discern between their right hand and their left hand; and also much cattle?" (4: 11).

the amassed dead (l. 61): Another reference to Anthony McNeill's poem "A Wreath for the Suicide Heart". See note for Chapter XVII, i, Epigraph.

Port Royal (l. 64): A reference to the earthquake and tsunami that destroyed the old capital of Jamaica in 1692, drowning and killing upwards of 5000 people. This was believed to be divine punishment for being the "wickedest place on earth". Perhaps, the poem suggests, it is not really God who has changed ("In the old days judgement was swift") but the kind of interpretation placed on such disaster. Much of what is known about Port Royal came from the marine archaeology begun in the late 1960s, in Kwame Dawes' youth, led by Robert Marx. There were further extensive investigations of the underwater site between 1981-1990. See R.F. Marx, "Excavating Port Royal (Part 1)" and "Divers of Port Royal", both 1968.

XV

the charred raven comes with meat in its beak (l. 1): Here there is a switch of prophets back from Jonah to Elijah, who like Jonah is sitting in lonely misery in the desert. This occurs because God has sent a drought to punish Ahab and Jezebel. However, God doesn't let Elijah die because he organises nature in his support: "And the ravens brought him bread and flesh in the morning, and bread and flesh in the evening; and he drank water of the brook" (1 Kings 16: 6). Here the bird is a charred raven, not only because ravens are black, like Clarice, but also because the charring signifies both that she has hubristically flown too near to the sun or, perhaps, that in falling she has burned up as she re-entered the earth's atmosphere. In this image, Dawes perhaps remembered either Wordsworth McAndrew's much anthologised poem "To a Carrion Crow" (1960) or Ted Hughes' "Crow's Fall" (*Crow*, 1972, p. 36). In the former, there's a final prophetic image, where the crow, once "the silver bird of the heavens" rises to mythological splendour in its Promethean daring to penetrate the mysteries of the upper sky, but is scorched for its pains as it passes through "that sacred blue fire" to "become this mendicant preacher" (*Kyk-over-Al*, 1960). In Hughes' poem there is a Promethean motif, too: "When Crow was white he decided the sun was too white" and attacks it. "But the sun brightened – / [...] and Crow returned charred black" (p. 36).

Clarice's panting like bloody Jezebel (l. 9): Jezebel has been Elijah's long-term enemy, an archetype for a cruel and devious woman who meets a predictably gory end: "So they threw her down: and some of her blood was sprinkled on the wall, and on the horses: and he trode her under foot... And they went to bury her: but they found no more of her than the skull, and the feet, and the palms of her hands. Wherefore they came again, and told him. And he said, This is the word of the Lord, which he spake by his servant Elijah the Tishbite, saying, In the portion of Jezreel shall dogs eat the flesh of Jezebel: And the carcase of Jezebel shall be as dung upon the face of the field in the portion of Jezreel; so that they shall not say, This is Jezebel" (2 Kings 9: 33, 35-37). That Thalbot should think of Clarice as a Jezebel is very plausibly Jamaican, where this archetype of conniving womanhood has maintained a lively presence in popular culture (reggae) and speech. See the note to Chapter IX (*Confessional*), i, l. 18 and to the critical commentary, p. 101.

Clarice has prophesied his dying (l. 12): At the same time that Thalbot is imagining Clarice's gory end, Clarice is engaged in the church ritual of "reading out", the formal disfellowshipping of Thalbot, declaring his spiritual death when, on her word, he is expelled from the church. See section xi of this chapter. The reading out probably consists of reading out 1 Corinthians 5: 11-13: "But now I have written unto you not to keep company, if any man that is called a brother be a fornicator, or covetous, or an idolator, or a railer, or a drunkard, or an extortioner; with such an one no not to eat./ For what have I to do to judge them also that are without? do not ye judge them that are within?/ But them that are without God judgeth. Therefore put away from among yourselves that wicked person."

the fallen Clarice (ll. 16-17): As Jezebel falls from the city wall, Clarice falls from her position as prophetess in the church. Whether this is really to be regarded as a fall is explored in Part Four of the poem.

the path of disobedient prophets/ now struck with powerless clairvoyance (l. 20): This relates both to the position of Jonah at the end of the Book of Jonah, where God has the last word, defending his right to use his power as he pleases (and we have no inkling of whether Jonah ends his sulk) – and to Thalbot who has clearly taken Clarice's denunciation of him as a reprobate, sexual offender and madman seriously, for which reason we may deduce that he thinks his prophetic career is at an end.

PART FOUR

Summary

The last part of *Prophets* moves out of the structure of narrative to offer
a series of metatextual commentaries, recaps and questionings. It comes
back to exploring the contrast between the "poetic realism" of quasi-
biographical experience and the construction of "poetic myth". This
is the alternative, imagined ending for Clarice's trajectory through the
poem.

The chapters in this last part of the poem are all "spoken" in the voice of
an "I", who is variously the Clarice of supposed experience, the Clarice of
myth; a prophetess who is not Clarice, who flies over Africa to the USA;
the "broken" student who reappears in this last part of the poem to reflect
on his experience; and finally an "I" whom the reader must suppose is the
poet. This last "I", as the presumed author of *Prophets*, comments not only
on the process of writing the poem, but also on the biographical figure of
"Kwame Dawes" as both writer and experiencer, the writer processing the
experiences of the younger self.

Overall, this fourth part of the poem comprises a meditation on how
questions about faith, the miraculous, the institutional practice of religion,
sexuality, power and gender, and the cultural and historical contexts of
contemporary Jamaica can be brought together in an imaginative whole.
Structurally, Part Four is located at points of departure: of Clarice from the
narrative (to Canada); of the unnamed prophetess to the USA; and of the
poet reflecting on the poem, as if from his writing desk, also in the USA.

The poem ends by asking what can be rescued from the "tricks, sin, the
betrayals, as if this was all" that constitute the experience of having been part
of Clarice's church. The poet asks where now does his faith stand, a faith
that is rooted in a belief in the possibility of the miraculous, in death
redeemed by resurrection, and in an openness to the minor miracles of
prophecy witnessed. He asks how he is to respond to the sincerity of literal
belief in the words of the Bible, to the sincere attempts of believers to lead
better lives, but also to the evidence of gullibility, of hubristic notions of
human saintliness in an institution that is inevitably susceptible to ordinary
human flaws. How can he deal with the fact that members of this church
believe themselves to be the true inheritors of the early Christians in
denying worldly things and preparing their souls for the hereafter, but who
are, perhaps inevitably, sliding into the corrupting thought that their pieties
make them deserving of earthly rewards. How is he to come to terms with
a church that is blind to its contradictions, that sets itself impossible and
self-denying rigidities of control over the body's sexuality, yet finds itself,
through acts of bodily abandonment, "labouring" to reach spiritual tran-

scendence through dance, jumping, falling and self-induced trance. How is he to make sense of a church that denies its Jamaican, creolised African cultural roots because of its often North American, white-derived notions of modernity, but which yet enacts those African cultural inheritances through their bodies. These are questions with national, institutional and deeply personal pertinence.

But perhaps the most central of these questions, for *Prophets*, is how to envision a treaty between spiritual and sexual transcendence. Here the master trope is the imagery of flight and falling, through which the poem constructs a mythical afterlife for Clarice as the prophetess who falls from one kind of grace through a sexual indiscretion – and yet rises to the grace of an enhanced personhood.

In structure and poetic mode, Part Four reminds us that *Prophets* moves in a space between epic narrative and the lyric poem, that it is as much an assemblage of lyric components as a linear narrative with a beginning, middle and end.

Notes

If my land cries out against me... if I have devoured its yield without payment (Epigraph): These two verses come towards the end of a long series of self-justifying questions from the suffering Job to God (Job 31: 38-39). Job claims that he is very willing to be punished for sins of omission and commission – if he has actually committed them – but he expresses his puzzlement about why, as a virtuous man, he is being punished.

How is one to read this epigraph to Part Four? At one level, it enters into the poem's debate about how the believer is to understand the mysteries of the relationship between God and man; but it can also be interpreted as a more personal statement, as part of Dawes' reflections on his decision/need to bid Jamaica farewell and his role as a writer in terms of his responsibilities to the country that has made him a writer. Having reflected on the flaws of the four apparitions, on the limitations of their arts' impact on Jamaica, as a consistently self-reflexive poet, Dawes cannot do other than ask whether what he offers in *Prophets* offers any more, or can even be regarded as due payment for what Jamaica has given him. At the end of his questioning, Job, the successful farmer, declares that if he has sinned, then: "Let thistles grow instead of wheat, and cockle instead of barley". In the context of leaving Jamaica, can *Prophets* be wheat and barley or is it fated to be briers and weed?

CHAPTER XXIV
Speaking for the First Time

Summary

Clarice speaks like a Pirandellian character claiming her independence from the author, yet speaking in a voice that is manifestly not her own – a disjunction that sends the reader back to reflecting on the different ways her writer/creator has shaped her image, in ways, for instance, that reflect shifts in point of view between the experiencing student and the author reflecting on that experience and constructing the poem as myth.

Notes

To speak my words would be to fracture/ the wings of myth (ll. 1-2): What Clarice *could* say must relate to the somewhat sordid deal she makes with the church brothers – the visa and blameless exit, in return for a non-disclosure agreement ("the vow to keep the tongue arrested"). But the statement also implies that if we were, at this point, to hear Clarice in her own voice, it would make implausible the mythical space that the writer wants to locate her in. The references to fractured wings and careering to the sunbaked earth clearly echo the fate of Jezebel and the raven that Thalbot pelts with a stone in Chapter XXIII, xv, ll.1-9. What Clarice displays, as an openly authorial construction, is an awareness of the contrast between the constructed image, of being "written into myth" as a saint in her church, a goddess, the performer of impossible miracles, and the reality of the woman who has stored secrets to her advantage, accepted the crumpled dollar bills, and who is now made ordinary as she heads as an immigrant to Canada.

The whore's hymen (l. 19): Compare the similarly irreligious speculations of Last Night concerning the handmaidens of the Lord on the beach (Chapter XXI, i, l. 22). Here Clarice alludes to leaving with no blemish on her reputation.

the three-day dead has stumbled forth (l. 21): See the note on Lazarus and the rolling of the stone from the tomb in Chapter XVI, l. 31. Here, the idea is that no more secrets will emerge.

role model, now player, now closed icon (l. 24): This summarises, self-referentially, the three stages in Clarice's transformation as a character in the poem: as admired prophetess, as the woman who cuts a deal, and now as a constructed piece of art, like a religious icon whose protective doors have been closed on the image.

to empty my heart to the wind... talking woman, gossiping herstory (ll. 28-29): This passage reviews the position of the prophetess who has sacrificed her selfhood and her personal desires in order to become the sacred vessel through whom the holy spirit speaks, who has had to deny herself, her individual personhood, but who is now becoming the woman who can speak for herself.

the tightly/ girded loins (ll. 30-31): She alludes to Ephesians 6: 14: "Stand therefore, having your loins girt about with truth, and having on the breastplate of righteousness".

a voice that deconstructs the metalanguage of God's clever narratives (ll. 31-32): At this point, the stylistic register directs us to recognise that this cannot be Clarice who is speaking, because its vocabulary exposes the author's ironic voice. This points to what follows as a different kind of myth, the creation of Clarice as the author would have wished her to be, very different from the church-constructed myth of the virginal prophetess with her blue-eyed Jesus, but no less a myth, no less an admission of wishfulness on the poet's part. The line quoted also points, self-reflexively, to the author as the writer of a chapter such as XV, with its deconstruction of the story of Legion and the Gadarene swine through the language of film.

But the air is too thin here at the gate of heaven (l. 34): This reverses the image in Chapter III, ii, l. 9ff and Chapter XIV, iii, l. 6ff, where the poem plays with the confusion between entry to heaven and the USA as jointly desired destinations of the faithful. Now it is entry to Christian heaven that is compared to the trials suffered at the US embassy (which plays the role of St Peter as the gatekeeper to heaven – as St Peter is often portrayed in Christian art – based on the words recorded in Matthew 16: 19: "I will give you the keys of the kingdom of heaven"). Clarice is now quite certain what kind of heaven on earth she wants to enter. She is "unlocking the tongue of my imprisonment", an ironic reflection on the fact that her capacity to speak in tongues has been her passport to perceived saintliness in the church.

longed to fall through (l. 37): From this point onwards, the poem reverses the usual connotations of rising and falling. Clarice will fall into her enrichment as a woman. To fall as a saint enables her to rise into the complexity of personhood.

let my hair snarl its unruly self (l. 39): The imagined Clarice is no longer the woman of Ponds lightening cream, corsets and the denial of her Africanness. (See Chapters II and VI.)

But they always knew… (l. 46): She asserts the complicity at the heart of the bargain between herself and the leaders of the church.

the pink and powder of my jewelled cage (l. 47): An image that connects back both to the epigraph of Chapter II, "In a shady cloister mew'd", and to the imagery of pinkness, coral and shells that accompany Clarice throughout the poem.

Now broken, my wings limping (l. 54): Images of herself as the raven, as Jezebel.

words tumbling forth (l. 56): An echo of speaking in tongues in the church, but also a contrast with the woman who is forced to constrain the Africa thick in her tongue, to twist it around King James' syntax, who has moved out of the rarefied atmosphere of the divine logos into the turbulent sensuality of the poetic word.

CHAPTER XXV
Miracles

Notes

I hear voices in my head: The present tense of this lyric poem, in Clarice's voice, locates it outside of historic time. Does it refer to how things were, to the pleasures of power and the temptations to corruption, or is it a flash-forward to Clarice in Canada, now an ordinary immigrant, remembering her gift? Perhaps, too, the action of slicing tomatoes takes her back to the room with Last Night (IX, *Confessional*).

and feel my face glow (l. 9): Another reference to Moses coming down from Mount Sinai (Exodus 34: 35). See the note to Chapter XXII, iii, l. 1.

CHAPTER XXVI
The Perks of Prophecy

Summary

Another lyric poem, again as if in Clarice's voice, and referring to the episode (seen then from the point of view of the "boy", the broken young man) in Chapter XII (*The Fear of Prophecy*) when he comes to church guilty over a sexual adventure, and fearful that Clarice will expose him, confessing: "Is it me she is reading, falling again, is it my// fantasy, flaming with its startling detail?/ How fully I repent, how deep my weeping,/ my lamenting before the altar" (XII, ll. 24-27). Clarice's memory of the episode neatly exposes the self-dramatising indulgence of the young man's guilt, his unconfessed feelings for Clarice, as well as confirming her human perceptiveness.

Note

Tonight, the spirit... is grieved (l. 4): There is no inspiration, no speaking in tongues.

CHAPTER XXVII
The Last Poem

Summary

As part of the vein of humour that runs through *Prophets*, this is not, indeed, the last poem, though it is a serious one that probably comes closest to Dawes' own voice, his own reflections on how, coming to the end of writing about the experiences of being a part of Clarice's church, he now approaches some understanding of the nature of that church and the nature of his faith. The poem is an admission, a disappointed one, that the sources of revelation may often be mundane and lack the splendour of miracle. Not the finger writing on Belshazzar's wall, but the words of a dead poet, whose High Anglican writing is about as far away as one can get from the thrill of prophecy. The poem is also about the process and hopes involved in writing *Prophets*. In using a paraphrase of a line from T.S. Eliot's *Four Quartets,* Dawes displays a neat ambivalence – somewhere between humility and ambition.

Notes

For us all there is the trying… (Paraphrasing Eliot) Epigraph: We may wonder whether offering a paraphrase rather than a quotation is an act of ownership or a declaration that the grand old man of modernism warrants no more? The paraphrase is actually close to the actual text drawn from East Coker V, which comes as the conclusion to this reflection:

> And what there is to conquer
> By strength and submission, has already been discovered,
> Once or twice, or several times, by men whom we cannot hope
> To emulate – but there is no competition –
> There is only the fight to recover what has been lost
> And found and lost again, and now under conditions
> That seem unpropitious. But perhaps neither gain nor loss.
> For us, there is only the trying. The rest is not our business.

As an epigraph, within its original context, what could be further from the passionate certainties of Clarice's Charismatic Pentecostalism than the polite modesty of this High Anglican declaration of faith? As such, is it a reproof to those certainties? An attempt to hold on to something after the mutual self-destruction of both the prophets of the poem, and a loss of trust in spectacular signs? But beyond this, we know that Eliot's poem was offered as an attempt to recover or construct the spiritual roots of an Englishness that could stand as a bulwark against the existential threats to the nation in the darkest periods of World War II (the poem was written between 1941-1943). *Prophets* is perhaps offered in the same spirit, to a Jamaica at an acute point of crisis as a post-colonial society.

This I heard (l. 1): I.e. the words paraphrased from Eliot.

the wind off the hills (l. 4): Cf. the rushing mighty wind of Pentecost. See note to Chapter XIII, l. 50.

the bloody cypher/ of his finger (ll. 5-6): I.e. a spectacular sign from God, as in Daniel 5: 5, the warning to King Belshazzar at his feast: "Suddenly the fingers of a human hand appeared and wrote on the plaster of the wall... The king watched the hand as it wrote."

no nick-of-time bleat (l. 6): This is another reference to the fortunate discovery of a ram that saves Abraham from killing his son Isaac as a sacrifice to God. See the note on p. 156 to X, ii, ll. 59-60.

words of a dead poet (l. 8): I.e. T.S. Eliot, who died in 1965.

backative (l. 9): A Jamaicanism, meaning that there has been no support, no offer of reward – as, for instance, results in the bitterness of the sybil mother who despite her faith and good works, has not been rewarded with a green card (in Chapter III, ii).

poet's flirtations with the cadence of a god (l. 11): As in the passage quoted above, Eliot imitates the rhythms of the book of Common Prayer. Perhaps this is also a reference to the way *Prophets* at times echoes the rhythms, the language, the tone and narratives of the Bible, but also makes several metatextual references to the act of creative myth-making – playing God – in the poem, for instance, in the play between the actual and the imagined in the portrayal of Clarice.

I sat among the roses/ and chewed at bitter leaves (ll. 12-13): The first line is an echo of a line from "Burnt Norton" from *The Four Quartets*: "Towards the door we never opened/ Into the rose garden"; and the second line perhaps references the "bitter herbs" to be eaten at Passover, from Exodus 12: 8 – here the bitter taste of experience, curative but difficult to swallow.

The slim volume of verse (ll. 15-16): I.e. *Prophets*, written in four books, like Eliot's poems, and hence also a quartet, though rather less slim than *The Four Quartets* (if rather slimmer than *Omeros*).

earth-makers, stone-breakers (l. 17): An allusion to the famous poem of Jamaican nationhood by George Campbell (1916-2002), "History Makers", from *First Poems* (2012 [1945], p. 101), which begins: "Women stone breakers/ Hammers and rocks / Tired child makers…" But unlike the ready embrace of George Campbell's work as defining the nation-to-be, the implicit question the comparison makes in these difficult post-colonial times seems to be: can *Prophets* hope for any more than to rustle impotently like the poem it is?

CHAPTER XXVIII
Flight

Summary

We might at first take the "I" to be Clarice, especially in the first couple of stanzas, and then suppose that it is the poet. It is neither, but perhaps a merger of the two. The "I" in the first four sections of the chapter is a woman, an unnamed prophetess, who makes a geographical passage from Jamaica, over the Blue Mountains, past Cuba, over Miami, over Africa, to halt at South Carolina, a flight that is purely of the imagination. It is the prophetess imagined as Dawes would like her to be. The temptation to read the "I" as Dawes arises because the flight echoes the actual migratory journey that Dawes made in 1992 to take up a post at the University of South Carolina. But this is a woman (not Clarice, since she is heading for Toronto), whose flight is made in fulfilment of the critique made in Toni Morrison's *Song of Solomon* (see the critical commentary, p. 69-70) that the flight back to Africa of the enslaved was could only be made by men. The slipperiness of identity here points to the poem's implication that the writing Dawes shares himself with Clarice, Thalbot and Last Night. The quasi-autobiographical, fictional "I" shares features with all these named characters: with Clarice's struggle between the pulls of sexuality and pious faith, with Last Night's woe-begoneness and guilt, and with Thalbot's instability between revolutionary blackness and spiritual prophecy. Again, like the second, third and fourth apparitions, the "I" as poet has to contemplate a vexed relationship with Jamaican society and the hope/ despair over whether writing prophetically makes any difference.

In the process of the flight, the poem reflects on the dreams of such a return to Africa and the intellectual self-deceptions involved in thinking that a complete, unchanged return to origins is possible. Even so, whilst acknowledging the onward rush of history and the constancy of change embedded in human culture, section i also acknowledges the impossibility of forgetting the dream, of overcoming the desire for a mythical lost wholeness, of knowing what and where is home – and where heaven is to be found. This section also explores the spiritual conflict within the speaking "I" between the cultural pulls that Africa exerts and her certainty in the revelation of Christianity and "blood shed for remission of sin" that makes it impossible for the prophetess to do other than turn away from Africa's own religious cosmology and belief systems.

In section ii, within a questioning of an Hegelian dialectic of history's unfolding, remote from individual human intentions (a nod, perhaps to Dawes' father's Marxism), the poem places the migratory person at the centre of concern, and in particular the person shaped by his/her emotions, by "heart", the indefinability of the deepest feelings, such as those brought on by "the stomp and rattle of the gospeller's Sunday" (XXVIII, ii, ll. 4-5).

Section iii is an announcement of an arrival, in the mode of a letter of introduction to various unnamed "you"s. It creates a mythic parallel to the actual journey that Dawes made to the new territory of South Carolina in 1992. But rather than discussing academic credentials, the prophetess reflects on the difficulties of bringing the gospel to these parts. There is a certain prickly rawness, a sometimes accusatory tone, that bears witness to arriving in a southern state that had been a slave state, that had fought on the Confederate, pro-slavery side in the Civil War, and that still flew the Confederate flag over the state capital; a state that had a large and under-privileged African American minority (around 30%), that manifested an historically embedded racism in its poor record on racial equality. The "I" who is in dialogue with the unnamed plural "you" is making it very clear that she is determined on change and not tokenism. As Dawes' later memoir, *A Far Cry from Plymouth Rock* (2007), makes clear, South Carolina was his first real experience of being perceived as black, as a minority man, as other. Ironically, this was an experience felt most acutely in the racially divided churches. One of the "you"s is undoubtedly some representative of the white churches with their "bloodless sermons" and the desire to "silence my songs", to exclude the emotional, bodily engagements of the African American churches.

But this is also an "I" who is committed (as Dawes was) to taking possession of the new landscape, who has already begun to find a place in the new soil, the piedmont of South Carolina ("I have wailed to the hills/ and my voice has returned dew soft/ with clear melody and harmony// of new trees, new brooks, new light…" (XXVIII, iii, ll. 37-40). This is a voice that finds its way into poems written at this time and published in collections such as *Jacko Jacobus* (1996) and most intensively in *Wisteria: Twilight Songs from the Swamp Country* (2006).

It is also, though, a voice that is engaged with the idea of migrancy and flight as a personal condition, "'cause I come to find a path – and this won't be/ a path you make, it will be a path you may offer,/ then I will decide and either walk the asphalt/ or ride the cobalt sky on that chartered journey back" (XXVIII, iv, ll. 6-9). The interviewing "you" is reminded: "Flying comes so natural to me these days…" (iv. ll. 32).

The last section (v) is an envoi to the poem itself, and the place where the poet is most clearly the "I" (as in "The Last Poem"). It reflects on a return to Jamaica ("How green is the island when it rains" (v, ll. 15), to the memories of spiritual transcendence, the miracles glimpsed behind "the tricks, the sin, the betrayals" (v, l. 2), the fearful acknowledgement that the poem itself has been in part Dawes' quarrel with God, but also a restatement of the conviction that there is a joy to be sought in the life of the spirit.

Notes

i

a bargain basement faith (l. 2): The phrase refers to the basement of a shop where goods are sold cheap, so it is an image that qualifies the nature of the experience, that expresses the recognition that the spiritual seeker must accept uncertainty and is destined to search amongst what may well turn out to be rubbish. At the least, the chapter makes it clear that it is a faith that must accommodate the cultural African-Jamaicanness of the "I".

my watertight goatskin satchel (l. 10): A deliberately archaic image, as if this was an enslaved person flying back to Africa. See the discussion of the trope of flight and *Prophets'* connection to Toni Morrison's *Song of Solomon* in the critical commentary, pp. 69-70.

cooling pebbles for under my tongue (l. 11): As an aid to allaying thirst in a desert; also as a cure, according to Demosthenes, for stuttering, and as an aid in training for effective public oratory.

stroking my chin (l. 14): Imitating Castro's beardedness.

defecting daughters (l. 15): Fidel Castro's daughter, Senora Fernandez, defected from Cuba to the USA in 1993 and spoke negatively of her father and the regime.

the boatload of criminals (l. 17): Over 100,000 Cubans were allowed to leave for the USA in the Mariel Boatlift of 1980. The number included a good many who had fallen foul of Cuban law.

sangre de dios (l. 19): An oath: God's blood!

scar-face badness (l. 20): A reference to the 1983 Brian De Palma film, *Scarface*, starring Al Pacino as a Cuban exile/ gangster who builds a drugs empire in the USA.

dusting the green with coke (l. 21): I.e. snorting cocaine from the American dollar bill.

South Carolina's low country: This is the agricultural region of Third-World levels of poverty along South Carolina's coast that was the centre of slave labour estates growing rice and *indigofera tinctoria* to make the dye indigo (see Jean M. West, "The Devil's Blue Dye: Indigo and Slavery" (nd), where there are still strong African survivals amongst the African American population.

turtle green islands (l. 29): The Sea Islands off the South Carolina coast, one of the centres of the Gullah/Geechee communities, peoples with a creolised African culture and language, with many resemblances to African-Caribbean creole cultures. (The word Gullah is possibly derived from Angola people.)

lodged in seed and stomach (l. 25): See, for instance, V.S. Naipaul's *The Mimic Men* (1967): "But we walked in a garden of hell, among trees, some still without popular names, whose seeds had sometimes been brought to our island in the intestines of slaves" (p. 147), and the line in Derek Walcott's *Omeros*, Chapter XXVIII, l. 10: "There were seeds in our stomachs…"

Sycorax… Caliban (ll. 26-27): As well as the obvious reference to Shakespeare's *The Tempest*, the lines allude to the use of these characters in, for instance, George Lamming's *The Pleasures of Exile* (1960), Aimé Césaire's *Une Tempête* (1969) and the use Kamau Brathwaite makes of Sycorax (as black mother) in *Barabajan Poems* (1994), where Sycorax's book parallels Prospero's.

Gabon (l. 31): A former French colonial territory in West Africa between The Congo and Equatorial Guinea, and one of the major sources of enslaved Africans.

akra (l. 32): A fried, seasoned dough dish brought to the Caribbean by enslaved West Africans.

kelewele (l. 33): Peppery fried ripe plantains, common in Ghana and, as fried plantain, a staple Caribbean food.

just legacies of the gifts we have left (l. 36): An allusion to the Sub-Saharan, black, Nubian contribution to the making of Ancient Egyptian civilisation – though the African presence is no longer readily visible in modern Egypt.

Black Atlantis (l. 42): This alludes to the thesis that the lost (undersea) continent of Atlantis was a black civilisation; part of a range of attempts to challenge, both scientifically and mythically, Eurocentric accounts of the development of world civilisations. Martin Bernal's *Black Athena* (1987) was perhaps the most seriously received of such challenges to Eurocentric history.

Whitewashed memories… clichés of a glorious race (l. 46): An allusion to the tendency of some accounts of Africa, written as anti-colonial texts, to focus only on the grandiose – Ancient Egypt and the West African kingships – rather than on the more quotidian reality of villages and agriculture. Whitewashed in the sense that they were still beholden to Western notions of what constituted a civilisation. See, for instance, J.C. DeGraft-Johnson, *African Glory: The Story of Vanished Negro Civilisations* (1954).

Egyptians wince at the kente and dashiki (l. 48): Amongst Arab North Africans, racial prejudice against sub-Saharan Africans (such as West African wearers of kente cloth and dashikis) is by no means unknown.

the Mahotella Queens… Mokola daughters (l. 51): The Mahotella Queens are a South African vocal mbaqanga group, first formed in 1962, still in existence in the 21st century, though no longer with any of the original members. They reached international success with records such as 1987's *Thokozile* with the gravel-voiced Malathini. "Mokola daughters" possibly refers to the women of the Makola market in Ghana who had protested against the anti-hoarding policies of the Jerry Rawlings' regime, which in 1979 destroyed the market in reprisal.

shabeens (l. 52): The name for African unlicensed bars in apartheid South Africa, like speakeasies in prohibition USA.

Masai's gaze (l. 54): I.e. the pastoralists of South Kenya and northern Tanzania. There are no doubt many iconic photographs of Masai gazing into the distance. See the Masai statue in Chapter XI (*Infidelity*), i, l. 7.

this is my dignity (ll. 55-60): An ironically absurdist account of an impossible homecoming (damp with tomorrow's rain), the deliberately ludicrous image of being sucked into the soil, and the imagery satirising the pompous respect for national flags.

the *brujo's* sharp recognition of healing (l. 63): The brujo is a worker of magic in Cuba (*brujo*=sorcerer), part of the country's Yoruba-derived

Orisha worship and healing practices, but here referenced as signifying a mere fragment of survival, rather than the wholeness of a living African culture.

Shrine of my deepest fears (l. 67): In Kwame Dawes' collection *Requiem* (1996), poems written in remembrance, as shrines to heal the suffering of slavery, he expands on the twin and conflicting emotions of the passionate urge to reconnect with Africa and the fear that slavery broke the connection, that there is no longer anything that can be recovered whole.

Split in my devotion (l. 70): Here, the speaker talks about feeling divided between the urge to draw on a belief system that is autochthonously African (the earth that beckons me with the smell of seed) and the fact of being a deeply convinced Christian, for whom much of such practice would be pagan.

blood shed for the remission of sin (l. 72): A reference to the central item of faith of Christianity, that Christ was crucified and shed blood to take on the sins of the world. The words echo the communion service where the priest offers wine to communicants, using Christ's words from the last supper before the crucifixion: "And he took the cup, and gave thanks, and gave it to them, saying, Drink ye all of it; For this is my blood of the new testament, which is shed for many for the remission of sins" (Matthew 26: 27-28).

another land, comely (l. 75): A reference to Ethiopia, imaged in the comeliness of the Queen of Sheba, and the Africa which is home for Rastafarians.

Jericho (l. 77): The Canaanite city that fell to the Israelites (see Joshua 5: 13 – 6: 27).

nigger Simon on Golgotha (l. 78): A reference to the man who, according to Luke 23: 26, was commanded to carry Jesus's cross: "And as they led him away, they laid hold upon one Simon, a Cyrenian, coming out of the country, and on him they laid the cross, that he might bear it after Jesus." Since Cyrene was in Libya, Simon was quite probably a dark-skinned man.

Kilimanjaro (l. 84): As the highest mountain in Africa (Tanzania), an iconic emblem seen as an African heartland.

ii

Culture is flux. Flux is culture. Absolute spirit (l. 1): An allusion to the language of the Hegelian dialectical concept of history as an unfolding process in which future change is latent in the present. The language points to the abstract and intellectual nature of this idealist attempt to comprehend history's movements in terms of formal logical proof.

Heart is the fire caught-up within my bones (l. 3): This sentence references Jeremiah 20: 9: "But if I say, 'I will not mention him or speak any more in his name,' his word is in my heart like a fire, a fire shut up in my bones. I am weary of holding it in; indeed I cannot." Jeremiah is here speaking of the impossibility of not speaking God's word, even though it brings his persecution at the hands of the orthodox temple priests. For the speaker, the clause tells of spiritual belief which feels physical in its intensity, which has nothing to do with the rational processes of logical proof.

Heart is not history [...] heart is prophecy: A counter proposition to the Hegelian "absolute spirit", charging that emotion and desire are the drivers of human existence, that there is a truth beyond historical time. This is a continuation of the language drawn from Jeremiah who distinguishes between false prophets and the destiny that derives from God's heart, using heart as a synonym for will: "The anger of the Lord shall not return, until he have executed, and till he have performed the thoughts of his heart: in the latter days ye shall consider it perfectly" (23: 20).

I arrive a stranger. I arrive dead (l. 9): An admission of the impossibility of a living return that overcomes the alienation of history.

...rustle their hymns, calling me back, calling me back (l. 11): This references a line from a song, "Chokota" by Ujamaa, the Canadian reggae band that Kwame Dawes led and wrote for, on the CD of that name, released in Fredericton, in 1991.

iii

dashiki... kente (l. 1): West African clothing and cloth. See notes to Chapter XXI, ii, l. 26, and Chapter VI, ii, l. 1.

There is no burden of guilt in my history (ll. 5-6): As one whose foreparents were brought to the Caribbean as enslaved persons and not one who sold Africans into slavery.

Sardining of humanity (l. 8): An allusion to the iconic engraving of a slave ship, seen from above, that shows all too clearly how slaves were packed like sardines in their holds. It was a cross-section of the slave ship *Brookes* of Liverpool, a woodcut published in 1789 (British Museum).

the all-seeing papal man (l. 11): Pope Nicholas V issued an edict in 1452 giving Spain and Portugal the right to enslave in perpetuity any unbelievers and heathens they captured.

the satchel of smallpox and rude disease (l. 12): The diseases brought by the Spanish that contributed to the wiping out of the indigenous Tainos from the Caribbean islands (as well as through deliberate slaughter, enslavement and enforced overwork).

Toussaint (l. 13): Noted here as a victim of betrayal. Toussaint L'Ouverture (1742-1803), the Haitian leader, was invited by Napoleon in 1803 to attend negotiations with promise of safe passage. In France, he was arrested and incarcerated in a mountain prison where he died of cold, hunger and neglect in the same year.

Sam Sharpe (l. 14): Also known as Daddy Sharpe (?–1832). He was a Baptist, an enslaved man who in 1831 attempted to lead a nonviolent revolt through strike action against slavery. As a literate man, Sharpe had read of the parliamentary debates on abolition and believed the local authorities and planters were denying the rights of the enslaved whom the British parliament was about to free. After the revolt there were reprisals and counter-reprisals and a military defeat of the insurgents. Sharpe was one of those captured and executed in 1832. He was made a National Hero of Jamaica in 1982.

Bogle (l. 15): Paul Bogle (1820-1865) was a deacon and preacher in the Native Baptist church who led a rebellion against the excessive taxation and repression of the African Jamaican peasantry in St Thomas in the East. In the savage repression of the uprising, following what became known as the Morant Bay rebellion of 1865, Bogle was one of around six hundred Jamaicans who were hung, many being brutally flogged before their execution.

the black and white churches (l. 15): A reference both to the need African Jamaicans felt to form their own churches (like the Native Baptists), since they were excluded from full participation in the mainstream churches such as the Anglicans, and even the Baptists, and to the way churches in the USA remain the most racially segregated institutions in the nation. See Dawes' chapter "Going to Church" in *A Far Cry from Plymouth Rock* (2007), pp. 183-197.

The rejected cornerstones falling (l. 16): This is an allusion to Bob Marley's song, "Cornerstone" on the album, *Soul Rebels* (1970): "The stone that the builder refused/ Will always be the head cornerstone". Marley is paraphrasing 1 Peter 2: 7-8: "Unto you therefore which believe he is precious: but unto them which be disobedient, the stone which the builders disallowed, the same is made the head of the corner,/ And a stone of stumbling, and a rock of offence, even to them which stumble at the word, being disobedient: whereunto also they were appointed."

black water of your hell (l. 17): This references the way the Eurocentric symbolism which allied white with innocence and black with sin infected and racialised Christianity.

the silencing of my songs (l. 17): Both an allusion to the attempted suppression of African-derived musical forms, particularly drumming, during the period of slavery and colonialism, and an observation on the distaste the contemporary white churches in the USA appear to have for African American musical expression in their liturgies.

I will not be no beast of burden for you no more (l. 18): This perhaps alludes to the Rolling Stones' song "Beast of Burden" (*Some Girls*, 1978), but adapted to speak for the patwa voice of one who will be a slave no more. The Stones' song begins: "I'll never be your beast of burden/ My back is broad but it's a hurting."

twilight schizophrenia (l. 18): Twilight states are used in psychiatry to describe mental states where the mind falsifies external reality, just as white Hollywood films falsify the image of the Middle-Eastern Jesus as a white, blue-eyed European. See note to Chapter VI, i, to Clarice, whose "bleeding Christ has crystal blue eyes".

the Academy of Regret (l. 24): The attitude, for instance, that whilst the past of slavery is regrettable, it has no place in current discourse – a refusal to acknowledge that its institutional violence and the racial attitudes it bred exist into present inequalities and prejudice.

your constant belief in the beauty and joy of Colon's accidental landing (l. 26): This refers to the white American view that Columbus's "discovery" of the New World was a matter for celebration; it had been instituted as a federal holiday in 1937. In 1992, the 500th anniversary, Native Americans in the two Americas showed very forcibly that this was a view they did not share, proposing instead an Indigenous People's Day.

the judgement of salt and fire (l. 29): An allusion to Mark 9: 49: "For every one shall be salted with fire, and every sacrifice shall be salted with salt." Also a reference to the fate of Sodom and Gomorrah, destroyed with brimstone and fire, and to the fate of Lot's wife, turned into a pillar of salt. What exactly Mark meant has been the subject of debate, but here it is used as an image of purification.

as if I had left nothing of beauty... (ll. 29-30): A critique of the denial that the African village world contributed anything to human culture. See the earlier passages portraying the African village in Chapter VI (*Denial*), i, l. 37ff; and ii, l.1 ff.

Trench Town bob (l. 32): A nice pun (celebrating Bob Marley who once lived in and sang about Trenchtown) and a description of a "skanking", loping, dipping, insouciant walk.

rhygin (l. 33): A patwa adjective that describes a behaviour or a person, with a range of meanings (depending on perspective) from the positive to the negative, but including: angry, spirited, raging, top-notch. Historically, it was the nickname of the real-life criminal of the late 1940s, Vincent Ivanhoe Martin, known as Rhygin, who is fictionalised as the main character in Perry Henzel's film (1972) and Michael Thelwell's later novel (1980), *The Harder They Come*.

the homelessness of the sea: An echo, perhaps, of David Dabydeen's long poem, *Turner* (2002 [1994]), which begins with image of the drowned slave floating in the sea, taken from J.M.W. Turner's painting, *Slavers Throwing Overboard the Dead and Dying* (1840), and ends with the lines: "No stars, no land, no words, no community,/ No mother" (p. 42). *Prophets*, in this respect, offers a respectful qualification of Dabydeen's poem.

take shelter in the green (l. 42): In *Jacko Jacobus*, the piedmont landscape of South Carolina is invariably imaged as green, as a landscape in which the poet's imagination can find sustenance.

my ancient garb (l. 44): The traditional dashiki.

to clear the table (l. 48): This and the stanza that follows suggest a combative kind of interview where the interviewee is very forcefully stating terms for accepting a post. No tokenism, no acceptance of the platitudes of "it was all in the past".

Oxford tongue (l. 58): Quite literally, the upper-class English accents of the Oxford Don.

clean sermon of bloodless salvation (l. 59): From the perspective of the Charismatic, evangelical churches, this is an evasive sermon that, in making no mention of the blood shed by Christ and the pain of the crucifixion (as the necessary sacrifice to redeem mankind), fails utterly to acknowledge what is central to Christian faith.

locked up in some closet [...] the muggy smell seeping through (ll. 61-62): This image envisages the painful history of South Carolina as being hidden away out of sight, like discarded junk in a lumber room, but its smell is seeping through.

iv

my cloth from Togoland (l. 2): I.e. the dashiki and kente cloth the poet as interviewee wears – Togo, a West African country between Benin and Ghana.

my raggamuffin gait (l. 3): The speaker's version of the Trenchtown bob; raggamuffin is the dancehall update of the rudies (rude boys) of early reggae, the disorderly youth enthusiasts of ragga (i.e. rough dancehall rhythms).

Finger me now (l. 3): As if she is a slave being auctioned, and prodded and poked to ascertain her health and fitness.

I won't cause no trouble (l. 4): The patwa syntax is designed to mock the assumption that this black woman could not possibly be highly educated.

the ushers (l. 5): Those church officials who show members of a congregation to their seats (but evidently show alarm in the presence of black faces).

See me sometime as your old black ancestor (l. 10): The implication is that the white churches might need to be persuaded that there is a route to heaven through recompensing the old black ancestor for the wrongs done to her in the past, by treating her descendants better.

paul, newton, augustine (l. 14): All three are significant figures in Christianity who underwent major reversals of what they had been before their conversions. St Paul (c. 5–c. 67) had been Saul the persecutor of Christians before the conversion on the road to Damascus in the first century. John Newton (1725-1807), the writer of the hymn "Amazing Grace", which became deeply connected with African American spirituality, had, before his conversion, been the captain of a slave ship. The North African Augustine of Hippo (354-430) had been a notable womaniser before becoming a saintly and celibate priest, as recorded in his *Confessions*.

like a comma to replace the closure... the end is somewhere in the middle (ll. 31-32): A neat, writerly metaphor that takes the idea of writing back to the Empire and gives it a concrete physical form, not simply as an act of reversal, black over white, but as a genuine treaty between races and cultures.

Sowetan gum-boot dancer, this Akan mother (ll. 35-36): Whether South African or Ghanaian, the implication here is that for the white South Carolinian these are all just black people, irrespective of their real differences of geographic origins and culture.

marching from the sea inland (l. 38-39): A reversal of the forced marches of slaves to the coast.

the smell clamouring behind the curtains (l. 42): The muggy smell seeping from the closet, as in iii, ll. 61-62. Perhaps also an allusion to Hamlet's claim that there is a rat behind the arras before killing Polonius.

o false prophet (l. 44): A reference either to Jeremiah (20: 1ff) who laments that false prophets have deceived the Israelites, or to Matthew 7: 15 who writes: "Beware of false prophets, who come to you in sheep's clothing, but inwardly are ravenous wolves."

ride this sun-full misty morning to Heartease (l. 48): A line that conflates (and inverts the meaning of) a phrase from Bob Marley's song "Misty Morning" which begins, "Misty Morning, I don't see no sun". See the note for Heartease in Chapter XX, ii, l. 9.

V

This song has wallowed in its grief (l. 7): Those elements of *Prophets* that have lamented the state of the nation, that have displayed the pain of faith undermined.

rising up like a fisherman's weighted seine/ to God (ll. 10-11): An image that implies that in reaching out to God (with the tambourines), something (as in the catch of fish) is received in return. See note on seines, Chapter XVIII (*On the Road to Emmaus*), i, l. 96.

How green is the island when it rains (l. 15): I.e. Jamaica, and perhaps alluding to Claude McKay's memoir *My Green Hills of Jamaica*, written in the 1940s, but not published until 1975.

Their feet skip on the mountains: An image drawn from Habakkuk 3: 19: "The sovereign Lord is my strength, he makes my feet like the flock of deer, he enables me to go on heights." Here, the line is used as a kind of apology to God, to avoid bringing down his wrath for abusing his prophets, who, of course, no longer groan through the stinking city.

ENDNOTES

Preface

1. See Sudeep Sen, *"Prophets"*, *World Literature Today*, 1996, pp. 1016-1017; Tilla Brading, *"Prophets"*, *Poetry Quarterly Review*, 1996; Chris Searle, *"Prophets"*, *The Morning Star*, 1996.
2. I am reminded of James Baldwin's prefatory comments to the publication of *The Amen Corner* (1998 [1968]), where he wrote, "Writing the *Amen Corner* I remember as a desperate and even rather irresponsible act." As his agent reminded him, "The American theatre was not exactly clamouring for plays on obscure aspects of Negro life" (p. xi).

One: Introduction

1. This refers to what U-Roy called "versions galore", where the DJ chants over a remix of an original vocal track (there could be half a dozen different DJs making their own versions), with the original vocal appearing only in interludes or as a ghostly background; or the use of the same rhythms to generate multiple and lyrically different songs; or to the dub version remix where the sounds are resculpted to bring up the drum and bass and apply a variety of sound devices such as echo or distortion to the original, where the vocal may be mixed in as just one of the elements. *Versions Galore* (Trojan Records, 1970) was U-Roy's first album, where he chanted, "Versions galore, you can hear them by the score, I could give you some more for sure…"

Three: Contexts

1. "A Brief Autobiography of an Ex-Playwright", Unpublished typescript.
2. See "Going to Church" in *A Far Cry from Plymouth Rock* (2007), pp. 161-173.
3. See, for instance, poems such as "Yap" in *Progeny of Air* (1994), p. 75.
4. See *Natural Mysticism* (1999), p. 134.
5. See the introduction, for instance, to Brian Meeks, *Caribbean Revolutions and Revolutionary Theory* (1993). For the sources of this account, see also Obika Gray, *Radicalism and Social Change in Jamaica, 1960-1972* (1991); Carl Stone, *Democracy and Clientelism in Jamaica* (1980); Obika Gray, *Demeaned But Empowered: The Social Power of the Urban Poor in Jamaica* (2004).

6. On the loss of political control of the posses, and the Green Bay incident, see both Gray, *Demeaned But Empowered* (2004) and Laurie Gunst, *Born Fi' Dead* (1995).

7. See, for instance, Maurice Cargill's *Jamaica Farewell* (1978) as an example of the wounded sense of self-entitlement some white Jamaicans felt about the social changes of the 1970s, in Cargill's case leading to an exit without regret.

8. On the use of reggae by both sides see Anita M. Waters, *Race, Class and Political Symbols: Rastafari and Reggae in Jamaican Politics* (1985), and Stephen A. King, *Reggae, Rastafari, and the Rhetoric of Social Control* (2002). Bunny Wailer sang, "It's getting dreader and dreader … My belly fill with white squall now" ("Crucial", Solomonic, 1980).

9. See Notes, p. 205, for Hearne's words in *The Gleaner*.

10. See Waters, *Race, Class and Political Symbols*, pp. 209-211.

11. But see Carolyn Cooper, *Sound Clash: Jamaican Dancehall Culture at Large* (2004) for a more sympathetic account of the dancehall years and a nuanced view of the issue of misogyny in lyrics.

12. See Robert Beckford's interesting thesis on the connections between dub music and evangelical spirituality: *Jesus Dub: Faith, Culture and Social Change* (2006).

13. The essential work on the post-war development of Kingston is Colin Clarke, *Decolonizing the Colonial City: Urbanisation and Stratification in Kingston Jamaica* (2006). More impressionistic but also valuable is David Howard, *Kingston: A Cultural and Literary History* (2005).

14. On the religious affiliations of Jamaicans, see Census 2001, Table 2.6, p. 56.

15. David R. Reagan, "The New Age Church: The World's Largest Church", c. 2010 (online).

16. On Jamaican Pentecostalism, see Diane Austin-Broos, *Jamaica Genesis: Religion and the Politics of Moral Orders* (1997) and Malcolm Calley, *God's People: West Indian Pentecostal Sects in England* (1965).

17. On the Afro-centric religious practices of Jamaica see Dianne M. Stewart, *Three Eyes for the Journey: African Dimensions of the Jamaican Religious Experience* (2005).

18. See Chevannes, "Revivalism: A Disappearing Religion" (1978), pp. 1-17.

19. Austin-Broos defines "eudemonism" most simply as the earthly pursuit of ecstasy through rite and performance.

20. See Christopher Hill, *The World Turned Upside Down* (1975) and E.P. Thompson's *Witness Against the Beast: William Blake and the Moral Law* (1993).

21. In his treatment of the church Dawes shows the same kind of questioning respect as James Baldwin does in *The Amen Corner*. See the discussion above, pp. 64-65.

22. George Eliot, *Silas Marner* (1861), p. 6.

23. See Mervyn Alleyne, *Africa: Roots of Jamaican Culture* (1997); Leonard Barrett, *The Sun and the Drum* (1976); Barry Chevannes, *Betwixt and Between* (2006); Dianne M. Stewart, *Three Eyes for the Journey: African Dimensions of the Jamaican Religious Experience* (2005); *Africa and the Caribbean: Legacies of a Link* (1979), ed. Margaret Crahan and Franklin Knight.

24. See Olive Senior, *Encyclopaedia of Jamaican Heritage,* p. 58.

25. For accounts of Paul Bogle, see Gad Heuman, *"The Killing Time": The Morant Bay Rebellion in Jamaica* (1994) and Devon Dick, *The Cross and the Machete: Native Baptists of Jamaica* (2009).

26. For H.E.S. Woods see A.A. Brooks, *A History of Bedwardism or the Jamaican Native Baptist Free Church* (1917).

27. For Bedward see Brooks, op. cit.; Veront A. Satchell, "Bedwardism" in *The Encyclopedia of Caribbean Religions* (2013), pp. 117-122; and Barry Chevannes, *Rastafari: Roots and Ideology* (1994), pp. 39, 78-80.

28. For accounts of Marcus Garvey that explore his contribution to the Jamaican tradition of prophecy, see Beverly Hamilton, "Marcus Garvey and Cultural Development in Jamaica: A Preliminary Survey", *Garvey: His Work and Impact* (1991), pp. 87-112.

29. For Leonard Howell, see Hélène Lee, *The First Rasta: Leonard Howell and the Rise of Rastafarianism* (2003).

30. For Claudius Henry see Barry Chevannes, "The Repairer of the Breach: Reverend Claudius Henry and Jamaican Society", in *Ethnicity in the Americas* (1976), and Brian Meeks, *Narratives of Resistance* (2001).

31. For Marley as prophet see Anthony Bogues, *Black Heretics, Black Prophets* (2003), pp. 187-205, and see Kwame Dawes, *Bob Marley: Lyrical Genius* (2007).

32. See Edward Baugh, "Warner-Woman" in *Black Sand* (2013), "Bell-mouthed and biblical/ she trumpeted out of the hills,/prophet of doom, prophet of God,/ breeze-blow and earthquake,/ tidal wave and flood" (p. 109).

33. A.A. Brooks, op. cit.

34. See also Kwame Dawes, "Ezekiel Chapter Twenty-Five" and "Dry Bones" in *Wheels* (2011), p. 40, p. 43.

35. See Gad Heuman, *"The Killing Time"*, p. 5.

36. See Chevannes, *Rastafari Roots and Ideology*, p. 39.

37. See Chevannes, "The Repairer of the Breach", p. 274.

38. Cyrus was the Persian king who delivered the Jews from Babylonian captivity. Isaiah 45:1 reports: "Cyrus is my anointed king./ I take hold of his right hand. I give him the power to bring nations under his control."

39. See Annie Paul on visiting the still existing church that Henry and

his followers built: "A Visit to Rev Claudius Henry's Church, Sandy Bay, Jamaica", *Active Voice*, 19 August 2012. Online.

40. Meeks, *Narratives of Resistance*, p. 25.

41. See Wayne Grudem, *The Gift of Prophecy in the New Testament and Today* (2000) for a more positive but evidently quite controversial view of New Testament prophecy.

Four: Literary Dialogues

1. See John Lennard for a concise survey of the verse narrative in the Caribbean and elsewhere: *Ralph Thompson: View from Mount Diablo, an Annotated Edition* (2009), pp. 10-18

2. *Sentinel Poetry* [online # 54, June 2007]

3. In reading Walcott's *Omeros*, I acknowledge the guidance of Edward Baugh, *Derek Walcott* (2006); R.D. Hamner, *Epic of the Dispossessed: Derek Walcott's* Omeros (1997); Maria McGarrity's *Allusions in* Omeros: *Notes and a Guide to Derek Walcott's Masterpiece* (2015) and Don Bernard's *Omeros: A Reader's Guide* (2014).

4. Walcott, *The Antilles: Fragments of Epic Memory. The Nobel Lecture*, n.p.

5. See Rhonda Cobham Sander's discussion in "A Enemy So Was a Complement" in *Interlocking Basins of a Globe*, pp. 100-102, on the shift from Walcott's early vituperativeness (see "What the Twilight Says" (1998 [1970], pp. 8-9) towards a greater openness to the traditions of Caribbean orality. *Savacou 3/4* itself drew a passionate and rather hysterical critique from another traditionalist formalist, Eric Roach ("Conflict of West Indian Poetry: Tribe Boys vs Afro-Saxons" (1971), p. 4), and an equally passionate defence from Gordon Rohlehr ("West Indian Poetry: Some Problems of Assessment" (1971). Dawes' strategies in *Prophets* can be seen as negotiating a position in between, though closer to Brathwaite.

6. See *Derek Walcott's Love Affair With Film* (2017), pp. 20, 145-147, 150-157.

7. This is the view very cogently explained in Northrop Frye's *The Great Code: The Bible and Literature* (1982), where he notes how, on the one hand, the books of the Old Testament constantly anticipate the master narrative of the New Testament – mankind's redemption by Christ – and, on the other, how the books of the New Testament constantly reference the predictions made in the Old Testament.

8. There were few who did not admire Walcott's poetry – including Kamau Brathwaite, though some of Walcott's criticism of Brathwaite's poetry was harsh – but Walcott's cultural poetics, as expressed in his essays, was in sharp disagreement with the criticism and essays

of Brathwaite and Gordon Rohlehr. For an unfortunate personalising of these differences see, Pat Ismond, "Walcott vs Brathwaite" (1971), pp. 54-70.

9. See, for instance, the obeah images in "Tales from the Islands VI", *In A Green Night*, p. 28, with the lines, "And it was round this part once that the heart/ Of a young child was torn from it alive/ By two practitioners of native art...". Or the crudely reductive verses of "Pocomania" (p. 35) on "The black sheep of their blacker Lord" ... seen as "the blind beast butts on the wall". And see too vituperative lines in *Another Life* such as: "I enclose in this circle of hell [...]/ Those who peel, from their own leprous flesh, their names/ who chafe and nurture the scars of rusted chains,/ like primates favouring scabs, those who charge tickets/ for another free ride on the middle passage..." (p. 127).

10. See *A Season of Adventure* pp. 25-35, 39-40, 44-45.

11. See pp. 68-69 above, for how this episode draws from Alice Walker's *The Color Purple*.

12. In *Nor Any Country* (2013 [1968]), set in the late 1950s, the returning character, Peter Breville, notes the changes in the economy. Peter's friend Colin tells him about "the big hotel they've built near La Colombe [...] you won't recognise the place", whilst his mother complains that she can't get lobster because the "fishermen selling all to the hotels". In the town, now full of consumer goods in the stores, Peter feels he "might have been walking in a hot, drab, imperfectly imitated miniature of a metropolitan shopping centre" (p. 119).

13. There is a consistent pattern in all Naipaul's African-Caribbean figures – from Man-Man, through Preacher in *The Suffrage of Elvira*, to Brown in *The Mimic Men* – of a psychopathology of prophetic Blackness that dwells on a disconnection with reality.

14. See my reading of Salkey's first novel in the entry on Salkey in St. James Press, *Contemporary Novelists* (1986). My view remains that Salkey expressed a middle-class brown Jamaican's alarm over what he saw as the wilder shores of Afro-centric Black Christianity. He confuses, for instance, Revival Zion with obeah.

15. Both Patterson (then a Marxist New Leftist) and Wynter were undoubtedly on the radical left, but see Dawes' critique of their positions in *Natural Mysticism*, p. 253, quoted below, of taking "cynical pot-shots at a working class community".

16. See *Natural Mysticism*, particularly the chapters on Burning Spear, Bob Marley and Lee Scratch Perry, pp. 185-256.

17. See Daryl Cumber Dance, *New World Adams: Conversations with West Indian Writers* (1992), pp. 298-305.

18. See Hélène Lee, *The First Rasta: Leonard Howell and the Rise of Rastafarianism*.

19. See *Natural Mysticism*, p. 250, where Dawes acknowledges the history oof too-many political figures who have assumed the roles of saviours of the people, whilst maintaining a strong allegiance to the ruling class. See the classic study of such figures, A.W. Singham's *The Hero and the Crowd in a Colonial Polity* (1968).

20. See for instance, Alex Gradussov, "Kapo: Cult Leader, Sculptor, Painter", (1969). Sylvia Wynter was herself a frequent contributor to *Jamaica Journal* between 1967-1984. For a mark of the distance Wynter travelled during the 1960s in grasping the reality of the Creolised African presence in Jamaica, see her later, ground-breaking essay on "Jonkunnu in Jamaica" (1970).

21. This is a confusion between Jamaican Pukkumina and Haitian Vodun, the former coming with BaKongo people from Central Africa, the latter from the West African area, with its heartland in Benin.

22. See for instance Ken Post, *Arise Ye Starvelings* (1978) and Colin A. Palmer's *Freedom's Children: the 1938 Labour Rebellion and the Birth of Modern Jamaica* (2014) for a sense of the dynamics of that period.

23. See Robert Hemenway, *Zora Neale Hurston: A Literary Biography* (1977), p. 197.

24. See Cheryl Wharry, "Amen and Hallelujah Preaching: Discourse Functions in African American Sermons" (2003), pp. 203-225.

25. Personal emails from Kwame Dawes 3rd, 5th February 2018.

26. Here, Shirley A. Stave, ed., *Toni Morrison and the Bible: Contested Intertextualities* (2006) had several useful essays.

27. On Morrison's use of Song of Songs in *Song of Solomon*, see Beth Benedrix, "Intimate Fatality: *Song of Solomon* and the journey Home", in *Toni Morrison and the Bible: Contested Intertextualities,* ed. Shirley A. Stave (2006), pp. 94-115.

28. Agnes Suranyi, "Bible as Intertext", in *Toni Morrison and the Bible: Contested Intertextualities,* pp. 122-123.

Five: Prophets as a Poem

1. Samuel Johnson, "The Life of Milton", *The Works of Samuel Johnson*, Vol. 9, (1820), p. 168.

2. "Mr Loverman" was written by Deborahe Glasgow, first released as a single in 1992, later on the cd, *Rough and Ready*.

3. See Cheryl Wharry, "Amen and Hallelujah Preaching: Discourse Functions in African American Sermons" (2003).

4. I'm thinking of lines like "While Expletives their feeble Aid do join/

And ten low words oft creep in one dull line/ [...] A needless Alexandrine ends the song/ That like a wounded snake, drags its slow length along." Alexander Pope, *The Poems of Alexander Pope*, ed. John Butt (1965), pp. 154-155.

5. For readers unfamiliar with the language of film, James Monaco's *How to Read a Film: The World of Movies, Media, Multimedia: Language, History, Theory* (2009) is still the best guide.

6. Smith, *Insanity, Race and Class and Colonialism*, quotes Thomas Allen, pp. 89 ff.

7. George Rosen, quoted in Andrew Scull, *Madness in Civilisation*, p. 15.

8. For instance, in "Ward" Dawes writes, "...and you drool, how you drool,/ your tongue, not yours, just a clumsy lump/ of meat in your mouth..." (p. 36); and in "Casting Out Demons", "... I imagine your/ valley: the gloom, you wondering about/ tomorrow: impossible equations" (p. 38). Both *Impossible Flying* (2007).

9. In thinking about madness and psychosis, I found Richard P. Bentall, *Madness Explained: Psychosis and Human Nature* (2003) the most insightful guide in the way it critiques the tyranny of diagnostic terms and locates personal psychic distress in the interaction between minds and societies, biology and culture.

10. See Frederick Hickling et al, eds., *Perspectives in Caribbean Psychology*.

11. See Orlando Patterson, *Slavery and Social Death: A Comparative Study* (Massachusetts: Harvard University Press, 1982).

12. Vincent Brown (*The Reaper's Garden* (2008)) makes the assessment that so high were the mortality figures in Jamaica in the 18th and 19th centuries, the population turned over almost completely every seven years. And see Saidiya Hartman, *Scenes of Subjection* (1997), pp. 154-161. Her account of the allegedly zombified state of enslaved Africans on the way to the slave coast, and the possibility that they may have been drugged, has disturbing resonances of accounts of the "liquid cosh" in the mental asylums of old and not so old times.

13. Randy Brown's study of court and other records in Demerara (*Surviving Slavery in the British Caribbean* (2017)) shows that enslaved people were very much engaged in matters concerning their sense of self, their rights and control of property that brought them most sharply into conflict with slavery's denial of those basic matters of human concern.

14. See Lyn Williams-Keeler, Michael McCarrey, Anna B. Baranowsky, Marta Young, Sue Johnson-Douglas, "PTSD transmission: A review of secondary traumatization in Holocaust survivor families," *Canadian Psychology 1998* < http://www.findarticles.com/p/articles/mi_qa3711/is_199811/ai_n8810928#continue>.

15. See F.W. Hickling, "Psychopathology of the Jamaican people", pp.

37-38; F.W. Hickling, Jacqueline Martin & Allison Harrisingh-Dewar, "Redefining Personality Disorder in Jamaica", pp.267-268; F.W. Hickling & Caryl James, "Traditional Mental Health Practices in Jamaica", pp. 476-478: all in *Perspectives in Caribbean Psychology* (2013).

16. Kwame Dawes' *Requiem*, which references the illustrations of Tom Feeling in his book, *The Middle Passage: White Ships/ Black Cargo*, moves backwards and forwards from poems about slavery to trace its aftermath in contemporary African American lives. It sings "requiems for the dead" to bring healing to the survivors.

Six: Allusiveness

1. See Kwame Dawes, *Natural Mysticism* (1999, 2008), pp. 66-67.

2. In the period immediately before *Prophets* was being written, Kamau Brathwaite published *Barabajan Poems* (1994) in the Sycorax video-style.

3. See, for instance, Judith Soares, "Fundamentalism" in *The Encyclopedia of Caribbean Religions* (2013), p. 290, on the "unflinching belief in millenarianism". And see Barry Chevannes, "Rastafari: towards a new approach" (1990), pp. 127-148.

4. My thinking about what allusion does draws, in the first place, from Christopher Ricks, *Allusion to the Poets* (2002).

5. Recorded in "A Brief Autobiography of an Ex-Playwright".

6. Grateful thanks to the websites <reggaelyrics.info>, and the even more excellent <https://www.jah-lyrics.com/biblical-reference>.

7. <https://www.reggaeville.com/artist-details/i-kong/news/view/interview-with-i-kong-part-ii/>.

8. See "The King James Bible's Language Lessons", *The Guardian*, 19 February 2011. Online. Johnson records that "This book, a most effective tool of colonisation, was the only one in my illiterate grandmother's house when I was a child in Jamaica. She would have me read it to her from time to time, and I got to like the language of the Old Testament and the Psalms in particular, her favourite book. That was my first real introduction to written verse. I was seven years old and could recite some Psalms from memory, having learnt them at Sunday school in the Baptist church of which my grandmother was a member. So it's not at all surprising that my verse has some biblical references."

9. Marilynne Robinson, "The Book of Books" (2011) (online).

10. This also includes such parables as the faithful servant, the lost sheep, the sower of seeds, the lost coin, the prodigal son, the wise and foolish builders, the talents, etc.

BIBLIOGRAPHY

Alleyne, Mervyn, *Africa: Roots of Jamaican Culture* (Chicago: Research Associates, 1997).

Antoine-Dunne, Jean, *Derek Walcott's Love Affair With Film* (Leeds: Peepal Tree Press, 2017).

Austin-Broos, Diane, *Jamaica Genesis: Religion and the Politics of Moral Orders* (Chicago: University of Chicago Press, 1997).

Baldwin, James, *The Amen Corner* [1968] (New York: Vintage International, 1998).

Barrett, Leonard, *The Sun and the Drum: African Roots in the Jamaican Folk Tradition* (London: Heinemann, 1976).

Barrow, Steve and Dalton, Peter, *Reggae: The Rough Guide* (London: Penguin, 1997).

Baugh, Edward, *Derek Walcott* (Cambridge: Cambridge UP, 2006).

Baugh, Edward, *Black Sand: New and Selected Poems* (Leeds: Peepal Tree Press, 2013).

Beckford, Robert, *Jesus Dub: Faith, Culture and Social Change* (London: Routledge, 2006).

Benedrix, Beth, "Intimate Fatality: *Song of Solomon* and the journey Home", in *Toni Morrison and the Bible: Contested Intertextualities,* ed. Shirley A. Stave (New York: Peter Lang, 2006), pp. 94-115.

Bentall, Richard P., *Madness Explained: Psychosis and Human Nature* (London: Allen Lane, 2003).

Bernal, Martin, *Black Athena: The Afroasiatic Roots of Classical Civilisation* (London: Free Association Books, 1987).

Bernard, Don, *Omeros: A Reader's Guide* (Colorado: Lynne Reiner Publishers, 2014).

Bilby, Kenneth M. and Bunseki, Fu-Kiau Kia, "Kumina: A Kongo-Based Tradition in the New World", in *A Reader in African-Jamaican Music, Dance, Religion* (Kingston: Ian Randle Publishers, 2015), pp. 473-528.

Bogues, Anthony, *Black Heretics, Black Prophets* (New York: Routledge, 2003).

Brading, Tilla, *"Review: Prophets"*, *Poetry Quarterly Review*, 1996.

Brathwaite, Kamau, *Rights of Passage* (London: Oxford University Press, 1967), pp. 16-20.

Brathwaite, Kamau, *Islands* (London: Oxford University Press, 1969).

Brathwaite, Kamau, *The Arrivants* (Oxford: Oxford University Press, 1971).

Brathwaite, Kamau, "The African Presence in Caribbean Literature", *Roots* (Ann Arbor: University of Michigan Press, 1993), pp. 190-258.

Brathwaite, Kamau, *Barabajan Poems* (New York: Savacou North, 1994).

Brodber, Erna, *Myal* (London: New Beacon, 1988).

Brodber, Erna, "Sociocultural Change in Jamaica", in *Jamaica in Independence,* ed. Rex Nettleford (Kingston: Heinemann Caribbean, 1989), pp. 55-74.

Brodber, Erna, *The Second Generation of Freemen in Jamaica*, 1907-1944 (Gainesville: University Press of Florida, 2004).

Brodber, Erna, Preface to *Obeah and Other Powers: The Politics of Caribbean Religion and Healing* (Durham: Duke University Press, 2012).

Bronfman, Alejandra, *On the Move: The Caribbean since 1989* (London: Zed Press, 2007).

Brown, Randy M., *Surviving Slavery in the British Caribbean* (Philadelphia: University of Pennsylvannia Press, 2017).

Brown, Vincent, *The Reaper's Garden: Death and Power in the World of Atlantic Slavery* (Cambridge MA, Harvard University Press, 2008).

Brown, Wayne, *On the Coast* [1973] (Leeds: Peepal Tree Press, 2010).

Calley, Malcolm, *God's People: West Indian Pentecostal Sects in England* (Oxford: Oxford University Press, 1965).

Campbell, George, *First Poems* [1945] (Leeds: Peepal Tree Press, 2012).

Campbell, Mavis C., *The Maroons of Jamaica: 1655-1796* (Granby: Bergin & Garvey, 1988).

Carberry, H.D., *It Takes a Mighty Fire* (Kingston: Ian Randle Publishers, 1995).

Carew, Jan, *Black Midas* (London: Secker and Warburg, 1958).

Cargill, Morris, *Jamaica Farewell* (Secaucus, NJ: Lyle Stuart, 1978).

Carr, W.I., "Roger Mais – Design from a Legend", *Caribbean Quarterly*, Vol. 13, No. 1, March 1967, pp. 3-28.

Carruthers, Jo, Knight, Mark and Tate, Andre, eds., *Literature and the Bible: A Reader* (London: Routledge, 2014).

Cassidy, Frederick, *Jamaica Talk: Three Hundred Years of the English Language in Jamaica* (London: MacMillan, 1961).

Cassidy, F.G. & Le Page, R.B., *Dictionary of Jamaican English* (London: Cambridge University Press, 1967).

Césaire, Aimé, *Une Têmpete* (Paris: Editions de Seuil, 1969).

Chevannes, Barry, "The Repairer of the Breach: Reverend Claudius Henry and Jamaican Society", in *Ethnicity in the Americas*, Ed. Francis Henry (The Hague: Mouton Publishers, 1976).

Chevannes, Barry, "Revivalism: A Disappearing Religion", *Caribbean Quarterly*, vol. 24, Nos. 3&4, 1978, pp. 1-17.

Chevannes, Barry, "Rastafari: towards a new approach", in *New West Indian Guide/ Nieuwe West-Indische Gids* Vol. 64, No: 3/4, Leiden, 1990, pp. 127-148.

Chevannes, Barry, *Rastafari, Roots and Ideology* (New York: Syracuse University Press, 1994).

Chevannes, Barry, "Crime and Drug-Related Issues in Jamaica", *Souls*, (Columbia University, 2001).

Chevannes, Barry, *Betwixt and Between: Explorations in African-Caribbean Mindscape* (Kingston: Ian Randle Publishers, 2006).

Clarke, Colin G., *Kingston Jamaica: Urban Growth and Social Change 1692-1962* (Berkeley: University of California Press, 1975).

Clarke, Colin, *Decolonising the Colonial City: Urbanisation and Stratification in Kingston Jamaica* (Oxford: Oxford University Press, 2006).

Cobham Sander, Rhonda, "A Enemy So Was a Compliment" in *Interlocking Basins of a Globe* (Leeds: Peepal Tree Press, 2015).

Conrad, Joseph, *Heart of Darkness* [1899], in *Three Short Novels* (New York: Bantam Books, 1960).

Cooper, Carolyn, *Noises in the Blood: Orality, Gender and the "Vulgar" Body of Jamaican Popular Culture* (London: MacMillan, 1993).

Cooper, Carolyn, *Sound Clash: Jamaican Dancehall Culture at Large* (New York: Palgrave MacMillan, 2004).

Crahan, Margaret and Knight, Franklin, eds., *Africa and the Caribbean: Legacies of a Link* (Baltimore: Johns Hopkins University Press, 1979).

Dabydeen, David, *Turner* (London: Cape, 1995).

Dance, Daryl Cumber, ed. *Fifty Caribbean Writers: A Bio-Bibliographical Critical Sourcebook* (New York: Greenwood Press, 1986).

Dance, Daryl Cumber, *New World Adams: Conversations with West Indian Writers* (Leeds: Peepal Tree Press, 1992).

Dawes, Alfred, "It is Madness How as a Society We Treat the Mentally Ill", *The Gleaner*, 5 October 2016. Online: <http://jamaica-gleaner.com/ article/health/20161005/dr-alfred-dawes-it-madness-how-society-we-treat-mentally-ill>.

Dawes, Kwame, "A Brief Autobiography of an Ex-Playwright", unpublished.

Dawes, Kwame, "Violence and Patriarchy: Male Domination in Roger Mais's *Brother Man*", *Ariel*, Vol. 25, No. 3, 1994, pp. 29-49.

Dawes, Kwame, *Progeny of Air* (Leeds: Peepal Tree Press, 1994).

Dawes, Kwame, *Resisting the Anomie* (Fredericton: Goose Lane Editions, 1995).

Dawes, Kwame, *Jacko Jacobus* (Leeds: Peepal Tree Press, 1996).

Dawes, Kwame, *Requiem* (Leeds: Peepal Tree Press, 1996).

Dawes, Kwame, *Natural Mysticism: Towards a New Reggae Aesthetic* (Leeds: Peepal Tree, 1999).

Dawes, Kwame, *One Love: A Dubaretta* (London: Methuen, 2001).

Dawes, Kwame, *A Place to Hide* (Leeds: Peepal Tree Press, 2003).

Dawes, Kwame, *A Far Cry from Plymouth Rock* (Leeds: Peepal Tree Press, 2007).

Dawes, Kwame, *Bob Marley: Lyrical Genius* (London: Bobcat Books, 2007).

Dawes, Kwame, *Bivouac* (Leeds: Peepal Tree Press, 2010).

Dawes, Kwame, *Wheels* (Leeds: Peepal Tree Press, 2011).

Dawes, Kwame, "Are We Related?" (19 February 2013, online: <ww.akashicbooks.com/kwame-dawes-asks-are-we-related>).

Dawes, Neville, *Fugue and other Writings* (Leeds: Peepal Tree Press, 2012).

De Graft-Johnson, J.C., *African Glory: The Story of Vanished Negro Civilisations* (New York: Praeger, 1954).

Dick, Devon, *The Cross and the Machete: Native Baptists of Jamaica: Identity, Ministry and Legacy* (Kingston: Ian Randle Pubishers, 2009).

Early, James, "The 'Re-communalization' of a Jamaican Kumina Drum", in the Smithsonian online *Folk Life* magazine: <http://folklife.si.edu/talkstory/2014/re-communalization-of-a-jamaican-kumina-drum>.

Edmondson, Belinda, *Making Men: Gender, Literary Authority and Women's Writing in Caribbean Narrative* (Durham NC: Duke University Press, 1999)

Eliade, Mercea, *Images and Symbols: Studies in Religious Symbolism* (Princeton, Princeton University Press, 1961).

Eliot, George, *Silas Marner* [1861] (London: William Blackwood, c1880).

Eliot, T.S., *The Complete Poems and Plays* (London: Faber and Faber, 1969).

Frye, Northrop, *The Great Code: The Bible and Literature* (San Diego: Harcourt Inc., 1981).

Escoffery, Gloria, "Osmund Watson's Masquerades", *Jamaica Journal*, Vol. 16: No. 1, 1983, pp. 40-43.

Goodison, Lorna, *Tamarind Season* (Kingston: Institute of Jamaica, 1980).

Goodison, Lorna, *Heartease* (London: New Beacon, 1988).

Goodison, Lorna, *To Us All Flowers Are Roses* (Urbana: University of Illinois Press, 1995).

Gradussov, Alex, "Kapo: Cult Leader, Sculptor, Painter", *Jamaica Journal*, Vol. 3 No. 2, 1969, pp. 46-51.

Gray, Obika, *Radicalism and Social Change in Jamaica 1960-1972* (Knoxville: University of Tennessee Press, 1991).

Gray, Obika, *Demeaned But Empowered: The Social Power of the Urban Poor in Jamaica* (Jamaica: UWI Press, 2004).

Grudem, Wayne, *The Gift of Prophecy in the New Testament and Today* (Westchester: Crossway Books, 2000).

Gunst, Laurie, *Born Fi' Dead: A Journey Through the Yardie Underworld* (Edinburgh: Canongate, 1995).

Hamilton, Beverly , "Marcus Garvey and Cultural Development in Jamaica: A Preliminary Survey", *Garvey: His Work and Impact*, ed Rupert Lewis and Patrick Bryan (Trenton: Africa World Press, 1991), pp. 87-112.

Hamner, Robert D., *Epic of the Dispossessed: Derek Walcott's* Omeros (Columbia: University of Missouri Press, 1997).

Hartman, Saidiya, *Scenes of Subjection: Terror, Slavery and Self-Making in Nineteenth-Century America* (New York: Oxford University Press, 1997).

Hartman, Saidiya, *Lose Your Mother: A Journey Along the Atlantic Slave Route* (New York: Farrar, Straus and Giroux, 2007).

Hearne, John, "Roger Mais: A Personal Memoir", *Bim*, No. 6, 1955, pp. 146-150.

Hearne, Shivaun, *John Hearne's Life and Fiction: A Critical Biographical Study* (Kingston: Caribbean Quarterly Monograph, 2013).

Hemenway, Robert, *Zora Neale Hurston: A Literary Biography* (Urbana: University of Illinois Press, 1977).

Heuman, Gad, *"The Killing Time": The Morant Bay Rebellion in Jamaica* (Knoxville: University of Tennessee Press, 1994).

Hickling, Frederick, et al., eds. *Perspectives in Caribbean Psychology* (London: Jessica Kingsley Publishers, 2008).

Hill, Christopher, *The World Turned Upside Down: Radical Ideas During the English Revolution* (London: Penguin Books, 1972).

Hopkins, Gerard Manley, *Poems and Prose of Gerard Manley Hopkins* (London: Penguin Books, 1970).

Hopkins, James K., *A Woman to Deliver Her People* (Austin: University of Texas Press, 1982).

Howard, David, *Kingston: A Cultural and Literary History* (Oxford: Signal Books, 2005).

Howard, Dennis, "Payola in Jamaica: Illegal and Unethical or Standard Practice", *Jamaica Observer*, 17 April, 2011. Online: <www.jamaicaobserver.com/ columns/Payola-in-Jamaica-Illegal-and-unethical-or-standard-business-practice_8646482>.

Hughes, Ted, *Crow* (London: Faber and Faber, 1971).

Hurston, Zora Neale, *Jonah's Gourd Vine* [1934] (New York: Harper Perennial, 1990).

Hurston, Zora Neale, *Their Eyes Were Watching God* [1937] (London: Virago Press, 1986).

Ismond, Pat, "Walcott vs Brathwaite", *Caribbean Quarterly*, Vol. 17, Nos. 3&4, 1971, pp. 54-70.

Jeffrey, David Lyle, ed., *A Dictionary of Biblical Tradition in English Literature* (Michigan: Wm. B. Eermans Publishing Co., 1992).

Johnson, Linton Kwesi, "The King James Bible's Language Lessons", *The Guardian*, 19 February 2011. Online at < https://www.theguardian. com/books/2011/feb/18/king-james-bible-language>.

Johnson, Paul Christopher, Ed. *Spirited Things: The Work of "Possession" in Afro-Atlantic Religions* (Chicago: University of Chicago Press, 2014).

Johnson, Samuel, "Milton", *The Works of Samuel Johnson*, Vol. 9 (London: G. Walker et al., 1820).

Josephs, Kelly Baker, *Disturbers of the Peace: Representations of Madness in Anglophone Caribbean Literature* (Charlotesville: University of Virginia Press, 2013).

Khan, Ismith, *The Crucifixion* (Leeds: Peepal Tree Press, 1987).

King, Stephen A., *Reggae, Rastafari, and the Rhetoric of Social Control* (Jackson: University Press of Mississippi, 2002).

Kosloski, Philip, "The Visible Church on earth is only one part of a much larger reality", *Aleteia*, online (22 October 2017).

Lamming, George, *Season of Adventure* (London: Michael Joseph, 1960).

Lamming, George, *The Pleasures of Exile* (London: Michael Joseph, 1960).

Lamming, George, *Natives of My Person* (London: Longman, 1972).

Lee, Hélène, *The First Rasta: Leonard Howell and the Rise of Rastafarianism* (Chicago: Lawrence Hill Books, 2003).

Lemon, Rebecca, Mason, Emma, et. al., eds., *The Blackwell Companion to the Bible in English Literature* (Oxford: Blackwell, 2012).

Lennard, John, *Ralph Thompson: View from Mount Diablo, an Annotated Edition* (Leeds: Peepal Tree Press, 2009).

Lewis, Rupert and Bryan, Patrick, eds., *Garvey: His Work and Impact* (Trenton: Africa World Press, 1991).

Lewin, Olive, *Rock It Come Over* (Kingston: UWI Press, 2001).

Lewis, M.G. (Monk), *The Monk* [1796] (Oxford: Oxford World Classics, 2008).

Libby, Ronald, "The United States and Jamaica: Playing the American Card", *Latin American Perspectives*, Vol. 17, No. 1, 1990, pp. 86-109.

Lovelace, Earl, *The Dragon Can't Dance* (London: Andre Deutch,1979).

Mack, Douglas R.A., "The Camps", in *Babylon to Rastafari* (Chicago: Research Associates, 1999), pp. 59-80.

Mais, Roger, "George William Gordon", *A Time and a Season: Eight Caribbean Plays*, ed. Errol Hill (Trinidad: UWI Extramural Studies Unit, 1976).

Mais, Roger, *The Hills Were Joyful Together* (London: Cape, 1953).

Mais, Roger, *Brother Man* (London: Cape, 1954).

Mais, Roger, *Black Lightning* (London: Cape, 1955).

Marquez, Gabriel Garcia, "A Very Old Man with Enormous Wings", *Leaf Storm and Other Stories* (London: Picador, 1972), pp. 105-112.

Marx, R.F. "Excavating Port Royal (Part 1)". *Jamaica Journal*, Vol. 2 No.

2, pp. 12-18; and "Divers of Port Royal", *Jamaica Journal*, Vol. 2, No. 1, pp. 15-23, both 1968.

McDaniel, Lorna, "The Flying Africans: Extent and Strength of the Myth in the Americas", *New West Indian Guide*, Vol. 64 No. 1/2 (Leiden, 1990), pp. 28-40.

McGarrity, Maria, *Allusions in* Omeros: *Notes and a Guide to Derek Walcott's Masterpiece* (Gainesville: University Press of Florida, 2015).

McKay, Claude, *My Green Hills of Jamaica* (London: Heinemann Education, 1979).

McNeill, Anthony, *Chinese Lanterns from the Blue Child* (Leeds: Peepal Tree Press, 1996).

Meeks, Brian, *Caribbean Revolutions and Revolutionary Theory* (Kingston: UWI Press, 1993, 2002)

Meeks, Brian, *Narratives of Resistance* (Kingston: UWI Press, 2001).

Miller, Kei, *Writing Down the Vision* (Leeds: Peepal Tree Press, 2013).

Miller, Kei, *Augustown* (London: W & N, 2016).

Monaco, James, *How to Read a Film: The World of Movies, Media, Multimedia: Language, History, Theory* (New York, OUP, 2009).

Morrison, Toni, *Song of Solomon* [1977] (London: Everyman Library Edition, 1995).

Morrison, Toni, *Sula* [1973] (London: Vintage, 2002).

Mulvey, Laura, "Visual Pleasure and Narrative Cinema", *Screen*, Vol. 16, Issue 3, 1 October 1975, pp. 6-18.

Naipaul, V.S., *Miguel Street* (New York: The Vanguard Press, 1959).

Naipaul, V.S. *The Mimic Men* (London: Andre Deutch, 1967).

Nenton, Lance, "Otherwise Known As", Lance Nenton talking to Charles Hyatt, *Jamaica Observer*, 1 November. 2014.

O'Callaghan, Evelyn, *Women Version: Theoretical Approaches to West Indian Fiction by Women* (London: MacMillan Caribbean, 1993).

Ovid, *Metamorphoses*, trans. A.D. Melville (Oxford: Oxford World Classics, 1986); for Cadmus, see pp. 51-55.

Palmer, Colin A., *Freedom's Children: The 1938 Labour Rebellion and the Birth of Modern Jamaica* (Chapel Hill: University of North Carolina Press, 2014).

Patterson, Orlando, *Children of Sisyphus* [1964] (Leeds: Peepal Tree Press, 2012).

Patterson, Orlando, *An Absence of Ruins* [1967] (Leeds: Peepal Tree Press, 2012).

Patterson, Orlando, *The Sociology of Slavery: An Analysis of the Origins, Development and Structure of Negro Slave Society in Jamaica* (New York: Humanties Press, 1969).

Patterson, Orlando, *Slavery and Social Death: A Comparative Study* (Massachusetts: Harvard University Press, 1982).

Paul, Annie, "A Visit to Rev Claudius Henry's Church, Sandy Bay, Jamaica", *Active Voice*, 19 August 2012. Online:<https://anniepaul.net/2012/08/19/a-visit-to-rev-claudius-henrys-church-sandy-bay-jamaica/>

Pope, Alexander, "An Essay on Criticism", *The Poems of Alexander Pope*, ed. John Butt (London: Methuen, 1963), pp. 144-168.

Post, Ken, *Arise Ye Starvelings: The Jamaican Labour Rebellion of 1838 and Its Aftermath* (The Hague: Martinus Nijhoff, 1978).

Poynting, Jeremy, "Andrew Salkey", *Contemporary Novelists* (London: St James Press, 1986).

Prahlad, Sw. Anand, *Reggae Wisdom: Proverbs in Jamaican Music* (Jackson: University Press of Mississippi, 2001).

Reckord, Verene, "Rastafarian Music – An Introductory Study", *Jamaica Journal*, Vol. 11, Nos. 1 & 2, 1977.

Reagan, David R., "The New Age Church: The World's Largest Church", c. 2010. Online: <christinprophecy.org/articles/the-new-age-church/>

Ricks, Christopher, *Allusion to the Poets* (Oxford: Oxford University Press, 2002).

Roach, Eric, "Conflict of West Indian Poetry: Tribe Boys vs Afro-Saxons", *Trinidad Guardian*, 12 January 1971, p. 4.

Robinson, Marilynne, "The Book of Books: What Literature Owes the Bible", *The New York Times*, 22 December 2011. <www.nytimes.com/2011/12//25/books/review/the-book-of-books-what-literature-owes-the-bible.htm>.

Rohlehr, Gordon , "West Indian Poetry: Some Problems of Assessment", *Tapia*, No. 23, 26 December, 1971.

Rubin, Vera and Comitas, Lambros, *Ganja in Jamaica: The Effects of Marijuana Use* (New York: Anchor Books, 1976).

Salkey, Andrew, *A Quality of Violence* (London: Hutchinson, 1959).

Satchell, Veront A., "Bedwardism" in *The Encyclopedia of Caribbean Religions* (Urbana: University of Illinois Press, 2013), pp. 117-122.

Scull, Andrew, *Madness in Civilisation* (London: Thames and Hudson, 2015).

Seaga, Edward, "Revival Cults in Jamaica: Notes Towards a Sociology of Religion", in *A Reader in African-Jamacan Music, Dance, Religion* (Kingston: Ian Randle Publishers, 2015), pp. 362-379.

Searle, Chris, Review: "*Prophets*", *The Morning Star*, 1996.

Selvon, Samuel, *The Lonely Londoners* (London: Longman, 1956).

Sen, Sudeep, Review: "*Prophets*", *World Literature Today*, 1996, pp. 1016-1017.

Senior, Olive, *Encyclopaedia of Jamaican Heritage* (Jamaica: Twin Guinep Publishers, 2003).

Shakespeare, William, *A Midsummer Night's Dream* [1595] (London: Arden Edition, 2017).

Shakespeare, William, *The Merchant of Venice* [1596] (London: Arden Edition, 2011).

Shakespeare, William, *Julius Caesar* [1599] (London: Arden Edition, 1998).

Shakespeare, William, *Hamlet* [1600] (London: Arden Edition, 2016).

Shakespeare, William, *Othello* [1603] (London: Arden Edition, 1996).

Shakespeare, William, *The Tempest* [1611] (New York: Norton and Company, 2004).

Shange, Ntozake, *for colored girls who have considered suicide: a choreopoem* [1975] (New York: Simon and Schuster, 2002).

Singham, A.W., *The Hero and the Crowd in a Colonial Polity* (New Haven: Yale University Press, 1968).

Smith, Leonard, *Insanity, Race and Colonialism: Managing Mental Disorder in the Post-Emancipation British Caribbean, 1838-1914* (Basingstoke: Palgrave MacMillan, 2014).

Soares, Judith, "Fundamentalism" in *The Encyclopedia of Caribbean Religions* (Urbana: University of Illinois Press, 2013), p. 290.

St. Omer, Garth, *Nor Any Country* [1968] (Leeds: Peepal Tree Press, 2013).

Stave, Shirley A., ed., *Toni Morrison and the Bible: Contested Intertextualities* (New York: Peter Lang, 2006).

Stewart, Dianne M., *Three Eyes for the Journey: African Dimensions of the Jamaican Religious Experience* (Oxford: OUP, 2005).

Stolzoff, Norman C., *Wake the Town and Tell the People* (Durham: Duke University Press, 2000).

Stone, Carl, *Democracy and Clientelism in Jamaica* (New Brunswick: Transaction Books, 1980).

Suranyani, Agnes, "Bible as Intertext", in *Toni Morrison and the Bible: Contested Intertextualities,* ed. Shirley Stave (New York: Peter Lang, 2006), pp. 122-123.

Taylor, Patrick and Case, Frederick I., eds., *The Encyclopedia of Caribbean Religions*, in two volumes (Urbana: University of Illinois Press, 2013).

The English Bible: King James Version, Volume One: The Old Testament, ed. Herbert Marks (New York: Norton & Co., 2012).

Thomas, Keith, *Religion and the Decline of Magic* (London: Penguin, 1973).

Thompson, E.P., *Witness Against the Beast: William Blake and the Moral Law* (Cambridge: Cambridge University Press, 1993).

Walcott, Derek, *In a Green Night* (London: Cape, 1962).

Walcott Derek, *The Castaway and Other Poems* (London: Cape, 1967).

Walcott, Derek, *Another Life* (London: Jonathan Cape, 1973).

Walcott, Derek, *Sea Grapes* (London: Cape, 1976).

Walcott, Derek, *The Star-Apple Kingdom* (New York: Farrar Straus Giroux, 1979).

Walcott, Derek, *Omeros* (New York: Farrar Straus Giroux, 1990).

Walcott, Derek, *The Antilles: Fragments of Epic Memory. The Nobel Lecture* (New York: Farrar, Straus and Giroux, 1992).

Walcott, Derek, "What the Twilight Says" [1970], *What the Twilight Says: Essays* (London: Faber and Faber, 1998).

Walker, Alice, *The Color Purple* (London: Women's Press, 1983).

Walker, Klive, *Dubwise: Reasoning from the Reggae Underground* (Toronto: Insomniac Press, 2005).

Warner, Marina, *Fantastic Metamorphoses, Other Worlds* (Oxford: OUP, 2002).

Waters, Anita M., *Race, Class and Political Symbols: Rastafari and Reggae in Jamaican Politics* (New Brunswick: Transaction Publishers, 1985).

West, Jean M., "The Devil's Blue Dye: Indigo and Slavery" (nd), online <teachers.sumnersd.org/shs/kmcguire/documents/download/indigo_and_slavery.doc>.

Wharry, Cheryl, "Amen and Hallelujah Preaching: Discourse Functions in African American Sermons", *Language in Society,* Vol. 32, No. 2 (April, 2003).

White, Garth, "Rudie Oh Rudie", *Caribbean Quarterly*, Vol. 13 No. 3 (1965).

Williamson, Karina, "Re-inventing Jamaican History: Roger Mais and George William Gordon", *The Society for Caribbean Studies Annual Conference Papers*, Vol. 3, 2002. <http://community-languages.org.uk/SCS-Papers/olv3p4.PDF>.

Wynter, Sylvia, *The Hills of Hebron* (London: Jonathan Cape, 1962).

Wynter, Sylvia, "We Must Learn to Sit Down Together and Talk About a Little Culture", *Jamaica Journal* Vol. 3, March 1969.

Wynter, Sylvia, "Jonkunnu in Jamaica", *Jamaica Journal*, Vol. 4, No. 2, 1970, pp. 34-48.

Yeats, W.B., *Collected Poems* (London: MacMillan, 1967).

INDEX